CULTURAL FACILITIES IN MIXED-USE DEVELOPMENT

by
Harold R. Snedcof

ULI—the Urban Land Institute

ULI Publication Staff

Director of Publications	Frank H. Spink, Jr.
Project Coordinator	Julie D. Stern
Editor	Duke Johns
Book Design	Watermark Design

Cultural Facilities In Mixed-Use Development

Study Staff

Director	Harold R. Snedcof
Manager	Sara W. Barnes
Associate	Leslie L. Flint

Editorial and Reporting Staff and Consultants
Kathleen Devaney
Margaret Lucke
Ernest W. Hutton, Jr., Partner,
  Buckhurst Fish Hutton Katz

Clerical Support
Eleanor Dugan

Real Estate Development Consultants
Keyser Marston Associates, Inc.

Michael Marston conceived the idea in 1982 for studying the arts as a part of urban development. His counsel and advice and that of Jerry Keyser have been most helpful. They and Robert Wetmore have provided real estate perspective throughout the project, especially in regard to Yerba Buena Gardens, California Plaza, and Horton Plaza, for which Keyser Marston Associates has served as real estate consultant in conceptualizing, structuring, and negotiating the transactions.

Fiscal Administration
The Institute for Urban Design
Ann Ferebee, Director

Funding for research and manuscript development is gratefully acknowledged from the following sources:

The Atlantic Richfield Foundation
The Chase Manhattan Bank
The City of Baltimore
The Cleveland Foundation
The Dallas Arts District Consortium
The Equitable Real Estate Group, Inc.
The Ford Foundation
Goldman, Sachs & Company
Ernest W. & Jean E. Hahn Foundation
Ernest W. Hahn, Inc.
The William & Flora Hewlett Foundation
The James Irvine Foundation
Kidder, Peabody Foundation
The S. H. Kress Foundation
Merrill, Lynch & Company
Metropolitan Structures
The National Endowment for the Arts
The Pittsburgh Foundation/The Howard Heinz
  Endowment
The Rockefeller Brothers Fund
Rose Associates
The Rouse Company
C. J. Segerstrom & Sons
Skidmore, Owings & Merrill
ULI — the Urban Land Institute

The inclusion of cultural facilities in mixed-use development is not a new idea. Certainly Rockefeller Center and its Radio City Music Hall can be described both as a predecessor of mixed-use development and as an example of the inclusion of cultural facilities. The term "mixed-use development"—or MXD—was given definition in 1976 when ULI published *Mixed-Use Development: New Ways of Land Use.* That report examined a then rapidly growing number of developments that were so different that they could be defined in a way that set them apart from other development concepts.

A definition was postulated: "Mixed-use development means a relatively large-scale real estate project characterized by: three or more significant revenue-producing uses (such as retail, office, residential, hotel/motel, and recreation—which in well-planned projects are mutually supporting); significant functional and physical integration of project components (and thus a highly intensive use of land), including uninterrupted pedestrian connections; and development in conformance with a coherent plan (which frequently stipulates the type and scale of uses, permitted densities, and related items)."

The MXD concept as thus defined proved so powerful that it was quickly accepted as a term that did in fact identify a new development form. By 1981 the ULI Urban Redevelopment Council had become the Urban Development/Mixed-Use Council. It became fashionable for any project that bore a close resemblance to the central definition to be labeled "mixed use," at least for marketing purposes.

The "such as" list of principal uses has continued to expand, as developers find new opportunities to include convention centers and cultural facilities, along with the primary retail, office, residential, hotel/motel, and recreation uses.

Not all the projects discussed in this book are mixed-use developments in strict definitional terms. The history and experience of these projects, however, can lead to more effective inclusion of cultural facilities in mixed-use projects.

This book also has a second and more subtle motivation—that of providing a bridge of understanding between the arts community and the development community. Increasingly, the art of development is replacing the business of development in the minds of its practitioners, while cultural organizations have found ways to be more businesslike in order to survive and to serve changing community needs. The inclusion of cultural facilities in mixed-use development is beneficial to both groups. For developers, the inclusion of cultural facilities can enhance value, instill a sense of place, provide animation, and add to the 24-hour cycle of activity that is a key element in a successful MXD. For cultural institutions, it can provide excellent locations, access to potential patrons, a less aloof relationship with the community, and the potential for increased community participation and support.

Mixed-use development continues to evolve as a concept. It is generally seen as the principal urban development form for the eighties and beyond. This publication is offered to further the understanding of cultural facilities as a land use appropriate for—and truly desirable for—inclusion in mixed-use development.

Frank H. Spink, Jr.
Director, Commercial and Industrial Research
ULI — the Urban Land Institute

This book presents case studies on the ways in which arts facilities and activities are being incorporated in mixed-use buildings, developments, and districts. It has been written for readers with a professional interest in real estate, urban development, and the arts and for public officials and foundation and corporate leaders who are concerned with making cities better places for residents, employers, and visitors.

The past decade has witnessed an increase in collaborative relationships among the public, private, and arts sectors—relationships that have resulted in new sources of funds for arts programs and facilities and for a broad range of public amenities that can help create vital urban environments. Since many of these projects are just bearing fruit, this book represents an initial attempt to view them through common lenses—tracing each project from its inception through its planning stages to its current status.

The idea for a book of case studies on arts-inclusive mixed-use developments emerged in the summer of 1982. Having recently completed a cultural plan for San Francisco's Yerba Buena Center, I initiated a series of discussions with some of the economic and program consultants who had worked with the San Francisco Redevelopment Agency on Yerba Buena. From those informal discussions, two ideas emerged: to contact the Urban Land Institute (which in 1976 had published a landmark study chronicling the emergence of the mixed-use development form) to explore its interest in a new volume on the ways in which arts facilities were being included in these projects; and to seek support from the National Endowment for the Arts' Design Arts Program for a preliminary research effort.

It was agreed that case studies could not fully evaluate the long-term economic impact of these projects on arts institutions, cities, or private developers. However, it was believed that a careful research effort could examine the common planning, design, program, and economic issues that each project must consider. It also could describe the financial mechanisms that underpin these complex projects and could define the steps that are necessary to meet the different expectations of the arts community, public policy, and the real estate marketplace.

Another reason for doing the study was to help raise the level of discourse concerning what is emerging as a small but influential new discipline—cultural and amenities planning. During the past fifteen years a group of urbanists, design professionals, planners, and arts administrators—notably including William H. Whyte, Jr., of the Street Life Project and Robert H. McNulty and Dorothy Jacobson of Partners for Livable Places—have tried to give definition and substance to the concept of cultural planning. Perhaps a rigorous case-study assessment could further define how cultural planning operates, and thereby argue for its inclusion in the real estate and development process at an early enough stage to make a difference.

In 1983, the Design Arts Panel of the National Endowment for the Arts recommended a grant of $25,000 for the case-study project, and the Urban Land Institute's Publications Committee agreed to publish and distribute the final work product—then envisioned as a collection of twenty short profiles. The Institute for Urban Design accepted responsibility for administration of any grant funds that might be given to the project by foundations. In the fall of 1983, with initial grants from the Rockefeller Brothers Fund, the Atlantic Richfield Foundation, the Kress Foundation, the Cleveland Foundation, and pledges of support from the Equitable Life Assurance Society's Real Estate Group and from the Ford Foundation, the study began.

Project Scope

An initial list of case studies had been selected before a research plan had been determined and before the realities of funding availability (from national and local foundations, public agencies, and corporations) had been tested. Gradually, the decision was made to organize the book into three categories descriptive of various kinds of real estate development—mixed-use buildings, developments, and districts. Attempts were made to ensure that projects exemplifying each of these development forms would be included in the book and that each case study would be presented in a common form.

By the summer of 1984, when the research phase was concluded, it was clear that a truly comprehensive survey of all significant current projects would not be possible. Hoped-for funding to underwrite research in several smaller cities such as Louisville, Milwaukee, and St. Paul, Minnesota, could not be found. Other projects, such as Carnegie Hall's planned mixed-use building, had not progressed to the point at which they could be publicly discussed. We regret these omissions and hope they have not adversely affected the final product.

The Staff and Research Process

As the research process progressed, discussions were held among the project's staff about the ways in which a uniform body of knowledge could be gathered for each project. Since little or no published material existed on the majority of these projects, the basic research method became interviews (many taped) with the individuals who have created and managed these projects, and analysis of the primary planning, design, financial, and public policy documents.

After the case studies, introduction, and tables were delivered to the Urban Land Institute, Frank Spink, Jr., ULI's director of publications, enlisted a group of members of the ULI's Mixed-Use and Urban Development Council to review the manuscript. Their comments and questions were reviewed by the project staff and incorporated into final drafts of the case studies.

Previously, copies of the initial drafts had been sent to informants in each city for review. This review process involved individuals from each of the three sectors (public, arts, development) and aimed to ensure that the facts were correct and that the study staff's analysis was in accord with the perceptions of those responsible for implementing the mixed-use projects.

Facts and figures regarding the size and cost of each project also were assembled. Since some of the projects have not yet been constructed, their final size, design, and costs are still undetermined. We have tried to present an accurate description of each project as of January 1985. In view of this situation—and the vagaries of building costs and construction schedules—readers may wish to contact individuals in each city before using the case-study data in new settings.

This study inevitably has left several tasks incomplete. We were not able to include all current projects representing partnerships among the arts, development, and public sectors. Many developed too late in our research period to be included; others remained at a stage of confidential negotiation. Still others were located in cities that could not provide the support necessary for the research team to visit them. Due to space and time limitations, we abandoned plans to include profiles of the individuals most responsible for the planning and implementation of each project.

The development community still awaits a book assessing the cost/benefit record of arts-inclusive MXDs. The relationship between the additional investments required to include arts facilities or programs and the returns that thereby accrue to cities and private developers remains a subject of much speculation but little documentation. Quite simply, filling this gap was beyond our capacity and scope of work. We hope that subsequent research will build upon our efforts and begin to answer these questions.

Harold R. Snedcof

Many individuals have contributed substantial time, energy, and knowledge to this book. They are named in various places throughout the text. At the risk of neglecting some who have been equally helpful, I would like to single out a few who have been particularly supportive from the beginning.

Michael Pittas, Charles Zucker, and their staff at the National Endowment for the Arts' Design Arts Program provided much of the project's initial impetus. Russell A. Phillips, Jr., executive vice president of the Rockefeller Brothers Fund, encouraged me to seek a variety of contributions from the corporate and nonprofit sectors and offered much wise counsel.

Charlotte L. Mayerson, senior editor at Random House, Inc., gave me a home base in New York City, encouragement during the fundraising process, and incisive criticism as we prepared the text. William B. Fleissig contributed a variety of suggestions to strengthen the manuscript's content and structure.

My colleague, Sara Barnes, who became project manager in mid-1983, provided indispensable administrative and financial management support. Leslie Flint, project associate, spent untold hours acquiring and organizing the visual materials and project data for each case study. Both worked tirelessly and unselfishly to make the project succeed. Once the case studies had been drafted, editor Kathleen Devaney organized and shaped the manuscript into publishable form.

My wife, Melanie, and my son, Jordan, have provided the love, understanding, support, and confidence without which this book would never have been completed.

Harold R. Snedcof

About the Author

Harold R. Snedcof is a cultural and development planner with a Ph.D. in American Studies from Brown University. A former program officer at the Rockefeller Brothers Fund and a cultural planner for the San Francisco Redevelopment Agency, he was a founder and principal of City Building–Urban Strategies, a cultural and amenities planning and consulting firm located in San Francisco. He now directs the New York Public Library's corporate and foundation giving program.

Advisory Council

M. J. Brodie, Executive Director
Pennsylvania Avenue Development Corporation
Washington, DC

William Bushnell, Producing Director
Los Angeles Actors Theater
Los Angeles, CA

David Childs, Partner
Skidmore, Owings & Merrill
Washington, DC

Patricia Jansen Doyle, Program Officer, Cultural Affairs
The Cleveland Foundation
Cleveland, OH

Larry Faigin, Executive Vice President
Shapell Associates
Beverly Hills, CA

John Gilchrist, President
The Ernest W. Hahn Company
San Diego, CA

Lawrence Goldman, Director
Real Estate Development and Planning
Carnegie Hall Society
New York, NY

William Hatch, Managing Partner
Metropolitan Structures
Los Angeles, CA

Edward Helfeld, Administrator
Los Angeles Community Redevelopment Agency
Los Angeles, CA

E. Eddie Henson, President
Williams Realty Corporation
Tulsa, OK

Benjamin Holloway, Chairman and CEO
The Equitable Real Estate Group, Inc.
New York, NY

Daniel Kenney
Sasaki Associates, Inc.
Watertown, MA

Ann R. Leven, Treasurer
The Smithsonian Institution
Washington, DC

Weiming Lu, Executive Director
Lowertown Redevelopment Corporation
St. Paul, MN

Robert McNulty, President
Partners for Livable Places
Washington, DC

Dr. Philip O'Bryan Montgomery, Coordinator
Dallas Arts District Consortium
Dallas, TX

Harry S. Parker, III, Director
Dallas Museum of Art
Dallas, TX

Norman Pfeiffer, Partner
Hardy Holzman Pfeiffer Associates
New York, NY

Milton Rhodes, President
American Council for the Arts
New York, NY

Daniel Rose, President
Rose Associates
New York, NY

Henry T. Segerstrom, Managing Partner
C. J. Segerstrom & Sons
Costa Mesa, CA

Charles Shaw, President
Charles Shaw & Company
Chicago, IL

James Snyder, Deputy Director for Planning
Museum of Modern Art
New York, NY

Hugh Southern (ex officio member)
Deputy Chairman for Programs
National Endowment for the Arts
Washington, DC

Jane Thompson, Vice President
Benjamin Thompson & Associates
Cambridge, MA

Gerald M. Trimble, Executive Vice President
Centre City Development Corporation
San Diego, CA

Homer C. Wadsworth, Former Director
The Cleveland Foundation
Cleveland, OH

Richard Weinstein
Richard S. Weinstein Associates, Inc.
New York, NY

ULI Review Committee

James E. Carley, Partner
Carley Capital Group
Madison, WI

Thomas J. Flynn, Chairman
Blackman Garlock Flynn & Company
San Francisco, CA

Gilbert J. Hardman, President
British Columbia Place Ltd.
West Vancouver, B.C.
Canada

Barry K. Humphries, President
Renaissance Group, Inc.
Columbus, OH

Clyde C. Jackson, Jr., President
Wynne/Jackson, Inc.
Dallas, TX

Don Nelson, Director, Construction
Plaza of the Americas, Inc.
Dallas, TX

Roy W. Potter, Executive Vice President
San Diegans, Inc.
San Diego, CA

F. C. Steinbauer, President
Mobil Land Development Corp./Eastern Division
Reston, VA

Nell D. Surber, Director of Economic Development
City of Cincinnati
Cincinnati, OH

Introduction

In U.S. cities of all sizes and locations, real estate developments of a new kind—large-scale, mixed-use projects that contain spaces for arts and culture—are gaining influence and popularity. Museums, concert halls, theaters, and outdoor performance plazas are taking their place beside such traditional uses as offices, hotels, retail space, and housing in complexes designed to make downtown areas better places to work and live.

These projects tend to be rich in amenities. Not only do they contain specialized arts facilities, but they usually feature large proportions of landscaped open space and ample opportunities for recreation and entertainment. They are people-oriented, with features intended to make them appealing destinations and to provide smooth and comfortable access for pedestrians. Their design standards are high, to ensure that they will achieve an image of quality and enhance the urban environment.

These are ambitious projects, conceived to meet a challenging set of goals. They are, of course, intended to be profitable investments, but their creators also hope that they will accomplish a broad range of public-policy objectives: These projects are supposed to help revitalize downtown areas, stimulate economic growth, and help ensure the viability of the arts in communities.

To manage and finance these projects, innovative partnerships are being forged among private developers, public agencies, and arts organizations. Multiple benefits seem possible for each sector:

■ Private developers, seeking ways to create a strong and distinctive market image, include arts and amenities to draw the desired consumers to these complexes and to extend the activity cycle to evenings and weekends.

■ Public agencies, whose goals are to strengthen downtown areas with development programs that attract residents, workers, and visitors, are willing to share the financial risks of including amenities and cultural uses in mixed-use projects.

■ For arts organizations, faced with operating costs rising higher than traditional funding sources can support, the use of real estate development rights or the opportunity to participate in major urban development projects can provide a way to gain new facilities and to supplement their funds.

This alliance of arts and economics reflects two important realizations. First, cities, as the traditional homes of the arts, can succeed best when they offer residents a rich variety of cultural experiences. Second, urban centers, though often maligned, can offer clear advantages as social, economic, and retail centers, in spite of the suburban growth of the past decade.

This book provides a comprehensive look at the phenomenon of the arts-inclusive mixed-use project and the collaborative relationships of the private, public, and arts sectors that bring it into being. It examines twelve projects in ten different cities, with particular attention to the planning process in each case. The projects can be considered examples of three different categories of the mixed-use form:

1) the mixed-use building, where an arts institution and one or more commercial uses become neighbors on a single site;

2) the mixed-use development, a large, integrated project on land assembled into a single parcel, in which several revenue-producing uses join with the arts in a mutually supportive, synergistic way; and

3) the arts district, a section of the city characterized by both arts and commercial uses, where public policy encourages both types and the creation of a coherent image for the area that will benefit the multiple owners and developers.

These case studies remain, however, stories of individual solutions to specific problems. It became clear during the course of research for this book that the arts-inclusive projects created to date are too new and too few for any clear-cut, universal formula for success to have emerged. However, the information and observations in this volume can provide readers with a greater understanding of this new development form and thus provide a frame of reference for other communities to take a creative approach to their own situations.

As a result of various forces at work in the arts, in real estate development, and in city planning and management, leaders in these three groups have found themselves learning to work together and discovering mutual benefits in doing so. For perspective, it's helpful to review the changes in the ways that arts organizations, private developers, and public agencies have done business over the past quarter century.

Trends in the Arts

Artists and arts organizations have two overriding needs: Appropriate spaces in which to create and present their works, and adequate funding to operate those spaces and to produce programs and works of high quality. In attempting to meet those needs in today's economic climate, arts organizations have become increasingly business-like.

The perpetual problem of funding shortages was compounded in the seventies and early eighties by inflationary pressures, a less-than-robust economy, and limitations in the growth of federal government support. Traditional arts patrons have continued to be essential sources of funds; corporations, for example, gave arts organizations $506 million in 1982, 32 percent more than in 1981. All private contributions to the arts and humanities totaled $3.95 billion in 1983. But even this strong support has not proven sufficient to meet arts organizations' needs, especially considering the capital costs for new facilities.

Arts managers therefore have been adventuring into the business world with profit-oriented ventures such as retail shops, mail-order services, and restaurants, usually located on the premises of their cultural facilities. The institutions that have chosen this path have had to confront both practical and philosophical dilemmas. They have had to deal with the fear that artistic products dependent on marketplace factors for their existence could be aesthetically compromised. Nonprofit organizations have had to learn how to carry on commercial activities without jeopardizing their tax-exempt status. Boards and administrators have had to recognize that significant income

may be a long time in coming, and that commercial enterprises require strong, steady commitment.

The business expertise of arts organizations also has grown as they have begun to use more sophisticated techniques to market their programs and administer their resources. For many such organizations, becoming involved in real estate development has been viewed as a logical next step.

The Search for Spaces

A new type of home for the arts began appearing in the early sixties—the performing arts center. The Lincoln Center in New York City, the Kennedy Center in Washington, D.C., and the Los Angeles Music Center are among the best-known examples, but they flourish in many other cities as well. The National Endowment for the Arts has estimated that as many as 2,000 such centers, large and small, now exist in the United States.

These often lavish complexes combine theaters, concert halls, and other facilities under one roof. The centers have been important not only in providing much-needed facilities but in making a symbolic statement of the importance of the arts to the community.

But the importance of the arts to the community is not merely symbolic. Critic Harold Schonberg, writing in the *New York Times* (July 10, 1983), noted that "Cultural centers have been responsible for growth of previously underdeveloped areas in the vicinity of the center. They have attracted developers, small businesses, and allied artistic enterprises, such as galleries and art movie houses. They have meant a tremendous upgrading of property values, more people downtown, more tax revenue for the city. The arts in America are big business." In 1981 John Mazzola, then the director of Lincoln Center, estimated that the center's financial impact on New York City in one year was $345 million.

Discussing the phenomenon of large arts centers in his 1970 volume, *Bricks, Mortar, and the Performing Arts,* Martin Mayer made two important points: First, "the largest single controllable factor in the health of the performing arts is the attractiveness, technical adequacy, and financial efficiency of their housing." The planning and management of physical facilities for the arts has come to exert unexpected and largely unrecognized leverage. Second, no major facility for the performing arts should be built unless the sponsoring group is assured that the maintenance and operation of the building will not become a burden on the performing groups, resident or touring.

Mayer suggested that a logical source for the needed arts dollars would be the real estate sector: "The most obvious source of supporting income is the facilities naturally ancillary to the theatrical function—garages, restaurants, and bars—to serve the audience drawn to the building, plus, ideally, others drawn to the neighborhood."

Since the presence of these arts centers had a strong stimulating effect on the economy of the surrounding areas, it was reasonable to expect that arts institutions themselves should participate in the boom. If the arts were indeed big business, as Schonberg argued, then arts managers, primed by their experience in smaller commercial ventures, were ready to become full-fledged businesspeople. By participating in the real estate development process, they could recapture for their institutions some of the financial benefits that their presence conferred upon communities.

Trends in Real Estate
The notion of funding the arts from the development process also relates to the real estate context that evolved after World War II. By the mid-sixties, two sophisticated types of real estate developers had emerged. The first emphasized joint ventures with landowners or sources of capital. The second had accumulated sufficient financial resources over several decades of activity to take on major mixed-use projects themselves.

Occasionally, a developer would enter into an arts program as a civic gesture or as a career capstone. Frequently, developers and their financial partners have had to muster enormous patience and investment staying power to see mixed-use projects

survive through several cycles of the real estate market.

Incorporating the arts in mixed-use projects also has related to the increasing involvement of the public sector in downtown development. The public sector's participation is often a prerequisite for a major development project with an arts component, because only the public sector owns or can gain control of the site, or can effect the financial mechanisms such as tax abatement that can make the project a reality.

These changes took root among developers and public agencies as two types of sophisticated real estate projects emerged. One is the mixed-use development (MXD), which, because of its complexity and scale, makes substantial public impact and demands public-sector participation in its creation. The other is the adaptive use project, by which a historic building is rehabilitated to serve a new purpose, frequently to provide a new home for an arts organization. The arts-inclusive MXD melds lessons learned from both types of projects.

Mixed-Use Development Projects
The Urban Land Institute's landmark study, *Mixed-Use Developments: New Ways of Land Use* (1976), defined these projects as those that share three characteristics:

1) a combination of three or more revenue-producing uses—such as retail, office, residential, hotel/motel, and recreation—that in well-planned projects are mutually supporting;

2) a significant functional and physical integration of project components (and thus a highly intensive use of land), including uninterrupted pedestrian connections; and

3) development in conformance with a coherent plan that frequently stipulates the type and scale of uses, permitted densities, and related items.

The prototype for the MXD was New York City's Rockefeller Center, begun in 1931, which set a precedent for mixing mutually supportive uses in a setting of architectural excellence. The ULI study called it a "pioneering development in concept, scale, physical design, and services."

The project originally was conceived to

provide and support a home for an arts institution—the Metropolitan Opera. Spearheading a drive to build a new opera house, John D. Rockefeller, Jr., supported a proposal for erecting a large office building as part of the complex, so that the Metropolitan could support itself from the rental revenues. Plans for the site included music studios, spacious landscaped plazas, and "the tallest skyscraper in the world."

The Great Depression put an end to this scheme, but Rockefeller went ahead to build an integrated development with office, retail, restaurant, and entertainment uses on a magnificently planned site. To attract visitors and tenants to its then-unfashionable location, the center's original design included surface-level gardens and promenades, plus direct access to the subway through a network of underground shopping concourses.

Although the Metropolitan Opera did not come to Rockefeller Center, art galleries and theaters did. Today the center, twice its original size, is filled with murals and sculpture. Radio City Music Hall still attracts enthusiastic audiences, and the center's gardens and ice rink have become legendary.

Another influence on MXDs was the postwar suburban shopping center. MXDs represented a reaction against the typical shopping center's lack of integrated design and planning. Early malls contained retail stores, fast-food outlets, and an occasional landscaped plaza, surrounded by paved acres of parking space. Small office buildings and movie theaters sometimes were constructed around their peripheries, but opportunities for recreation and culture generally were not pursued.

Some expanded shopping malls built in the sixties, such as Newport Center in Orange County, California, and suburban Detroit's Northland Center, began to include office, residential, and hotel uses. But even these centers showed little coordinated planning or functional integration, and people-centered activities were not encouraged. Suburban residents continued to rely on television for much of their routine entertainment.

By the late sixties, suburban mixed-use projects began to evolve. Though still serving a suburban clientele, they offered a more sophisticated range of stores and restaurants. Gerald Hines's 1967 Galleria in Houston typified the goals of the mixed-use shopping complex. With three levels of shopping, surrounding an ice rink and topped by a barrel-vault glass roof, the first phase of the Galleria provided connections to an adjoining department store, an office building, a hotel, and two movie theaters. It was described by its developer as "a whole new urban form that the American public doesn't know exists." The Galleria's considerable appeal sprang from its compact orchestration of a mixture of uses in a setting of elegance and refinement.

As MXDs were developed in cities, they tended to be designed as self-contained, secure domains where people could work, play, live, and shop apart from the perceived unfriendliness of an unsafe downtown. But even if most of these projects presented themselves as urban fortresses, divorced from street life and pedestrian activity, many enjoyed popular and financial success.

The best of the major MXDs have succeeded in creating strong identities for themselves while making a positive contribution to their surroundings. City dwellers have proven to enjoy well-designed, active environments where they can shop, eat, and be entertained. Developers have gained experience in establishing and staffing multitalented organizations capable of planning, financing, and managing these intricate projects.

The increasing complexity of MXD projects has called for an extensive planning process involving considerable participation by the public sector. Projects as elaborate as these are expected to provide public benefits, but the nature and extent of those benefits has had to be defined, along with the means for financing them. For a combination of reasons, these ambitious developments pose too great a financial burden for the private sector to bear alone, and because the scope of public benefits desired has grown so large, many steps are required beyond the traditional public support techniques. Zoning incentives, infrastructure improvements, tax abatements, and writedowns thus have

played key roles in most MXDs. The 1976 ULI study noted:

Without public-sector support, many mixed-use projects will never be developed, much less make a meaningful contribution to the community. While it is true that financial return on investment to private developers in mixed use may eventually be higher (as compared to single-purpose projects), mixed-use developments are much more difficult to initiate and entail much higher initial exposure—hence greater risks—than less ambitious single-purpose projects.

Both the public and private sectors have recognized the need for a successful MXD to include a complex mixture of diverse uses. This blend enables a project to contribute to a city's life at all hours, not just during the business day. Furthermore, it creates a desirable level of "market synergy"—the interplay among a project's components that benefits each and creates a sense of identity and excitement greater than any single use could achieve alone. The ULI study observed:

Diversity in a mixed-use development also means drawing people after the close of the business day. A variety of eating and drinking facilities is one means. A second means may be through emphasis on entertainment through provision of facilities (e.g., movie houses and legitimate theater) and programming of a busy schedule of events (such as specially designated mall and plaza areas). Still another way may be through the incorporation of waterfront esplanades, museums, libraries, land-intensive recreational facilities, and other public and institutional uses in MXDs.

With this growing recognition of the need to ensure that MXDs make a positive contribution to the urban environment, it has become feasible and desirable to expand their uses to include the arts.

The Historic Preservation Movement
American preservationists of the thirties, forties, and fifties were concerned primarily with saving Presidents' homes and other buildings that played clearly significant roles in the nation's history. By the sixties,

however, many less revered older structures were being leveled as part of the widescale land clearance inspired by urban renewal programs, or were being replaced by new structures. People began to realize that these vintage buildings were an irreplaceable resource that gave cities much of their character and distinction.

In an effort to conserve something of this heritage, many projects aimed to give new life to buildings that were historically or architecturally significant but that were no longer needed for their original use. As the value of these adaptive use projects became more apparent, a variety of federal and state tax incentives were created to attract the participation of private investment dollars.

A number of adaptive use projects became lively multiple-use complexes, successfully attracting a large and enthusiastic public. One of the earliest and best-known is San Francisco's Ghirardelli Square, where a collection of warehouses and industrial buildings was converted during the sixties into a successful complex of specialty retail shops, restaurants, offices, gardens, and plazas. The Rouse Company later spent nearly $30 million to transform an 1826 wholesale food market next to Boston's Faneuil Hall into a modern marketplace whose three buildings house shops, restaurants, and office space. Pittsburgh's Station Square saw a 1901 railroad terminal become luxury office space and its old freight house become a specialty shopping center; to complement them, a 250-room hotel was constructed.

Many more of these recycled structures became homes for the arts. The ULI's 1978 volume, *Adaptive Reuse*, cited numerous instances in which old movie palaces have been transformed into performing arts centers, city halls and police stations have been converted into children's museums and institutes of contemporary art, and railroad stations have been remodeled as arts and science centers.

Arts organizations had established themselves as a major occupant of rehabilitated buildings by the mid-seventies. By working together on adaptive use projects that provided homes for the arts as well as business investment opportunities, arts administrators and real estate developers had made strides in understanding their various needs, objectives, and strengths.

Trends in Public Policy and Urban Development

City officials grappling with urban problems increasingly have come to regard their downtowns as resources for at least some of the solutions. A healthy central core—economically strong, lively at all hours, activity-oriented, pedestrian-focused, containing a rich mixture of uses—now is perceived as key to the vigor of the city as a whole. A variety of economic and social forces have combined to change perceptions of the needs and goals for downtowns, and to bring public agencies in closer alignment with the private and arts sectors.

Shifts in Federal Spending

Federal efforts over the past 30 years aimed at alleviating urban ills have reflected changing diagnoses of the causes and appropriate solutions. In the fifties and early sixties the focus was on slum clearance, based on the belief that through improving patterns of land use, downtown areas could be revitalized and protected and the social problems of ghettos could be eased. With federal assistance, local governments took on a role that had once been the purview of private developers: They acquired tracts of land, sometimes entire neighborhoods, and razed all the buildings. Through newly created redevelopment agencies, cities then encouraged private investment in these leveled areas.

When this approach proved not to be a panacea, federally funded programs such as Community Action and Model Cities were initiated to provide direct assistance to neighborhoods. These programs aimed to help meet the needs of low-income citizens for housing, neighborhood improvements, and social services. While there were many individual successes, the problems and their root causes proved intransigent.

As the federal role in the cities grew larger in the sixties, efforts increasingly concentrated on downtown areas. According-

ing to Dennis R. Judd and Margaret Collins, in their article "The Case for Tourism: Political Conditions and Redevelopment in Central Cities" (from *The Changing Structure of the City*, G. A. Tobin, ed., 1979):

Of the broad purposes contained in the federal approach, the promotion of economic growth and downtown redevelopment attracted the greatest support from a very large coalition within all of the large cities. The coalition was similar in city after city. It included city politicians working with a new breed of bureaucrats, large corporations, metropolitan newspapers, and often construction trade unions. . . . In the 1960s, the coalition stabilized to such an extent that it was virtually the only unified political interest which spoke for the central cities. In comparison, inner-city neighborhoods were split on the basis of social class, racial, or geographical differences to such an extent that they could rarely come together to articulate an alternative to the central business district development. The consequence was that the downtown coalition dominated central city politics. Partly because the interest groups represented in the downtown coalition agreed so fundamentally on the problems of the central cities, the urban agenda was singularly defined as the problem of economic growth and middle-class flight to the suburbs.

This agenda predicated the revitalization of the central business district as the solution to urban problems. But that revitalization was a larger matter than federal and city governments could handle alone; the projects also needed the support of private developers. They received that support because they offered the likelihood of a substantial return on the investment. Thus the private and public sectors found themselves partners in a mutually profitable alliance.

The Attraction of Tourism

As the industrial base in many cities has declined, and production of services has become the dominant segment of the economy, tourism has began to take on a new importance. Competition among cities for tourist dollars has grown fierce, demonstrated by the rush over the past two decades to build convention centers, sports arenas, and other visitor attractions. Tourism is perceived to generate both skilled and unskilled jobs, to add substantial tax revenues to city coffers, and to pump significant sums into the local economy.

Judd and Collins succinctly described tourism's appeal:

Aside from the direct economic benefits to downtown interests, cities seek tourists because the convention industry seems uniquely beneficial, essentially a "free" commodity. Presumably, tourists spend money without taking anything out of the economy. The convention industry has frequently been described as "the industry without a smokestack."

Cities therefore have pursued providing the types of facilities that draw visitors. Those that succeed in pulling in substantial numbers of conventioneers and vacationers not only provide a strong tourism infrastructure of hotels, restaurants, meeting spaces, and trade show halls, but also a variety of recreational, commercial, cultural, and artistic attractions. These cities in turn are perceived in the tourism marketplace as places that are lively, exciting, and fun, with their own distinctive and characteristic flair.

Seeking new ways to reinforce such an atmosphere, cities began to look to the arts. Healthy cultural organizations with strong programs are powerful attractors of people; because of the economic benefits they generate, cities have become increasingly willing to lend them public support.

Large mixed-use projects, often featuring a combination of hotel, restaurant, and retail uses, meet many of the needs of tourism. Including arts facilities or activities in these projects makes the one-stop package more complete and that much more of a magnet.

The Europeanization of American Cities

In a recent article, "Restructuring the American City: A Comparative Perspective" (from the G. A. Tobin book, *The Changing Structure of the City*), Norman I. Fainstein and Susan S. Fainstein articulated a change that has been occurring in a few older American cities:

Until midway in the last decade, two metaphors captured the physical contrast between major European and American cities: a shallow bowl and a doughnut. European metropolises displayed a preserved historic center, serving expensive consumption, surrounded by high-rise commercial and residential development. . . . The American city, in contrast, revealed a partially abandoned, desolate core, dominated by low-income, minority populations threatening an increasingly beleaguered central business district. . . . Suddenly, however, the U.S. picture appears to have changed.

The Fainsteins identified a number of older American cities—New York, Chicago, Boston, San Francisco, Pittsburgh, Minneapolis, and Denver among them—as "converting" cities: communities in which social-class composition and economic function are changing in significant ways. These cities, according to this analysis, represent a countertrend to the deterioration prevailing in most older urban locales and a movement toward convergence with European models. Central to this process of conversion and convergence is the transformation of the urban core:

These cities have witnessed massive new public and private investment in the core, resulting in displacement of the poor and transformation of function. Downtown has become a source of profit once more as its uses have changed—the factory, the port, and the working-class district have been replaced by the office, the tourist center, and the upper-class neighborhood. . . . The difference between old cities in general and the subset undergoing conversion is created by the interaction among the three factors of demography, housing, and occupation within the context of increasing private investment, which facilitates major changes in the utilization of land in the urban core. . . . Thus, converting cities are defined by transformation of core land use in a positive investment situation.

These economic and demographic shifts have resulted in a change of activity from production of goods by the working class to the production and consumption of services by the upper classes. The arts-inclusive MXD benefits from this conversion phenomenon and helps to further it, because the uses it contains and the market it attracts are those characteristic of the "Europeanized" city.

The Metropolis Syndrome

A common ambition of elected officials and civic-minded business leaders is to establish a strong civic identity and cosmopolitan image for their city and to participate in the tradition of the world's great cities. This goal might be called the "metropolis syndrome."

The metropolis syndrome has several components. The first is a recognition of the contribution that the arts can make to both the image and the economic health of a city. It can be argued that among American cities only New York has the kind of comprehensive arts presence that marks a world-class metropolitan center. But others, working hard to catch up, are emerging as strong regional and even national arts centers.

A second component is a pedestrian focus, with people actively mingling on the streets, squares, and plazas. On foot, people can interact with each other and their surroundings. The potential for this interaction can inspire street performances and vending that further enlivens the city.

Related is a third component—a 24-hour activity cycle. Great metropolises do not die at night, as many American downtowns do. Rather, they offer a broad spectrum of activities beyond purely economic ones, meeting a multitude of residents' and visitors' needs.

In European and some American cities, these qualities have evolved over a long period. But in other cities that aspire to such a status, civic leaders have had to search out ways to create them more quickly. A major arts-inclusive project offers one possibility for launching such an effort.

Public Participation in Real Estate and the Arts

As goals for the revitalization of downtowns have evolved, the public sector has found it necessary to become an active participant in the development projects that would help meet those goals. MXDs have demonstrated substantial potential for combining desirable commercial uses with public amenities, but as the scope and objectives of these projects have grown more complex, so have the difficulties of initiating them, financing them, and carrying them through the development process.

The 1976 ULI study on MXDs described the public sector's participation as follows:

Broadly conceived, possible public-sector roles range from *passive* (e.g., no public action apart from zoning approval, warranted where benefits of public action are thought to be inappreciable), to *catalytic* (for example, public "seed money" to finance particular project components such as parking facilities or a convention center), to *comprehensive* public (re)development (such as through existing renewal authorities or creation of a public corporation).

Cities where arts-inclusive MXDs are being created have tended to move from a passive to a catalytic posture. A few city agencies have achieved a comprehensive involvement, to the point of participating in the ongoing management of particular uses in a project.

The public sector also is in the business of helping to support arts organizations. All 50 states, plus the District of Columbia and five special jurisdictions, have state arts

agencies, which for 1984 received a total of more than $136 million from their legislatures. The National Endowment for the Arts estimates that there are 1,500 local arts agencies—some private, many public—that collectively provide more than $300 million in annual support for the arts. About 17 percent of the earnings gap of professional nonprofit arts organizations is filled by the public sector.

The argument sometimes is raised that the arts are elitist, and that those who participate should be willing to bear the costs. This attitude ignores the benefits, both economic and intangible, that the arts provide to communities. As Helen Sause, the San Francisco Redevelopment Agency's project director for the Yerba Buena Center, has said:

It is critical for cities to provide a variety of experiences for their citizens, and the arts have long been an essential part of this experience in the great cities of the world. The arts draw people together, give them a means to communicate, create a sense of participation and involvement. Cultural resources are a crucial part of the city's infrastructure, as much as schools, transportation, and the physical structure of the city. Because arts facilities and programs are so significant to a major urban area, the public sector has an obligation to provide such opportunities.

All arts-inclusive MXDs to date have evolved through a collaborative effort of the private, public, and arts sectors. The process is much like a partnership (though not in the legal sense); although the parties involved may not be equal participants, the project cannot come into fruition unless all three groups are committed, supportive, and willing to share risks. In large-scale developments they also must be willing to provide a framework for fulfilling future needs, rather than focusing simply on the present.

The Needs and Strengths of Each Player

Each party has certain needs that it hopes a project will meet, and each brings certain strengths to the relationship that can aid a project in meeting its goals. The result is that the team is far more capable of handling a complex project than any one player would be acting alone.

The Arts Sector

The arts participant, whether a single institution or a coalition of a community's cultural groups, needs the state-of-the-art facilities that can be included in an MXD, and it needs the financial participation of the other team members to create and operate these facilities. It also can benefit from the exposure to potential new audiences it can achieve by being a highly visible part of a prestigious development. However, the arts sector is seldom able to take financial risks typical of real estate endeavors.

In return, the arts, by their presence in the project, provide it with that valuable commodity—people. They attract not only audiences for their own programs, but customers for the retail shops and restaurants, guests for the hotels, tenants for the office buildings, and buyers for the residential units. The arts audience, largely educated and affluent, is precisely the type of consumer needed by a project's other uses.

The arts also give an MXD a strong identity, marketing focus, and image of quality. This result is partly due to the high regard in which highly educated consumers hold cultural endeavors. But the inclusion of the arts also frequently raises a project's design standards.

The Private Sector

Developers, of course, participate in an MXD to generate profits, and they need precisely that sort of marketing advantage. The presence of the arts can differentiate a project from a whole host of competitors—single-use and mixed-use developments, downtown and suburban—and can enhance the public's perception of it. This kind of strong, positive image and appeal to the desired consumer may enhance a project's profitability.

A developer's contribution to a project is professional know-how in assembling and structuring real estate developments: from planning to design, financing, construction, operation, and marketing. Developers also are a major supplier of the investment needed to get the job done, but they are seldom willing or able to assume unaided the entire financial burden for an arts-inclusive MXD.

The Public Sector

Local government's goals for an arts-inclusive project generally include the economic objectives it would have for any development: an increased tax base, revenues from the sale or lease of publicly owned land, revitalization of an underused area, and the creation of new jobs. Public planners often hope to stimulate economic activity in areas surrounding a project, and they sometimes aim to provide benefits and amenities to citizens and visitors and to enhance a city's reputation as a center for cultural activity.

The public sector's strengths include control of the approvals needed for a project to be completed, the ability to provide appropriate infrastructure, and often the ownership of the land. The agencies involved may not necessarily play the role of a full financial participant, contributing dollars directly. More frequently they provide tools that make a project's financing feasible, such as writedowns of the land price, bond issues, and so on. Often the public sector also becomes the key manager of the complex preliminary planning process required for an arts-inclusive MXD.

What Makes the Partnership Work?

Several ingredients are essential for making such partnerships work: strong leadership, genuine cooperation among the three parties, and a favorable or potentially valuable location.

Leadership

Arts-inclusive projects generally succeed in part because one or more of the individuals involved maintains an extremely strong dedication to making it happen.

■ In San Diego, Gerald Trimble, executive director of the Centre City Development Corporation, the public partner in the creation of Horton Plaza, has said:

The most important reason for including the arts in Horton Plaza is my strong interest in art, music, and theater. This frame of reference on a personal level is essential in understanding and implementing projects which integrate art and cultural attractions.

■ Dr. Philip Montgomery, prime mover behind the Dallas Arts District, put in hundreds of volunteer hours to coordinate cultural organizations' needs for new homes, the city's needs for a revived downtown district, and private developers' needs for a sound investment opportunity.
■ For San Francisco's Yerba Buena Center, Helen Sause of the city's redevelopment agency led the city government, the developer, and the arts community through four years of comprehensive cultural planning. She began with an undefined requirement that some land in the project be set aside for cultural purposes and evolved a feasible plan for a cultural center with a realistic budget, a management structure, and an innovative programming concept.

In each of the projects described in this book's case studies, some individual has taken this sort of leadership role, with deep personal commitment to the goals of the project, its vision, its possibility, and its potential for meeting true needs. To these leaders, achievement of the project's goals came to be more than just a professional task. It became a matter of intense conviction, for which they committed generous amounts of talent, persistence, and professional resources.

Cooperation

The three partners in an arts-inclusive MXD must be willing to collaborate on shaping the development and to share the risks and costs of creating it. For such projects to succeed, the expectations and goals of each party must be shared and incorporated in a comprehensive vision of the project's potential, underpinned by a firm strategy for managing the development process. This vision should guide the process and sustain the partners through the inevitable ups and downs.

The public and arts sectors must acknowledge, for instance, that a developer will participate only if a project meets certain standards of financial feasibility: they must share the economic risk in order for a developer to gain the needed return. Frequently the arts participant is responsible for providing or raising planning funds to instigate the project, or for providing the capital or endowment funds to make the arts component possible. The public-agency landowner may have to make certain compromises in the financial negotiations with a developer to guarantee a place for the arts in the project. Developers, for their part, must understand that even with the risk shared, such projects frequently require an extraordinary commitment on the part of the private sector.

Similarly, the public and private parties must recognize that arts institutions, whatever their fundraising or programming talents, rarely have the trained staff or other resources to manage the construction, maintenance, and operation of complex real estate projects. Even if they do, day-to-day involvement in a development process is likely to raise serious questions about possible compromises to an organization's artistic mission and integrity. Therefore, for the arts to be a viable part of these projects, the other public and private participants must assist in managing the cultural component's development process.

Location

The best intentions of all the parties will not make an arts-inclusive MXD succeed if it is not a financially viable project in the first place. The project must meet a market demand for its major revenue-producing uses as well as its arts component. This requirement is far easier met in a location where the real estate market is strong and land values are rising, or where the area has a potential for becoming attractive within a reasonable period of time.

What constitutes a reasonable period, however, can be hard to define, and how long it will take to create a positive real estate market in a particular place can be difficult to predict. In Los Angeles, uptown from the established financial market, the California Plaza project benefited from a surge in developer interest in downtown Los Angeles. But the site still presented some pioneering risk. In San Francisco, the opportunity to comprehensively develop 22 acres of downtown land represented an unusual opportunity, but here, too, the site was not a prime location. Baltimore's Inner Harbor was developed over a period of many years; success came incrementally, and the Charles Center–Inner Harbor management could use the success of earlier parts of the project as a selling point to attract new developers and new uses to the remaining parcels. In Cleveland, the Playhouse Square Foundation believed that the rehabilitation of a group of historically significant theaters would help create the image of distinction and quality needed to spur the upgrading of the surrounding neighborhood.

Just as a synergistic effect exists among the various uses in each one of these projects, so is there a dynamic relationship between an MXD and its environment. The existence of the project is likely to stimulate economic growth and market vitality in the project area. These positive effects in turn benefit the project itself, strengthening its own market position. This potential for synergy is frequently one of the objectives that prompts public agencies to participate in a project.

In addition to a potentially strong real estate market, an arts-inclusive MXD requires an existing cultural market. It cannot create an audience for the arts where none exists. It is possible, though, that in a location where there appears to be no arts market, that market is hidden because its needs are not being met. The cultural programming of an MXD may stimulate a local flowering of the arts beyond a project's boundaries.

Real Estate Context

Arts-inclusive MXDs have been developed in widely varying real estate environments, and at widely different cycles in the market. In some situations, such as Dallas or Orange County, California, the project has been phased or keyed to an expanding commercial real estate market. In others, such as Cleveland or Baltimore, the project has been part of a strategy to revitalize a decaying downtown core.

In all successful situations, however, the principal participants have been fully aware of the real estate context in which the project took shape. And in all of these projects, an understanding has existed of which transactions could be struck to make projects financially feasible. The components of a feasible deal include projected capital costs and operations expenses that can be borne by the project, with a capping of the exposure to the developer and a public program for development of major urban land holdings or major arts facilities that has genuine political support in the community.

The political support that may be forthcoming for an arts-related MXD will reflect community values. It can range from an interventionist role for the public sector in making New York's South Street Seaport feasible, to solutions that rely almost exclusively upon the private sector, as with real estate negotiations within the Dallas Arts District.

Mixed-use projects that include arts components differ from those that do not in fundamental ways. Making room for the arts affects the planning and development process, the financial structure, and the management and operations of the project after it is built.

Effects on the Nature of the Development

The most obvious difference between a project with the arts and one without them is the need to include specialized arts facilities, designed to meet the requirements of the particular disciplines they are intended to house. These facilities can be costly to build and maintain, and the construction and operating funds probably will need to come from the development process. If the costs are skimped on, or if the facilities are planned, designed, and built without a full understanding of the arts organization's needs, the result will be to undermine the quality of the organization's programs, which may have a detrimental effect on the entire MXD project.

Moreover, there are likely to be land use considerations for a project beyond the arts facilities themselves. Arts-inclusive projects typically are intended to serve broad public-benefit goals, of which the arts constitute just one part. Permitted densities are often much lower than they would be otherwise, and there frequently is a high open-space requirement. In San Francisco's Yerba Buena Gardens, for example, roughly half the land will become gardens, plazas, and terraces to serve the objective of providing a pedestrian focus. Some mitigations may be made—an office building may be permitted to rise taller than otherwise would be the case, for instance. But overall the parcel is likely to be developed at considerably less than its "highest and best use." If historic buildings lie within or adjacent to the site, there may be a requirement that they be preserved and incorporated into the project.

Because such projects are envisioned as civic centerpieces, quality design generally is expected. Strong design can integrate the diverse uses, create the image of a prestige destination, and foster a public perception

that the project will enhance rather than compromise its surroundings. Superior design also can further the public approval process and generate excitement in the corporate and investment communities.

Effects on the Development Process

The predevelopment stage for an arts-inclusive MXD can be extended and time-consuming, generally averaging seven to fifteen years instead of the three to five years more typical of non-arts MXDs. Intensive negotiations among the developer, the public agency, and the arts sector are needed to establish the nature of the arts program for the project and its fit with the revenue-producing uses.

Public participation is essential in the planning process. The public will be footing a great part of the bill, either directly through public treasuries or through enabling mechanisms such as bond issues. Many residents also participate in the project as volunteers. Traditional arts supporters such as foundations are also likely to be involved in planning the nature of the arts component and its financial support.

The planning for arts components therefore must be collaborative from start to finish, with each participant maintaining a focus on overall needs and goals. In some of the cases in this book, the relationship among the participants has been highly structured, in others more informal. In either case, the planning process must be carefully managed, with appropriate commitments of staff and consultant time. One party should take the responsibility for this managerial role.

Effects on the Financial and Management Structures

Arts-inclusive projects involve more complexities than their non-arts counterparts for a number of reasons:

■ They are larger, both in size and in purpose.

■ More participants are involved whose interests must constantly be addressed. Each sector may include, in fact, several different individual agencies or players.

■ They incorporate a greater variety of uses, which must be coordinated and made complementary.

■ Some of the uses—primarily the cultural ones—will not produce net revenue, which raises the financial risk associated with the project. Moreover, it is extremely difficult to quantify the total value of the contribution that the arts can make to the project, which can complicate efforts to allocate the costs and risks equitably among the participants.

■ The initiation and preconstruction stages take much more time, because the level of planning detail is far greater. Accordingly, these projects require a considerably higher upfront capital investment, while the return on the investment is likely to be delayed.

Financial negotiations for these projects, not surprisingly, have tended to be protracted, intense, and occasionally acrimonious. In the cases described in this book, the financial arrangements that finally have been struck have been individual solutions, highly specific to the project and the parties involved.

Management issues also can revolve around the need for fair allocation of the responsibility for maintaining and operating the various project components. The cultural component presents problems not shared by its commercial neighbors—in particular the need to maintain artistic independence and the need for unearned revenue to ensure its viability. The management structure for an arts-inclusive MXD therefore cannot be an afterthought, but should be carefully worked out, with accountabilities clearly defined before implementation begins.

What Types of Projects Are Created?

The projects described in this book fall into three general classifications, with each type involving increasingly complicated issues of design, financing, management, and operations. From the simplest to the most complex, they are: (1) mixed-use buildings; (2) mixed-use developments; and (3) arts districts.

Mixed-Use Buildings

Smaller in scale and less ambitious than mixed-use developments, these projects combine two uses—one arts-related and one revenue-producing—in a single building or on a single site. The two examples discussed in this book both involve art museums: New York City's Museum of Modern Art, with its residential tower, and the Whitney Museum annex, which is being incorporated into the Equitable Life Assurance Society's new headquarters building, also in New York.

Combining uses in this way requires a relatively simple transaction between an arts institution and a developer. Rather than being a direct financial participant, the public sector may limit its involvement to the establishment of public policies—such as zoning variations or mechanisms for the transfer of development rights—that favor such arrangements when they benefit the arts. An ongoing management relationship may not be necessary once the project is completed. The parties sharing the site are close neighbors with common interests, but they maintain separate and distinct management structures.

Mixed-Use Developments

An arts-inclusive mixed-use development unites a developer, a city agency, and one or more arts organizations in an effort to meet complementary goals. What these parties create is a complex of many uses, each of which must reinforce and support the others.

In each of this book's case-study cities featuring such MXDs, the project has been intended to strengthen the downtown. Costa Mesa's South Coast Plaza, located in suburban Orange County south of Los Angeles, is in fact intended to create a downtown for a region where none exists.

Because the uses are unified into a single complex, the success of the whole depends on the success of each part. Therefore, effective management of ongoing operations is critical, and the relationship of the three parties must be extended into the operational phase.

Arts-intensive MXDs tend to involve an extremely diverse range of uses. San Francisco's Yerba Buena Gardens, for example, is planned to include offices, a major hotel, residential units, specialty retailing, an extensive amusement/recreation/entertainment package, and public amenities such as open space and plazas, as well as a generous presence for the arts.

Arts Districts

An arts district might be defined as a formally designated area that has a special and desirable cultural character and for which public policies have been established to encourage the preservation or further development of that character. Historic districts set the precedent for this approach. Now several cities are creating arts districts to revitalize downtown or near-downtown areas where arts facilities are clustered. Revenue-producing uses are being incorporated to give the district economic viability, while the arts uses attract the consumers. The objective is to combine these uses in a way that gives the entire district a cohesive identity and a public image of quality and excitement.

Districts may encompass a number of properties, which remain separate rather than being combined into a single parcel (as is the case with mixed-use developments). So the number of actors involved, particularly from the real estate and arts sectors, is likely to be high. The need to coordinate all their various interests and objectives, while ensuring that the larger goals of the district are met, raises extremely challenging issues of planning, land use, design, finance, and management. As a result, these projects take even longer to create than mixed-use buildings and mixed-use developments.

Some cities, in creating such arts districts, are building directly on the historic-district model by making old but significant buildings keystones of the project. They thus can serve twin goals of preserving both architectural and cultural resources. Often the buildings involved are theaters, but the oldest structures do not have to be arts-related. In the South Street Seaport project, landmark buildings, piers, and historic vessels have been restored to create a museum that recalls the maritime history of New York City.

Arts districts, unlike historic districts, are intended to serve economic as well as artistic purposes. In Cleveland's Playhouse Square, three historic theaters on Euclid Avenue are being rehabilitated in the largest theater restoration project in the nation. The project is an attempt to reassert cultural and allied commercial uses around a major downtown thoroughfare, recently declining but with a proud past. Similarly, Pittsburgh planners are using the scheduled renovation of one performing arts space and the expansion of another nearby to spur the development of a multiblock cultural and entertainment district in the city's Golden Triangle. The presence of the arts is being encouraged specifically to generate economic development in the downtown area.

The public policy legislation that designates such districts does more than set its boundaries. Special zoning provisions usually are included to establish strict controls on land use, density, design, permitted uses, and overall planning.

Types of Facilities Included

The arts can be included in a project for two different reasons: to provide new facilities for an existing recognized cultural institution, or to create opportunities for smaller or new arts groups to establish a presence in the community.

In some cases both purposes are served. The Performing Arts Center in Tulsa's Williams Center includes facilities both for major resident companies and for smaller community groups. Its Chapman Music Hall is home to the Tulsa Ballet, the Tulsa Opera, and the Tulsa Philharmonic, which have grown from local to regional stature since the opening of the center in 1977.

The center's John H. Williams Theater features performances by the professional American Theatre Company as well as several college and amateur groups. Two small "black box" studio theaters provide space for rehearsals, workshops, and experimental works. Many special events also have been held at the center, which serves multiple community and cultural functions.

The Tulsa project is typical in that its arts presence is large and substantial. Except in the case of the smallest examples—the mixed-use buildings—most arts-inclusive developments provide multiple facilities. Usually these are performing arts spaces, in some cases accompanied by a major museum. The emphasis is on first-rate, state-of-the-art facilities, designed to meet the specific needs and potentials of the particular arts disciplines involved.

The programming concepts for these cultural components reflect the reasons why the arts were included in the project. The facilities may house a resident organization, or they may permit a variety of arts groups to enjoy access to space not otherwise available to them. The South Coast Plaza in Costa Mesa, California, includes a home for a resident repertory theater company, a theater for use by Orange County's 250 local arts groups, a performance hall to attract world-class arts organizations on tour, and a sculpture garden featuring a permanent display of works by Isamu Noguchi.

In San Francisco, an innovative programming philosophy evolved through a comprehensive planning process that encouraged broad participation from the arts community. Recognizing an abundance of local artistic talent and activity, along with a lack of accessible, suitable spaces, Yerba Buena's planners created a concept for a multifacility cultural center with an ambitious mandate to showcase the Bay Area's arts. This showcasing, as defined in their planning process, will have several key components:
■ presentation of professional-level, high-caliber work in arts-specific facilities of the highest possible quality;
■ a diverse program of events encompassing all artistic disciplines—a mixture of formal and informal and traditional and avant-garde, with a variety that will appeal to

people of all ages, races, income levels, and cultural backgrounds; and
■ emphasis on giving local artists presentation opportunities that do not presently exist in the city.

A chart accompanying this section summarizes the range of arts facilities included in this book's case-study projects.

Baltimore: Mixed-Use and Culture in a Revitalized City

The Charles Center–Inner Harbor complex in Baltimore does not fit neatly into the project categories just described. Instead, Baltimore's experience might be seen as a culmination of the trends and development approaches considered in this book and an illustration of their potential for transforming a city's downtown.

Charles Center and Inner Harbor are actually two projects, about two blocks apart in downtown Baltimore. But a single nonprofit corporation, Charles City–Inner Harbor Management, Inc., orchestrated the development process in each instance, has managed both projects, and united the two in the public's perception. Moreover, the projects have had a strong synergistic effect on each other.

Charles Center, begun in the late fifties and developed over a long period, includes office, retail, and hotel space, as well as housing. The Morris Mechanic Theater and two performing plazas provide an arts presence. The components are joined by extensive walkways, providing the development with a pedestrian focus.

Inner Harbor, a redevelopment project initiated in the mid-sixties, has become a festive place rich in educational and entertainment opportunities. Built around a picturesque waterfront and bordered by plazas and gardens, the project includes a major science museum, an aquarium of national stature, and a festival-retailing and specialty-food complex. A marina offers paddleboats and other craft for rentals, and a floating museum of historic ships. Still under development is an innovative urban entertainment center, designed as much for adults as for children, which promises to be a prototype for other cities. Housed in an old rehabilitated power plant, it will use

Case Study Projects

City	Name of Project	Name of Arts Facility	Type of Arts Facility	Programming Concept
MIXED-USE BUILDINGS				
New York	Museum of Modern Art/ Residential Tower	Museum of Modern Art	Art museum	Resident institution
New York	Equitable Center	Whitney Museum Branch	Art museum	Resident institution
MIXED-USE DEVELOPMENTS				
Tulsa	Williams Center	Tulsa Peforming Arts Center	Concert hall Main theater Two black box theaters Art gallery	Resident and touring companies; Community access
San Diego	Horton Plaza	Horton Plaza Theatres	Theater and black box	Resident institution & other companies
Los Angeles	California Plaza	Museum of Contemporary Art	Art museum	Resident institution
		The Dance Gallery	Dance theater	Resident institution
		Performance Plaza	Outdoor festivals, performances, activities	Community access
Costa Mesa	South Coast Plaza	South Coast Repertory Theater	Theater	Resident company
		Orange County Performing Arts Center	Concert hall Theater	Visiting artists and companies; Community access
		California Scenario	Sculpture garden	Permanent exhibit
San Francisco	Yerba Buena Gardens	Theater Visual arts Video facility Multiple-use forum		Showcasing of local arts
ARTS DISTRICTS				
New York	South Street Seaport	South Street Seaport Museum	Cultural/ historical museum	Resident institution
Dallas	Dallas Arts District	Dallas Museum of Art	Art museum	Resident institution
		Morton H. Meyerson Symphony Center	Concert hall	Resident company
		Dallas Theater Center	Theater	Resident company
Cleveland	Playhouse Square	State Theatre	Performing arts spaces	Resident and touring companies
		Palace Theatre	Performing arts spaces	Resident and touring companies
		Ohio Theatre	Theater	Resident company
Pittsburgh	Pittsburgh Cultural District	Heinz Hall	Performing arts spaces	Resident and touring companies
OTHER PROJECTS				
Baltimore	Charles Center/ Inner Harbor	Morris Mechanic Theater	Theater	Touring artists and companies
		National Aquarium in Baltimore	Aquarium	Resident institution
		Maryland Science Center	Science museum	Resident institution
		Mayor's Flotilla	Historical/ cultural exhibit of ships	Permanent exhibit
		Pier 6 Pavilion	Outdoor theater	Touring artists and companies

Disneyland-style techniques to portray today's city from the point of view of a turn-of-the-century scientist.

At the time of these projects' inception, their location was considered a liability, since downtown Baltimore was deteriorating, economically and socially. New project components were phased in slowly, and success came incrementally, until finally it was substantial enough that highly financed developers could be attracted to the remaining parcels. A major factor in the ultimate success was an original planning study for Charles Center commissioned by the Greater Baltimore Committee and headed by architect and planner David Wallace from the Philadelphia firm of Wallace Roberts & Todd. Drastic and dramatic, the plan emphasized the need to create open spaces and pedestrian access, to insist on outstanding architectural design, and to make the project of sufficient scale to create an interest in downtown investment. The plan generated essential support from the mayor's office and downtown business leaders, and it provided a vision to sustain the extended development process.

By design, not all of Baltimore's cultural facilities have located in the project areas. The city has a strong group of museums that have been encouraged to remain in their traditional facilities. The donor of a new home for the symphony was urged to consider a location elsewhere in the center city. By spreading the cultural riches, Baltimore planners hope to help keep its whole downtown vital.

Certainly Baltimore retains many problems not addressed by the success of Charles Center and Inner Harbor. But it also has achieved a new confidence in its problem-solving ability. Such optimism is a powerful byproduct of its arts-inclusive development initiatives.

The development process for any large-scale mixed-use development has four stages: initiation and conception; preconstruction; construction; and management and operations. In the first two stages, the planning of the project takes place; the second two focus on implementation.

In the initiation and conception stage, the task is to define the project. The participants are chosen and begin working together, goals for the project are shaped, and a development strategy is created.

In the preconstruction stage, concepts are refined and made concrete. The feasibility of specific ideas is tested, the negotiations are conducted, and the financial deal is structured.

In the design and construction stage, detailed architectural plans are created and approved, the project is built, and marketing begins.

In the management and operations stage, the completed project becomes and remains functional.

The work in the first two stages, when the essential planning is accomplished, must be handled carefully if the project is to proceed smoothly in the implementation stages. For this reason, and because most arts-inclusive MXDs have not yet had enough experience with the later stages from which to draw meaningful conclusions, the following discussion concentrates on the planning stages.

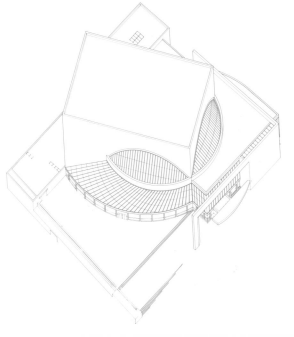

Initiating the Project

While no standard models have been developed for the precise ways in which the public, private, and arts sectors should work together, a number of approaches have been used with apparent success. In each case, one party has served as the project's principal initiator and catalyst. That party creates the initial vision, then seeks the collaboration of the others to realize the vision.

A preliminary economic analysis of a site will not necessarily generate such a vision, because economic analyses typically review a site's potential for specific uses—as office space, retail outlets, residential outlets, or hotels. In a successful MXD, such activities support each other in a synergistic manner. But how uses will interact and build on each other is nearly impossible to measure or predict.

Any one or a combination of the possible parties might become the initiator of a project.

Public Agencies

Often a city redevelopment agency will be the instigator of an arts-inclusive project. Since unusual ranges of public benefits are called for, the agency can take an active role that may include front-end planning and development, land acquisition, or zoning incentives. It may even move beyond previously established boundaries of active participation by sharing the financial risks of providing arts and amenities.

San Francisco and Los Angeles both illustrate cases in which a redevelopment agency initiated the development of major mixed-use projects on long-vacant tracts of urban-renewal land. In each case, the agency established ambitious public-policy objectives for the project before issuing a solicitation to developers. Then it directed a collaborative process that led to the creative planning and financial solutions needed to ensure that those objectives would be met.

Private Developers

The impetus for an arts-inclusive development usually does not come from the private sector, although there are notable exceptions. In Tulsa, the Williams Realty Corporation acted as the catalyst in the creation of Williams Center. The firm worked with the city to establish a need for the performing arts center that is the centerpiece of the project, and it purchased land, managed construction, and provided ongoing subsidies to ensure the development's success. Another example is South Coast Plaza in Costa Mesa, California, where developer Henry Segerstrom is creating an unusual mix of office, retail, hotel, and arts uses on 2,000 acres of former lima-bean fields owned by his family. The Segerstrom contribution has included land for theaters and a performing arts center, financing for an Isamu Noguchi sculpture garden, and a multimillion-dollar donation for the performing arts center's construction costs.

Many developers who might be interested in initiating such projects simply do not have the resources; this type of development requires substantial front-end investment, complex phasing, and intricate management systems once the project is open. A developer must be prepared to defer immediate returns for longer-term rewards, some of which may be difficult to quantify. Real estate organizations therefore often prefer to concentrate on more traditional opportunities. The developers who do get involved with arts-inclusive projects tend to be large, multitalented organizations that have gained the requisite expertise through their work on smaller MXDs or elaborate adaptive use projects.

Any developer who initiates such a project is likely to exhibit strong entrepreneurial leadership. Developers may be most open to the challenge of doing something grand and magnificent when it can be considered a capstone to their careers. In such situations, while the demands of return-on-investment still must pencil out, developers tend to be more willing to include a range of amenities that may not be immediately profitable.

The Arts Sector

The impetus for a project also can come from a cultural institution or a private foundation concerned with the arts. The Museum of Modern Art in New York, faced with a need to renovate and expand its facilities, conceived a way to generate funds by selling development rights to the air space over its building. This transaction led to the creation of a residential condominium tower and an ongoing revenue source for the museum.

For foundations, the active development role is relatively new. In Cleveland, a community foundation with a record of helping the arts—the Cleveland Foundation—took the lead in the creation of Playhouse Square. Spurred by the desire to save and rehabilitate three historic theaters, the foundation realized that their deteriorated downtown location could deter potential audiences. It perceived the need for ancillary commercial uses to strengthen and enhance the theaters and revitalize the district around them. The foundation therefore purchased commercial property in the neighborhood, supported feasibility studies, and defined strategies for creating and marketing both the arts and commercial uses.

In Pittsburgh, the Heinz Foundation took the initiative in generating funds for the restoration of the Stanley Theatre by acquiring land on an adjacent site and leasing it to a major corporation for a headquarters building. This idea evolved into a plan for a downtown cultural district that will aim to serve broad public objectives and generate considerable economic activity.

Foundations and cultural institutions often work in concert, with foundations providing funds for the institutions to prepare the master plans or feasibility studies needed to rally public-agency and private-sector support for a project.

Other Initiators

Arts-inclusive MXDs may be initiated by other entities, such as intermediary organizations established for precisely that purpose. These groups commonly combine elements from the public, private, and arts sectors.

The Centre City Development Corporation is a quasi-public agency, a nonprofit development corporation created by the city of San Diego to coordinate redevelopment efforts and reverse stagnation in the downtown area. The corporation performs all predevelopment and development activities—acquiring land in the name of the San Diego Redevelopment Agency, negotiating with developers, and entering into contracts for architectural, legal, planning, and economic services.

Horton Plaza, a retail/office/hotel mix, is one of a number of projects in which the corporation is involved. Recognizing the project's need for a special marketing niche in the face of tough suburban competition, the corporation planned and helped finance the construction of two theaters at the site, provided an ongoing subsidy for their operation, and encouraged the project's developer to set aside substantial funds for an arts program. When an adjacent theater was identified by a citizens group as a potential site for an art museum, the corporation found a developer to join with the museum in developing the building.

The *Downtown Development Handbook*, published by ULI in 1982, said of this approach:

Public or quasi-public corporations are often created to stimulate general downtown activity and may be empowered to support or participate in specific projects. . . . In addition to the general advantages of corporate status, [they] have important powers that can be used to initiate downtown [development] projects: the power of eminent domain, the power to sell tax-exempt revenue bonds, the right to receive revenues from the sale or lease of property, and the authority to levy property taxes, special assessments, or fees for specific public improvements. . . . A separate development corporation increases the city's effective management and its ability to coordinate public and private actions.

In Dallas, where a strong tradition of voluntary cooperation between the public and private sectors exists, an ad hoc committee called the Dallas Arts District Consortium was formed to create a forum within which development objectives for the city's proposed arts district could be prioritized. The arts district has required thoughtful and innovative approaches to planning, design, land use controls, cost-sharing, and site assembly. The consortium, whose members represent public, private, and arts interests, established financing mechanisms, public-policy objectives, zoning and planning guidelines, and a nonprofit management structure for the district.

Charles Center–Inner Harbor Management, Inc., is a private nonprofit corporation formed to provide the city of Baltimore with management services for the downtown development process. It operates on an annual contract with the city and is relatively free to carry out management decisions in implementing the city's downtown policies.

Managing the Planning Process

Since arts-inclusive development projects extend over many years, ongoing management must sustain the development process through all its stages. Usually the project initiator takes on this orchestration role as well. This leadership is not an iron-clad assignment, however; it may shift from one party to another. The Dallas Arts District Consortium, for instance, was formed only after an arts institution failed to float a bond issue for a much more modest version of the project than the one the consortium eventually planned.

The close relationship that evolves among the involved parties may produce not only significant benefits but also significant confusions. It is necessary to clearly define the roles and responsibilities that each participant will take on—who coordinates which aspects of planning, who pays for what kinds of feasibility studies and test programs. A mechanism for ongoing communication must be provided.

Creating a Development Strategy

Once a project has been initiated and a private/public/arts coalition has been established, it is necessary to formulate a preliminary concept and a development strategy. The development strategy must be flexible enough to allow for several possible variations in composition, phasing, cost, management, and participation of the coalition members. At the same time, the basic concept should be clear enough to catch the imagination of the participants and to provide the public with an idea of the project that it can understand and support.

The development strategy is likely to change and evolve as the planning process proceeds. Over time, its components could include:

■ a statement of the goals and objectives of the project;

■ a clear expression of the image and identity desired for the project;

■ a listing of the project components—what uses and amenities will be included, who will be responsible for financing them, when they will be phased, who might be potential major tenants—and a

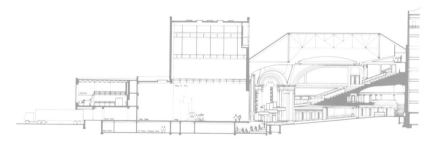

plan for achieving the desired synergy among them;

■ a general plan for proceeding with the project, including dates for completion of planning, design, construction, and occupancy, the composition of the development team, design review, and so on;

■ a marketing plan, including an articulation of the project's distinct market identity;

■ a first estimate of the nature of public participation in the development process and the project itself; and

■ a management plan.

Issues

Some of the issues likely to arise during the planning process include:

■ How to define a mix of uses that will best meet the overall objectives of the project. In particular, how to define the nature and extent of the arts and amenities packages.

■ How to position the revenue-producing uses in relation to the cultural uses that do not produce revenue, so as to give each its appropriate emphasis and image and to ensure market synergy.

■ How to provide people-oriented spaces and easy pedestrian access throughout the project. Increasingly, many public agencies expect MXDs to provide outdoor urban recreation areas.

■ How to create and maintain the exciting, active atmosphere that will make an attractive destination. How to make the project appealing to residents as well as visitors, so that it will not come to be perceived as a tourist trap.

■ How to encourage a 24-hour activity cycle.

■ How to provide adequate parking without having it become unsightly and intrusive.

In an arts-inclusive mixed-use project, a substantial portion of the site is devoted to uses that consume rather than produce revenue, a situation that magnifies the financial risk. The challenge in financial negotiations therefore is two-fold: The parties must find a way in which the risks—and the rewards as well—can be shared equitably, and they must ensure that all the objectives for the project, including the cultural ones, can be met.

For many of this book's case-study projects, the negotiation process has been protracted and sensitive. In typical real estate developments, many financial issues are resolved by custom (as when a municipality traditionally pays for certain improvements in and around the project site), or by law (as when a developer is required to allocate one percent of the construction costs to fine arts). Adding the cultural factor, however, raises a number of new issues, and no clear formula has emerged for resolving them. In each situation, the participants have had to hammer out an individual solution that addresses their particular needs.

The issues that arise can be as basic as how the arts uses are to be defined. This became a sticking point in the planning for San Francisco's Yerba Buena Gardens, where separate budgets had been established for the cultural component—a multidisciplinary arts center to be paid for by the city—and for the amusement, recreation, and entertainment uses, to be paid for by the developer. The developer maintained that certain community-oriented activities such as ethnic festivals and neighborhood fairs were cultural in nature, and that they and their facilities therefore should come under the cultural budget. The arts planners, on the other hand, contended that these activities should be considered as recreation or entertainment, and they were adamant that the arts center should be limited to professional-level presentations from traditional arts disciplines. The matter ultimately was resolved by increasing the arts center's budget and including the disputed uses under that banner.

Capital Costs

Arts-inclusive projects usually require public improvements and amenities far in excess of those provided in typical real estate developments. The cultural facilities are of course a major element in this requirement, but there are others. Land may be allocated for open-space plazas and gardens, which must be accompanied by lighting, landscaping, paving, water, and street furniture. Design requirements often are high, resulting in a need for higher-quality materials and costlier architectural and engineering fees.

The financial arrangements must be structured so that the burden of these costs is apportioned fairly among the participants. The simplest way may be to calculate a formula for a straightforward cost sharing. However, the nature of the relationship of the participants and the resources available to each rarely permit this approach.

The experiences of Dallas, Los Angeles, and San Francisco have been particularly instructive. In Dallas, whose arts district encompasses a number of separately owned parcels, the city agreed to pay for those items that are normally identified in the development process as city costs, such as normal street paving, lights, and signs. The costs for amenities—trees, drainage, irrigation, special paving, street furniture—would be split between the city and adjacent property owners, who would be responsible for that portion of the improvements to be made directly along their respective frontages. In many instances the city scheduled improvements such as water and sewer mains prior to the development of the adjacent properties. As these essentials were completed, responsibility shifted to the property owners to complete development of their sites.

The California Plaza project in Los Angeles has required careful financial structuring to compensate for extraordinary financial commitments required of the developer, estimated by a consultant at $58.6 million in October 1981. Most of this sum related to the cultural and open-space components of the project. One feature of the financial package that was arranged was a writedown in the cost of the land. On the assumption that the developer eventually would re-

ceive some benefit from the Museum of Contemporary Art and the project's other amenities, an adjusted cost burden of $30.8 million was assigned. The full value of the land was estimated at $89.1 million, but the city agreed to treat the developer's adjusted costs as in-lieu payments, bringing the land cost down to $58.3 million.

In San Francisco a similar land-cost writedown had been anticipated as part of the financial arrangements for Yerba Buena Gardens. But despite extensive negotiations, the city and the developer were unable to come to an agreement on the dollar value to be assigned to the public-amenity portions of the project. The final arrangement called for the developer to pay full market value for any land it bought or leased. The redevelopment agency will use the proceeds to fund construction of the cultural center and gardens.

Operating Costs

With nearly all of this book's case-study projects, a principal objective has been for the commercial uses to generate an ongoing subsidy for the cultural component. Several mechanisms have been created to achieve this result.

One means is tax abatement. In the case of the Museum of Modern Art, the city of New York agreed to forgo property tax revenues from the condominiums in the residential tower. Instead, a Trust for Cultural Resources is authorized to collect payments in lieu of taxes from the condominium owners, with these funds earmarked for the museum's expansion program and ongoing operations.

Another approach involves the creation of a subsidy from the revenue generated by commercial uses. In San Francisco, the plan is to combine lease payments from some of the Yerba Buena project's land with participation payments from the office building (whose site will be sold) to provide an annual budget for the security, maintenance, and operations of the gardens and cultural center. Both the lease and participation payments will be tied to income percentages. New York's South Street Seaport uses a similar concept: The Rouse Company, which operates the project's three-level specialty food market, pays a base rent; then, after recapture of operating costs and receipt of a preferred return, the remaining income from the market is split fifty-fifty between Rouse and the Seaport museum. The museum shares its revenue with the city and the state.

In Los Angeles, by contrast, the projected subsidy will be tied to the success of the arts program. The developer has agreed to a partial subsidy of the Museum of Contemporary Art, with the payments calculated on a formula based on the museum's attendance record.

The success of an arts-inclusive mixed-use project depends on both the success of its individual components and on a reinforcing relationship among the various uses. To ensure that the needs of all the segments, commercial and cultural, are met once the project is complete, a comprehensive management structure should be devised. Management issues should be resolved as much as possible during the project's planning stages, because the answers to management questions may affect design, financing, and other matters.

Several key issues must be addressed:
- What entity will be responsible for the ongoing maintenance and security of the public-benefit portions of the project?
- How should promotional efforts be structured to yield maximum results for the project and its individual parts?
- How can the arts component be managed to guarantee its artistic independence and integrity, yet ensure that it complements the overall project?
- How can the long-term viability of the arts component be ensured, if it is not expected to be profitable or self-sustaining?

Arts-inclusive MXDs represent a new phenomenon with little management history. Of the cases examined in this book, several remain in the planning stages, while others are under construction. A few have been operational for a short time or in a limited way, but there have not been enough fully operational, fully phased developments to create a definitive management model.

Nevertheless, a few observations can be made. Tom Flynn of Zuchelli, Hunter & Associates, in his article, "Maintenance and Management Agreements: Implementation of Mixed-Use Developments" (*Urban Land*, June 1984), identified three general management approaches for MXDs:

1) division of responsibilities among public and private participants for specific components or geographic sectors of a single project;

2) the creation of a distinct management/maintenance entity, separated from either of the two principal parties and probably representing wider interests when other participants are involved; and

3) the delegation of public responsibilities to the developer himself or to a third party.

Flynn cautioned, however, that:

It would be misleading to indicate that there is some exact body of knowledge on this subject when, in fact, agreements on the matter of mall maintenance and management have only evolved in recent years and only by the trial-and-error process of striking a deal which is acceptable to all major actors—developer, city officials, quasi-public corporations, and others—in typical mixed-use projects. In fact, the process of evolving an agreement which is perfectly acceptable to all parties is probably an unreachable goal.

The Museum of Modern Art achieved the simplest solution: There *is* no ongoing relationship between the museum and its residential tower, each being independently responsible for its own maintenance and management. But this entire project had a simpler, more straightforward structure than the typical arts-inclusive development, and the two uses have no overlap either in the space they occupy or their function.

For other projects, some sort of ongoing relationship among the parties will remain essential in the operations stage. In San Francisco, the participants in Yerba Buena Gardens chose to combine Flynn's first and second approaches. The redevelopment agency and the developer divided responsibility for the different project components, with the agency assuming the operation and maintenance of the gardens and cultural center and the developer handling the hotel, office, residential, retail, and amusement/recreation/entertainment uses. The cultural center actually will be managed, however, by a nonprofit organization (still to be formed), working under contract to the redevelopment agency. The city, the developer, the arts community, and other constituencies all will be represented on the nonprofit group's board of directors.

Such nonprofit intermediary organizations may emerge as one viable management model for an arts-inclusive MXD—or at least for the arts component, particularly when a single existing cultural institution is

not involved. The nonprofit Pittsburgh Trust for Cultural Resources, for instance, coordinates the development process for that city's downtown cultural and entertainment district, and it is expected to provide ongoing services and promotional activities for the district, including management of the renovated Stanley Theatre and other arts facilities. In San Diego a nonprofit corporation is projected to lease the Horton Plaza theaters from the developer for a dollar a year and to operate and maintain those facilities. A study commissioned by the city of Dallas recommended the formation of three separate nonprofits to administer the Dallas Arts District: (1) a management organization to handle leasing, maintenance, and other business matters; (2) a policy-making body that also would be responsible for promoting the district and its activities; and (3) a membership organization that would provide a forum for the public's views.

Whatever form a management structure ultimately takes, it is critical that these matters be resolved early and well. The Project for Public Spaces, Inc., a New York City consulting firm that conducted the Dallas study, emphasized in its report that "a strong management organization can be the single most important factor in the success of a downtown district or public area."

Arts-inclusive mixed-use projects offer the prospect of exciting benefits both for the public/private/arts coalition that creates them and for the citizens of the urban areas where they are located. However, they are extremely complicated and time-consuming to develop. They will succeed only when a clear, mutually accepted vision of specific goals is established for the project at the outset, and when a strong, committed leadership directs the development process.

Only when mixed-use projects make financial sense apart from the arts should plans be made for including cultural components. The arts activities should be carefully integrated with the commercial uses. This comprehensive planning will help establish a successful market image. It also will ensure that the cultural presence will provide quality programs. Most important, it will guarantee that all the project uses, revenue-producing and non-revenue-producing, will support and augment each other.

It remains difficult to quantify the added dollar value or increased return on investment achieved by integrating the arts into mixed-use projects. The cumulative economic impact of the arts industry on a city is measurable. The tools do not yet exist, however, to calculate precisely the increased economic benefit of arts components to specific projects. Cultural institutions and amenities do seem to improve retail and restaurant business, increase the use of hotel rooms on weekends, stimulate employers' interest in office space, and enhance a project's overall image. Michael Marston of Keyser Marston Associates, a real estate consulting firm with extensive direct experience in assembling arts-inclu-

sive MXDs, summarizes the real estate context as follows:

I have always advised our clients to build quality projects and hold them for the long term. Nowhere is this more true than in a large mixed-use project with an arts component. Real estate projects that include the arts appropriately have the opportunity to offer commercial space that is unique, thereby achieving a highly desirable position in the marketplace. I personally feel that mixed-use projects including the arts have, over the longer run, stronger value appreciation potential than more standard forms of real estate development.

Public agencies and private developers must anticipate extensive and costly negotiations. Since agencies often must take the lead in land assembly, program formation, and developer selection (as well as in joint financing tasks), the public side usually must acquire new expertise. A ready supply of trained public-sector professionals does not yet exist to plan and operate such projects. Frustration and delays often plague projects with poorly planned amenities that do not correspond with developers' requirements. Projects also suffer when an arts organization's ability to deliver quality exhibitions or performances is unknown.

As MXDs incorporating the arts become more sophisticated, so do their financial requirements. Extended development schedules are often necessary. Realistic timeframes must be figured into estimates of project planning costs to ensure that good work will be done and that unnecessary disappointment will be avoided.

Once developers and public officials agree on substantial commitments of space

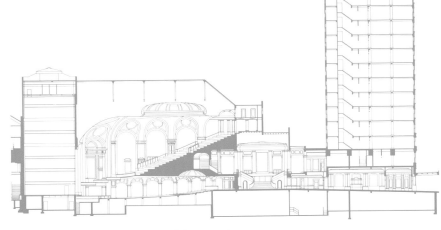

and funds for the arts, the cultural community has a responsibility to provide a superior product. Spaces for the arts cannot easily be rehabilitated into stores or offices. Cultural organizations must meet the challenges of working with public officials and private developers. They frequently will need new programs and audience-development schemes to hold up their part of the bargain. Innovative programs must build audiences from neighborhood residents, office workers, hotel guests, and conventioneers as well as from traditional arts patrons.

The costs of these kinds of programs are likely to be high, and the funds will not easily be obtained from the usual arts contributors. Some of the arts component's costs, however, can be recovered from the development itself. Part of the project's capital and operating funds should accrue to the participating arts institutions. And in return, the arts should attract significant numbers of consumers to the marketplace.

Excellent design is critical to these projects. Commenting on the lessons that other localities might learn from San Diego's Horton Plaza, Gerald Trimble of the Centre City Development Corporation has said:

An important transferable item is that the urban design aspects of the project have to be considered along with the business transaction. Both of these elements have to be monitored all the way through to completion of construction and then through leasing. We also have to think about the function and operation of these various developments, how they mix together, and how they will function for years to come. We have spent a great deal of time figuring out how performance art, theaters, movie theaters—all

the people-oriented portions of these projects— can be included so that the developments will receive people very well and consumers will be willing to come past other large developments to shop and dine and be entertained in Centre City.

These design requirements include the need for first-class arts facilities able to accommodate superior presentations of particular arts disciplines. However, as the arts enter the mixed-use arena, the definition of "culture" may need to expand to include festivals, outdoor recreation, popular concerts, and fairs that will attract large numbers of people. Neither cultural elitism nor traditional forms of popular entertainment will fill the bill completely. New art forms may in fact evolve out of such projects' operating experiences.

In spite of all the complicating factors, the emerging partnership of the arts, private development, and supportive public policy is likely to have mutually reinforcing benefits for all. Just as the visual arts world has decentralized outside New York City, so can the rest of the arts find new places for themselves in these innovative mixed-use projects where people live, work, and play. This phenomenon cannot help but create a genuinely enlivening influence on cities.

The Museum of Modern Art

Between 1975 and 1984, the Museum of Modern Art (MOMA)—the world's premier museum of the modern period's visual arts—added a wing on the west of its famous building at 11 West 53rd Street in midtown Manhattan; remodeled the existing wing on the east, slightly reducing but not marring its hallowed sculpture garden; and, all in all, doubled its exhibition areas and study, work, education, and retail spaces.

All this modification was undertaken not in a spirit of profit-making or contemporary changefulness, but simply to preserve MOMA's tradition as a keeper of the modern art heritage and to enhance its function as an arbiter of taste by making its superb collection more available to its burgeoning audiences. The museum had so outgrown its gallery spaces (40,500 square feet) that by the mid-seventies it could display only 15 percent of its painting and sculpture collection at any one time. And it had so outreached its financial resources that it could not realistically undertake a conventional capital fund campaign for construction moneys without depleting future contributions to its endowment, which subsidized operations. Furthermore, without more space, MOMA could not increase its self-support from admissions and retail sales.

The impasse was broken by a real estate deal. MOMA sold its air rights above an adjacent property for $17 million, a transaction made possible by MOMA's political skill in persuading the city and the state to pass legislation creating a Trust for Cultural Resources. The trust could receive the air-rights money without jeopardizing the museum's tax-exempt status. It also receives payments in lieu of taxes from the developed property, and from unit owners when condominium units are sold. Thus the air-rights sale has, in part, enabled the museum to expand and to develop an operating subsidy.

A 52-story luxury condominium apartment tower was built by the Charles H. Shaw Company of Chicago, the purchaser of MOMA's air rights. Museum Tower operates independently from the museum, and it was constructed separately though simultaneously. The two buildings share only transfer floors that house separate mechanical systems for each.

The construction costs of the 168,000-square-foot museum expansion totaled $55.7 million. The trust paid for the expansion by issuing two series of bonds totaling $60 million in anticipation of the in-lieu-of-tax payments. Both the apartment tower and the new museum are completed and occupied.

The history of the enterprise demonstrates creative intelligence, perseverance, aesthetic and fiscal integrity, and collaborative good will between MOMA and Shaw.

Midtown Busts, Then Booms with Finance, Arts, Entertainment

Midtown Manhattan, bounded by 34th Street on the south, 60th Street on the north, and by First and Eighth avenues on the east and west, has long been regarded as a centerpiece of New York City's—and thus the Western world's—cultural life.

Although Lincoln Center and the Metropolitan Museum of Art are located outside this core area, hundreds of art galleries and theaters lie within its boundaries. Many Midtown locales have become generic descriptions of entire American industries: "Broadway" for theater, "Seventh Avenue" for fashion, "Madison Avenue" for advertising. "Fifth Avenue" is universally understood to mean fine retail stores, while "Park Avenue" is a synonym for luxurious residences. Office buildings, department stores, restaurants, and hotels located in Midtown contribute to its overall vibrancy. It has always boasted a rich mix and variety of uses.

In 1980, a Midtown Development Project draft report summarized those unique qualities:

The dominance of the Midtown skyline by its agglomeration of tall office towers mirrors its dominant function: national and international business management and finance. New York's preeminence as a national and international center of business and finance in turn is supported by—and helps support—a wide variety of other functions: professional and business services of all kinds; a marketplace of ideas; an international center of arts and culture; a home of renowned educational, medical, and religious institutions; a shopping bazaar with an unsurpassed variety of goods and services; an entertainment "smorgasbord" offering everything from Broadway theater to honky-tonk; a popular and growing center of tourism, hotels, and restaurants.

. . . The quality of Midtown that defines it as a place, its unique and urbane character, is more than the sum and variety of its parts. It flows from the style and ambience of its avenues, streets, and places: Fifth Avenue with its stately limestone buildings, elegant department stores and shops, great churches; Rockefeller Center; the Broadway Theater District, particularly just before curtain time; the sculpture garden of the Museum of Modern Art and the quality and scale

of the midblocks to the immediate north of it; restaurant row; the sweep of Park Avenue— these are a few of the parts whose special qualities and differences contribute so much to the exciting whole.

This combination of attributes helps keep midtown Manhattan functioning as the economic heart of New York City. It is a workplace for more than 600,000 people, almost one out of every four jobs in the entire city, the greatest concentration of jobs and productive wealth on earth.

The Museum of Modern Art is located on West 53rd Street, between Fifth and Sixth avenues. Considerations of how to expand it had to be made within two contexts:
■ the expansion of private Midtown development to the west and south of the museum, which increased the value of the museum site and adjacent property; and
■ a number of municipal zoning ordinances, including the potential for sale or transfer of air rights, developed since 1961, which had been designed to protect and to enhance the quality of Midtown and to make sure that the needs of private development and of the public interests were jointly served.

The current history of Midtown development on the west side of Sixth Avenue may be said to have begun during the four years of 1969–72, when New York experienced the greatest burst of office construction in its history. During that period, almost 18.8 million square feet of office space were built west of Sixth Avenue. However, soon after this building boom, the city entered a period of economic decline. From 1970 to 1977 it suffered a net loss of more than 600,000 jobs. By the middle of the decade, New York neared bankruptcy. The normal credit markets were closed to it. It survived largely because of various emergency financial measures, the most visible being the Municipal Assistance Corporation, which administered a variety of unusual public/private strategies to help return the city to health.

During this recovery, Manhattan made a distinct shift in economic emphasis from manufacturing and production jobs to financial and corporate headquarters, particularly in information and publishing. This

trend was part of a national evolution in which urban areas and their central business districts would begin to function more as business and communication centers than as production sites.

At the same time this shift was taking place, two other trends emerged. A 1981 Department of City Planning document described these two new and interrelated factors:

After the bicentennial in July 1976, the city emerged once more as a great tourist attraction from its temporary depression, media bad-mouthing, and exaggeration of urban problems.

Tourism has boomed. Its rapidly increasing foreign component is related both to New York's role as an international center, and to the favorable rates of exchange which make it a good buy for foreigners. In 1979, a record number of tourists, 17.5 million, visited the city. They spent $2.25 billion and generated $180 million in direct tax revenues for the city government. Hotel occupancy reached an all-time-high rate of 83 percent.

The national and international function of the city generates business services—legal, accounting, and advertising among the most important. Tourism and the hotel and restaurant industries that it helps to support in turn generate blue-collar services and help to fill the gap in the job market left by the decline of manufacturing.

The symbiotic relationship of the arts, culture, and entertainment to both the city's business and finance headquarters function and to tourism need not be belabored. Neither should it be underestimated. The arts/cultural/entertainment function is an important industry in its own right. It contributes, according to a study by Professor Dick Netzer, some 3 percent of the city's gross domestic product—as much as the securities industry. It also helps bind together and reinforce the vast constellation of disparate activities that make up New York's CBD.

Thus the city recognized that its cultural institutions benefited tourism, and that the high-level business decision making that had come to characterize so much of Midtown was enhanced by amenities ranging from plazas in front of office buildings to through-block arcades that eased access between midblock streets.

MOMA Becomes a Victim of Its Own Success

The Museum of Modern Art was established in 1929 to "cultivate in the public a sound understanding of modern art." Because it owned no paintings and only one work of sculpture when it first opened its doors in rented space in the Hecksher Building on Fifth Avenue and 57th Street, MOMA was not so much a museum as a prospectus for one, and its first home contained ample space for gallery exhibitions and educational activities. During its early years, the museum established a virtual monopoly on the American public's interest in the modern arts. Only a small handful of New York galleries exhibited paintings and sculpture of the 20th century; popular criticism of contemporary art was rare; and scholarly investigation of current art was almost nonexistent. The public's enthusiastic response to MOMA's temporary exhibitions and publications therefore astonished even the most ardent of its supporters.

While the museum educated the public, it also built up a permanent collection under the guidance of its first director, Alfred Barr, Jr. By 1939, when MOMA moved into its fourth and final home at 11 West 53rd Street, its collections numbered 2,500 works in all media. Between 1939 and 1941, the collections doubled; in each of the next two decades, they doubled again.

The museum's single auditorium eventually became inadequate to house its film, lecture, and other educational programs. Rooms for showing prints, drawings, and examples from the museum's architecture and design collections also proved limited. Its facilities for scholars and its restaurants grew chronically overcrowded, and the efficiency and profitability of its retail operations were impaired by the cramped space. The museum also found it needed a library and archives for research by its own staff and a growing scholarly community.

By the seventies, the museum was clearly becoming a victim as well as a beneficiary of the explosive interest it had helped create. In no small measure because of the work of Alfred Barr and MOMA's founders, New York has become the world capital of contemporary art. It has more than 500 art galleries showing contemporary paintings, sculpture, photographs, prints, and posters. Other museums and universities in the city cater to the tastes in art and design that MOMA first cultivated.

MOMA now had to deal with ever-increasing requests from scholars, students, and practicing professionals for use of its study centers. Because much from its collections could not be seen in its own galleries, it offered an extensive program of circulating exhibitions, and it was generous with its loans. Between July 1974 and June 1976, MOMA circulated 15 different exhibitions containing more than 1,500 works of art to 31 cities and made nearly 1,500 individual loans to 147 U.S. institutions.

At the same time, the museum faced growing financial pressures. During the decade between 1965 and 1975, MOMA's membership declined from 32,000 to 25,000, partly because it could afford no vigorous promotion effort and partly because of a surge in popularity and in membership of the Metropolitan Museum of Art. By some other measures, MOMA's vitality was being called into question. *New York Times* art critic John Canaday expressed his ungenerous opinion (in August 1976) that "the Metropolitan has taken over from the Modern as the city's cultural midway, while the Modern has settled into a conservative historical stance. MOMA is one of the great museums of the world, but there is no longer anything very modern about it. . . . What changed the Modern during the last 17 years," he went on, "was that American art caught up with it and passed it."

As attendance declined, annual deficits were approaching the $1 million mark and the declining stock market threatened a dwindling endowment. From every standpoint in the mid-seventies, the museum found itself short of space and funds.

A number of suggestions were made to generate additional revenue—from freezing the museum's collection and simply displaying already held art to "deaccessioning" or selling of some paintings to generate operating cash. None of these ideas were deemed appropriate, because the trustees believed that MOMA should not become static, and that the museum's collection was really public property, donated specifically so that others could view it. To

Fund Drives Succeed but
Never Satisfy

use the collection as a salable asset was considered to be immoral if not illegal. Trustees and staff determined instead to remain faithful to the original concept of the museum and to keep the collections together on West 53rd Street. They cut staff, introduced operating economies, and increased revenues, but proved able only to prevent deficits from rising above the $1 million level during 1975–77. Evidence mounted that the museum would never be self-supporting in its existing space. The deficit was projected to pass the $1.2 million mark by 1979–80 and to "increase rapidly thereafter."

That MOMA should have reached such a precarious financial state was not a total surprise. It had been undercapitalized since its early years, and it had on several occasions mounted funding efforts designed both to alleviate its continuing need for physical expansion and to strengthen its endowment base.

Between 1959 and 1961, the museum had raised $25.5 million to expand its building and endowment. With these funds, the museum had opened a Philip Johnson–designed wing, the renovated Abby Aldrich Rockefeller Sculpture Garden, new galleries, and study centers in May 1964. In 1968, an additional stage of expansion had been completed when the museum bought a building behind it on 54th Street that had housed the Whitney Museum of American Art. This building, called the North Wing, was remodeled as a library, a conservation laboratory, and art storerooms.

But a continual shortage of gallery space continued, caused by MOMA's commitment to exhibiting the entire range of modern visual arts. In the late sixties, for example, the museum's department of photography acquired the magnificent Bernice Abbott collection of photographs by Eugène Atget. But after a show at the time of the acquisition, only a token representation of the Atget works could be displayed.

During the late sixties, several studies had investigated converting the air rights above the property adjacent to the museum into a profit-making venture. One scheme had suggested that the development of a commercial office building above the museum could net the equivalent of an increase of between $10 million and $15 million in the museum's endowment. This income, combined with a $35 million capital campaign, could be sufficient to cover the museum's operating expenses.

Before these studies could be developed further, however, the recession of the seventies set in. This economic slowdown, coupled with a projected oversupply of office space in midtown Manhattan, convinced MOMA's trustees to postpone the proposed building plan. Most important, the size of the annual operating deficits continued to mount, and the trustees decided that all new contributions should be added to the endowment fund to cover annual deficits. No substantial new construction would be undertaken until this primary goal had been achieved and the cost of operating any newly constructed space had been adequately endowed.

MOMA's fundraising goal therefore was reduced to $21.5 million, all for the operating endowment. This sum was met by 1974 from private donor pledges. At the same time, however, the value of the museum's endowment portfolio diminished through a declining stock market and through withdrawals to cover operating deficits. The $21.5 million campaign, intended to ensure the museum's fiscal stability, became instead only a holding action against current losses.

In 1975, the museum therefore began to consider two additional options for restoring its financial health: intensifying its appeal to the city government for financial support as a cultural and economic asset; and developing its real estate potential. The estimated annual revenue needed to put the museum in the black was approximately $1 million. If MOMA could obtain this amount each year from either the city or from its real estate, it could rely on traditional donors for funds to replenish its endowment.

MOMA Sells Air to Buy Floor Space

Unfortunately, before the museum could ask city agencies for support, the city suffered one of its worst fiscal crises ever. With municipal officials laying off police, teachers, and other employees by the thousands, closing museums and libraries, and struggling to avert bankruptcy, it was hardly the time for MOMA to request an operational subsidy of $1 million a year.

Instead, MOMA turned to its second plan, the commercial development of its 66,000 square feet of prime Midtown property. Initial feasibility analysis suggested favorable results. Just a few blocks away, the recently built Olympic Tower, a luxury residential and retail building, had nearly sold out before its construction had been completed. Encouraged, MOMA focused its plan on the construction of a luxury apartment building above a long-proposed new west wing for the museum that would solve its spatial difficulties.

The plan for increasing the museum's gallery spaces was based on a strategy that originally had been developed in 1969 during the administration of Mayor John V. Lindsay: to encourage private developers to construct legitimate theaters in new office buildings on Broadway in exchange for increased building heights. This principle of using air rights to provide a cultural amenity had already been suggested to MOMA by Richard Koch, general counsel and director of administration for the museum, but was shelved when the office market declined. It now appeared, however, that the late seventies would witness a strong market for luxury apartments in the Midtown Fifth Avenue area. There were doubts that an office building, with its large elevator core, could be accommodated above the museum, but a residential building might work—if MOMA could sell its air rights to a developer without jeopardizing its tax-exempt status.

MOMA assembled a talented consultant team to assist it in this real estate challenge. Richard Weinstein, an urban designer and architect who had been responsible for the theater district program under Mayor Lindsay, was working as a consultant at the Rockefeller Brothers Fund when he learned of the museum's interest. By the end of 1975, working with Donald H. Elliott, who had been Lindsay's commissioner of city planning, Weinstein arrived at a new formulation for an air-rights strategy:

■ construction of a west wing of the museum on its adjacent property along 53rd Street;

■ construction of an all-residential tower (instead of a mixed office and residential building) on top of the west wing;

■ conveyance of MOMA's air rights to a private developer under new zoning regulations; and

■ creation of a special state agency—the Trust for Cultural Resources—to act on behalf of the museum in funding its expansion through tax-exempt financing secured by dedicated in-lieu-of-tax payments from the apartment development.

After an initial building concept had been prepared, the museum asked Weinstein to direct a full-fledged feasibility study. Elliott prepared a financial plan, and

MOMA's Trust Wins
City/State Advocacy, Court Ruling

Peter E. Pattison directed the real estate component. All worked closely with the mayor's staff, and together they formed a task force that reported to Richard E. Oldenburg, director of the museum, and Mrs. John D. Rockefeller 3rd, its president.

Critic Paul Goldberger described the key elements of Weinstein's design concept in the *New York Times* of February 13, 1976, as follows:

The design [also] suggests some dramatic changes in the museum building itself. The rear wall of the main building facing the sculpture garden would be removed, and a wall of glass would be erected several feet out from the present wall. The glass area would be open to all floors and would function as a circulation spine, with escalators rising to the top, permitting a view both of the garden and of the galleries as the visitor rides upstairs.

The Weinstein plan also calls for the transfer of the museum's restaurant to the east end of the sculpture garden, where the present D'Harnoncourt temporary exhibition gallery is. The sculpture garden would be reduced only slightly in size, however.

The financial scheme required a new state law to provide for the creation of the Trust for Cultural Resources, which would have limited condemnation powers and the authority to issue tax-exempt securities and to receive payments in lieu of real estate taxes. The proposed trust would sell the museum's air rights to a private developer. Once the tower was built and occupied, the bulk of more than $1 million a year in taxes that would ordinarily go directly to the city would be paid to the trust. This anticipated stream would allow the trust to issue tax-exempt notes to finance the construction of the expanded museum spaces.

Bills to create MOMA's Trust for Cultural Resources went before the New York State legislature in June 1976. They were written to permit all cultural institutions in New York State that met certain qualifications to establish similar trusts to administer real estate projects as a means of improving their cultural operations.

The bills received wide support from public officials and leaders of cultural institutions. Mayor Abraham Beame endorsed the legislation on the advice of Martin E. Segal, the present chairman of Lincoln Center, who became closely involved with the project. Beame stated the reasons for his support of the expansive program:

It is important to note that the museum is trying to come to terms with its own difficult financial problems without asking the city for cash payments. At this point in our history, that's a relief. It's like money in the bank.

In spite of this high-level support, the state assembly voted down the legislation after it was passed by the senate. The *New York Times* reported that "The issue of balancing the need and desire to foster those things which make New York City a center for the arts with the needs of a city in financial 'extremis' dominated the hour-long debate." Oliver G. Koppell, a Democrat from the Bronx, put the issue this way: "We can't build palaces of gold when we can't feed our children, finish new schools, and keep hospitals open."

Immediately after the bill's defeat, an intense lobbying effort was mounted by Mayor Beame, museum advocates, and cultural leaders. Some legislators feared that the legislation represented a "Trojan horse"—that it would enable powerful museums to muscle their way into the development industry. Donald Elliott countered that the payments to the trust in lieu of taxes would be no greater than if they went directly to the city, and that the trust's condemnation powers were not so awesome as to enable cultural institutions to gobble up taxable land.

Elliott stressed the tremendous hope within the cultural community that the plan would succeed: "I think we all feel we

Museum of Modern Art
Project Data

Physical Configuration
Component—Income Generating

Residential Tower	263 condominiums 409,129 sq. ft. residential space 44 stories beginning at the 7th floor above the MOMA wing (7 & 8 are mechanical and service floors, 9–52 are residential) 580 ft. high

Component—Arts/Culture/Open Space

Museum of Modern Art	168,000 sq. ft. new space 203,000 sq. ft. renovated space 371,000 sq. ft. total Construction of six-story West Wing facility adjacent to MOMA's main facility and renovation and improvement of rest of museum.
Location	West 53rd Street, New York City
Master Developer	Museum Tower Associates—Charles H. Shaw Company and Leon DeMatteis Construction Corp.
Architects	
Museum	Cesar Pelli, Cesar Pelli & Associates, New Haven, Conn., project designer in collaboration with Gruen Associates, New York, architect of record
Tower	Cesar Pelli and Gruen Associates in collaboration with Jacquelin Robertson. Edward Durell Stone Associates, New York, architect of record
Development Period	1979–84

Estimated Total Development Cost

Museum Expansion	
Development Cost	$55,700,000
Financing Cost	8,880,000
Residential Tower	
Air Rights Purchase	$17,000,000
Development Cost	$100,000,000

Source: MOMA

have to find ways of raising money other than asking for it. We can no longer go to the big contributors because the money isn't there."

Two days later, the legislature reversed its position and approved the trust. The only difference was the addition of a requirement that the New York City Board of Estimate approve the concept of the trust before its creation. The effect of the amendment was to move the debate from the state to the city. Governor Hugh Carey then signed the bills approving the trust, paving the way for the city Board of Estimate to review the project.

The project then was examined by the New York City Planning Commission prior to Board of Estimate consideration in September 1977. The planning commission approved the museum tower plan, but not without expressing concern about the huge tower in the middle of the block, which would alter the character of 53rd Street. It also heard criticisms of the proposed reduction in the sculpture garden's size. Commissioner Gordon Davis explained why the commission voted for the plan: "Because of the complex and difficult design issues, I do not believe the commission would have approved the project if it was not convinced that it was essential for the museum's survival."

At the same time as the planning commission and Board of Estimate were reviewing the plan, a lawsuit challenging the constitutionality of the law came before the appellate division of the New York State Supreme Court in Manhattan. It had been brought by the Dorset Hotel, whose property lies adjacent to a portion of the museum on West 54th Street. The hotel's views would be obstructed if the apartment tower were built, and the hotel owned an easement on a brownstone at 29 West 53rd Street that gave it the right to setback restrictions for any construction on that site. MOMA needed to use this property and others at 31, 33, and 35 West 53rd Street to build its new tower.

The state supreme court ruled that the law was unconstitutional on three grounds:

1) because the state constitution requires tax exemptions to be made on a "general" rather than specific basis;

2) because the power of condemnation could only be used for a "public use," and "no public use was involved here"; and

3) because the legislature had violated the state constitution by passing a special law affecting New York City without obtaining a "home-rule message" from the city council.

MOMA then requested a special court hearing by the New York State Court of Appeals. The Whitney Museum of American Art filed an amicus curiae brief contending that the law was constitutional. A Whitney spokesman explained that although they were "not contemplating a like project, it's always nice to have the law available if we wish to do something similar."

At the end of December 1978, the state court of appeals upheld the legislation's constitutionality. Judge Domenick Gabrielli, writing for the majority, argued that "the new law does not grant an exclusive privilege or franchise and cannot under the circumstances be deemed a private bill, since it satisfies the constitutional fiat of generality." He also emphasized the "state public interest" in assisting cultural institutions.

Charles Shaw Chosen as Condominium Developer

With the favorable court ruling, MOMA was ready to move ahead. The Arlen Development Corporation, developer of the Olympic Tower, had signed a letter of intent with the museum in the spring of 1978, but that had been allowed to lapse, by mutual agreement, during the constitutionality litigation. By the spring of 1979, inflation had raised cost projections considerably, which in turn now required a larger fund drive for the new wing than the $36 million campaign previously planned. The market for condominiums, however, had improved, so the tower concept was changed from a part-rented, part-condominium building into an all-condominium structure. This revision required extensive changes in apartment layouts. Design difficulties in "marrying" the facade of the new tower with that of the expanded museum building also had to be solved.

The healthy condominium market helped stimulate interest in the project from more than two dozen potential developers, but by May 1979 the museum was negotiating only with Charles Shaw, a Chicago developer with a strong financial position, a reputation for reliability, and a record of high-quality mixed-use projects. Frederick and Alfonso De Matteis were brought into the project by Shaw to serve as general contractors, and their joint venture was called Museum Tower Associates.

Shaw faced the challenge of attracting condominium buyers to a part of the city that had not seen luxury residential apartments for decades, and of establishing an identity for the project separate from but related to the museum. Despite these drawbacks, he secured substantial funding from

the Continental Illinois National Bank and Trust Company of Chicago and purchased the museum's air rights outright for $17 million.

Museum Tower Associates' outright purchase of the air rights immediately insulated MOMA from any financial risks in the development. But to make certain that the long-delayed project would move ahead, the museum got Shaw and the De Matteis brothers to guarantee the tower's comple-

Project Data: Museum of Modern Art

Location	North side of 53rd Street between Fifth Avenue and the Avenue of the Americas, New York	
Completed	Spring 1984	
Architects	Cesar Pelli, Cesar Pelli & Associates, New Haven, with Gruen Associates, New York, the architect of record for museum portion	
Consultants	Mechanical Engineer:	Cosentini Associates
	Structural Engineer:	Rosenwasser Associates
	Lighting:	Donald Bliss
	Landscaping (Sculpture Garden):	Zion & Breen Associates
Contractor	Turner Construction Company	
Building Cost	$55 million	
Gross Area	168,000 sq. ft. of new space	
	203,000 sq. ft. of renovated space	
	371,000 sq. ft. total for the expanded museum	
Breakdown of Interior Area	Galleries	87,000 sq. ft.
	Public Areas	
	Main Lobby and Education Center	12,200 sq. ft.
	Garden Hall	18,000 sq. ft.
	Department Study Centers	15,000 sq. ft.
	Library	9,000 sq. ft.
	Auditoriums	13,400 sq. ft.
	Theater I (seating 460)	
	Theater II (seating 217)	
	Conservation Labs	8,000 sq. ft.
	Restaurants	20,700 sq. ft.
	Garden Cafe (seating 220)	
	Members Dining Room (seating 240)	
	Museum Store	8,000 sq. ft.
	Storage	17,000 sq. ft.
	Shops	8,000 sq. ft.
	Offices	65,000 sq. ft.
	Mechanical	37,000 sq. ft.
Exterior Features	*West Wing and Museum Tower Facade:* concrete frame; aluminum and glass curtain wall patterned with 11 shades of opaque ceramic glass and tinted vision glass.	
	Garden Hall: Steel frame with aluminum and glass curtain wall. Glass type: PPG insulated clear with an ultraviolet screening interlayer.	
	Facade of West Wing was designed to balance the overall composition of the museum exterior along 53rd Street. The original white No. 11 building containing the expanded lobby entrance is now flanked by the dark gray West Wing and the similarly dark East Wing.	
Interior Features	Circulation is organized horizontally via a tier of escalators rising from the main No. 11 building into the new West Wing. This system is housed in the new four-story glass-enclosed Garden Hall. A light and airy space that opens views to the sculpture garden, 54th Street, and midtown Manhattan.	

tion with their personal assets as well as their companies'.

In December 1979, the Trust for Cultural Resources issued $40 million in collateralized revenue bonds to get construction started. To obtain a Triple A rating for this initial offering, the bonds were guaranteed by a collateral fund to which MOMA contributed $31 million of its own unrestricted funds, to be held in escrow for the life of the bonds. Proceeds from the bond sale were to be allocated in the following manner:

Proceeds from Trust Revenue Bonds

Land acquisitions	$ 4,000,000
Construction and fixed equipment	25,000,000
Fees and other	7,000,000
	$36,000,000
Capitalized interest and cost of insurance	4,000,000
	$40,000,000

MOMA's trustees had been convinced that Charles Shaw could develop a distinguished luxury residence that would meet the architectural standards of the late Edward Durell Stone and Phillip Goodwin, designers of the museum's original 1939 building. Shaw had participated in the development of United Nations Plaza and in the initial stages of Tulsa's Williams Center. He knew Manhattan real estate, as well as the difficulties inherent in a mixed-use development.

Shaw agreed to a highly unusual series of design criteria and review processes. Because Cesar Pelli had already been selected as the museum's architect, Shaw had to work with Pelli's basic massing of the tower and with the concept of a curtain wall for the tower and museum. While the museum and the condominium remain functionally separate, they constitute a single architectural unit. Luckily, MOMA's insistence on quality architecture and design tallied with Shaw's perception of the residential market.

Shaw's attitude toward working with the museum during the five-year period of the tower's planning and construction was unfailingly cooperative: "You have to trust one another for it to succeed." That trust was well earned by the MOMA staff and by the trustees' expansion committee, chaired by Donald Marron, chairman of Paine Webber. They worked hard to make the museum's schedule for planning and construction mesh with Museum Tower Associates'.

Although one could not quantify precisely the added value of a museum address for the condominium apartments, Shaw acknowledged a beneficial relationship: "This identification . . . with the cultural force of the Museum of Modern Art is, in the city and in the world, a decided plus. When all is done, Museum Tower and the [MOMA] expansion will clearly be perceived as an integrated whole."

It is an open question whether the air-rights partnership between MOMA and Shaw's organization could be replicated by other cultural institutions and other developers. Museum Tower Associates paid a record price for the air rights—an upfront investment many other developers might not accept. Shaw also had to work with two different architects (Pelli for the museum expansion and tower facade and Edward Durell Associates for the tower's interiors). Several million dollars were spent on plans alone before the deal was finalized, and strong personal guarantees that the tower would be completed were required. In exchange for these rigorous commitments, the developers obtained both the opportunity to build on one of mid-Manhattan's choicest sites and the prestige of association with a world-famous museum.

Although other nonprofit institutions in New York City, such as the New-York Historical Society and St. Bartholomew's Church, have since proposed placing towers over their buildings, final agreements have not been reached. Such a project requires a rare relationship of trust and care between a nonprofit institution and a private developer.

The concept of constructing apartment towers over cultural or nonprofit institutions also is limited by the small market for luxury housing, and by the long time (seven to ten years) needed to produce such a building from inception to selling. This extended timeline hampers most developers' abilities to obtain financing.

MOMA Builds Next To and Under the Transfer Floors

In February 1977, one month after having assumed the duties of dean of the Yale University School of Architecture, Cesar Pelli was commissioned by MOMA to design its expansion and renovation project. Pelli previously had been a partner in Gruen Associates in Los Angeles, for whom he had directed such projects as the Pacific Design Center in Los Angeles and the Courthouse Center in Columbus, Indiana.

Pelli chose to use the basic features of the schematic design developed by Richard Weinstein during the feasibility study: a garden hall circulation spine linking the old and new buildings, and the relocation of the restaurants to the garden wing. He faced design difficulties that had been identified in the feasibility study:
■ the need to integrate the existing museum buildings into the new scheme for an expanded museum and apartment tower;
■ the need to preserve the museum's famed sculpture garden and still create a circulation pattern throughout the expanded museum; and
■ the need to create a building with bulk and height for a tower, yet one that would not block out the sunlight to the garden.

Pelli preserved the facade on the 1939 building at 11 West 53rd and blended it with his new west wing and the 1964 east wing designed by Philip Johnson. Pelli believed that at all costs:

... the facade had to be preserved. It may be our first example of modern architecture for an important institution and it has become a universally recognized symbol for the museum. The facade means "Museum of Modern Art" as much as "Demoiselles d'Avignon."

Pelli's glass wall, with escalators that carry visitors from the ground-floor entrance to the top gallery level, solved the circulation problem, making movement upward through the entire building more pleasant. The glass wall has an added effect of reorienting the museum from 53rd to 54th Street. Paul Goldberger of the *Times* described the impact of this reorganization as follows:

The effect of this is a subtle but powerful change. The museum was formerly a medium-sized building that faced 53rd Street and had a pleasant backyard. Now, thanks to the creation of the Garden Hall and to the relocation of the museum's restaurants at the east end of the Sculpture Garden, it is a U-shaped complex that is oriented toward 54th Street and the Sculpture Garden. Fifty-third Street, though it is still the formal front door, is really now the museum's back. Its front is its own exquisite garden with the view across the street to the eclectic and gracious architecture of 54th Street—a streetscape very much like the one that 53rd Street itself presented before the museum grew so big.

When it came to the interior design, Pelli chose not to impose strong preferences on those spaces. Rather, he treated the new galleries like the existing ones. Pelli combined the small-scale galleries sought by the curators with a circulation pattern that moves large numbers of people up the side of the building, without interfering with the gallery intimacy.

For the condominium tower, extensive design studies explored the best possible apartment layouts for each floor. Finally Shaw and his associates settled on a layout that reduced the number of apartments per floor from nine to six, positioning the living rooms of four of these in the corners of each floor. This arrangement gave many of the apartments a fine view of the museum's sculpture garden.

Shaw also had to build a platform on which to construct his project. In essence, he had purchased a lid plus 44 stories of space on top of the museum's proposed expansion; he had to make certain that the underlying shell would be constructed in a time sequence that would correspond with his own plans for the condominium tower.

Accordingly, Shaw and MOMA entered into a five-year agreement during which the structure that would house the new museum wing would be built, forming the shell over which the apartment tower construction would proceed. The agreement

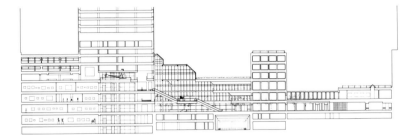

Cross section of the expanded museum complex behind the facades of 53rd Street. Part of the original six-story edifice (center) has been removed to show the glass-enclosed garden hall behind it. The north wing on 54th Street is not shown.

MOMA's new sculpture garden with a view of the new garden hall.
Credit: Terry Sanders

View of the MOMA abstract expressionist galleries on the third floor of the new West Wing.
Credit: Adam Bartos

The Museum of Modern Art's expanded facade along West 53rd Street includes the new West Wing on the far left, the original 1939 building in the middle, and the 1964 East Wing on the right.

reflected two important aspects of the project:

■ Although the expanded museum facilities were independent of the condominium tower, certain spaces could be constructed more economically under a single construction plan.

■ The museum had certain aesthetic standards for the apartment tower's exterior and lobby areas the developer had to meet.

Under the agreement the entire project was divided into three sections:

■ the six-floor lower building that would house the expanded museum's west wing (exclusive of the residential tower's lobby and elevators);

■ the 44-floor tower parcel for condominiums; and

■ two transfer floors, housing mechanical equipment.

The agreement established a development schedule for the entire project, a reciprocal easement agreement, a joint review process for those design issues affecting both the museum and tower, and the standards for a "distinguished luxury residential building." Both parties agreed to pay their proportionate share of the lower building and transfer floors. Finally, the agreement provided for an arbitration mechanism to settle any disputes and a termination date for the completion of the lower building shell (exclusive of the facade) and issuance of a certificate of occupany for the tower. This agreement confirmed the already established pattern in which the developer and the museum each operated and managed their own project separately, but both cooperated in jointly important decisions.

Upon completion of the west wing's shell, work on the museum building continued separately. This relationship permitted structural, mechanical, and electrical engineers to work on the museum's and the condominium's basic needs at the same time and to speed construction of the condominium tower, which was finished before the museum.

MOMA as Agora

The Abby Aldrich Rockefeller Sculpture Garden in 1984.

T
he expanded museum opened in spring 1984 and launched its first full exhibition program the following fall with " 'Primitivism' in 20th-Century Art." Having doubled its exhibition space from 40,500 to 87,000 square feet, MOMA now can display its permanent collection as a complete history of modern art. William Rubin, curator of painting and sculpture, told *Artnews* what the museum's expansion means to art lovers and scholars:

Whether you put the beginnings of modern art as Alfred Barr did, in the 1880s, which is where our collection begins, or a little earlier with Manet, we are dealing essentially with about 100 years of art. . . . And in a world in which contemporary art is being widely shown, and in which it's much more difficult for anyone but us to organize a show of, let's say Picasso, or Rousseau, or even a show of Surrealism or Abstract Ex-

MOMA's new garden hall overlooks the Abby Aldrich Rockefeller Sculpture Garden. The hall, housing a bank of escalators, connects the museum's new West Wing with its original building and the East and North wings.
Credit: Adam Bartos

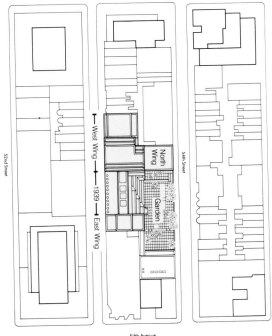

Site plan, MOMA.

pressionism, the exhibition program of this museum is responsible to the entire history of modern art, not merely, or even primarily, to what is happening today.

The new painting and sculpture galleries retain the intimate scale and setting that the museum has always had yet enlarge the number and diversity of works on view. The most important examples of an artist's achievements are juxtaposed with others' work in an appropriate historical context. In specially designed galleries with wood floors, space has been provided for a rotating exhibition of contemporary works that require an atmosphere more like an art gallery or loft studio than a collector's apartment.

MOMA's other principal departments—architecture and design, photography, prints, and illustrated books and drawings—have doubled their display space, so that they can mount temporary shows and reveal works that previously had been impossible to display. Other improvements include study facilities in each exhibit area, a second auditorium, an enlarged library, and an education center for groups. Two new restaurants, one for members and one for visitors, have been created at the garden's east end. The museum's store has expanded to include more than 8,000 square feet on the ground floor and lower level of the renovated east wing, as well as an annex at 37 West 53rd Street.

The circulation patterns of the building have improved significantly through the construction of the glass-walled escalator hall along the building's garden facade. While the experience of the garden, designed by Philip Johnson, has been altered by the larger size of the expanded museum and apartment tower, its essential quality as a sophisticated oasis in the city's heart has been preserved.

The impact of the new building on 53rd Street has been less positive. To keep its garden intact, MOMA was forced to expand along 53rd Street and, in the process, to demolish four brownstones. As Ada Louise Huxtable wrote in the *New York Times* of June 29, 1980:

But what bothered most people—and still does—was the destruction of 53rd Street that the expansion entailed. This has been one of midtown Manhattan's most attractive side streets, with its varied uses and styles and small-scale, older buildings, its brownstones and town houses converted to shops, galleries, and restaurants, in a fine architectural, commercial, and cultural mix. It is the kind of street that supplies much of New York's characteristic appeal.

The character of 53rd Street has indeed been changed forever by the new MOMA, by the tower, and by other new tall buildings that are being erected along the street.

The Museum Tower condominiums came on the market in early 1983 with purchase prices ranging from $247,000 to more than $5 million. Initial sales were slow, but because the building offers quality materials and a dedication to owners' privacy, the apartments now seem to have found a unique niche within the New York market. Almost all the apartments have been sold, a high percentage to foreign nationals. "Museum Tower is designed for that small, upscale segment who appreciate quiet luxury and an elite address in the center of the world's most exciting city," says Shaw.

Though the architectural and demographic impacts of the expanded museum upon 53rd Street are viewed by some as negative, fears that an involvement with commercial real estate would compromise the integrity of the museum have thus far proven groundless. By means of provisions of the Trust for Cultural Resources legislation, the museum has been kept at a distance from the commercial aspects of the tower's construction and the sale of its apartments. Charles Shaw and his associates have proven to be superior developers, not only in their respect for the museum's sensitivities and design requirements during construction, but also in their pursuit of quality for the apartment tower.

In 1984–85, the museum expected to balance its operating budget at $15 million. With tax equivalency payments contributing $290,000 in 1984–85 and expected to rise substantially over the coming years, the museum stands a good chance of paying for its expanded functions and increased operating expenses through its new combination of assets: increased revenue from its endowment, income from the Trust for Cultural Resources, growing attendance and memberships, ongoing contributions from the private sector, and revenues from its expanded retail operations. Although Richard Oldenburg, MOMA's director, reports that some financial problems persist, the museum now can work to solve them with resources it never had before.

Oldenburg explains:

The real purpose of the entire project was never to make us a profitable institution, but to assure more adequate space for the museum. The problem was how to do all of this, how to get more space, when we really could not afford to maintain the space we had before. We all know we will not solve our financial problems with this expansion, and we will not eliminate our deficits—but we will have the space we need. And we will have expanded income from more visitors. That plus the money from the capital campaign should put us in decent shape.

And so it appears that this complicated transaction has succeeded. The new condominium tower project has enabled the museum not only to survive but to expand— and expansion of its curatorial and exhibition functions is the key to its continuing success.

That MOMA turned to a real estate project in seeking to solve its space and financial problems in 1975 is not surprising, if the developments of modern art and of the public's appreciation for it are considered. The museum's original patrons were able to provide their own dollars to build MOMA's original home. When enough private dollars could no longer be secured for the museum's expanding operations, the museum needed a business plan and help

from government.

The real estate transaction completed an organizational transition from a first-generation museum supported by a small group of donors to a full-fledged public institution with significant support from government and corporate sources. The expanded building also symbolizes the evolution from a highly personal administration directed by visionaries such as Alfred H. Barr, Jr., and René d'Harnoncourt to a management structure that must concern itself with new sources of revenue, polical influences, and fiscal expertise. The museum has been ably guided in these transitions by Richard Oldenburg, its director, and Mrs. John D. Rockefeller 3rd, its president.

The entire project has been possible because of the public perception of MOMA's value to New York City, to the nation, and to the world. The new building eloquently manifests this factor as well, as described by critic Calvin Tomkins in the October 15, 1984, *New Yorker:*

**Museum Tower from
53rd Street.**

People come to museums for many different reasons, and with many different expectations, but they come in ever greater numbers, and their presence has changed the essential nature of museums. Traditionally, in this country (although not in Europe), the primary function of a museum was thought to be educational—the museum was a temple of knowledge and an arbiter of taste. No museum has played that role more effectively than MOMA, of course, and MOMA's teachings, refined and codified, are now enshrined for all time in the galleries of the permanent collection. But MOMA has also played other roles through much of its history. More than any other museum in the city, it has served as an agora, a gathering place, and it is this function that the new Garden Hall, incorporating and extending the garden itself, is designed to enhance. The importance of the agora should not be underestimated. New York has relatively few gathering places of this nature, and no city can ever have too many of them. The pleasures that such an environment offers, moreover, are by no means unrelated to the experience of looking at works of art. It is perfectly possible to approach art on a level that has nothing to do with education—or with reverence, for that matter—and everything to do with pleasure.

Equitable Center

I n its new headquarters at Seventh Avenue between 51st and 52nd streets in Manhattan, the Equitable Life Assurance Society will provide an unusually extensive array of public sculpture, murals, and museum exhibitions, as well as a 500-seat theater. This commitment to including a variety of arts and public amenities in a corporate office building represents a collaboration among the Equitable's top executives, the Whitney Museum of American Art, several visual artists, and the building's architect, Edward Larrabee Barnes. The art program, a series of landscaped plazas, and underground concourse-level connections to the original buildings in Rockefeller Center will serve to make Equitable Center an extension of Rockefeller Center to Seventh Avenue.

Equitable Tower, a 54-story skyscraper, projected to cost $200 million and due for completion in the fall of 1985, adjoins the Equitable headquarters built in 1959 at 1285 Avenue of the Americas (Sixth Avenue). The new building, opening onto Seventh Avenue, fills the rest of the block. The full-block complex will contain three million square feet of institutional office space. Among its art features will be Thomas Hart Benton's 1930 ten-panel mural *America Today* and a 6,000-square-foot branch of the Whitney Museum, divided into two galleries. One gallery will display works from the Whitney's permanent collection and the other will feature temporary exhibits.

The building's entrance—a five-story atrium—will display a 68-foot Roy Lichtenstein mural and a Scott Burton sculptural centerpiece. The 124-foot-high walls of the galleria, running through the building from 51st to 52nd Street, will feature a Sol LeWitt mural. Other works of art already purchased for public display include Alexander Calder's *Les Trois Barres* and Paul Manship's *Day.* (Manship created the much-beloved *Prometheus* statue at

Rockefeller Center's skating rink.) The theater will present public lectures and recitals.

The new headquarters will be the first office tower in recent times featuring a main entrance on Seventh Avenue, where aging hotels and dilapidated storefronts have presented a woebegone streetscape. For the past two decades developers have confined their Midtown activities to the more attractive areas adjacent to Rockefeller Center on Park and Madison avenues and along the East Side. Equitable Center and important new zoning changes now are shifting builders' attention westward. Even before the project's negotiations had been finalized, city planners and real estate professionals were calling the skyscraper a catalyst for construction in the district. A series of new office, apartment, and hotel projects subsequently were announced and started nearby. They include income-producing towers for two of the city's important cultural institutions, City Center and Carnegie Hall.

The Equitable building raises to a more sophisticated level than in other Midtown buildings what Calvin Tomkins has called "the new art of public spaces." Tomkins believes that collaborative relationships among artists, sculptors, and architects have moved beyond merely placing paintings and sculpture in building lobbies and on plazas:

Rather than impose an aesthetic statement on a public space in the form of a sculpture, they seek to make the space itself more interesting, more alive, or more useful to the people who pass through it or congregate there.

City Revises Zoning to Encourage More Authentic Amenities

This Roy Lichtenstein mural will hang in the new Equitable Tower lobby.

Midtown Manhattan, a sprawling area bounded by Second and Ninth avenues from 34th Street to Central Park South, remains the major source of New York City's retail economy and cultural vitality. Within its boundaries, Manhattan's skyline has been fashioned into the world's most recognizable cityscape. The shape of its most recent development has been guided largely by the city's 1961 zoning ordinance, which introduced a new tool to govern building density: the concept of floor/area ratio (FAR). The ordinance set the basic floor area for the largest office building at 15 times the lot area, or FAR 15, and controlled exceptions or additions to a building's height and bulk by a specific series of bonuses.

The Seagram Building, Ludwig Mies van der Rohe's 1959 bronze-clad masterpiece, became the city's favorite model for new buildings. Its spacious plaza provided sitting space, light, and air in Midtown's congested streets. Thus the 1961 ordinance offered bonuses to buildings with plazas: they could be 20 percent higher. Incentive zoning became the means by which the city offered builders additional building height and bulk in exchange for "bonusable amenities."

Bonuses also were offered for vest pocket parks, modeled after Paley Park and Greenacre Park, both provided by philanthropists for reflection and relaxation. Through-block arcades and galleries, modeled after Milan's Gran Galeria and London's Burlington Arcade, also were encouraged to improve mid-block pedestrian activity with shops lining the passageways. An extremely high bonus range was offered for "covered pedestrian spaces" that combined the pedestrian circulation requirements of a through-block arcade with climate-controlled spaces, greater heights, and larger dimensions. Such spaces could lend themselves to public art displays, musical performances, lavish plantings, and cafes with movable seating and informal food service. Architects and developers integrated these amenities into many of the skyscrapers built in New York City during the seventies.

More than 140 towers with close to 80 million square feet of space arose between 1960 and 1980 in Midtown alone, jamming buildings together, blocking out sunlight, and bringing tens of thousands of workers into an already crowded area. By 1980 it became apparent that the incentive zoning process had produced too many unattractive and bulky buildings conforming to the letter but not to the spirit of the ordinance and offering little or no genuine public benefit. A plaza might be provided, but it would be cold; a through-block arcade would be designed, but it would be dim and dull. Architecture critic Paul Goldberger wrote that many of the zoning amenities "have been poorly designed, poorly executed, and poorly maintained, and it is not difficult to question now whether we would not have been far better off without the amenities and therefore without the bigger buildings that came along with them."

In 1980, under the direction of New York City Planning Commission Chairman Robert Wagner, Jr., a working group of planning and design professionals reviewed the 1961 ordinance and drafted a new set of guidelines to regulate Midtown development. Among other goals, they hoped to encourage a transfer of development from the overbuilt East Side to the West Side, which had excess subway and utility capacity, underused land areas, and steadily declining neighborhoods.

By May 1982 the city's Board of Estimate had incorporated many of the study group's recommendations into a series of new ordinances that simplified the city's development review procedures, eliminated FAR bonuses for amenities that did not provide tangible public benefits, and offered stronger incentives for West Side development, including significant density differentials for new building construction in designated "growth areas" west of Sixth Avenue.

At the same time that the city was working to revise its zoning procedures and to shift office development to the West Side, private builders were constructing three skyscrapers on the East Side that greatly increased the sizes of their office towers in return for providing spaces for the arts and for enclosed, landscaped atriums on the ground floors. These buildings were the 43-story, green granite IBM Building (one million square feet) at Madison and 57th Street, designed by Edward Larrabee Barnes & Associates; across the street, the 37-story American Telephone & Telegraph Company headquarters (with its much-discussed Chippendale roof) by Philip Johnson and John Burgee; and the 26-story Philip Morris headquarters, by Ulrich Franzen Associates, at 42nd Street and Park Avenue.

At IBM, a glass-enclosed atrium displays a bamboo garden with other unusual vegetation, courtesy of the New York Botanical Society, and a cafe encourages sitting, eating, and conversation. From the atrium, escalators take visitors to a below-ground art gallery. Michael Heizer's granite fountain, set at the corner of 56th Street and Madison Avenue, needles the typical corporate fountains in and around so many Midtown buildings; his cataract rushes sideways through its stone basin.

The AT&T building includes a pair of arcaded public plazas on the 55th and 56th Street sides of the building, plus space for a museum of communication at the building's western base. Movable public seating is provided underneath the building's Madison Avenue loggia.

The Philip Morris building provides amenities in the Grand Central Station area, plagued by congestion and awkward street-level circulation. Two of its large public areas are administered by the Whitney Museum: a three-story, 5,200-square-foot sculpture court and an adjacent 1,000-square-foot gallery for changing exhibitions.

West Side builders like the Equitable and its development manager on Equitable Center, Tishman Speyer Properties, have been able to benefit from the example of these three East Side towers. But the specific model the Equitable's senior executives have had in mind is a close neighbor, admired for nearly 25 years, its vast and beautifully designed facility used by most of the Equitable's employees at one time or another during the average week: Rockefeller Center.

A grand monument of Art Deco design, Rockefeller Center combines first-class office space with a below-street concourse system that links buildings with accessible shops and restaurants. Stirring murals and

Rockefeller Center, New York, in 1976. On the lower plaza are located Paul Manship's *Prometheus* sculpture and an outdoor cafe (surrounded by a Bicentennial flags display).

Rockefeller Center, New York, in 1978. *American Progress*, Jose Maria Sert's mural in the RCA Building, depicts America's reliance on brains and brawn.

sculptured panels make its entrances and lobbies elegant. Its formal Channel Gardens, rooftop plantings, promenades, plazas, and sunken skating rink provide outdoor areas of quality and vivacity.

When Rockefeller Center's original limestone towers were erected in the mid-thirties they faced severe competition from two awe-inspiring skyscrapers, the Empire State and Chrysler buildings. Moreover, its west of Fifth Avenue address then was considered unfashionable and inconvenient. But the center's arts and tenant services overcame any liabilities of location. It even originally housed the Museum of Science and Industry, whose displays of scientific models, replicas, and visitor-operated machines attracted half a million persons annually after it opened in 1936.

Equitable Center's developers kept all this in mind as they began to plan their own expansion west to Seventh Avenue in the late seventies.

Corporations Embrace Art, While a Museum Branches Into Business

New York City's tradition of architectural sculpture and decoration, murals, mosaics, and statues has sprung from a rich heritage of public patronage. Midtown Manhattan's enormous amount of office building construction has offered substantial opportunities for corporations to install major outdoor artworks. Some pieces have been merely larger versions of sculpture that can be seen in museums and gallery collections. Others have been monuments commemorating public events or statesmen and heroes. But until the early seventies, developers and architects devoted little thought to designing public spaces inside buildings for the display of art. Acquisitions typically were afterthoughts; art was not considered so much an integral part of a development as a decoration.

The public art introduced into Manhattan since 1970 breaks with this tradition. Surveying a range of contemporary art in public places, fine arts consultant Nancy Rosen describes the contributions made by such pieces as Louise Nevelson's *Night Presence IV*, a 22-foot-high Cor Ten steel structure installed on the Park Avenue mall at 92nd Street:

The challenge of matching the style and spirit of public works of art to their adopted sites, of successfully integrating the artist's personal vision with public space, is formidable. The selection and placement of public art requires an unusual sensitivity and sense of responsibility, so that in the most fortuitous instances, large-scale objects, installed in public spaces, seem appropriate, even invited, and hence their works hold their own in adopted environments with dignity.

Artists increasingly are becoming involved in collaborations with architects and developers at the start of a project's design, rather than midway in its process. Rosen suggests why this is important:

When artists are involved early and when their ideas and concepts are valued by developers and architects rather than treated merely as decoration, public art has the capacity to reveal [itself], fulfilling our need for surprise, relief, diversion, contemplation, or delight.

The opportunity for installing major artworks in a private commercial building was one important part of the arts context that shaped the Equitable Center project. Equitable Center also was able to build upon an emerging relationship between New York corporations and museums. For the past fifteen years, several New York corporations have included space for galleries and branch museums in the lobbies of their office buildings. Such facilities bring exhibitions to areas where cultural respites from office routines are not typical.

The Whitney Museum of American Art pioneered in this area in 1973 by opening a downtown museum in 4,800 square feet of space in a new Wall Street office building at 55 Water Street. Operating funds were provided by corporate donors, foundations, and the National Endowment for the Arts. The branch, now located at 26 Wall Street in the Federal Hall National Monument, provides extra space for Whitney's growing collection and serves a population that largely lives outside of Manhattan and therefore finds it difficult to visit the main museum on the Upper East Side.

In 1978, Ulrich Franzen, architect for Philip Morris's new headquarters at 42nd Street and Park Avenue, suggested that a portion of the building's covered pedestrian space, for which an FAR bonus had been granted, be devoted to a museum or gallery. Since Philip Morris had long been a major supporter of both the visual arts in general and the Whitney Museum's exhibition programs in particular, an agreement was reached rapidly. Tom Armstrong, the Whitney's director, described his interest in launching a Midtown branch as follows:

The branch museum enables us to expand our opportunities to present our programs. It gives us an opportunity to do things perhaps not appropriate for the Whitney, or which we otherwise might not have time to do. The branch museum was conceived as a way of reaching more people. Midtown Manhattan has a great public that is probably only in that part of the city during the day.

Five years later, in 1983, the Philip Morris Whitney branch museum opened. Its 5,200-square-foot space displays works by

The Equitable Spurs Midtown's Move to the West

Alexander Calder, John Chamberlain, Claes Oldenburg, and George Segal, among others. An additional 1,100 square feet in an adjoining gallery hosts six temporary exhibitions per year. Philip Morris annually contributes about $200,000 to the Whitney to cover all costs associated with the branch, although it exercises no control over the content of exhibitions. The experience of the Whitney at Philip Morris demonstrated that a branch museum could succeed in bringing art to a business environment without compromising the integrity of the exhibition process.

The arts program at Equitable Center resulted from an expansion and redirection of the Equitable corporation's earlier involvement in art acquisition. It was initiated in mid-1980, under the impetus of the late Nancy Hanks, former chairman of the National Endowment for the Arts and then a member of the Equitable's board of directors. With the approval of the Equitable's president, Coy Eklund, and the help of his chief of staff, David Harris, Hanks redirected the company's patronage to the acquisition of younger artists' work. A variety of prints and works on paper was purchased for the company's executive dining room. Paintings by Kenzo Okada and Jack Youngerman were added to its burgeoning collection. Contemporary art cropped up all over the 38th floor, in reception rooms, and in corridors in other executive areas. Approximately 164 works were accumulated until the program terminated in early 1984, to make way for an even more ambitious art program for the new headquarters complex.

Since its founding by Henry Hyde in 1859, Equitable Life Assurance has been headquartered in New York City. Its first official home office opened in 1871 at 120 Broadway and featured the city's first elevator system, which made the nine-story granite and brick Victorian structure a major visitor attraction. When fire destroyed the building in 1920, the Equitable lost no time in erecting a 36-story, Italian Renaissance skyscraper on the same site. Designed by Ernest R. Graham, its twin towers and limestone facade added distinction to the Lower Manhattan skyline, already dominated by the towering Woolworth Building. But the massive new Equitable building rose up straight from the street with no setbacks, and its bulk above the fifth floor covered 90 percent of the site.

Partially in response to criticism of the new building's bulk, the city established height districts to protect streets and avenues from being turned into dark canyons. These regulations limited the height a building could rise in proportion to the width of the street it fronted on, until it had to set back. This law shaped New York's architecture, producing a plethora of "wedding cake" buildings whose repetitive dullness led in turn to the 1961 "bonusable amenities" ordinance.

The Equitable did not stay at 120 Broadway for long, moving uptown in 1924 to a 22-story building at 393 Seventh Avenue, between 31st and 32nd streets across from Pennsylvania Station. When, decades later, the company had grown into the nation's third largest life insurer, its executives studied expanding the building and then settled on a site at 51st Street and Sixth Avenue. Land was acquired at 1285 Sixth Avenue and, in 1959, construction began

The Whitney Museum of American Art at the Philip Morris world headquarters on Park Avenue at 42nd Street.
Credit: Geoffrey Clements

on a 42-story aluminum and glass L-shaped tower with more than 1.5 million square feet of usable space. It became the largest single-tenant building in New York when the Equitable's 7,000 employees moved uptown in 1961.

In the 20 years that followed, Manhattan experienced a building boom. The Avenue of the Americas (Sixth Avenue) became one of the world's most prestigious addresses, as Rockefeller Center continued its expansion on the west side of the avenue and CBS and ABC built headquarters. A financial crisis in the mid-seventies proved short-lived. A huge surplus of office space, which some analysts had predicted would take 15 years to absorb, vanished by late 1978, setting off another spate of construction activity. Average Midtown rental rates rose above $30 per square foot, rushing toward the $40 level and beyond.

The Equitable, meanwhile, had evolved into one of the nation's leading pension fund managers while maintaining its position in the life and health insurance markets. Some operations areas were regionalized, and some back office functions moved out of New York. The company began exploring the various financial service markets, and its real estate operations shifted investment strategy from commercial mortgage lending to property ownership, soon establishing the Equitable as the leading institutional real estate investor in the city. Among its acquisitions were the St. Regis and Sheraton Centre hotels, the Corning Glass Building on Fifth Avenue, and several high-rise office buildings purchased as part of a liquidation of Tishman Realty and Construction Company. In 1980 the company announced plans to develop Trump Tower with Donald Trump, and launched an acquisition strategy that has brought its New York regional portfolio to a value of $2 billion. It also acquired all the parcels on the remainder of the block behind the home office between Sixth and Seventh avenues and 51st and 52nd streets, including the aging Abbey Victoria Hotel.

All these factors led to the Equitable's senior management to evaluate the company's future space needs. One of the first conclusions they reached was to develop the remainder of the block behind the home office. As *Real Estate Forum* reported:

[By 1979] it was decided to start redeveloping the balance of the Equitable Center block. "Our decision," comments [Benjamin] Holloway, "was based on the observation that the Avenue of the Americas was pretty much built out between 42nd and 57th streets, and the prime Midtown district, having gone about as far eastward as it could, had to start moving to the west. With the Times Square/42nd Street renewal looming, for which we have been an early consultant, and the convention center in the works, we felt confident that it was only a matter of time before there would be a great revival in West Midtown . . . and our building would be part of it. Although we began our planning before these projects had fully jelled, all of this is now coming to pass."

A 1981–82 limit was placed on leases for the site's buildings, and a closing date was negotiated for the principal property on the parcel, the Abbey Victoria Hotel. In January 1981, John T. Walsh became head of the Equitable's internal development team. Edward Larrabee Barnes & Associates signed on as architects; Turner Construction Company, which had built the 1285 building, became construction manager for the new building; and Tishman Speyer Properties, a leading national developer in which the Equitable purchased a limited partnership interest, assumed management responsibility for the entire project, including leasing and property management. Benjamin Holloway, the Equitable's executive vice president, who became chairman of Equitable Real Estate Group when realty operations assumed the status of an independent subsidiary in 1984, has overseen the development from the start.

Art Can Confer Prestige
Status on an Investment Building

The Equitable's decision to build on the site behind its home office forced its senior management to determine whether "Tower West" would be an investment property, a headquarters, or a combination of both. Another issue was whether to sell or lease the 1285 building. The company also had the opportunity to study a series of employee redeployment alternatives—including moving most operations out of Midtown to potentially more cost-effective locations. Executives met with city officials to examine options for moving offices to the boroughs outside of Manhattan. Divisional chiefs scrutinized the benefits of relocating to other cities. In 1982 the company's real estate operation, with board approval, moved its national headquarters to Atlanta prior to its becoming a subsidiary.

John Carter, who replaced Coy Eklund as the Equitable's president in 1982 and as chief executive officer one year later, began accelerating the company's diversification into a full range of financial services. He also came to the conclusion that no major financial institution could afford to leave New York, which by then clearly had surpassed London as the world's business capital. In February 1983, the Equitable board acted on Carter's recommendations for the new building. Tower West would be renamed Equitable Tower and become the company's world headquarters. About 1,000 employees would move into the new building, while others would be shifted to less expensive space, mostly in Manhattan. The remaining two-thirds of Equitable Tower (unused by the Equitable) and the entire 1285 building would be leased to tenants, taking advantage of Manhattan's strong commercial rental market. With modest architectural redesign in the 1285 lobbies, an 800-foot corridor would be created, extending from the Avenue of the Americas to Seventh Avenue. The lobbies would be narrowed and the 51st and 52nd street sidewalks widened to ten feet on each street, strengthening the identity of the entire complex as Equitable Center.

But these architectural features would not by themselves create a corporate headquarters setting commanding premium Midtown rents at a yet-to-be proven Seventh Avenue address. Something more would be required to make the new Equitable Center one of New York's most prestigious commercial addresses.

Under the leadership of Ben Holloway, the Equitable decided that this "something more" should be a public art complex of daring dimension—combining gallery space with spectacular commissions and acquisitions in the new building's galleria, lobby atrium, and ground-floor corridors.

In the early spring of 1983, Edward Larrabee Barnes met with Holloway and Tom Armstrong, the Whitney Museum's director, to discuss the possibility of incorporating a museum branch into the new Equitable Center. The Whitney's latest branch had just opened at the Philip Morris building, and John Russell, art critic of the *New York Times*, had commented favorably:

The Whitney Museum of Art at Philip Morris will be a blessing to anyone who likes modern art, [or] finds himself with a little time to kill. It is an enclave of serious art in an area that has hitherto been notably short of it. It looks pretty, the initial choice of art is quite distinguished, and the views—whether from outside in or from inside out—are consistently provocative.

Holloway told Armstrong that he wanted art at Equitable Center to be more than just an amenity. Armstrong reacted positively:

I realized that the Whitney's branches were something that corporations wanted; that they helped develop audiences for art who didn't normally get to the main Whitney Museum at Madison Avenue and 75th Street. Seventh Avenue could be as good a location for a branch museum as 42nd Street and Park Avenue, and the building itself had extraordinary potentials.

Soon after, the Whitney formally agreed to operate two 3,000-square-foot galleries in the two wings off the Equitable Tower entrance atrium. The process of melding architecture and art was now well underway.

1285 Avenue of the Americas (Sixth Avenue): Home office of the Equitable Life Assurance Society of the United States from 1961 to 1985.
Credit: Wurts Brothers, Huntington, Long Island, N.Y.

The Company, Museum, and City Coodinate Architecture with Art

Formal announcement of the Equitable's decision to remain in New York and to build a new world headquarters was made on February 17, 1983. "We intend to remain a very strong part of New York," Carter declared. "We looked over every option we could find around the United States and this one made the most sense."

Turning the Equitable Center into a commercial location that would attract tenants of Rockefeller Center's quality began with the selection of Edward Larrabee Barnes as architect. The Barnes office recently had completed two new Manhattan skyscrapers: the IBM headquarters at 590 Madison Avenue and the 36-story 535 Madison Avenue building for George Klein. Barnes was also in the midst of designing the 210,000-square-foot new Dallas Museum of Art. He was familiar with the revisions being made in New York City's zoning regulations, and he understood how to gain additional footage for the building by including two urban plazas along 51st and 52nd streets.

When it signed on the Whitney Museum as a collaborator in the development of a first-class art center, the Equitable gained a knowledgeable and enthusiastic partner. Lisa Phillips, associate curator for the Whitney's Branch Museum program, summarizes the history behind the Whitney's involvement with the branch museums:

Over ten years ago we opened our first branch—a radical experiment in educational outreach and museum decentralization. Almost everyone (trustees, the director, art professionals) was skeptical about the value of the program and whether high professional standards could be maintained. In 1973, the concept of a branch museum was visionary—and one whose time had not yet arrived. Now it is one of the most vital, important, distinctive programs at the Whitney. We have negotiated very profitable, favorable contracts with corporate sponsors in return for providing an extremely exclusive service—operating a branch of a national museum in their headquarters. It works for the sponsor—as a relatively inexpensive promotional device and public amenity which engenders tremendous good will in the community—and it works for the Whitney—as a way to extend the name and influence of the institu-

tion, exhibit more of the permanent collection, and develop a broader audience for American art.

Finally, the audience benefits tremendously—and the audience varies for each branch. All of our branches are free and there are complimentary brochures, free lectures, and symposia accompanying every exhibition. Art becomes part of the flow of daily life in a context that is familiar—people feel comfortable wandering in and out, 30 percent of the museum's overall attendance is branch museum atttendance. People who might not have the time, patience, confidence, or inclination to visit a larger museum can drop by their local branch for something pleasing, provocative, newsworthy. What started out as a sixties "radical education" project has over the last decade taken root, become institutionalized, professionalized, and has given hundreds of thousands pleasure in a way that is enormously gratifying.

For both parties concerned, the Equitable branch museum's frontage on Seventh Avenue constitutes a strong commitment to the future of art and real estate in the west Midtown area. The planned exhibition program will take advantage of two spaces totaling 6,000 square feet on the north and south sides of the new building. Three thousand square feet will be set aside for displays from the Whitney's permanent collection and 3,000 square feet will house temporary exhibitions. The Equitable will compensate the Whitney for all staff costs relating to the exhibition areas and also will cover maintenance and operations costs—a major investment estimated at $100,000 for the first year the branch will be open. It also will make an annual contribution underwriting a major exhibition at the Whitney itself.

One particular event already has catapulted the Equitable into the limelight as an art patron and set directions for commissioning new works for Equitable Center's atrium and galleria. This event was the purchase of the Thomas Hart Benton mural *America Today*.

The mural, painted in 1930 for the New School of Social Research, consists of ten scenes painted with egg tempera on linen and glued to panels, all but one measuring seven feet high and ranging in width from eight to 13 feet. The murals depict pre-Depression America, from the pulse and excitement of the big city, with its dance halls, subways, boxing matches, and revival meetings, to the technological expansion in the industrial belt and the slower pace of life on farms and in small towns. Over the years, the paintings had ceased to be viewed much by the public and had suffered damage and neglect. Needing funds and believing that the mural could be better displayed elsewhere, the New School had sold it in May 1982 to Christophe Janet, director of the Maurice Segoura Gallery.

After trying for a year to keep the mural intact and in New York, Janet approached collectors outside the city. The price for the total mural was prohibitive for most museums, and its large size ruled out private collectors. It appeared that the panels would have to be sold individually and possibly abroad.

At this point, aides in Mayor Edward Koch's office, concerned that the city would lose another of its artistic treasures, asked a lawyer, W. Barnabas McHenry, to help keep the Bentons in Manhattan. They suggested he approach real estate developers who were planning new buildings and who might be willing to incorporate the mural into a space designed especially for it. To make the mural more attractive as an

Equitable Tower
Project Data

Physical Configuration
Component—Income Generating

Office	1,400,000 sq. ft.
Retail	26,000 sq. ft.

Component—Arts/Culture/Open Space

Galleries (2 @ 3,000 sq. ft. each)	6,000 sq. ft.
Theater	500 seats
Galleria	51 ft. wide × 91 ft. high
Acreage	1.84 acres (80,333 sq. ft.)
Floor/Area Ratio	17.18 (average)
Location	East side of Seventh Avenue between 51st and 52nd streets, New York City
Total Development Costs	Over $200 million
Architect	Edward Larrabee Barnes
Master Developer	Equitable Life Assurance Society of the United States

investment, the city proposed offering potential buyers an amount of additional floor space comparable to the purchase price of the mural. A 38-page proposal for a zoning amendment that would allot an FAR in return for the preservation and display of landmark artworks was rejected, however, by the city planning commission, though it endorsed in principle a development scheme that would incorporate the mural into its plans. The commission suggested that builders be approached who were planning a headquarters building as opposed to speculative projects, and it offered names of several candidates, including the Equitable.

Impatient with this course of action and with the financial burden of carrying the Bentons, Janet signed a contract with Sotheby's to auction the mural in May 1984. The city then requested time until January 15, 1984, to buy out the auction without penalty. Sotheby's agreed.

In December 1983, Herbert Rickman, special counsel to Mayor Koch, met John Carter of the Equitable at a social function and told him of the Benton mural. After investigating the situation, the Equitable decided to purchase the Bentons on January 27, 1984. Discussions with architect Barnes indicated that the mural could be accommodated on the north wall of the elevator

Extensive underground concourse system links Equitable Tower and 1285 Avenue of the Americas building.

Two parts of *America Today*, a ten-panel mural by Thomas Hart Benton. The mural, created from egg tempera, distemper, and oil glazes on linen, will extend along the north elevator lobby of Equitable Tower.

lobby, where it would run 90 feet along the corridor, dramatically affecting the movement and aesthetic impression of the space. The highly positive response to the acquisition from the press and the general public encouraged Holloway to focus attention on using additional mural art to enhance Equitable Center's public spaces. He enlisted the help of Jerry Speyer, managing partner of Tishman Speyer Properties, the building's development manager, and a trustee of the Museum of Modern Art. He also hired art historian Emily Braun as an art advisor to serve as a liaison to the Whitney and to coordinate the commission and acquisition process.

Rather than decorating its plazas, lobbies, and pedestrian access areas with isolated pieces of sculpture, the Equitable now embarked on a policy of commissioning works from artists who would design for a particular space in Equitable Center. Holloway encouraged fresh approaches for public areas—lobbies, plazas, and arcades—whose aesthetic value had so often been neglected in recent office developments. Monumental sculpture, the traditional filler for such spaces, seemed inadequate, and Holloway began seeking alternatives.

Full-Block Center Links
Midtown to Rockefeller Center

The Equitable became the first major developer to move into Midtown west of the Avenue of the Americas following the adoption of the city's sweeping zoning revisions to promote commercial development away from the congested East Side. The new building also was located inside a theater subdistrict that has its own special set of zoning incentives.

The zoning permitted a basic floor/area ratio (FAR) of 16.5 for the site. The Equitable's FAR was increased to an average of 17.18 because of such "as-of-right" incentives as the through-block galleria. Additional FAR bonuses were permitted because of the company's commitment to upgrade existing urban plazas on the north and south sides of the 1285 building by new plantings and trees. The zoning also mandated retail and storefront-line continuity along Seventh Avenue—a problematic requirement that eventually was relaxed to permit an equally desirable use: the inclusion of the Whitney Museum branch along the Seventh Avenue frontage.

Barnes designed a classical structure faced with bands of buff-colored stone and glass, linked with Rockefeller Center both physically, through its underground concourse, and aesthetically, through its commanding spaces, murals, and other artworks. Besides setbacks from the street, he provided a five-story skylit atrium at the Seventh Avenue entrance and a through-block galleria to connect the new skyscraper with the existing 42-story building behind it. This arcade of shops also will link 51st and 52nd streets at midblock. A 400- to 500-seat theater on the concourse level, available for tenant meetings, will provide a place for concerts, recitals, and lectures—a need that was communicated to the Equitable management by Barnes after conversations with William Schuman, president emeritus of Lincoln Center, and Norris Houghton, founding director of the Phoenix Theater.

The design of an urban space in New York remains inextricably connected to the bonuses received by the developer for providing pedestrian amenities. At the initial stages of planning, the Equitable hired Alex Cooper as a consultant for the building's streetscape. The through-block

Plan for renovations of 1285 Avenue of the Americas building lobby by Skidmore, Owings & Merrill.
Credit: Raoul De Armes

galleria, the urban plazas on 51st and 52nd streets, the atrium lobby of the new headquarters tower, and the lobby of the existing 1285 building all were considered prime spaces for imaginative art and design.

For the lobby of 1285, which will become the headquarters for Paine Webber, Inc., and the law firm of Paul Weiss Rifkind Wharton & Garrison, the Equitable hired Raoul De Armes of Skidmore, Owings & Merrill, the original architects of the building. SOM's solution was to remodel the interior of the lobby and design an art gallery down both sides. The original 1959 interior is being transformed from its cool, metallic tones into a warmer decor of mahogany and rich granite surfaces. The gallery design breaks up the corridorlike effect of the previous modernist interior. The addition of the gallery also changes the lobby from a mere conduit to an elegant passageway.

The idea to exhibit art in 1285 evolved partly from Paine Webber's interest in moving uptown. Paine Webber chairman and chief executive officer Donald Marron has fashioned an outstanding corporate collection of avant-garde art over the years, and he and Equitable officials agreed that a Paine Webber gallery would be an excellent counterpoint to the Whitney branch. Besides displaying part of the Paine

Webber collection, the gallery also will exhibit shows for local and national museums, community organizations, and archives lacking Manhattan exhibition space.

The Equitable, meanwhile, engaged the Whitney to advise on art commissions for the Equitable Tower lobby—an atrium flanked by the two Whitney galleries, surmounted by a skylight, and walled by limestone articulated with polished red granite. Through a huge arch entrance from Seventh Avenue stretches a facing limestone wall measuring approximately 68 feet by 32 feet, an ideal site for a large mural that could dominate the expansive lobby space. Working with the Whitney and Emily Braun, Equitable officials decided to commission Roy Lichtenstein to create a work for this wall that will provide continuity with the Benton panels. It will be Lichtenstein's largest work to date.

The enormous space of the atrium, with its vast floor area, needed to be addressed as well—to impart a more human scale, to provide seating, and to establish a formality appropriate to the entrance of a world corporate headquarters. The Equitable turned to artist Scott Burton to deal with these concerns. Burton is known for his art furniture and in particular for his collaboration with architect Cesar Pelli and artist Siah Armajani in designing the forthcoming World Financial Center public plaza at Battery Park City in Lower Manhattan.

In Burton's concept for the Equitable atrium, a curving green granite settee, punctuated by pink onyx lights and articulated by low relief, will form the main seating element, facing a curving screen of trees. Together they will form two arcs of a delineated circle that defines a more intimate space. They also will enclose a central oversized green granite table, also for seating, which will hold an enormous basin filled with water plants. Burton's creation can be described as a huge salon with an elegant settee, table, and vase of flowers to welcome the thousands of visitors to the center.

The Equitable Tower's galleria offered another focal point for an art commission in the building's challenging architectural space. Spanning an entire block length and soaring to a height of more than 100 feet,

the arcade's massive walls provide yet another natural surface for a large mural. The long, funnel-like space needed a sense of rhythm to liven up its monotonous flow. With elegance, modularity, and wall surface as key specifications, the Equitable commissioned Sol LeWitt, a conceptual artist and muralist, to create an enormous five-part mural. LeWitt's geometric design will be color-stained into the galleria's limestone wall fields. The major center section measures 106 by 32 feet. Five other wall areas each measure approximately 20 by 38 feet. The separate surfaces will relate to each other with color, scheme, and design and to the overall environment.

On either end of the galleria, red granite fountain basins will provide settings for whimsical animal bronzes by British artist Barry Flanagan. The sculptures—*Hare on Bell* (1983) and *Young Elephant* (1984)—will lighten the high formality of the galleria. The Equitable also acquired a Paul Manship bronze, *Day*, which will be mounted on a specially designed pedestal and placed on the Avenue of the Americas frontage. The work is one of four sculptures Manship created as fountain figures for the 1939–40 New York World's Fair.

Builders and Artists Create Art That's More Than an Ornament

The new Equitable skyscraper, under construction, is due for completion by the end of 1985. Lichtenstein and LeWitt will create their murals, for which maquettes already have been approved, beginning in the late summer. They should be finished in time for the center's grand opening in mid-October 1985, which will include the opening of the Whitney branches and the unveiling of the Bentons.

Still in the design stage are the urban plazas flanking the existing Avenue of the Americas building on 51st and 52nd streets. An original Barnes design for the plazas' seating and planting fulfilled the 1982 city ordinance requirements for securing FAR bonuses for the tower. The design provided fixed seating for the public. A later opinion of the city planning commission, however, called for movable chairs, allowing for flexible individual and group use. This requirement presents logistical problems—moving 80 chairs out and in each day, storing them, and providing security and, inevitably, frequent replacement.

As an alternative, in December 1984, the Equitable commissioned Scott Burton to prepare a new plaza design, still with fixed seating, but offering increased benefits to walkers, office workers, and neighbors. This scheme must be resubmitted to a community review board and to the planning commission to justify the FAR bonuses. In place of unfixed seating, Burton has designed plazas with attention to needs of seating, sociability, traffic, pedestrian patterns, and volume. These will be plazas of radically different design than has been the tradition on the Avenue of the Americas.

With the exception of Burton's plazas, Equitable Center's artworks and gallery spaces have been integrated into the architectural plans before construction began. Most of them have been designed in direct relation to their architectural environment. They will not be part of a museum or civic hall, nor have they been accumulated by a philanthropist interested in creating a distinguished monument. Rather, these murals, sculptures, and paintings will be striking modifiers of the architecture and of visitors' experience of the building's space. It is this blend of art and architecture,

rather than the mere presentation of prestige art objects, that the Equitable intends to pursue in all its real estate ventures.

While Equitable Tower will help spur a desired neighborhood revitalization, the entire focus of the project from its earliest conceptualization was to develop a property that would be more than just another office building and corporate symbol. "What we wanted to do," says Benjamin Holloway, "was to give the city a development in the tradition of Rockefeller Center, which could be an inviting urban oasis providing workers and visitors with an environment that could be spiritually uplifting and exciting, a place that underscores the dynamism of New York—its size, its architecture, its culture."

Paul Manship's *Day*, a 1938 bronze sculpture, will be mounted on a pedestal on the sidewalk in front of the 1285 Avenue of the Americas building.

Williams Center

Williams Center is a $200 million mixed-use project developed by the Williams Realty Corporation, a wholly owned subsidiary of the Williams Companies. Located at the northern edge of Tulsa, Oklahoma's central business district, Williams Center covers nine blocks (21.5 acres)—approximately 30 percent of the downtown area. It has acted as a catalyst to reverse Tulsa's downtown decline, stimulating substantial new investment by additional public/private sources. It includes the Bank of Oklahoma Tower, a multitenant, 52-story office building; the Westin Hotel, Williams Center, a 450-room luxury hotel; the Williams Center Forum, an enclosed three-story retail center with The Ice (the only year-round ice rink in Oklahoma); the Tulsa Performing Arts Center, containing four theaters and an art gallery; two multilevel parking garages (with space for 1,684 cars); and The Green, a 2.5-acre park linking the components together. The project totals just under three million square feet.

The Tulsa Performing Arts Center, the result of a tenacious and trusting public/private partnership among citizens, the city, and the Williams Companies, provides a home for the Tulsa Philharmonic, the Tulsa Opera, and the Tulsa Ballet Theatre, which all stage their seasons exclusively in the center's Chapman Hall. The American Theatre Company, Tulsa Junior College, Theatre North, American Indian Theater Company, Oklahoma Sinfonia and Chorale, Concertime, and other professional and amateur groups also perform there, but not exclusively. The arts center also serves as a multipurpose community facility where recitals, graduations, awards presentations, gala benefits, social gatherings, and corporate meetings take place. Owned by the city, the arts center operated in 1984 on a budget of $1.4 million.

Phase I of Williams Center, containing the components listed above, started in 1973 and was completed between 1976 and 1978. On its west, Phase II includes the Williams Center Towers I and II, first-class office buildings completed in 1982 and 1983 at a cost of $75 million, plus a 350-car parking garage and a one-acre public plaza. During the years between the construction of Phases I and II, the Williams Realty Corporation renovated three buildings on blocks immediately adjacent to Williams Center: the Kennedy Building (205,098 square feet), the 320 South Boston Building (473,149 square feet) and the Tulsa Union Depot (45,615 square feet), for a total investment of $15.1 million.

Stores Follow
Homeowners to the Suburbs

No longer considered the "Oil Capital of the World," Tulsa nonetheless retains more than 1,000 oil-related businesses and a 1983 per-capita county personal income of $14,484—33 percent above the national average. In 1983 the population of the city totaled 369,500; its metropolitan area numbered 728,000. Aviation, aerospace, computers, and data processing rank among Tulsa's strongest industries, and the port of Catoosa links Tulsa to the Mississippi through barge shipping.

The city occupies 187.5 square miles primarily on the east bank of the Arkansas River. Downtown Tulsa, where 55,000 people work daily, encompasses 1,000 acres bounded by the Inner Dispersal Loop, which links all incoming highways. Because of Tulsa's tremendous growth during the teens and twenties, the downtown boasts a rich collection of Beaux Arts and Art Deco buildings.

Tulsa is the largest city in the nation still using the mayor–commission form of local government, adopted there in 1908. Its five-member board of commissioners includes the mayor and commissioners of finance and revenue, police and fire, streets and public property, and waterworks and sewerage. The city auditor sits on the commission but does not vote. The state of Oklahoma requires an annual balanced budget. A city cannot incur debts beyond the funds that are available for expenditures, unless its citizens vote a tax for the repayment of that debt. For projects requiring contracts for more than one year, therefore, Tulsa does business through nonprofit authorities or trusts that can incur indebtedness for longer periods of time and that have as their beneficiary the city or other government entities.

Tulsa was incorporated as a city of the Creek Indian Nation in 1898; the population then was 1,100. Oil was discovered in June 1901, and a major strike at Glenn Pool in November 1905 proved eventually to be the world's most productive small oil field. By the time Oklahoma became a state on November 16, 1907, Tulsa was booming, and its region led the nation in oil production during World War I. Between 1916 and 1920 alone, $336 million was spent on downtown construction.

After World War II, Tulsa boomed again and built water and sewer systems, streets, and expressways. But because of its legal difficulties in financing public improvements, it deferred amenities like a new city hall, a convention center, and a public theater.

Downtown Tulsa remained a dynamic commercial center until the mid-fifties, when suburbanization began draining the city's consumer and tax base. In 1958 Sears relocated its only Tulsa store some five miles from downtown, starting a trend of downtown store emigration. As the once-proud residential neighborhood abutting the downtown gradually lost its class and polish, Tulsa's after-hours downtown came to be synonymous with cheap hotels, greasy spoons, winos, and panhandlers. This image chilled the investment climate in central Tulsa, and in 1958 Mayor James Maxwell's 150-member Committee for Community Conservation produced a report calling for three coordinated long-term strategies to staunch the loss of jobs and tax revenue: (1) urban renewal, (2) minimum housing codes, and (3) a comprehensive city plan.

Williams Center. Clockwise: The Bank of Oklahoma Tower, Tulsa Performing Arts Center, The Green, Westin Hotel, Towers I and II, and the Forum.

Artists and Patrons Decry the Unlovely "Old Lady on Brady"

After oil was discovered in Tulsa, fortune-seekers flocked to the city from all over the nation, bringing with them an interest in the arts. Tulsa's first opera house opened in 1906, and as early as 1911 the New York Symphony came to the city. The Chicago Civic Light Opera Company performed in the city in 1924, and by 1929 music enthusiasts had organized an unpaid local orchestra. The Tulsa Opera, the Tulsa Philharmonic, and the Tulsa Ballet Theatre were founded in 1948, 1949, and 1955 respectively. The opera company presents three productions a year. The ballet's 20 dancers present 15 performances annually and tour to 13 cities in six southwestern states; in 1983 the company made its New York City debut. The 85-member orchestra draws music lovers from 500 miles around.

Tulsa also boasts a wealth of local drama groups. Theatre Tulsa, formed in 1922, is one of the six oldest community theaters (in which the performers are local, non-professional actors) in the nation. In the early seventies the American Theatre Company emerged as the only professional resident theater company in Oklahoma. The American Indian Theater Company of Oklahoma casts Native American actors and actresses in works by Native American playwrights. Theatre North presents performances by the black community.

Tulsa's facilities for these performing groups, however, were woefully inadequate. As early as 1913, the citizens passed a bond issue to finance a combination convention hall and municipal theater. The Tulsa Convention Hall, constructed just north of the railroad tracks on Brady and Main streets, opened in 1914, but it proved unsuited for convention purposes and only barely suited for cultural events. Eventually the hall was converted into the Municipal Theater, but its lack of air conditioning, its 2,700 wooden seats, its minimal backstage dressing room area, and its location next to the railroad tracks caused civic leaders and performing groups to disparage the "Old Lady on Brady."

A Civic Center Master Plan developed in the fifties for the western side of downtown included plans for a performing arts center. However, two successive bond issues calling for a combined convention/arts center failed. A third issue passed by eliminating the theater and reducing the budget from $10 million to $7 million.

In the sixties, the newly created Arts Council of Tulsa, established as a clearinghouse and guide for local arts organizations, began to muster public support for a performing arts center. In 1966, the old Municipal Theater was blackballed by the American Guild of Musical Artists and the Actors Equity Guild. The unions cited the theater's dangerous stage floor and its lack of both running water and proper heating. According to union rules, artists and organizations under union contract can be fined or subjected to disciplinary action for performing in facilities not meeting union standards.

Later that year, Mayor James Hewgley appointed a mayor's committee to investigate the need for a performing arts center. The committee's 45-page report, submitted to a city–county citizens advisory committee in May 1969, stated that "the present Municipal Theater is . . . 'unworkable, hazardous, and incredibly unlovely,' . . . with antiquated stage facilities, lack of parking, poor access, and totally depressing patron accommodations." The report called for the inclusion of a new arts center in an omnibus bond issue containing 15 other projects. The center it proposed would contain a large, 2,500- to 3,000-seat auditorium suitable for ballet, opera, and concerts, and a smaller 1,000-seat proscenium theater with a stage house.

Mayor Hewgley and the city commission backed the arts center proposal against strong opposition. Leading the campaign to win approval of the proposal was the Arts Council of Tulsa, which pledged the support of its 15,000 members. When the tally was complete on the omnibus bond, however, it was apparent that the arts council's votes may have been the only support the proposal received. It was defeated by a 72 percent margin, with 14,610 votes in favor and 38,407 opposed.

Plans for Downtown and Theater Renewal Proceed Separately

In 1959 a comprehensive plan for central Tulsa had recommended a downtown pedestrian mall—a 12-block area where auto traffic would be removed and trees planted. Because of tight economic resources, however, only four blocks of Main Street were refurbished into a semi-mall in 1966.

In 1970 Downtown Tulsa Unlimited, a private nonprofit organization founded in 1956 to help downtown retail operations promote and revitalize the central area, joined with the Metropolitan Tulsa Chamber of Commerce to form a task force to update the 1959 plan. Their study, *Central Tulsa: A Plan for Action,* conducted by Barton-Aschman Associates of Chicago, was released in 1973. The plan identified three principal downtown activity centers—the Civic Center (containing all major local, state, and federal agency offices), the central business district core, and a proposed nine-square-block, mixed-use redevelopment project—with recommendations that these areas be connected by attractive pedestrian links. The report also called for public performances or events to stimulate excitement in the downtown area; replacement of housing that had been torn down near the downtown core; creation of intimate parks and plazas; a shuttle service; and establishment of one-way paired streets to improve circulation and to compensate for streets closed for the pedestrian mall.

The Tulsa Urban Renewal Authority already had initiated a Downtown Northwest Urban Renewal Project, encompassing 309 acres that included the heart of Tulsa's central business district. The authority had amassed strong evidence on the downtown's decline: from 1950 to 1962, almost 40 percent of new office space and 93 percent of all new hotel rooms in Tulsa had been constructed outside the city center. Over five years, the agency acquired and cleared about three-fourths of the lots on nine contiguous blocks on the downtown's northern edge, from the railroad tracks on the north to Third Street on the south, and from Cincinnati Avenue on the east to Boulder Street on the west. On these nine blocks had stood marginal buildings dating back to Tulsa's early days—mostly half-vacant flophouses, beer joints, and pawn shops. The tax revenue generated on the entire nine-block area prior to redevelopment had been $175,000. The area wasn't as blighted as the skid rows of many cities, according to Paul Chapman, executive director of the Urban Renewal Authority. But "nice girls didn't go north of Third Street."

When the authority made its first public offering in 1965 for development of this land, the only viable proposal was presented by Metro Center, Inc., a well-financed corporation of local investors, an architect, and a general contractor. Metro Center's plans called for a $25 million redevelopment of an eight-block area with parking, high-rise office buildings with stores on the lower floors, a hotel, restaurants, theaters, and an intermodal transportation center—a project then unprecedented in the Southwest. The corporation proved unable, however, to generate sufficient tenant interest to finance the undertaking.

In November 1971 the Williams Companies of Tulsa and the Harnett-Shaw Development Company of Chicago unveiled proposals for a $200 million office, hotel, and retail complex on the cleared downtown site. Under this plan, the Williams Companies, with Urban Renewal Authority approval, would acquire ownership of Metro Center, Inc., and assume its redevelopment rights. The authority estimated that the projects—collectively called Williams Center—would generate more than $5 million in tax revenues, more than the entire area inside the downtown Inner Dispersal Loop did at that time.

That same year, Mayor Robert Lafortune, a member of an established Tulsa oil family and a former commissioner of streets and public property, formed a Municipal Theater study committee to carry forward the continuing interest in a new performing arts center. Charles Norman, former city attorney, and William Waller, a local financier, both board members of the Arts Council of Tulsa (which renamed itself the Arts and Humanities Council in 1972), co-chaired the committee, which spent two years assessing what the city needed and how it might be financed. The committee and a staff person assigned by the Arts and Humanities Council reviewed previous pro-

A Local "Challenge Grant" Finances Theaters in Williams's MXD

posals for a Tulsa arts center, as well as plans for centers that had been built in the last 15 years all over the world. They researched the needs and availability of touring attractions and road companies. After interviewing four local user groups, they decided that the two-theater plan that had been defeated in the 1969 omnibus bond issue had been inappropriate. The 1,000-seat theater would have been much too small for traditional Broadway shows that might travel to Tulsa, yet too large for local theater groups. The proposed larger hall would have been too small for opera and private promoters but too large for the orchestra and the ballet, which both preferred 1,800 seats.

The study committee concluded that a 2,000-seat theater would provide the minimum capacity suitable for Tulsa's needs, and that the Municipal Theater on Brady Street remained beyond repair. It also recommended that a $10,000 study be conducted by the American Institute of Architects to determine the feasibility of renovating the Akdar building across from the Civic Center, as opposed to building a new facility. The Akdar building, opened in 1925 as a Masonic temple, contained an 1,800-seat, fully equipped auditorium, though its sloping floor had been leveled. The city board of commissioners financed the feasibility study, which concluded that renovation would cost $3.5 million to $4.5 million and, because of its limited size, would not fully meet the needs of all arts groups.

In 1972 Mayor Lafortune formed another committee to coordinate the celebration of Tulsa's 75th anniversary in 1973. In March 1973 a weekend community workshop was conducted by Paul Chapman of the Urban Renewal Authority and Lawrence Halprin of Lawrence Halprin Associates of San Francisco to explore ways to commemorate the anniversary and act as an energizer for positive downtown development. The mayor made sure that Tulsa's top business leaders attended, including Joseph H. Williams, president and chief operating officer of the Williams Companies. The workshop participants spent the weekend downtown, visiting all its activity centers (including the Akdar, which was being used as a country dance hall), and trying to visualize what it could become. Their Monday-morning conclusion was succinct: What could be done in downtown Tulsa on the weekend? Nothing.

One of the principal notions generated by the workshop was that an arts center could help Tulsa "physically exhibit that cultural activity is part of the quality of life available to its citizens." But the memory of the 1969 bond defeat made public support for a new facility questionable at best. Local business leaders supported the concept of a new theater, but none came forward with a financial plan.

Downtown Tulsa, showing location of Williams Center and the Civic Center joined by the mall on Main and Fifth streets.
Credit: Downtown Tulsa Unlimited

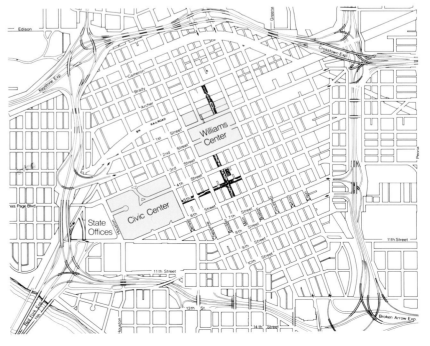

Williams Center
Project Data

Component—Income Generating

Office

Bank of Oklahoma Tower	1,100,000 sq. ft.
Williams Center Tower I	310,000 sq. ft.
Williams Center Tower II	450,400 sq. ft.

Retail

Bank of Oklahoma Tower	40,000 sq. ft.
The Forum	152,442 sq. ft. NLA
Cinema	700 seats
The Ice	85 ft. × 185 ft.
The Westin Hotel	450 rooms

Component—Arts/Culture/Open Space

Tulsa Performing Arts Center	161,653 sq. ft.
Chapman Music Hall	2,450 seats
John H. Williams Theater	450 seats
Multiform Theaters—Studio I	up to 288 seats
—Studio II	up to 210 seats
Visual Arts Gallery	4,000 sq. ft.
The Green	2.5 acres
Williams Center Towers Plaza	1.0 acres

Other

Parking	2,134 spaces
Gross Building Area	3,000,000 sq. ft.
Floor/Area Ratio	3.2
Acreage	21.5 acres
Location	Downtown Tulsa
Master Developer	Williams Realty Corporation
Master Planner and Architect	Minoru Yamasaki
Development Period	1973–83
Total Development Costs	$243.4 million

Source: Williams Realty Corp.

Williams Center
Development Cost Summary

	Private	Public
Office Buildings	$163.0 million	
Retail	16.5 million	
Hotel	25.5 million	
Tulsa Performing Arts Center	9.0 million	$ 9.0 million
Parking		20.4 million
Total	$214.0 million	$29.4 million

Source: Williams Realty Corp.

After the Williams Center had been announced, the Arts and Humanities Council's president, Kathleen Westby, suggested to John H. Williams, chairman and chief executive officer of the Williams Companies, that the new project might be a suitable place for an arts center. According to Westby, Williams told her: "I'll give you the land if you raise the money." She said she couldn't imagine raising $10 million, considering what had happened to previous bond issues.

The Municipal Theater study committee persevered. After further input from citizens, it concluded that for maximum programming flexibility, Tulsa should aim for a 2,400-seat theater (as originally proposed), as well as three "black box" facilities that would have seating capacities of 100, 150, and 350–400 seats.

The committee also proposed including a gallery space for visual arts and some multipurpose space for educational programs, and it suggested the possibility of locating a theater complex in the suburbs, where parking would be more accessible—perhaps even moving it to the University of Tulsa and making it a joint-use center.

But no funds were available to purchase the land in the suburbs, while the land still nominally available in the downtown Civic Center parcels had become less desirable, since many new buildings had been built since the sixties with competing focal points and relationships.

Meanwhile, the Williams Companies quietly reviewed Kathleen Westby's thoughts about an arts center. The Williams Center's neighborhood, though close to the city's most important business locations, retained a stigma of crime and decline. Incorporating cultural facilities in the project held out the potential for attracting people to the area at night. But John Williams also knew that Tulsans might not be willing to vote support for an arts center in a private commercial development rather than in the Civic Center, the long-designated use area.

John and his cousin, Joseph H. Williams, asked Charles Norman to help them review the idea of renovating the Akdar. They asked whether, given the choice, Tulsans would want to renovate an old facility or build a new one. Norman said there was no question that a new facility would be preferable. John Williams then gave him three weeks to determine how much an effective multipurpose facility would cost.

With the help of the Arts and Humanities Council staff and the Williams Companies' estimating and construction departments, Norman developed a budget of $14 million—$12.5 million in hard costs, the remaining for architects' fees and land costs—for a center containing a large concert hall, three black-box theaters, and a 200-car parking garage.

Williams proposed a challenge grant to finance the theater: If he could come up with $7 million in private funds, would the citizens of Tulsa support the other half? The mayor endorsed this strategy, and Williams presented the following plan:

■ that the arts center be located in Williams Center;
■ that the city approve a program prepared by the Municipal Theater study committee, and that a facility be built that met those needs;
■ that the Williams Companies designate the center's architect; and
■ that a small arts center committee be formed, with two representatives from the private sector and two from the public sector, to manage design and construction. The representatives were to be John Williams; Ralph Abercrombie, a lawyer representing a major private donor; Harold Miller, the city engineer; and Charles Norman.

When revised plans for Phase I of Williams Center were announced, they included the arts center in addition to: (1) a 52-story office building to serve as the corporate headquarters for the Williams Companies as well as the the Bank of Oklahoma. The remaining one-third of the building would be available for lease. (2) A luxury 400-room hotel on the western boundary of the project. (No new hotel rooms had been built in downtown Tulsa in more than 50 years.) (3) A multilevel parking garage on the north serving the Forum, a three-story specialty retail center and ice rink. (4) A second multilevel parking garage to the south, with The Green, a two-and-a-half-acre park, built above it to serve as a focal point for the project.

Project Data: Tulsa Performing Arts Center

Location	Williams Center, Tulsa, Oklahoma	
Completed	March 19, 1977	
Architect	Minoru Yamasaki	
Consultants	Wozencraft, Mowery, Sanders—Associate Architects Bolt, Beranek & Newman, Inc.—Acoustical and Theatrical	
Contractor	Flintco Inc., Tulsa	
Building Cost	$17,650,000 construction costs $350,000 land costs	
Gross Area	161,653 sq. ft.	
Breakdown of Interior Area		
Chapman Music Hall	Seating:	2,450 seats (1,402 orchestra; 62 forestage lift; 618 mezzanine; 368 balcony)
	Proscenium Height:	34 ft.
	Proscenium Width:	60 ft.
	Grid Height:	84 ft., 6 in. + 71 line sets
	Stage Width:	100 ft.
	Stage Depth:	53 ft.
	Orchestra Pit:	60 musicians
	Dressing Rooms:	Space for 72 persons
John H. Williams Theater	Seating:	450 seats on one level
	Proscenium Height:	22 ft.
	Proscenium Width:	38 ft.
	Grid Height:	51 ft. + 50 line sets
	Stage Width:	72 ft.
	Orchestra Pit:	25 musicians
	Dressing Rooms:	Space for 20 persons + makeup rooms for 16 persons
Studio I	Seating:	Flexible; up to 280 seats depending on stage area required
	Room Dimensions:	60 ft. × 60 ft. × 20 ft.; Can accommodate end-stage, arena, and thrust stage
	Dressing Rooms:	Space for 24 persons
Studio II	Seating:	210
	Room Dimensions:	52 ft. × 52 ft. × 19 ft., 6 in.
	Dressing Rooms:	None normally assigned
Art Gallery	Approximately 4,000 sq. ft. including storage and offices	
Exterior Features	Outdoor patio spilling onto Williams Center Green Two separate entrances for four theaters	
Interior Features	In addition to the above, the facility includes box office; dressing rooms for 160 people; two green rooms; costume shop; scene shop.	

The City and Williams Perceive the Common Good

Without the tenacity and collaborative commitment of the Tulsa Urban Renewal Authority, Mayor Lafortune, the Williams Companies, private philanthropists, and the Tulsa arts community, the vision of an arts center never would have been realized.

The Williams Companies

The "original" Williams brothers formed their company just after the turn of the century, when a general contractor who had employed them went bankrupt and turned over his equipment in lieu of past-due wages. The Williams Brothers Company's first project was to build a concrete bridge over the Arkansas River to the region's oil fields. It soon began building pipelines for the oil companies, and by 1935 it was a significant pipeline contractor. From the end of World War II until 1966 the Williams Brothers Company worked principally for international clients, building pipelines in the Middle East, South America, and Alaska. During the fifties, the founding Williams brothers retired and sold the company to their nephews and sons, who renamed it the Williams Companies. In the sixties the firm acquired the Great Lakes Pipeline, owned by a consortium of eight oil companies, for $287 million.

In 1971 and 1972 the Williams Companies purchased the fertilizer divisions of both Gulf and Continental Oil, thus becoming the nation's largest fertilizer company. By 1972 its assets totaled just under $1 billion. This rapid growth required offices in five separate buildings in downtown Tulsa. When the firm purchased 20 percent of the stock in the Bank of Oklahoma (then called the National Bank of Tulsa), it knew it had a potential need for at least two new office buildings.

The company considered Dallas and Houston as possible sites for a new corporate headquarters but, as John Williams puts it, "We couldn't come up with any sound reason for moving." The firm's roots were in Tulsa, the overall quality of life was high, and the tremendous infrastructure of the oil industry remained. Two of the top four drilling contractors and the dominant supplier of pipeline equipment in North America all still were located in Tulsa.

The Williams Companies then considered the city's suburbs, but it decided to stay downtown. The decision was "altruistic," says E. Eddie Henson, president of the Williams Realty Corporation: "A major company has an obligation to the community to not be a part of the deterioration of the downtown."

Before publicly announcing their plans for Williams Center, the Williams Companies bought or took options on two of the four privately owned tracts of land within the proposed superblock, and then assumed the Metro Center redevelopment contract with the Urban Renewal Authority for the publicly owned land. The authority also agreed to acquire two other privately owned properties to complete nine full blocks.

The project then became contingent on the Urban Renewal Authority's ability to obtain a few remaining properties that had to be condemned, on closing Main Street and Boston Avenue between First and Third streets, on Williams' purchase of air space over Boston and Main, and on permission for the project to dovetail with the city's expressway and major street plans. The authority officially approved plans to include the Williams Center in the Downtown Northwest Urban Renewal Project, and in December 1971 the city commission approved the closing of two blocks of Main Street and two blocks of Boston Avenue to accommodate the project.

Final plans for Williams Center were announced in October 1972. Because of the project's size, John Williams felt it was important to choose an architect with an international reputation: Minoru Yamasaki.

The City Acts Fast

On May 3, 1973, Mayor Lafortune announced that Tulsa had received the largest cash gift in its history. John Williams had negotiated a pledge of $3.5 million from Mrs. Leta Chapman, a member of a family of oil-rich philanthropists, in return for his promise to raise another $3.5 million in private donations, and in expectation of public passage of a $7 million bond issue. The mayor noted that the bonds had to be voted by August 22, 1973, to meet a Williams Center construction deadline.

The City Buys the Arts Center, the Developer Provides Amenities

On June 8 the city commission approved an ordinance creating a Tulsa Municipal Theater Authority, composed of the mayor, the commissioner of finance and revenue, and the commissioner of streets and public property, whose purpose was to finance, construct, own, and maintain "a municipal theater and community arts center facility with appurtenant parking"; to issue bonds for the facility and to secure their payment with its anticipated revenues; to receive gifts from private donors; and to enter into contracts with the city and others to construct and operate the arts center. Billed as "an offer the city couldn't refuse," the bond election was held August 7, 1973, and passed by a margin of 6,658 votes: 19,112 yes, 12,454 no.

Tulsa's comprehensive plan was amended to move the publicly designated theater site from the Civic Center area to the Williams Center complex on a block bounded by South Boston, Cincinnati, Second, and Third. Although it was one of the most valuable parcels in the project, the Williams Companies sold it to the city for $350,000, the exact price it had paid for the land.

Within four months the private money was raised—much of it in the form of pledges of $50,000 to $500,000, payable over a three- to five-year period. To ensure adequate cash flow for the project, donors were required to provide a letter of credit equal to the pledge and then to sign a legal form binding against their estate. The Theater Authority thus could borrow against the pledges to pay construction costs as they arose.

Because of the small size of the arts center's site (140 feet by 300 feet), a significant difference in elevation from Third to Second streets, the necessity of including a parking garage to help support the center, and the desire to include four separate theaters acoustically and functionally isolated from each other, architect Yamasaki had to prepare more than 20 different design schemes to fit all the elements together. Each space had to be designed so that when activities took place in all four theaters simultaneously, no sound would "leak."

In February 1974 Theatre Tulsa, an amateur group that had been considering building its own facility in the suburbs, asked the four-member arts center steering committee to consider changing one of the three black boxes into a small stagehouse theater. The committee therefore recommended converting the 400-seat black box to a 450-seat theater with a proscenium arch and fixed stage, and deleting the 200-car parking garage, which represented about $1 million in costs. Because of the availability of nearby parking—notably under the proposed adjacent Green—the city commission approved the changes.

Yamasaki's 22nd design received the approval of the arts center committee and the city commission in March 1974. The estimated cost of construction totaled $12,202,750. Engineering and architectural fees would amount to $945,000. Yamasaki guaranteed that even with land costs and interior furnishings included, the arts center could be built for $14 million. At the same time, Lawrence Kirkegaard of Bolt, Beranek & Newman, Inc., joined the design team as accoustical consultant, and Ron Jerit was named theater design consultant.

Bids were solicited in early October 1974, and three firms responded by mid-November. They ranged from a low of $19,540,000 to a high of $20,400,000—$5.5 million over budget. When all nonconstruction costs for furnishings and equipment were added, the total projected cost for the theater exceeded $22 million. After two weeks of technical review with the architects and bidders, the arts center committee concluded that, while significant

The Green, a 2½-acre park that serves as the focal point of Williams Center.

cost reductions could be made, it would not be possible to produce a building with the funds available without major redesign and elimination of broad categories of community space, such as the balcony in the orchestra hall, the small theater, one or more of the multiform spaces, or the entire gallery wing.

Redesign, however, seemed unacceptable for more reasons than just the loss of various functions. Redesign and rebidding would have created a six-month delay. In addition, after January 1, 1975, the project would be subject to new federally required environmental impact review procedures. With construction costs escalating at that time at a rate of 9 percent per month, the arts center committee knew that the center would begin to flounder if construction did not start immediately.

Fortunately for Tulsa, John Williams, Charles Norman, and Mayor Lafortune mustered fresh reserves of tenacity. They believed the arts center was necessary, that the public wanted it, and that Williams Center was a good location. There just had to be a way to build it. Williams describes it as "one of those moments of truth—you've got to get on with it."

A Nonprofit Intermediary Is Born

On December 5 the arts center committee presented a new proposal to Mayor Lafortune and the board of commissioners. It suggested that, by working closely with Flintco, the low construction bidder, costs could be reduced $4 million without major redesign and without eliminating any principal functions, leaving a $15.5 million building cost. This total still exceeded the funds available (from bond proceeds, private contributions, and earned interest), but only by $3 million.

To accomplish an immediate beginning in the construction of the Performing Arts Center, the committee recommended:

1) . . . that a new nonprofit corporation be formed for the purpose of constructing the Performing Arts Center. The new corporation would construct the facility [and contract with Williams Realty to provide construction management services] in substantial accord with the plans and specifications approved by the Board

of Commissioners of the City and by the Authority, subject to cost reduction changes necessary to reduce the cost to the level of funds available. The corporation would be named Performing Arts Center, Incorporated, and would have as its officers and directors the current members of the Committee for the Performing Arts Center [Williams, Abercrombie, Miller, Norman].

2) The corporation would enter into an agreement with the low bidder under the previous bid process in which the contractor, the nonprofit corporation, and the architects and engineers would agree on cost reduction changes necessary to construct the building within the funds now available and those to be obtained.

3) . . . that the City of Tulsa and the Tulsa Municipal Theater Authority enter into an agreement to purchase the Performing Arts Center from Performing Arts Center, Incorporated, for a purchase price which will not exceed the total of funds to be available to the two bodies (bonds proceeds, current and future donations, future city appropriations, and interest thereon); and that these two entities make periodic payments toward such purchase as the work is completed in accordance with the agreement.

4) . . . that the City Commission appropriate $1 million in additional funds in fiscal year 1975 and an additional $1 million in fiscal year 1976.

This course of action offered a number of advantages. The most important was that construction could begin immediately. Second, the nonprofit construction management entity, Performing Arts Center, Inc., would be committed to producing the building within the funds available—any risk of overruns would be absorbed by the nonprofit entity rather than by the city or the theater authority. Third, the format would provide continuity of management and supervision for the project.

Included with the proposal was a letter from John H. Williams pledging to raise more private gifts to match the city's new $2 million commitment, and a letter from Williams Center, Inc., offering to arrange interim financing from Tulsa area banks.

In a rare display of municipal efficiency, the city issued a building permit for the center a week later on December 12. On December 13 it pledged $2 million in general revenue-sharing and sales tax capital funds, to be issued in 1975 and 1976. On

December 18 the city commission passed a resolution calling for the construction of the center by Performing Arts Center, Inc., and its purchase by the city after completion. On December 20 ground was broken.

Mall and Williams Center Meet

While the arts center began construction, other components of Williams Center already were being developed. Ground had been broken for Phase I in 1973, and the buildings opened between 1976 and 1978. Although planned jointly by the Williams Companies and Harnett-Shaw Development Company of Chicago, the project actually was completed under the direction of the Williams Realty Corporation, formed as a wholly owned subsidiary of the Williams Companies in 1974 after Harnett-Shaw's interest was purchased by the Williams Companies.

As Williams Center began, the city was designing a new downtown mall with the assistance of Lawrence Halprin Associates of San Francisco, which conducted a series of three "Take Part" workshops in the spring of 1974 to enable citizens to contribute to the design process. After the mall concept was agreed upon, the Williams Companies agreed to modify design specifications for the Williams Plaza Hotel and Williams Center, to enable the mall to extend visually north across Third Street alongside the hotel and into the mixed-use complex.

A seven-block Central Tulsa Pedestrian System plan added new trees and shrubs, benches, pedestrian lighting, drinking fountains, informational kiosks, eating areas, a clock and weather station, trash containers, a public address system, and a self-service postal station. At the intersection of Main and Fifth streets, a large fountain was installed, evoking the rolling countryside of northeastern Oklahoma and the sights and sounds of water rushing over river rock. Three blocks of Main Street closed to public vehicular traffic, and Fifth Street was redesigned to limit traffic through the use of cul-de-sacs on two blocks and one-way, serpentine, 24-foot roadways on two others. Williams Center and the mall were coordinated, discussed, and compared thoroughly, so they would complement each other.

The major components in Williams Center's first phase were as follows:

■ The Bank of Oklahoma Tower on South Boston Avenue between First and Second streets offers 52 stories of first-class office space, financed by an $86 million loan from the Equitable Life Assurance Society of the United States—at that time the largest mortgage ever made by the Equitable.

■ The Westin Hotel, Williams Center, the first new hotel in downtown Tulsa in more than 50 years, is owned by a subsidiary of Williams Realty and operated by Westin.

■ Williams Center Forum, a three-story, enclosed specialty retail center, contains 152,442 square feet of net leasable area, connected to the Bank of Oklahoma Tower and to the hotel by skywalks. Among its features is The Ice, the only year-round ice skating rink in Oklahoma.

■ Two multilevel parking garages, accommodating 1,684 vehicles, are owned by the Tulsa Parking Authority (a public trust) and operated through a management agreement by Williams Realty Developments, Inc., operators of Williams Center. Williams Realty Corporation sold the land under the two parking structures to the parking authority, which then designed and built the structures. The Williams Companies, with the

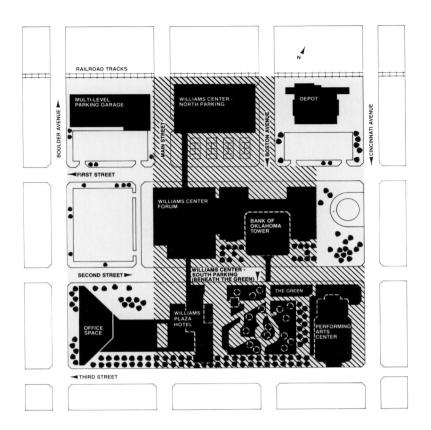

Williams Center, showing initial development and proposed full density/master plan.

▧ Initial Development
☐ Full Density / Master Plan

Williams Center, Arts Center, and Mall Spur Restoration

The Forum, a three-level specialty retail center with The Ice, the state's only year-round ice rink.

The Bank of Oklahoma Tower.

Bank of Oklahoma, underwrote a $20.4 million bond issue (serial notes expiring over a 20-year period), since there was no guarantee that, even with a 52-story office building and a 400-room hotel, the parking structures could produce enough revenue to make an attractive investment. To make the bonds marketable, the Williams Companies and the Bank of Oklahoma guaranteed on a 70/30 percent basis the payment of any debt service deficiency after payment of the operating expenses.

■ The Green, connected to the bank tower by a second-story skybridge, was financed as part of the parking structure underneath it and is owned by the Tulsa Parking Authority. The bond issue limited maintenance expenditures to 5 percent of the gross garage revenues. The Williams Companies and the Bank of Oklahoma agreed to pay all additional maintenance costs for The Green.

To separate vehicular and pedestrian traffic, all the components of Williams Center are linked by climate-controlled tunnels and skybridges, constructed and owned by the Tulsa Parking Authority. Because the hotel, the arts center, the two garages, and The Green are owned by three different entities (the city, the parking authority, and Williams Realty Corporation), reciprocal easement agreements had to be developed to handle the connections through the east wall of the parking structure into the lobby of the arts center, through the west wall of the parking structure into the hotel, from the west lobby of the arts center onto The Green, between the north garage and the Forum, and between the south garage and an office building to the south.

In 1977 the Tulsa Board of Commissioners formally received title to the arts center from Performing Arts Center, Inc. The building opened to the public on March 19, 1977, with Ella Fitzgerald singing in Chapman Music Hall to a sellout crowd.

The Tulsa Performing Arts Center today houses four separate performing areas under one roof: the 2,450-seat Chapman Music Hall; the 429-seat John H. Williams Theater; and Studios I and II, two multiform black-box spaces with capacities ranging from 184 to 288 seats depending on the physical arrangement of the event. The center also includes a visual arts gallery that hosts traveling exhibitions. Fifty-five artworks in a variety of media, representing 44 artists, remain on permanent display throughout the center.

The mechanisms for managing and programming the arts center had been put into place several years earlier, so that once the building was completed, it began functioning smoothly. The city owns, operates, and is responsible for managing the building as a public events facility. The managing director (Sidney McQueen) is a city employee who works under the city director of public events, who in turn reports to the commissioner of streets and public property. The 1984–85 operating budget totaled $1,456,862; 75 percent was provided by the city from the general fund, the convention fund, the short-term sales tax fund, and (to a very limited extent) revenue-sharing. The remainder was generated by facility and equipment rental and in-house services. The city works hard to keep rental costs low, and there are different rental rates for nonprofit and profit-making groups.

During 1983 the schedule offered 910 "event days" (days when something was happening in the facility, though not necessarily attended by the public) and 382 public days. In 1984, it was estimated that the event days would total 1,200 and the public days 450. Estimated attendance at all events during the 1984–85 season was 250,000.

About 75 to 80 percent of the arts center's programs are locally produced, delivered by the Tulsa Ballet Theatre, Tulsa Philharmonic, Tulsa Opera, Tulsa Performing Arts Center Trust, Tulsa Alliance for

Classical Theatre, American Indian Theater Company, Tulsa Junior College, Tulsa Park and Recreation, Theatre North, Concertime, Oklahoma Sinfonia and Chorale, Tulsa Town Hall, and American Theatre Company.

Tulsa Performing Arts Center Trust

With the completion of the arts center, the Tulsa Municipal Theater Authority had accomplished its principal objective of receiving private funds and scheduling payments toward the construction and furnishing of the facility. Once the center was conveyed to the city, it was decided that the theater authority could continue to be effective as a catalyst for obtaining private funds to support increased programming and staff expenses. The trust indenture therefore was amended, and the authority's name was changed to the Tulsa Performing Arts Center Trust. The number of its trustees expanded from three to 15, still including the mayor, the commissioner of streets and public property, and the commissioner of finance and revenue. The purposes of the trust broadened to:

. . . rehabilitate, repair, reconstruct, remodel, improve, enlarge, alter, rebuild, operate, maintain, administer, equip, furnish, and decorate the Tulsa Performing Arts Center. . . .

. . . provide financial assistance, direction, and other assistance in connection with cultural, artistic, or other entertainment events . . . in the Tulsa Performing Arts Center, or in . . . contiguous public spaces and to carry on, sponsor, produce, finance, arrange, present, manage, and represent attractions of various kinds and nature as the Trustees may from time to time elect.

Performing Arts Center, Inc., had been able to construct and furnish the facility for $600,000 less than contracted, and that savings formed the nucleus of an endowment that by 1984 had grown to $1.1 million. The trust uses the interest income from the endowment for three purposes:

1) capital improvements to the center that the city might not otherwise undertake;

2) programming to bring attractions to Tulsa that no other group can provide or that might not otherwise come; and

3) providing grants to small groups that

The 2,400-seat Chapman Music Hall, in the Tulsa Performing Arts Center.

for economic reasons would not otherwise appear at the center.

The city treasurer manages the trust's funds and investments, and the city auditor handles accounting functions on a reimbursement basis.

Since 1977 capital improvements funded by the trust have included replacement and upgrading of the original carpeting, enlargement of the women's rest room, modification and expansion of the visual arts gallery, construction of a 30-person barrier-free elevator from the parking garage, installation of handrails, improved signage on the exterior canopies and on the interior, and additional sound amplification equipment for Chapman Music Hall.

The trust sponsors a broad range of programs, which in 1984–85 featured 11 different series for a total of 93 events, including a film series, guitar series, jazz series, modern dance, Celtic music, and performances by such artists as Ray Charles and the National Theatre of the Deaf. Special children's programming includes workshops for teachers and students. Artist Interaction provides an opportunity for students to meet visiting artists and to discuss careers, life on the road, and professional training. "Brown Bag It" offers free lunchtime programs featuring local professionals in recital.

The 10-story atrium in the Kennedy Building.

The Kennedy Building, a restored 1913 building with a completely new interior.

The trust also sponsors events with and provides limited grants to local organizations. In 1983–84, it awarded more than 20 grants totaling more than $50,000 to area performing groups.

Williams Center Forges Ahead

The Bank of Oklahoma Tower, the first building to be completed in Williams Center, opened in October 1976. Twenty percent is occupied by the Bank of Oklahoma, 40 percent by the Williams Companies, and the remaining 40 percent has been fully leased since the day it opened.

The Green opened in April 1977, offering a variety of entertainment during the lunch hour. Every day for three months throughout the first summer, some activity enlivened The Green at noon. By providing a beautiful front lawn and something to listen to, Williams Center quickly overcame the notion that "nice girls didn't go north of Third Street." Since the completion of Bartlett Square in Main Street Mall and the Williams Center Towers Plaza in Phase II, The Green primarily is used for annual events that have become community traditions, such as a three-day Chili Bluegrass Festival (combining bluegrass bands and a chili cookoff), the Tulsa Run (in 1984 it had grown to 9,000 runners), and Mayfest, a four-day arts and crafts festival that attracts 400,000 visitors.

The stores, restaurants, ice rink, and movie theater in the Forum opened in the fall of 1978, just after completion of the hotel. In 1980, two floors of executive suites were added to increase the hotel's capacity from 400 to 450 rooms.

Tower Plaza, to the west of these buildings, encompasses one acre of public space with tables, chairs, and trees. Workers gather there for lunch to enjoy programs offered once a week during the summer. The plaza connects with both the Main Street Mall and the Forum. Towers I and II, built during Phase II of the project, were designed by 3DI of Houston and H. C. Wang & Partners, Inc. Tower I rises 17 stories, and Tower II reaches to 23.

Restoration and Renovation

Downtown Tulsa retains a handsome collection of Art Deco and Beaux Arts buildings built during the rapid-growth years between 1910 and 1930. In the years between Phases I and II of Williams Center, the Williams Companies renovated two such structures. "When it makes sense economically to keep them and when they work, they're dynamite," explains Eddie Henson of the Williams Realty Corporation.

The 320 South Boston Building had served as the home of the National Bank of Tulsa—now the Bank of Oklahoma—and it contained some Williams offices. After both

Mayfest, an annual arts, crafts, and visual and performing arts festival on the plaza in front of Williams Center Towers I and II.

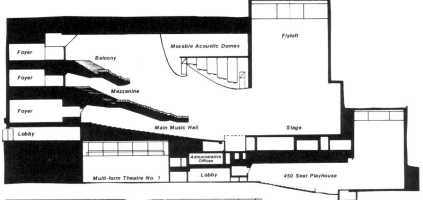

Cross section of Tulsa Performing Arts Center, showing the stacking of facilities: Chapman Music Hall, John H. Williams Theater, and Multiform Theater 1 (Theater 2 is behind Theater 1).

Bartlett Square, at the intersection of Fifth and Main streets.
Credit: Downtown Tulsa Unlimited.

tenants moved out, it was only 30 percent occupied. The Williams Realty Corporation remodeled it for $1.8 million and thereby reintroduced 345,423 square feet of prime office space to the downtown market in 1978.

The Kennedy Building across the street had been purchased by the Williams Companies in the mid-sixties, about the time it bought the Great Lakes Pipeline. Williams Realty spent $6.5 million renovating this U-shaped, functionally obsolete building. A new exterior wall was built and a translucent glass sky roof added to create a 10-story atrium, on which all offices open. Finished in 1979, the exterior remains true to its 1916 self, while the 205,098-square-foot interior has become useful, dramatic space.

Both buildings were completed shortly after the enactment of the federal rehabilitation tax credits, when monies became available for restoration of historic buildings. The creative remodeling of the Kennedy Building, plus renovations of the old City Hall and Central High School a few years earlier, stimulated a positive preservation trend in downtown development. Tulsa was able to meet all its office-space requirements from 1979 to 1981 through restoration and renovation. Since the restoration of the Kennedy and 320 South Boston buildings, every office building ex-

cept one in downtown Tulsa that offers more than 100,000 square feet has been restored or renovated. More than $73 million has been spent on rehabilitation projects since 1977.

The Tulsa Union Depot, part of the original Northwest Urban Renewal Project, had been built in 1931 in the Public Works Administration Art Deco style. Then one of the most modern passenger terminals in the nation, it serviced as many as 36 trains daily until after World War II. When the station closed in 1967, many residents believed it would never open again. Transients used it as sleeping quarters, and burned its fine wood and cabinetry as firewood. But when the Urban Renewal Authority proposed demolishing the station, community leaders came to its defense and urged the city to explore alternatives. A plan finally evolved whereby Williams Realty, with city support of $327,000 (of the $6 million total cost) would adapt the depot as an office building. In addition, the Urban Renewal Authority undertook conversion of an obsolete Boston Avenue overpass (spanning the railroad tracks adjacent to the depot) to a landscaped pedestrianway linking Williams Center, the depot, and the area to the north. The bridge conversion cost of $600,000 was split three ways, with Williams Realty and the city

The Tulsa Union Depot's interior.

each paying $61,250, and the balance coming from a federal Economic Development Administration grant.

The building, completed in the spring of 1983, was occupied by the architect and engineering firm that performed the restoration work. Care was taken to preserve the depot's original elegance and character; as new limestone pieces were required, they were obtained from the original quarry in Indiana, and the exterior was cleaned with water and detergent rather than being sandblasted.

Catalyst and Synergy

Although plans exist to include another office building, a parking structure, and a department store, Williams Center as it stands today already has made a significant positive impact on Tulsa.

As John Williams describes it:

Tulsa was dying on the vine. I have friends who later told me, "John, I can't imagine anybody being such a damn fool to go down to skid row and start a 52-story building without any tenants. It was the craziest thing I ever heard anybody doing."

Yet, you develop an idea. We're not always right, but when we get an idea, we go ahead and act on it. On hindsight—I didn't realize it at the time; it seemed like such a natural deci-

sion—it probably was a fairly courageous thing that we did to go ahead and build this thing. But once we got started, we couldn't stop.

It had an impact on Tulsa that even we couldn't visualize . . . the owners of other buildings began sprucing them up and recognizing that they had values downtown.

When you look at it from the point of view of utilities—all the power, gas, and water, all those things that make a city function, were already here. We were crazy to let it wither. It did act as a catalyst—there's no question about it.

Thanks to this private-sector leadership and commitment, the Tulsa Urban Renewal Authority took only 15 years—a short time compared to many other cities—to complete its ambitious Civic Center complex, achieve its goal of a superblock mixed-use development in the most blighted area of downtown, and link them together through the central business district with a pedestrian mall. Most important, the completion of Williams Center inspired both new construction and renovation of old buildings throughout the business district. As Paul Chapman, executive director of the authority, puts it, "The Williams Companies, in my mind, has been the making of our program, by their presence and dedication. Every urban redevelopment director needs a Williams Companies."

Although much has been accomplished in Tulsa, large portions of the downtown remain a sea of parking lots—the result of wholesale clearing of housing in the mid-sixties. Because Tulsa lacks a substantial public transit system, most Tulsans drive to work. Thus, almost every parcel cleared twenty years ago became a parking lot. Downtown Tulsa Unlimited would describe those sites as "opportunities for development," but even with the revitalization of downtown, substantial new growth will be needed to fill in these gaps. Fortunately, future plans include construction of new housing downtown.

In late 1984 Tulsa, like many cities, was experiencing an economic lull; its unemployment was the highest in the state, and its oil companies and related services were experiencing a recession. Downtown Tulsa is, in fact, currently overbuilt. Since 1970, $389 million has been invested in new private construction, and $80 million in private renovation. Today, Eddie Henson concurs, "would not be a good time to start a big mixed-use project in downtown Tulsa. There's no apparent need for the product."

The Williams Realty Corporation nevertheless has established an enviable reputation because of its creative approach to Williams Center and related downtown investments. Each element in Williams Center has been designed and marketed to strengthen the overall project by filling a specific set of human needs. Its office buildings provide customers for its shops and restaurants; its hotel houses business visitors; its arts center, cinema, ice skating rink, and tennis courts invite participation by office workers, visitors, and shoppers.

Contributing to the synergy has been a sense of human scale. Minoru Yamasaki, architect and master planner for Williams Center, has said that "A man spends 80 to 90 percent of his life in buildings, and those buildings should be a pleasure to him. A building should contribute to a man's happiness."

John Williams describes the lessons he and his collaborators learned as follows:

"I think . . . there's a better chance of success if it is a self-contained project that has enough critical mass that will create an atmosphere where people want to come to it. One building isn't enough. I think it was luck, if not skill, but we did a lot of things right on this one and to that extent we've copied the same concept in other places.

The arts have proven to be an important ingredient. The Tulsa Performing Arts Center remains one of the finest performance facilities in the Southwest. Sidney McQueen, its managing director, describes its impact:

In the seven years since the opening of the Performing Arts Center, many of the performing arts organizations have grown and developed into strong regional companies. The use of a quality facility and the services provided by trained professionals have enabled the groups to increase both the quality and quantity of their offerings. The opera, ballet, and Philharmonic have increased their audiences, as the hall is so superior to the Old Lady on Brady. The aesthetics of the space has made the evening a social night out and the continued growth of new restaurants and clubs has aided in the new enthusiasm for the arts.

The Tulsa Philharmonic has steadily increased the number of paid musicians and is now touring outside the state of Oklahoma. The Tulsa Ballet Theatre is receiving national recognition and is planning a major west coast tour. The budgets of each of the major performing arts groups have expanded greatly and range from $1 million and up. The arts in Tulsa have bloomed and their presence is being felt outside the state of Oklahoma.

Downtown Tulsa may still be mainly a daytime place, but arts enthusiasts flock to the center in the evening and on weekends. Each year more than 250,000 people have attended an event at the center—equivalent to almost everyone in Tulsa coming at least once.

Eddie Henson argues strongly that there aren't any "cookie-cutter" formulas for arts-inclusive MXDs, and that it takes some "enlightened unique solution to each particular opportunity." John Williams points out that "you have to realize that you can't do it all yourself. You have to surround yourself with good people, motivate them, and provide leadership. There are a lot of smart people in the world, and there are a lot of people who have brilliant ideas—but there are darn few who say 'Okay, let's go ahead and do it now.'"

Fortunately, Tulsa has a generous share of just those kinds of leaders.

Horton Plaza

Horton Plaza, in the heart of San Diego's downtown, is the fruit of a collaboration between the city, working through the nonprofit Centre City Development Corporation, and a private developer, Ernest W. Hahn, Inc. Together these partners are creating a major mixed-use development that breaks the mold of the stereotypical shopping center and brings major retailing, restaurants, offices, entertainment, and cultural amenities back downtown.

Occupying an 11-acre site near the San Diego Bay waterfront and between the central business district and the civic center, the project's costs are anticipated to reach $140 million by the time it opens in late 1985. Its components include a multilevel regional shopping center containing 412,000 square feet of shops, restaurants, and entertainment uses, and 460,000 square feet of department store space. Four department stores—Mervyn's, Robinson's, The Broadway, and Nordstrom—never before located in downtown San Diego will anchor the six-and-a-half-block complex, organized around a European-style, open-air street. Horton Plaza aims to resemble an Italian hill town more than a American shopping mall—except that it will have 3,000 parking spaces. In addition, an entertainment zone extending through Horton Plaza and linking the Gaslamp Quarter on the east to First Avenue on the west will inject a vitality long absent from the city's core.

No arts institution was an early participant in the Horton Plaza project, but the opportunities inherent in the development stimulated the creation of the new San Diego Art Center, which will exhibit contemporary art, architecture, and design in an adjacent restored movie theater. Two new performing arts theaters with a combined seating of 775 are being constructed by the city within a Horton Plaza Theatres shell donated by Hahn. Following the Centre City Development Corporation's design guidelines and public art requirements, the project's edges will be characterized by street-level retail, restaurants, and entertainment that welcome and reinforce pedestrian activity, and Hahn has funded a substantial program of outdoor sculpture.

Horton Plaza also expects to benefit from a 450-room Omni International Hotel on an adjacent 1.5-acre site. A projected Phase II will include 300,000 square feet of terraced office space on the project's upper levels. Historic Horton Plaza Park at the Broadway side of the project has been restored after years of neglect.

Considered as a whole, this mix of retail and restaurant uses, a strengthened arts presence, and imaginative architectural design should strongly reinforce San Diego's long-term strategy of reclaiming its downtown from unemployed transients and sailors on liberty.

Suburban Malls Sap Downtown Vitality

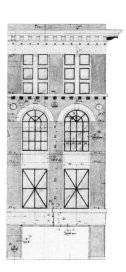

San Diego, the second largest city in California, experienced a 40 percent growth rate between 1970 and 1980, and it shows no signs of slowing down. The Standard Metropolitan Statistical Area population is 1.9 million; family income averages $28,000. Both the new downtown office buildings and the industrial parks outside the city demonstrate a shift in San Diego's burgeoning economy from agriculture and the military to finance, aerospace, wholesale and retail trade, health science, government, and service businesses. Convention and tourist spending exceeds $1 billion annually, and the city's proximity to Mexico remains a strong asset for the city's retail business.

The region is blessed with natural beauty and a varied landscape of beaches, hills, and mesas. Its relaxed lifestyle has evolved out of ideal weather, efficient freeways, and year-round water sports and other recreation. "Affluence with an eagerness to spend money and enjoy life characterizes the youthful San Diego citizenry," says a promotional brochure, "and most live and work within a 30-minute drive of the heart of the city."

But these very qualities have adversely affected San Diego's downtown. It has been easier to live, shop, and work in the suburbs than to drive to a deteriorating downtown. Shopping opportunities at suburban malls meet all a typical family's consumer needs. In the sixties Mission Valley, seven miles north of downtown, supported two major shopping centers totaling 2.25 million square feet, while downtown there remained only a few hundred thousand square feet of operating retail businesses.

Ernest W. Hahn, the developer of Horton Plaza, built Fashion Valley, a mall in Mission Valley, and developed Parkway Plaza. His company also worked on University Towne Centre and Escondido's North County Fair. With ironic honesty, today Hahn calls Fashion Valley "one of the culprits that helped to decimate the retail still left in the downtown in the sixties and seventies."

As middle-class residents abandoned the center of the city for the suburbs, downtown buildings deteriorated at so rapid a rate that the taxes generated by the area fell far short of the cost of required public services. Clearly, the city needed a strategy to reverse the flight to the suburbs and to restore its tax base. In the mid-sixties, therefore, the city planning department, working with a nonprofit advocacy group, San Diegans Incorporated, established five objectives for downtown revitalization:

1) Reinforce existing retail business and promote new retail development.

2) Link the new retail to the older retail and office districts.

3) Expand financial and governmental services.

4) Build downtown residences.

5) Build a convention center.

The planners understood that no single project alone could transform the city; instead an array of projects, carefully phased, would be necessary. Although at first no mixed-use developments were planned, the basic principles of creating a variety of complementary uses were present. It became apparent, for example, that public agencies were outgrowing their offices and that a performing arts theater and convention center were badly needed. After the failure of a bond issue in 1962 that was to have funded the land acquisition and construction costs for such projects, San Diegans Incorporated took options on the land necessary for a multiuse center and urged the city to borrow from its employee pension funds. A gap of $1.6 million was provided by local corporations, and by 1965 the downtown Charles C. Dail Community Concourse was complete. It included a new City Hall, the City Operations Building, a 3,000-seat Civic Theater, an 80,000-square-foot exhibition space, and a parking garage.

Once the concourse was finished, a new group of problems could be faced. Principal among them was the unhappy reality that one of the world's most beautiful urban waterfronts and the downtown next to it were languishing.

Two Old Theaters
Inspire an "Arts Presence"

The history of two old theaters, the Lyceum and the Balboa, illustrates the pattern of San Diegans' initial enjoyment, subsequent neglect, and gradual rediscovery of the downtown. In quite different ways, the theaters stimulated the incorporation of performing and visual arts into Horton Plaza's development.

In anticipation of the opening of the Panama Canal, San Diego prepared for the Panama–California Exposition of 1915 by launching an intense downtown building campaign. The Lyceum Theater opened on May 5, 1913, at the corner of Third Avenue and F Street, as an intimate 430-seat legitimate theater. In the same building was the Robert E. Lee Hotel. Between 1913 and 1932, the Lyceum presented a rich variety of vaudeville, burlesque, musicals, drama, and motion pictures. From 1932 to 1970, as the Hollywood Theater, its offerings were wholly burlesque.

Early in 1971, the Lyceum reopened as the Off-Broadway Theater, featuring Hollywood stars in productions such as *You're a Good Man, Charlie Brown, 40 Carats,* and *The Last of the Red Hot Lovers.* But in 1975, the theater was incorporated into the Pussycat Theater chain, and it showed the X-rated movie *Deep Throat* for four years. In 1979, the Downtowners Ltd. assumed the lease on the theater and immediately began restoration in preparation for the *Lyceum Follies,* which opened in October 1979 and ran until 1981. The theme of the *Follies* was the history of an old theater about to be torn down. At one point in the show, the emcee would appeal to the audience to "save this beautiful theater," urging them to pick up postcards in the lobby and mail them to their city council representatives.

The public by this time showed tremendous support for the Lyceum. Not only was it the only theatrical/hotel building ever built in San Diego, but it was the city's oldest dramatic theater and the only downtown small facility with a full stage and fly gallery. Nevertheless, in 1981 the Centre City Development Corporation purchased the building to tear it down, because it sat where the Horton Plaza parking facility was to be.

Shortly after the corporation took over, Sam Woodhouse, artistic director of the San

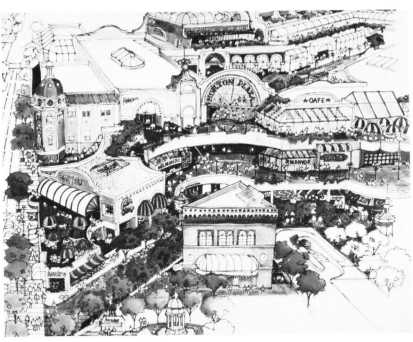

Jon Jerde's 1977 plan for Horton Plaza.

Diego Repertory Theater, wrote asking that his group be allowed to rent the Lyceum at $1 per year on a month-to-month basis until it was torn down. The Repertory Theater had been founded in 1976 and was performing in a refurbished former mortuary chapel. The company was presenting more than 200 performances a year and wanted to play in a larger space. An agreement was reached, and in May 1981 the company opened *Working,* which ran at the Lyceum until October 1981—the longest-running legitimate show in the history of San Diego. That was followed by *The Elephant Man, Tintypes, Death of a Salesman,* and an annual production of *A Christmas Carol.* The company performed at the Lyceum until October 1982, when the theater finally was torn down.

The Repertory's experience at the Lyceum proved that, despite the building's sleazy past as a porno house in a decayed district, well-produced live theater could draw large audiences downtown. The loss of the Lyceum—and the quality of the Repertory's performances in its dying days—created pressure for new theater facilities in Horton Plaza.

The Balboa Theater and the San Diego Art Center

By contrast, the Balboa Theater, on the corner of Fourth Avenue and E Street contiguous to the Horton Plaza site, had achieved landmark status, and it was considered an essential visual keynote for the Horton Plaza site because of its ornate Spanish Renaissance Revival exterior. Its entrance floor of mosaic tile commemorates Balboa's discovery of the Pacific Ocean in 1513. Major features of its elaborate interior include two twenty-foot-high waterfalls, one on each side of the proscenium, and a polychrome-tiled dome soaring above the roof.

Built in 1924 primarily as a movie house, the Balboa also had facilities for live stage performances. In its early years it hosted plays, vaudeville shows, and even circus performances. In 1930 it became a deluxe Spanish-language theater, but in late 1932 it returned to screening Hollywood films. The theater shared its building with 34 offices and six stores.

During the seventies, several attempts were made to encourage the city to buy and restore the Balboa as either the Old Globe Shakespeare Company's third theater, an extension of the Civic Theater for smaller productions, or an auditorium for the Civic Light Opera Association. But a renovation estimate of $1.9 million cooled the city's interest, and the Balboa continued to operate as a second-run film house.

Future plans for the Balboa now are quite different and relate not to the performing arts, but to the visual arts. The region has two major art museums—the San Diego Museum of Art and the La Jolla Museum of Contemporary Art. The San Diego Museum of Art lies just north of downtown in Balboa Park, another result of the 1915 Panama–California Exposition and now home to a collection of science, art, natural history, anthropology, sports, and photography museums, sports facilities, theaters, botanical gardens, and a renowned zoo. The museum's permanent collections include Asian, Renaissance, Baroque, neoclassical, 19th- and 20th-century, modern, Dutch, English, and American art. The La Jolla Museum of Contemporary Art, located about 12 miles from downtown San Diego in an area some consider inaccessible, maintains an excellent reputation for mounting exciting shows of 20th-century architecture and contemporary product design. This reputation is due, in part, to the efforts of Sebastian "Lefty" Adler, who served as director of the museum from 1973 to 1983.

Danah Fayman, an art patron and board member of the La Jolla museum for 15 years, urged the board for several years not only to change its name to the San Diego Museum of Contemporary Art, but also to locate a branch in downtown San Diego, where its excellent programs might reach a larger audience. Neither of these ideas proved acceptable to the board. When downtown revitalization plans began to gather steam—and after Adler was fired from the La Jolla museum in 1983—Fayman took the idea for a new San Diego contemporary art museum to Gerald Trimble, executive vice president of the Centre City Development Corporation. She believed that a downtown art center could make a substantial contribution to a vital downtown. Trimble took Fayman and Adler on a tour of possible sites for a museum, stressing the virtues of the Balboa Theater—its architectural uniqueness and its proximity to the forthcoming Horton Plaza complex and the western edge of the historic Gaslamp Quarter district, currently undergoing redevelopment.

Adler and Fayman were struck by the attractiveness of the Balboa, its location, and the importance of preserving it. They immediately retained architect Richard S. Weinstein of New York City to study the feasibility of converting the Balboa into a museum space. He proposed that an art museum use the two floors at the top, with the lower floors devoted to design-oriented retail businesses.

The San Diego Art Center was incorporated on August 28, 1983. Adler, hired as director, defined its role as a design-oriented contemporary art museum. A curator, John Lloyd Taylor, formerly the director of the Fine Art Galleries at the University of Wisconsin in Milwaukee, came on board in September 1984. The goals of the art center are to emphasize international and Ameri-

The Balboa Theater in 1983, with Horton Plaza under construction in the background.

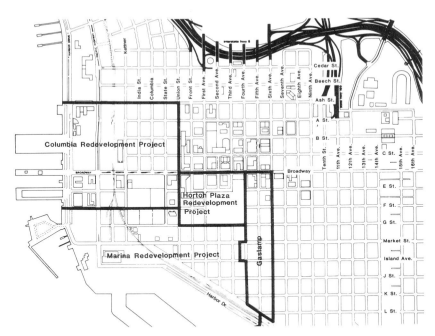

Map of downtown San Diego showing Horton Plaza and redevelopment area.

can architecture and design, especially contemporary California art:

> . . . from the design of furniture to the design of cities, from the clothes we wear to the buildings we live in, to the painting, sculpture, books, films, and television we look at, to how we think about them.

Unlike the cases of Los Angeles and Dallas, for instance, there thus was in San Diego no initial pressure from strong arts constituencies to attain new buildings in return for their potential to help animate the downtown. Instead, the demand for the arts came from the public-sector leadership of San Diego's center-city revival. Gerald Trimble of the Centre City Development Corporation explains:

> A number of years ago I realized that in order for downtown San Diego to become an attractive urban environment and draw people from the suburbs, its development could not just focus on office buildings, retail, a convention center, hotels, and housing. We had to appeal to people's emotional senses and expand the arts in downtown. This means public art, legitimate theater, cultural institutions like museums, and commedia dell'arte companies doing performances on the sidewalks and plazas. This is a relatively simple statement, but to implement this becomes very difficult.

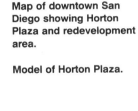

Model of Horton Plaza.

Omni International Hotel at Horton Plaza.

The City Council Initiates Conventional Redevelopment

An Inner Pedestrian Passageway Links Department Stores

Government-sponsored redevelopment had encountered strong resistance from the San Diego business community for years, but in July 1972 the city council adopted a comprehensive redevelopment plan for the Horton Plaza area. It reasoned that the development of a large district around the historic Horton park and fountain south of Broadway might succeed in creating a vibrant urban center for the city where piecemeal beautification efforts had failed.

The objectives of the Horton Plaza redevelopment plan included:
■ providing an environment where "a full range of activities and uses will take place;"
■ preserving artistically and architecturally worthwhile structures and sites; and
■ establishing design standards to ensure quality and provide unity and integrity.

The plan called for eliminating such "blighting" conditions as "obnoxious" land uses, congested streets, and inadequate parking facilities. The project's area included 15 city blocks from Broadway south to G Street and from Union to Fourth Avenue—a size sufficient to attract prominent developers and investors.

Using traditional redevelopment procedures, the city's redevelopment agency was charged to purchase land within the project area from private parties. The project was characterized by mixed uses, including office, hotel, retail, service, entertainment, education, and related auxiliary uses. "Landscape criteria, fine artworks criteria, and criteria for street and exterior furnishings" were to be established; old buildings were to be restored and rehabilitated; and the Horton fountain and plaza were to be restored, improved, and, if feasible, expanded.

To finance this project, the agency was authorized to use a range of tools including property tax increments, bonds, interest income, and the lease or sale of agency-owned property. The goals established for the project, in other words, were conventional for public redevelopment—but the method of implementation in a historically conservative city like San Diego had to be carefully gauged.

In 1973 an urban design program for the Horton Plaza area was drawn up by the redevelopment agency with the assistance of Rockrise, Odermat, Mountjoy & Amis (ROMA), planning consultants, and Keyser Marston Associates, Inc., financial consultants. Their program (which became known as the ROMA plan) recommended assembling a superblock of properties for an MXD including retail, office, and hotel uses, preserving several architecturally worthwhile structures and sites in the process. Stressing the advantages of including arts and amenities in private development projects, it recommended that 1 percent of the building costs be allocated toward purchasing public art. The consulting team favored the mixed-use development form because they believed it offered the best chance of extending southward the economic revival stimulated by the Community Concourse and city government offices, and of making the downtown more active on nights and weekends.

The ROMA plan called for up to two million square feet of office buildings, first-class hotel rooms, retail spaces, and entertainment. The consultants believed that the area would not be conducive to high- or middle-income housing until Horton Plaza was clearly established. They urged a high-impact concentration of at least 200,000 square feet of specialty retail and restaurant uses, to attract not only weekday workers but nighttime and weekend visitors as well. Their report devoted particular attention to the quality of public open space and to the blending of low elements such as restaurant, retail, and entertainment with higher tower units for office and hotel uses. And it called for the remodeling and restoration of two theaters on the Horton Plaza site, the Lyceum and the Spreckels, as well as the refurbishment of the adjacent Balboa Theater for off-Broadway shows.

The consultants also recommended that the adjacent Gaslamp Quarter be upgraded to include a mix of small office space, retail outlets, entertainment facilities, restaurants, and bars, and that strict zoning and design controls be implemented to maintain the architectural integrity of this historic district. They suggested closing E Street where it ran through the project and

The City's Agent and the
Developer Deal and Re-Deal

converting it to a pedestrian passage bordered by entertainment, large retail stores, and small shops and restaurants. They believed that a perception of safety, business, and excitement could be created by concentrating and closely connecting the active interior spaces of Horton Plaza. This interior space was conceived as a multilevel pedestrian passageway, covered but not wholly enclosed, onto which the various uses would front, and behind which extensive parking facilities would be provided.

The report included a thorough discussion of the project's open spaces, landscaping, street furniture, signs, lighting, art, and kiosks vending flowers, tickets, and news. It was somewhat atypical of consultant documents in the early seventies for so much attention to be devoted to the importance of creating "a character that is . . . friendly to people, especially people on foot."

The ROMA plan proposed that the project developer be given the opportunity of contributing the required 1 percent art assessment as cash rather than providing the artworks. This procedure would enable art to be commissioned especially for the site. The plan also called for a series of city actions: creating land parcels large enough to serve multiuse development, retaining architecturally significant theaters, and upgrading the adjacent Gaslamp Quarter into a low-rise retail and entertainment area. The project would have to be implemented in phases, during which the agency would assemble blocks large enough for private retail development and would construct public parking facilities funded by tax increment bonds. Since the agency did not yet own property in the area, it would need to wait until after a developer had been selected to determine the nature and extent of its purchases. Anticipated tax-increment financing was proposed to subsidize land acquisition and improvements.

In February 1974 the redevelopment agency invited developers who had expressed interest in Horton Plaza to submit formal proposals. Developers received copies of the redevelopment plan and the ROMA urban design and development plan to guide them in the preparation of their proposals, along with a draft form of a participation agreement.

Of four proposals submitted by April from International Six, the M. H. Golden Company, Arcon, Inc., and Ernest W. Hahn, Inc., Hahn's was the most extensive. It suggested a mixture of uses that met the agency's goals, but it also required a range of public commitments. Hahn initially proposed creating 250,000 square feet of retail space, plus hotel, office, and housing uses in an expanded project area that could include 200 acres between Horton Plaza and the San Diego Bay. The proposal went on to suggest those actions or development activities that should take place in the surrounding areas for the full potential of Horton Plaza to be realized.

Hahn's development concept thus called for the creation of high-quality retail and commercial uses as well as a comprehensive city effort to change and clean up the downtown as a whole. Faced with this challenge to coordinate a much more sophisticated set of development activities than the redevelopment agency could manage on its own, the mayor and city council responded to a proposal put forward by San Diegans Incorporated that a nonprofit corporation of professional managers from the business community be established to assemble joint ventures and to monitor development needs in the city's central core. By early 1975, when the Hahn proposal for Horton Plaza had been accepted and was being refined, the Centre City Development Corporation had been created, modeled on Baltimore's Charles Center–Inner Harbor management entity.

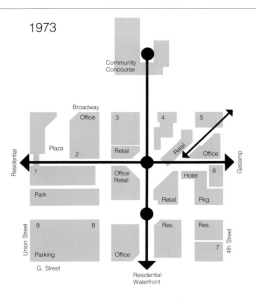

1973

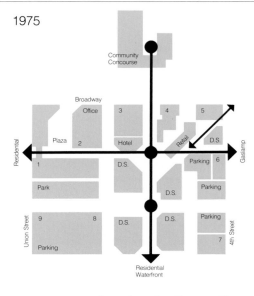

1975

Four drawings show the basic evolution of Horton Plaza from an enclosed mall to an open one; from the ROMA plan through the Hope plan to Jon Jerde's designs.

1973

1 Federal Building
2 Office
3 Spreckels Building
4 Central Federal
5 Horton Plaza Park
6 Balboa Theater
7 Golden West Hotel
8 Parking
9 Parking
Ret - Retail
Off - Office
Res - Residential
Pkg - Parking
D.S. - Department Store
    Activity Linkages

1975

1 Federal Building
2 Office
3 Spreckels Building
4 Central Federal
5 Horton Plaza Park
6 Balboa Theater
7 Golden West Hotel
8 Parking
9 Parking
Ret - Retail
Off - Office
Pkg - Parking
D.S. - Department Store
    Activity Linkages

The City's Agent in Collaboration

Centre City Development Corporation was created by Mayor Pete Wilson and the city council as a public, nonprofit corporation with responsibility for managing all of San Diego's downtown development efforts, not just Horton Plaza. It is governed by a seven-member board of business and real estate professionals. Gerald Trimble, the corporation's executive vice president, has described the purpose of the organization as follows:

From the beginning, Centre City Development Corporation's major role has been to streamline the redevelopment process. Thus its staff, along with consultants, work on behalf of the Centre City Development Corporation board to represent the city and its redevelopment agency in a contractual relationship, handling all negotiations with property owners, businesses, and developers. Centre City Development Corporation also implements property acquisition, relocation, clearance, public improvements, public facilities, public financing, and design review of all private improvements in the downtown's redevelopment area.

Centre City Development Corporation's role is a broad one. The premise is that, while cementing the business transaction with developers and ensuring public financing are important steps in the redevelopment process, they should not override other important concerns: urban design, amenities, public art, and people-oriented uses. These concerns cannot be lost in the eagerness to make a business deal.

Thus, although the San Diego Redevelopment Agency initiated the developer selection and evaluation process for Horton Plaza, the ongoing responsibility for managing the negotiations with the Hahn Com-

pany was transferred to the Centre City Development Corporation. Using a design review program, the corporation evaluated public and private development plans on the basis of the following goals:

■ linking the core of the center city area to the waterfront with a series of connections—major streets, pedestrianways, small parks, and plazas;
■ emphasizing amenities such as pavement treatments, signs, and furniture that support pedestrian activity;
■ retaining historic buildings, by preserving interesting and diverse examples of old architecture; and
■ encouraging arts facilities, cultural programs, and outdoor events to enhance the experience of walking through the central city.

The corporation's specific design and planning goals for Horton Plaza were:

. . . to create a window on Broadway, to encourage the revitalization of the area to the south, to support and relate to the Gaslamp Quarter . . . to develop an active street scene, to preserve select land uses and buildings, and to organize development around existing and proposed open spaces by linking Horton Plaza Park to the Federal Building's plaza and park.

Much of the new corporation's time between 1975 and 1977 was spent negotiating a disposition and development agreement with the Hahn company. The evolution of the project's design has reflected both an increasing willingness by the developer to make the project integrate with the rest of San Diego's downtown, and a growing readiness of the downtown area to welcome and support private development.

After these two years of intensive negoti-

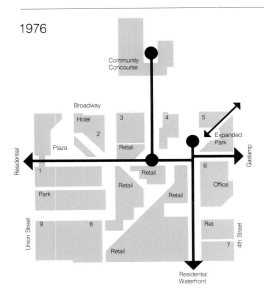

1976

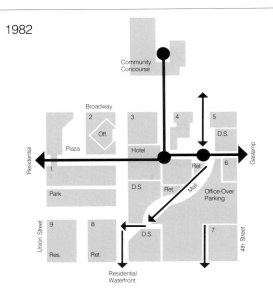

1982

ations, an initial development agreement was signed by the Hahn company on October 21, 1977. (It would be amended eight times before final agreement on the project was reached in September 1982.)

The first agreement described the responsibilities of both parties and outlined a time schedule for the entire project. The developer was required to obtain four department store participants (which together with other specialty retail and restaurants would produce 563,000 square feet of gross leasable area), to arrange private financing for the project, and to design and construct all private improvements. The city was required to assemble the site, secure public financing, and to provide public improvements and public parking facilities. In 1977 these public costs were estimated at $17.4 million for the land and $11.1 million to build parking facilities. Funds were to be raised through tax allocation bonds; lease revenue bonds for the design and construction of public improvements and parking; interest income from invested bond proceeds; Hahn's $4.2 million purchase price for the land; and a $4 million loan from the city of San Diego.

In these first years, attracting major department stores and settling planning and financial issues occupied the collaborators' attention more than design concerns. By the fall of 1977, Hahn had commitments from Robinson's (for 90,000 square feet), Buffums (60,000 square feet), and Mervyn's (80,000 square feet), even though such stores generally are loath to invest in an inner city. The development agreement required the city to reassure these tenants with improvements to the area surrounding Horton Plaza. To this end, the Gaslamp Quarter was to be designated a redevelop-

ment district; a developer was to be selected to build 3,000 residential units (a mix of condominiums and low- to moderate-income housing) on 73 acres in the Marina and Columbia projects adjoining Horton Plaza; the Navy's recreation facilities on 28 acres in the Marina were to be moved south of the center city and replaced by hotels, specialty stores, and boatslips; and a downtown convention center was to be constructed.

Proposition 13

Representing the redevelopment agency, the Centre City Development Corporation assembles land for its projects either by condemnation or by negotiated sale, under the right of eminent domain. But its property has to be paid for. More than half the revenue the corporation needed to acquire the land and to build parking facilities at Horton Plaza was projected to come from increased property taxes. The passage of California's Proposition 13 in June 1978 placed a sudden ceiling on property taxes of 1 percent of market value, cutting the available revenues almost in half. To make matters worse, by the summer of 1978 the price of the Horton Plaza land (including the expense of assembling it) had risen to $29.2 million. The cost of the parking construction had risen from $11.1 million to $19.3 million, bringing the total public obligation to $48.5 million. Within two years this total would soar to $53.9 million.

Projected interest rates for 1979 and 1980 proved to be much higher than originally calculated. Because the initial $8 million tax allocation bond issue was now insufficient to meet the costs of the project, the city considered selling more bonds. But new bonds had to offer a higher interest

1976

1 Federal Building
2 Hotel
3 Spreckels Building
4 Central Federal
5 Horton Plaza Park
6 Office
7 Golden West Hotel
8 Parking
9 Parking
Ret - Retail
Off - Office
Res - Residential
Pkg - Parking
D.S. - Department Store
     Activity Linkages

1982

1 Federal Building
2 Wells Fargo Building
3 Spreckels Building
4 Central Federal Building
5 Horton Plaza Park
6 Balboa Theater
7 Golden West Hotel
8 Retail
9 Residential
Ret - Retail
Off - Office
Res - Residential
Pkg - Parking
D.S. - Department Store
     Activity Linkages

View of the Gaslamp Quarter to the east of Horton Plaza.

rate if they were to compete on the market, and San Diego simply lacked the cash with which to pay off new bonds plus interest.

One might have thought this situation would cripple the Horton Plaza project. Not so. The Centre City Development Corporation, its real estate consultants, Keyser Marston Associates, and the Hahn company found ways to bypass the roadblock.

One route to increase tax revenue from the project was to boost density. So in 1978 the area devoted to retail and parking was reduced from 16 to 11 acres, and 1.5 acres were set aside to enable another developer to build a 450-room hotel spanning E Street behind the Spreckels Building. While the project's total site area thus was reduced, its scope and components remained the same.

Furthermore, Hahn persuaded the participating department stores, which already were enjoying much lower taxes after Proposition 13, to make in-lieu-of-tax payments to the redevelopment agency for 30 years, thereby guaranteeing the agency's debt service for lease revenue bonds. The fee was 2 percent of the property's market value. According to Hahn, the department stores seemed "content to pay the in-lieu-of-tax fee, since they were enjoying good business in the San Diego area." As the project continued to evolve and as the local economy changed, however, this strategy was

modified and eventually abandoned.

The payments in-lieu-of-taxes were incorporated in an amended development agreement on August 1, 1979. It also was agreed that the Centre City Development Corporation would still be responsible for assembling the land but that the developer would buy it for $4.8 million (much less than it cost the corporation). Hahn would build approximately 650,000 square feet of gross retail area, an increase since the original arrangement.

The Developer Builds More, Pays Less, and Rescues the Deal

A year and a half of further negotiating between Hahn and the Centre City Development Corporation produced yet another amended development agreement, signed on November 2, 1981. Important changes were as follows:

■ The basic land price was reduced from $4.8 million to $1 million. (Needless to say, many San Diego taxpayers were angered by this apparent giveaway to private interests. But the corporation was convinced that the entire Horton package would benefit the city and that the long-range contribution of the project to the downtown would more than compensate for the reduction in Hahn's payment.)

■ Hahn agreed to pay the city annually, for 50 years, 10 percent of the overall rents collected from the non-department-store retail space, as well as 25 percent of all parking revenues.

■ Hahn agreed to design, finance, construct, and operate all parking facilities and to include retail shops facing the street on the ground level of all parking structures. These stores would help to eliminate blank facades and link the development with the pedestrian life of the area.

The corporation was happy to shift onto Hahn the considerable risk of constructing and operating the parking. For his part, the developer expected to build the parking structure for 25 percent less than the city had estimated. Because the construction of Horton Plaza's retail center would eliminate many on-street parking spaces, and because the city had failed to provide alternative parking nearby, the developer could count on high demand for his parking facility. Furthermore, if Hahn maintained control of the parking structure, he also could control the hours it was in use and the number of spaces reserved for patrons of his retail tenants.

■ Until conveyance, Hahn would loan the Centre City Development Corporation $5 million interest-free. After conveyance, the interest would be 10 percent; the loan was due in 24 years.

■ Hahn would allocate $1 million for public art and building restoration at Horton Plaza. He also agreed to consider incorporating physical details of the old buildings (castings, cornices, and so on) in the structure of the new buildings.

■ The gross leasable area of retail would be increased to 780,000 square feet, and there would be an additional 350,000 square feet of office space. These additions would regain some of Hahn's lost profits and would boost the city's tax increment.

The Developer Makes a Personal Loan

In the summer of 1982, just when all seemed well—the developer's financing was fully in place; the site was cleared and ready for conveyance—one more hitch occurred. The Hahn company was acquired by Trizec Corporation, and Trizec's board of directors disapproved of the plans for Horton Plaza for financial reasons. The board instructed Hahn to tell the Centre City Development Corporation that it could not go forward with construction unless Hahn, Inc.'s 24-year loan of $5 million was paid off at conveyance. But where was the development corporation going to find that much money in so little time? The solution was intriguing—and gracious. The corporation structured a subordinated tax allocation bond issue for $5 million, which was bought personally by Ernest Hahn. The Hahn company was paid in August 1982, clearing the way for an October groundbreaking.

A new amendment to the development agreement raised the development corporation's share of parking revenues from 25 percent to 31 percent and provided the city with 10 percent of the net cash flow generated by the 300,000-square-foot office space scheduled to be built above the parking facilities as part of the second phase.

The spring of 1982 had witnessed the completion of a new 420,000-square-foot office tower, the Wells Fargo Bank Building, built by the Koll Company and Intereal next door to Horton Plaza in the block bordered by Broadway, First Avenue, and E and Front streets. The new building promised to contribute considerable foot traffic to the retail center, but it also provided the city with a new negotiating opportunity. Though the office tower already had 385 parking spaces on its own block, the Koll Company wanted more. In a move that must have appeased some of the residents who blamed the city for having "given" Hahn the Horton Plaza land for $1 million, the Centre City Development Corporation now proposed to sell Koll air rights to build 450 additional parking spaces beneath the Horton Plaza retail center for $1.3 million. A long-term lease then was negotiated with Ernest W. Hahn, Inc., to use these additional spaces for Horton Plaza parking.

At first the Hahn company resisted this plan, but it finally acquiesced because it would help the development of the downtown without impairing Horton Plaza's image. The Koll parking would effectively elevate the retail parking, thereby expediting shoppers' access to the upper retail levels. Generally shops located above a second story draw less foot traffic. With Horton Plaza's retail parking raised, even the highest retail levels would be more accessible.

Retail "Neighborhoods" Lure Pedestrians, Public Art and Theaters Attract Consumers

In 1976, while the initial development agreement was being negotiated, Hahn hired first Archisystems, Inc., and then the Hope Consulting Group to develop a design concept for Horton Plaza. Hahn approved the Hope plan, but when it was shown to the Centre City Development Corporation, it was criticized for being too low in density and for failing to provide enough street-level activity. Perhaps a more serious flaw was the design's fortress-like effect: modeled after suburban malls, the buildings were projected to turn in on themselves and away from the surrounding city.

Responding to these criticisms, Hahn hired Los Angeles architect Jon Jerde, who had considerably more merchandising experience than Hope. In December 1977, Jerde unveiled a new design in which the size of the retail center had increased dramatically and the entire eight-block area was treated as a megastructure. Since the Hahn company had used ice rinks successfully at its University Towne Centre to boost activity on weekends and in the eve-

nings, Jerde proposed a rink inside an enclosed, climate-controlled mall area. The links between the Gaslamp Quarter and the Federal Building were retained, but no direct access into the project from its other sides was proposed.

A retail market analysis by Keyser Marston Associates in the spring of 1978 identified three market segments that could patronize Horton Plaza: (1) customers for popular-priced retail goods, who would travel to the area to shop (by 1987, a projected consumer population of 310,000); (2) customers for higher-priced, fashion-oriented goods, who would travel even farther (60,000 customers); and (3) downtown office workers (between 60,000 and 100,000) as well as new residents and tourists who would buy both popular and fashion-oriented goods.

Hahn spent years assembling the right mix of stores to appeal to all three market segments. At last, in 1981, he found a desirable combination: two fashion stores (Robinson's and Nordstrom), one popular-priced store (Mervyn's), and one mixture (The Broadway), providing a grand total of 420,000 square feet. Much of the delay stemmed from the hesitancy of several leading department stores to locate in downtown San Diego, no matter how much redevelopment took place. In effect, Hahn had to leverage his suburban shopping centers with their known sales potential against Horton Plaza. He told department stores that if they wanted to locate branches in his suburban centers, they would have to come downtown also.

After Proposition 13 passed in 1978, the project's area was reduced because of diminished revenues available for land acquisition. This reconfiguration was accompanied by a slow series of improvements in the areas surrounding the project, raising the possibility that there might be other ways to meet department store operators' concerns for security other than by turning the project away from the streets.

By 1981, as construction costs kept rising, Hahn asked Jerde to prepare a design plan that offered an alternative to creating an enclosed central space with expensive air conditioning. Removing the project's lid would permit the internal parts of the

Map of Horton Plaza complex.

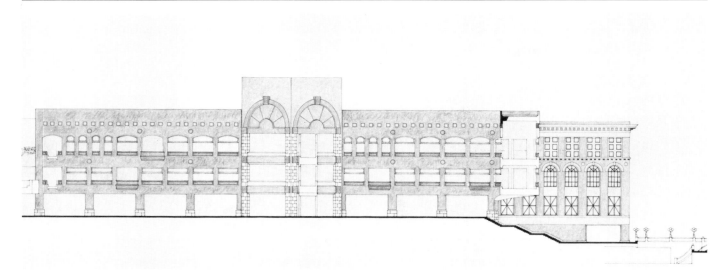

project to take advantage of San Diego's sunlight, and the diagonal element that had been proposed to link the department stores at each end of the project could thereby function more like a city street.

The continuing concerns of the prospective department-store operators also came into play as the project's design evolved. Why, they asked, would customers want to drive downtown to an environment they wouldn't like as much as their nearby, familiar malls? Horton Plaza's parking would be multilevel and cost-regulated. The complex would not offer the convenience of single-level store entrances or traditional "anchor store" patterns. It would attract a more varied, less homogeneous mix of people.

Gradually, and with positive support from the Centre City Development Corporation and Keyser Marston Associates, the Jerde office and the Hahn organization developed a design approach that treated these differences not as deficiencies but as assets that could form the basis for a truly competitive shopping environment. Rather than trying to restrict street-level access from the city into the project, perhaps the design could encourage access with show windows and retail entrances on all four sides. Such an approach would connect the project to the 60,000 downtown workers and visitors who were expected to be the plaza's primary market, and it would reinforce the city's goal that the project act as a catalyst for further downtown development and animation.

In 1982 the Jerde Partnership's final plan arranged the buildings along a strong diagonal open street intersecting with E Street, now called Broadway Circle. A full-scale model made deliberate allusions to the liveliness of a European hill town—multi-

level streets, colorful awnings and banners, specialized store facades, and elaborate signs and symbols. The design represented Jerde's conviction that only an ever-changing, dynamic, people-centered scene could lure shoppers away from the successful but commonplace regional shopping malls.

The new design moved beyond the department store operators' preference for the familiar to a concept that organized shops and restaurants into a series of "neighborhoods" along layered streets and plazas that would encourage exploration and traffic flow. Each level would be organized around a special series of uses, with restaurants open to the sky at the uppermost levels, and retailing located at the ground and plaza levels. Shops would be "tucked under stairways, placed on bridges, attached to parking garages, and located in carts and kiosks scattered throughout the project." Individual buildings could be designed as separate elements rather than blending into an overall visual formula.

This design approach also aimed to meet three goals of the city: making the project an integral part of the downtown by blending its edges into the existing streetscape; encouraging pedestrian linkages; and including significant artworks in new commercial development.

The Centre City Development Corporation had designated Broadway Circle, which runs through the project's northern boundary, as a central city corridor that should function day and night as "a social space where people [can] gather to talk or meet friends, shop, enjoy the night life, or to stroll in this active urban atmosphere." Hahn responded by planning a series of restaurant, entertainment, and retail uses along Broadway Circle. To further encourage pedestrians, he suggested that the two

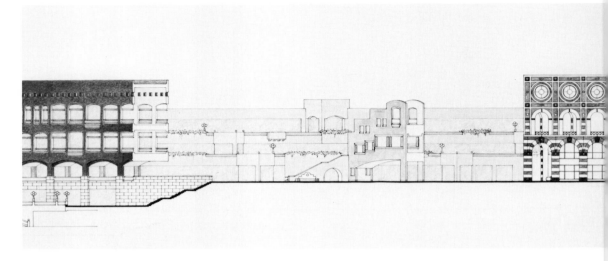

proposed theaters locate their entrances at the intersection of Broadway Circle and Horton Plaza's major diagonal. This strategy would create an entertainment focal point at the ground level, balanced by a seven-screen, 35,000-square-foot movie theater proposed for the project's upper level.

Hahn's willingness to open up the project to adjacent streets led to consideration of providing further substantial amenities. Dale Nelson, project manager for the Hahn company, described the link between downtown and Horton Plaza as follows:

As other elements in the downtown plan improved (the provision of residential housing and the upgrading of the Gaslamp Quarter), the need for further enhancement became apparent. When dealing with a blighted area, you are talking about the removal of objectionable uses, not putting up pieces of sculpture.

Horton Plaza's Fine Arts Program

In 1982, the Hahn company retained Tamara Thomas, a Los Angeles–based fine arts consultant, to advise it on how art could be incorporated into the project. The development agreement required Hahn to allocate approximately $350,000 toward artworks for the project.

Thomas met with architect Jon Jerde to study the project, establish a direction, and identify appropriate sites for art. They reached an agreement at the outset that the art should be an integral part of the project, even to the point of influencing parts of the architectural design, and that the artists should be identified and involved as early as possible in the process.

Thomas then reviewed the past work of approximately 100 artists whose work had

potential for such integration, narrowing this group down to approximately 15. Input also was received from a fine arts advisory committee. Eventually three artists were selected and asked to make site-specific proposals. They were Loren Madsen, Peter Alexander, and Judy Pfaff. Each was paid a design study fee, enabling them to visit the site, study the general area designated for their work, and produce a proposal. The situation presented to each artist was much more fluid than usual; although general areas for the work were indicated, the sizes and materials were left to each artist, and many structural and design changes were still possible.

Each artist thus benefited by visiting the site and understanding the context of the total project and the city's fabric. All had the opportunity to familiarize themselves with the architecture and the rationale behind the overall design. Thomas believes that this careful and early selection process will result in an outstanding example of a mixed-use project with major sculptural works:

If public sculpture is to be successful, it is imperative that this interaction [among the artist, the site, and its architecture] exist. A sculpture designed to be viewed in a museum or gallery setting, blown up to public scale, and insensitively deposited out of context on a building plaza serves neither art nor the public. The keys to success are an early start, the range and knowledge of the consultant, a spirit of willing collaboration on the part of the architect, and the vision and sensitivity to the environment of the artist.

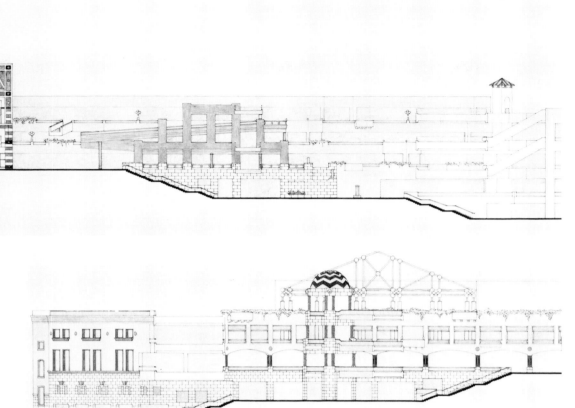

Hahn Replaces the Lyceum with a Live Theater Shell

To compensate for the loss of the Lyceum, Hahn offered to provide space in Horton Plaza for a 450-seat theater. The space could be leased to a nonprofit theater company for $1 per year; the company was expected to build and operate the theater.

The Centre City Development Corporation worked to find a local theater company that could finance, design, build, and operate the facility in Horton Plaza. However, it became apparent that this task was virtually impossible for any small theater group in San Diego to finance.

In 1982 the development corporation hired Arthur H. Ballet, of the Guthrie Theater in Minneapolis and a professor of theater arts at the University of Minnesota, to provide objective, out-of-town guidance. He reported in July that:

■ San Diego needed and would support a "wide diversity of theatrical fare, ranging from the great classics of the past through the contemporary plays of the commercial and the not-for-profit, professional theater, all the way to the 'cutting-edge' playwrights and play producing units." The mix was all-important, for it would feed and nourish theater in general as well as specific theaters.

■ A focal point for those theaters was needed so that a joint public image could be projected.

■ The prospect of raising large sums of money for the arts appeared dim.

■ Horton Plaza was "an ideal chance to take national leadership in returning the arts . . . and the artists . . . to the central city to live and to work."

■ There was a great scarcity of middle-sized theaters seating 200 to 500 people. To achieve a good theater mix, it was important to develop a range of theater spaces to accommodate experimental and growing companies.

Ballet recommended that the Horton Plaza theater space be converted into a "black box" to permit a variety of configurations, seating arrangements, and capacities, "permitting approximations to a proscenium, a thrust, and an arena arrangement as well as anything in between." In fact, he estimated that two theaters could be accommodated in the space—one up to 500 seats, the other less than 100 seats, and that it should not be built to accommodate any single production company.

He recommended that a nonprofit organization be formed to administer and run the Horton Plaza theater, one-third of the board of directors coming from active per-

Horton Plaza
Project Data

Physical Configuration Component—Income Generating	Completion	Profile at Build-Out
Retail—Department Stores		
Mervyn's	83,000 sq. ft.	83,000 sq. ft.
Robinson's	127,000 sq. ft.	127,000 sq. ft.
The Broadway	138,000 sq. ft.	138,000 sq. ft.
Nordstrom	142,000 sq. ft.	142,000 sq. ft.
Retail—Shops/Restaurants	403,000 sq. ft.	403,000 sq. ft.*
Office		300,000 sq. ft.
Hotel—Omni International (being developed by separate developer)	450 rooms	450 rooms
Component—Arts/Culture/ Open Space		
Two Performing Arts Theaters	796 seats	796 seats
Rehab of Balboa Theater for San Diego Art Center		100,376 sq. ft.
Open-Air Mall		
Other		
Parking	2,800 spaces	2,800 spaces
Acreage	11 acres	11 acres
Location	Downtown San Diego	
Development Period	1982–85	late 1980s
Estimated Total Development Costs	$220 million	$250 million
Master Developer	Ernest W. Hahn, Inc. (does not include Balboa and Omni Hotel)	
Master Planner/Architect	The Jerde Partnership	

*includes 34,000-square-foot, 7-screen United Artists Theatre and also the two performing arts theaters, which total about 34,000 sq. ft.

Source: Centre City Development Corporation
Ernest W. Hahn Company

Horton Plaza
Development Cost Summary

	Private	Public
Retail and Parking	$136 million	
Hotel	45 million	
Office	30 million	
Site		$25.5 million
Site Improvements		7.5 million
Theaters	1 million	4.0 million
	$212 million	$37.0 million

Source: Centre City Development Corporation

forming arts institutions within the city.
He concluded by saying:

The "mix," to misquote Shakespeare, "is all." And, while I am at it, quoting the Bard, I think that San Diego has the chance to make an exciting contribution to the national stage, to make a dream become a reality. After all, "we are such stuff as dreams are made of" and after we are gone, we hope fervently, all of us, that we leave some memory for future generations . . . some footnote that is remembered. An imprint in sand is what the buildings are, but what the artists create is what memory is made of. And history as well.

During the summer of 1982, S. Leonard Auerbach & Associates, San Francisco theater design consultants, provided a schematic design and cost estimate for a flexible 500-seat theater. As a result of many meetings with theater groups in San Diego, they decided that rather than a large, flexible black-box theater—which none of the potential users wanted—two theaters should be built: one with 500 seats, the other with 200, and both with flexible seating and performance areas. The architect later selected to work with Auerbach to design the space was Liebhart Weston & Associates, the architect of the new Old Globe Theatre in Balboa Park.

The redevelopment agency, on September 21, 1982, approved a third amendment to the development agreement with Ernest W. Hahn, Inc., which provided for a theater space of 30,000 square feet below the plaza level at Third and E streets. The developer would construct this basic shell at a cost of approximately $750,000 if the agency agreed to finance and begin construction of a drama facility by July 1, 1986. The estimated cost for the two theaters, support areas, theatrical equipment, architectural design, and administrative costs totaled $4.35 million. On October 26, 1982, the city council approved in concept this expenditure of $4.35 million, as well as the creation of a nonprofit corporation to operate the theaters on a self-supporting basis, leasing the space from Hahn for $1 a year for a period of 30 years.

The Centre City Development Corporation suggested three alternatives for financing the theater: lease revenue bonds; a loan from the city to the redevelopment agency to be repaid from tax increments in Horton Plaza; or tax allocation bonds in the nearby Columbia redevelopment project.

A Horton Plaza Theatres design advisory committee was created in late 1982 to assist the development corporation and the design consultants. After a complete analysis of "flexible" vs. "fixed" seating, the committee opted for fixed seating in the main stage house and flexible seating in the smaller, black-box theater.

In October 1983 the city council adopted the articles of incorporation and bylaws for the formation of the Horton Plaza Theatres Foundation. The foundation advises the Centre City Development Corporation on the design and development of the theater, but it has no power to select plays or to make other artistic or literary decisions. It will, however, select the theater companies that use the facility.

In February 1984 the development corporation approved a financing plan for the theater shell's initial capital expenditures. Funds will come from the corporation's Horton Plaza retail budget ($750,000) and from the sale of tax allocation bonds backed by the tax increment of the Columbia redevelopment project ($3.6 million). In addition, the corporation approved $200,000 to cover potential operation deficits incurred by the foundation during its first several years. A portion of the transient occupancy tax generated from the Horton Plaza hotel development may be used to fund any operating deficits in subsequent years.

Early in 1984 the Horton Plaza Theatres Foundation met with members of the arts community to help it decide the theaters' management. It was advised not to embark on the business of booking and producing theater. Rather, it was urged to find a tenant that would perform in residence most of the year, making the space available to other groups the remainder of the season.

In February 1984 the foundation issued a Request for Proposals to 90 groups in southern California, soliciting plans for the use of the Horton Plaza Theatres. Seven groups responded; among them was the San Diego Repertory Theater. Shortly there-

Project Data: San Diego Art Center

Location	Balboa Theater, Horton Plaza
Projected Opening	Fall 1986
Architect	Richard Weinstein
Developer	Balboa Building Partnership (Lincoln Land Investment Corp. plus San Diego Art Center)
Consultants	Pegasus Architecture and Design The Jerde Partnership
Building Cost	$1.5 million estimated $6.5 million conversion of Balboa $2 million new wing
Gross Area	100,376 sq. ft. 73,770 total square footage of the Art Center

Breakdown of Interior Area (in sq. ft.)		Balboa	Annex	Total
	Art Center			
	Gallery	20,096	5,168	
	Administration	1,141		
	Circulation	9,993	6,579	
	Service/Storage	6,501	7,187	
	Dining/Reception		4,209	
	Terrace		2,443	
	Bookstore	1,624	530	
	Coats	117	58	
	Control/Information	528		
	Lobby/Gallery		1,708	
	Auditorium		2,888	
	Total	43,000	30,770	73,770
	Retail			
	Retail	15,010	3,026	
	Circulation	6,977	1,189	
	Service/Storage	108	296	
	Total	22,095	4,511	26,606
	Total			100,376

Project Data: Horton Plaza Theatres

Location	Horton Plaza, San Diego
Projected Opening	October 1985
Architect	Liebhardt Weston & Associates
Consultants	Theater Design: S. Leonard Auerbach & Associates
Building Cost	Construction of shell—$750,000 Completion of interior—$4,350,000
Gross Area	34,000 sq. ft.
Breakdown of Interior Area	Main Theater—546 fixed seats Black Box Theater—250 seats (flexible seating)

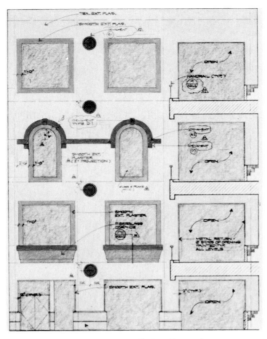

after, the Repertory and the foundation entered into exclusive negotiations to come to an agreement whereby the Repertory would be the major tenant for nine months of the year, and would manage and book the theaters for the remaining three months. As of September 1984, those negotiations were still in progress, pending resolution of the length of the lease and the financial terms.

San Diego Art Center Develops the Balboa

The adaptive use of the Balboa Theater was not included in the Hahn development of Horton Plaza. It remains part of a separate, 15,000-square-foot site adjacent to the plaza. As Jerry Keyser of Keyser Marston Associates explains, "The initial thinking of preserving the Balboa by integrating the building directly into Horton Plaza didn't work for architectural and economic reasons. The decision was made to treat the building independently and to find a separate sponsor for its preservation and restoration."

Thus, once the Centre City Development Corporation had outlined the Balboa's possibilities to Danah Fayman and Sebastian Adler, stimulating the creation of the San Diego Art Center, the corporation worked with the museum board to secure a developer, Lincoln Land Investment Corporation, that could convert the ground floors of the old theater to retail space linked with Horton Plaza, and the two upper floors to the museum and a gallery.

Fayman tried to arrange the museum's purchase of the building, but its owners considered the appraised price—$1.6 million—too low. Consequently, the Centre City Development Corporation arranged for the redevelopment agency to condemn the Balboa and to sell the land and building to the Balboa Building Partnership, a limited partnership consisting of Lincoln Investment and the San Diego Art Center. Lincoln acts as the general partner, and the museum as the limited partner.

The art center also has plans to locate expansion space, storage, a theater, and restaurants in a 35,200-square-foot Fourth Avenue annex. This structure will be developed from the Balboa Theater down to the Horton Plaza garage entrance on air rights above the plaza stores. The annex will be built by the agency with lease revenue bonds and leased to the art center. Revenue to pay the annual debt service will come from the agency's Horton Plaza tax increments. The $6.5 million conversion of the Balboa Theater and the $2 million new wing have been designed by Richard Weinstein & Associates in conjunction with Pegasus Architecture and Design and the Jerde Partnership, both of San Diego.

Retailers Aim to Spark
Downtown Shopping Revival

On October 18, 1982, groundbreaking for Horton Plaza finally was celebrated, with a heavy equipment parade. Spaces in the development are being marketed enthusiastically by the Hahn company as "the keystone in the continuing revitalization of downtown San Diego." By the end of 1984, 55 percent of the retail space had been committed, in addition to the four department stores. Ninety percent of the restaurant, fast-food, and entertainment area was committed. Hahn also has begun to commission the sculptural works for the plaza. The stores will open in August 1985.

In October 1984, San Diego's Historic Sites Board approved a request for the demolition of the interior of the Balboa Theater. Construction on the theater is to start in August 1985, and construction on the Fourth Avenue annex by the end of 1985, with completion of both buildings as the new San Diego Art Center scheduled for mid-1986. When both components of the art center are completed, the museum will have 30,000 square feet of exhibition space at an extremely reasonable price—almost one-third the cost per square foot of the new museums in Dallas and Los Angeles.

The center is gathering an international collection of painting, sculpture, design, and architecture that will emphasize California artists and constructivist–minimalist style. Its permanent collection will be at least 25 percent devoted to architecture and design, and it will allocate at least half of its annual exhibition schedule to these aspects of contemporary arts.

While waiting for its new playhouse to be started in 1986, the San Diego Repertory Theater is negotiating with the Centre City Development Corporation for assistance in meeting the deficits it estimates will reach nearly $200,000 a year in the new space. Sam Woodhouse of the Repertory argues that the earnings the theater will bring to the shopping center should be compensated. People will come to Horton Plaza not only because certain department stores are located there, Woodhouse maintains. He believes they will come downtown because it will be the only place besides the Old Globe in Balboa Park where they can see live theater.

The long-term significance of Horton Plaza is its imaginative reintroduction of major department-store retailing downtown. It constitutes the first attempt in the United Sates to merge the department-store–based shopping center model with festival retailing, public art, and live theater. It holds the potential to attract suburban residents because it will be strikingly different from malls closer to their homes.

The Centre City Development Corporation and the Hahn company have worked hard over a decade to craft an ingenious financial plan whereby the public agency and the developer share the costs of the more traditional functions (such as land assembly and parking construction), and both provide capital and operating support for the cultural facilities.

The project also has been marked by a shared realization that Horton Plaza could best succeed as part of a long-term plan to change the nature of downtown San Diego—a realization that is bringing new housing, public transportation, hotels, offices, and a convention center to the city's core. This comprehensive development strategy will help increase the number of workers, residents, and visitors using the downtown, so that Horton Plaza's retail and arts businesses can grow and flourish.

The Centre City Development Corporation has been an active participant in the development process, rather than expecting the developer or the arts community to produce the ideas or the funds alone. Although the extensive nature of this collaborative development process has involved heavy staff and dollar demands on the Centre City Development Corporation and on the Hahn company, it appears to be justified by the quality of the planning and design, by the increased revenues that are accruing to the city, and by the vitality that an enhanced arts presence will offer. In the words of the Repertory's Sam Woodhouse, Horton Plaza will be "enlightened redevelopment. It addresses the spirit of the city as well as the physical construct—the soul instead of just the body."

Fred Colby, development director of the art center, expects that when Horton Plaza is completed, "San Diego will not only *be* a major city, it will *act* like one."

California Plaza at Bunker Hill

California Plaza at Bunker Hill constitutes an attempt by the city of Los Angeles and a private developer to create a regional magnet—a mixed-use project with significant arts places and watching, walking, and buying spaces to draw people on foot. Within its eleven hilltop acres on the northeast edge of the central business district, new homes will be provided for the Museum of Contemporary Art and for the Bella Lewitzky Dance Gallery, so that these visual and performing arts can be presented downtown in state-of-the-art facilities. The total public and private cost of California Plaza at completion of the project is projected to be $1.2 billion.

Another unusual feature of the development will be a performing arts plaza located on a major bridge spanning Olive Street. It will provide a focal point for nearby shops and restaurants, and, reflecting the major role played by Los Angeles's entertainment industry, it will offer a variety of events—from noontime concerts to major evening concerts.

California Plaza is a multiphased joint project of the Los Angeles Community Redevelopment Agency and Bunker Hill Associates, a partnership including Metropolitan Structures, Cadillac Fairview, Shapell Industries, and Goldrich & Kest. Construction began on the first office building and the new Museum of Contemporary Art in September 1983. Both facilities are expected to open in 1985–86 at an expected cost of $205 million in 1983 dollars.

The project will link the city's Civic Center, the Music Center (one block west of Bunker Hill), and Los Angeles's new business core. The pedestrian route through California Plaza will be enlivened by festive spaces designed to invite office workers, residents, and evening and weekend visitors. A new historical museum will be built beside the reconstructed Angel's Flight, a historic single-track funicular that once ran up and down the hillside between Hill Street and Upper Bunker Hill.

While California Plaza lies adjacent to office development occurring elsewhere on Bunker Hill, it remains removed from the central core of the city's business district. The participating arts organizations collaborated with the redevelopment agency during bidding and negotiations with developers, indicating the importance the agency has attached to a cultural presence that can compensate for the site's relative isolation from the city's commercial district.

Major corporations, banks, hotels, retailers, and public employers, however, are located within walking distance of the museum site, and the museum has received contributions toward its capital campaign from companies who view the museum as a cultural drawing card. Because of the project's land area, financial participation from the developer, and broad community participation via public, corporate, and individual philanthrophy, California Plaza should make a major contribution to Los Angeles's arts. In return, the arts are expected to create a quality and verve that will attract tourists and residents who otherwise might not visit the area.

No "Heart" in the Southland

Angel's Flight Funicular, circa 1904.
Credit: California Historical Society/Ticor Title Insurance (Los Angeles)

The Los Angeles Standard Metropolitan Statistical Area incorporates the second largest concentration of population, employment, income, business, industry, and finance in the United States. In 1984 the 12.4 million people in Los Angeles's five-county area (Los Angeles, Orange, Riverside, San Bernadino, and Ventura counties) enjoyed a per-capita income of $14,442—17 percent above the national average. Although the city and its suburbs have grown steadily since World War II, until recently its downtown—the area bordered by the Hollywood, Santa Monica, and Harbor freeways, and by Alameda Street— has not. The region that calls itself the Southland (meaning southern California) lacked the central urban focus that confers genuine metropolitan status.

In an attempt to stimulate the downtown's revitalization, the Los Angeles Community Redevelopment Agency has orchestrated a number of development plans over a period of 25 years, beginning in March 1959 when the city council passed an ordinance mandating a Bunker Hill project. City officials recognized that this once-fashionable neighborhood of Victorian-era homes and buildings was deteriorating and that a height limitation on the site was keeping new construction off the hill. Nearby, across First Street, the then-planned Music Center project (begun in 1964 and now including the Dorothy Chandler Pavilion, the Mark Taper Forum, and the Ahmanson Theater) made the hill's down-at-the-heel housing and habitués even more unseemly. The redevelopment agency therefore cleared the area and divided the land into 30 parcels, to be sold separately to developers for a variety of office buildings, condominiums, and high-rise apartments.

While Bunker Hill awaited such development, the area immediately to the south of it gradually became the city's new business core. In 1969 ARCO Plaza was built at a cost of $190 million by the Atlantic Richfield Company and the Bank of America, to house their national and southern California headquarters, respectively. Other office buildings soon followed. Projects built downtown since 1964 represent more than $1.1 billion worth of construction.

Downtown Los Angeles thus seemed ready to enter the eighties as a regional focal point for business growth. However, it still needed a special kind of development program if the city was to create, in the midst of the downtown high rises, an active "heart"—an environment that could lure people out of their cubicles and cars with a mixture of commercial and cultural activities during the workday, after hours, and on weekends.

The redevelopment agency had made an important and symbolic statement when in 1969 it dismantled but saved the historic Angel's Flight, a tourist attraction that had been carrying Angelenos and visitors up the eastern slope of Bunker Hill from downtown since the 1890s. Any development concept for the remaining parcels on the hill would have to include restoration of the funicular and its placement among the new office buildings as a symbolic link between Upper Bunker Hill and the commercial activity on Broadway, Hill Street, and the Pershing Square area below. The Angel's Flight could carry only 30 people at a time, and elevators and escalators would have to be the principle people-movers; but planners hoped it could link the city's bustling past with a new era of urbane, cosmopolitan activity.

No Homes for the Moderns

Los Angeles has seemed close to becoming a major international art center since the mid-fifties. Today it boasts a large community of contemporary artists, a number of wealthy collectors, and many innovative and effective galleries. In the early sixties, Los Angeles artists began to be noticed outside California. They experimented in many media besides painting: ceramics as sculpture, assemblage, light and reflective surfaces, space, and pop images. This art attracted attention not only in museums, but also in studios and private collections.

But Los Angeles lacked a full-scale museum of contemporary art to support this movement. The Los Angeles County Museum of Art and the Pasadena Art Museum, after important showings of contemporary art, ceased to devote much attention to it. The Los Angeles County Museum of Art's Contemporary Art Council gave cash awards in the sixties to developing Los Angeles artists, supported exhibitions of modern art, and acquired important contemporary works for the museum's collections. Major exhibitions of Peter Voulkos, Edward Keinholz, Morris Louis, Jackson Pollock, and others were mounted. But after 1968, the trustees began to shift the emphasis to earlier periods of art history and other aspects of their permanent collections, as well as to special traveling exhibitions. Following the passage of Proposition 13 in 1978, plans to build a new facility for contemporary art were modified to a wing primarily for "classic modern" art.

Other Los Angeles art activity centered around the Pasadena Art Museum, founded in the twenties and originally located in a modest structure in Pasadena's Carmelita Park. In 1951, the internationally known Galka Schever Collection of 600 paintings, drawings, and documents, including works by Vasily Kandinsky, Paul Klee, and Lyonel Charles Adrian Feininger, was deeded to the museum. This gift and important exhibitions of American contemporary art catapulted the Pasadena museum into a position of national prominence.

Plans for a larger facility were launched, but even before its new building opened as the Pasadena Museum of Modern Art in 1969, the institution became plagued with

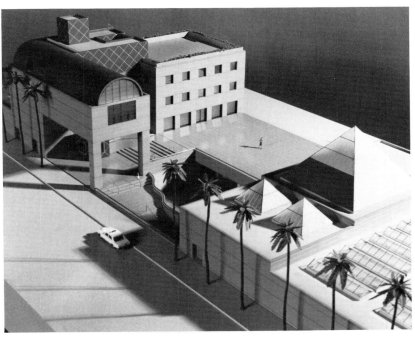

Model of the Museum of Contemporary Art.

financial problems. Later, increased costs of operation, past deficits, and unpaid construction costs forced its closing. When in 1974 Norton Simon acquired the building and its collections for his own extraordinary collections of historical and early 20th-century art, an agreement was reached to emphasize old masters, impressionists, and other noncontemporary artworks.

Marcia Weisman, Norton Simon's sister, and her husband, Frederick, who have built a substantial personal collection of post–World War II art, made a number of efforts to start something in the Pasadena museum's stead. Mrs. Weisman helped to find rent-free space for the Los Angeles Institute of Contemporary Arts, organized by Robert Smith to provide an arena for experimental artists. The institute opened in 1974 and remains in business, but it has operated more as a gallery than as a museum, and two other Weisman-sponsored museum ventures failed to take hold.

In 1979, at Weisman's urging, Los Angeles attorney William A. Norris formed a group of six major contemporary art collectors who signed an agreement "to pledge individually a portion of [their] collections up to a collective amount of $6 million, to create a museum of standing and repute." Mayor Tom Bradley appointed a mayor's museum advisory committee to look into

A Museum Dream Fills the Box Labeled "Culture"

the city's need for a full-fledged museum of contemporary art and to investigate possible sites.

Los Angeles Nurtures but Does Not Showcase Modern Dance

Similarly, Los Angeles has neglected to showcase the work of its local dance artists. Much of American modern dance took shape in California—developed by Martha Graham, Alvin Ailey, Twyla Tharp, Lester Horton, Bella Lewitzky, and Ruth St. Denis among others—and by the early eighties nearly 100 dance companies existed in the Los Angeles area. But when a leading dance group was chosen to be housed in the Los Angeles Music Center, it was a New York–based company, the Joffrey Ballet.

It may be that Los Angeles's appreciation for its own performing artists was stifled for decades by the film industry's overwhelming dominance, and that only when that industry began to relocate outside Los Angeles could local interest in the performing arts revive.

Bella Lewitzky alone of the major modern dance originators chose to stay in southern California and to build her reputation there. Her early training was with Lester Horton, and with him she cofounded one of the few institutions in the nation with both a school and a performing theater of dance in a permanent house. In 1951 she founded Dance Associates, a school and performing concert group. In 1966 she formed her nationally acclaimed present company, the 12-member Bella Lewitzky Dance Company. The Lewitzky Dance Foundation, a nonprofit organization, was founded in 1968 to support the company and to promote concerts of modern dance.

In early 1979 Edward Helfeld and Donald Cosgrove, administrator and deputy administrator of the Los Angeles Community Redevelopment Agency, initiated a planning process for the agency-owned property that remained on Bunker Hill: four contiguous parcels (R, S, T, and U) totaling 8.75 acres, located directly across Olive Street from the Angelus Plaza housing for the elderly. A fifth parcel, Y-1, was added in December 1979, after an earlier commitment to that parcel fell through. This final package totaled 11.2 acres.

In its scheme for the site, which after some name changes came to be called California Plaza, the redevelopment agency departed from policy for the other acreage on Bunker Hill. Instead of being sold individually to developers with unrelated interests, it was decided to offer these last five parcels as a single entity. The staff was hesitant at first, because earlier efforts to market "the Hill" in one piece had failed. But the agency's real estate consultant, Keyser Marston Associates, Inc., judged the current real estate context to be favorable, and argued that the single-unit strategy offered the best opportunity to achieve a dynamic mixture of uses and create a "people place." In accordance with existing agency policy, the developer of California Plaza would be required to spend 1 percent of the construction budget on works of art.

In the agency's March 1979 development offering, the invitation for proposals suggested that the Bunker Hill site possessed a number of unusual potentials and represented the last available uncommitted land close to the downtown business and civic core. With anticipated mass transit systems, planners expected that the site would not require elaborate internal parking facilities.

In June 1979, Cosgrove read a *Los Angeles Times* story that reported on the problems the mayor's museum advisory committee was encountering in locating a home for a contemporary art museum. Cosgrove wrote to William Norris, chairman of the committee, offering the redevelopment agency's help. Cosgrove mentioned several downtown buildings within the agency's control as possible sites for what he assumed would be a renovation rather than a new structure. He also proposed exploring

One-Percent-for-Art Is Defined
Not as Artworks, but as a Museum

"other means by which the agency might participate in the realization of this most significant project."

Norris responded eagerly, and within a few days the committee met at the agency's offices to discuss possible sites. The agency staff described several vacant buildings on Spring Street that could be rehabilitated as a museum, as well as the Brunswick Building in Little Tokyo, the center of the city's Japanese-American community. At the end of the meeting, the idea of new construction on Bunker Hill emerged as a backup alternative.

The agency already had thought of including a minimum of 1.5 acres of public open space on Bunker Hill. A park was envisioned as being a center of pedestrian and cultural, as opposed to commercial, activity. But no one at the agency had given much thought to what those cultural uses might be. For the time being, a box simply labeled "culture" had been incorporated in the drawings.

Bunker Hill intrigued the museum committee, and when the preliminary drawings of the project were unrolled, there was the "culture" box, just waiting to become a museum.

The intersection of the needs of an emerging cultural institution to find a home and the desire of a development agency to create a lively pedestrian environment was appropriate but unplanned. The museum committee had budgeted no more than $11 million for restoring a building; it could not afford a new structure at downtown rates.

The agency's staff suggested that the project's required 1-percent contribution for art might possibly be combined into a lump sum that the developer of California Plaza could be required to pay toward building a museum. Since the agency knew major developers were interested in the project, it believed that the arts requirement could even be raised to 1.5 percent of the projected construction costs.

Meanwhile, Keyser Marston Associates had advised the agency that the public policy objectives for California Plaza significantly increased the development risk for the project and that the level of risk had to be reflected in shaping the developer selection process and the negotiation of business terms. The agency decided that it would remain in charge of developer designation, but that the museum committee should participate in evaluating the full proposals—not just those aspects that concerned the museum structure, but rather

Master plan of California Plaza at Bunker Hill.

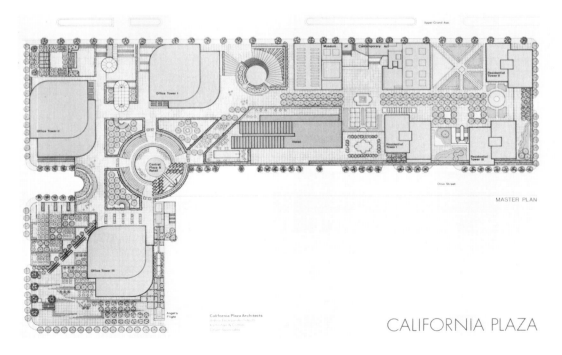

CALIFORNIA PLAZA

the entire site. In other words, both the agency and the museum committee would share in a precedent-setting process: the selection of the developer, the third partner in an arts-inclusive MXD.

In the executive summary of its Request for Proposals, the agency outlined the scope of the proposed development: "3.5 to 4.2 million square feet of office, retail, and residential buildings as well as a 100,000-square-foot museum to house a world-renowned collection of modern art; [and a] central park . . . connected to the various elements of the development by a unifying 'greenbelt' or linear spine . . . owned and maintained by the developer [but with] public pedestrian easements . . . affording access to the activities and amenities." The agency also required prospective developers to incorporate the restored Angel's Flight funicular.

Although the agency expected that overall construction would be time-phased, the Request for Proposals required development of the central park and museum at the start of the project, to create an initial

Bunker Hill redevelopment project parcels R, S, T, U, and Y1. Illustrative development plan dated May 1982.

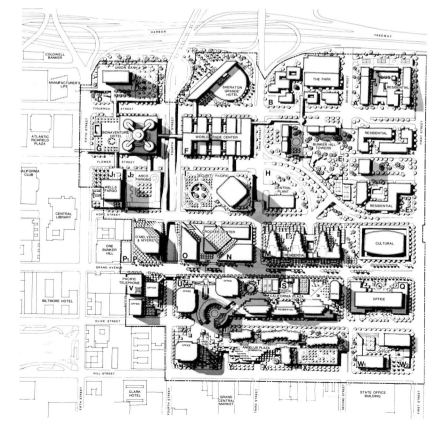

showpiece. The developer was to be awarded a 180-day exclusive right to negotiate. The agency envisioned that the property would be leased to the developer for 99 years. The land lease payments were projected at 9 percent of the determined fee value (that is, gross market value, minus developer's cost for amenities, plus value of amenities to developer). They included a formula to reflect future changes in the real estate and money markets and an upside participation in the developer's profits in return for favorable terms in the early years of the project.

The museum committee drew up a letter for inclusion as an appendix in the Request for Proposals. It expressed the committee's interest in a collaborative effort and summarized their intentions as follows:

. . . that the museum be a nonprofit corporation with a board of trustees representative of the ethnic and economic diversity of the city; that there be working artists on the board; that the museum be privately financed and, towards that end, that $10 million in endowment funds be raised; that the museum open with at least $25 million worth of art, donated by private collectors; that at least 100,000 square feet of space be available for exhibits, shows, storage, and other uses.

The possibilities for highlighting the cultural element of the development are numerous; artists' studios might be incorporated into the housing units, while office and residential tenants could be offered special museum benefits.

On October 4, 1979, the redevelopment agency issued its Request for Proposals. The original due date for receipt of proposals, January 31, 1980, was changed to February 29, 1980, after Parcel Y-1 was added to the offering on December 7, 1979. Museum committee members began to meet with prospective developers to negotiate directly for the best possible rendering of their vision into developer proposals.

In the meantime, someone else had read the June 1979 news story in the *Los Angeles Times* about the mayor's museum advisory committee. This was Bella Lewitzky, who had been looking for a facility for her dance company for two years. The story gave Lewitzky the idea that the incipient

The Agency, the Developers, the Art Collectors, and the Dance Company

contemporary art museum might share space with her company. She talked to Sheri Geldin, a member of the museum committee, who advised Lewitzky to speak directly with the redevelopment agency. However, the Lewitzky company manager and production designer did not talk to the agency until the following October—two days after it had mailed its Request for Proposals—and so the dance company lost its chance to be written in as an element of the project.

Nevertheless, the agency indicated that it was interested in including a dance facility at Bunker Hill, suggesting that once the agency had selected a developer, the Lewitzky Foundation could help plan California Plaza. Instead, Lewitzky followed the example of the museum committee and talked directly with the developers, arguing the importance of a "dance gallery" and outlining her requirements: a freestanding building with a theater built specifically for dance, studios for classes, a library, and offices.

The Los Angeles Community Redevelopment Agency, which exercises jurisdiction over the city's downtown development, has established itself as one of the most aggressive development planning agencies in the nation. It requires a variety of public benefits from developers who wish to build downtown. Subsidies and density exemptions have been used, and the agency has allowed builders to exceed zoning density requirements in exchange for land gifts that can be made into neighborhood parks.

In the early seventies, the agency had adopted a policy that required developers to contribute 1 percent of hard construction costs for public artworks. In addition, it encouraged the establishment of nearly 1,000 artists downtown in both living and work situations and in 25 galleries, even providing funding for housing and loft space. With its own funds, the agency had been purchasing works of downtown artists, and in constructing public parks—such as the Isamu Noguchi plaza and sculpture in Little Tokyo—it had demonstrated a commitment to the arts.

At California Plaza, this arts advocacy expanded far beyond previous agency projects, due both to the extraordinary size of the project ($1.2 billion in 1983 dollars) and to the readiness of two arts organizations to participate in the planning.

This partnership was also possible because, at a time when development approvals were becoming increasingly costly to achieve in California, the agency was able to offer an 11-acre parcel of downtown land with a mixed-use program already approved. Most of the city's comparable, centrally located sites already had been developed. And because the land had been vacant for many years, no broad public support campaign was necessary. The agency's major concerns were the quality of the design, the nature of the arts-and-amenities package, and the experience and financial capacity of the developer. For the developer, the much-increased costs to include arts facilities were offset greatly by the benefits of being able to invest $1.2 billion in a single location.

The agency recognized that the financial terms of the land lease should not be based

upon the market land price—that is, on its highest and best economic use—but would have to take into account the programmatic and open-space uses that would meet the agency's social and economic objectives. The agency also was willing to agree to a base lease rate and "holding rent" favorable to the developer during the construction period. These economic terms served as incentives for the developer to undertake the art museum during the first phase, and to undertake the other extraordinary obligations of open space, arts, entertainment, minority-business enterprise, and energy efficiency required by the agency.

In January 1980, Chairman Andrew W. Wall of the redevelopment agency's board appointed a Bunker Hill Task Force of three board members to work with agency staff in evaluating the proposals received from developers. The task force consisted of Marilyn Hudson (chair), Alan Goldstein, and Everett Welmers.

Bunker Hill Associates
Wins on Image and Staying Power

Although this project held out the promise of financial success, it was, of course, a high-risk venture. In spite of its recent commercial success, downtown Los Angeles remains largely an untried market for mixed-use developments. The Bunker Hill site was being offered on a lease, not purchase, basis, and the Request for Proposals indicated that the redevelopment agency would, therefore, remain as a partner in the project's design and development. Even after designation, the process of working with a public agency on design and construction approvals was bound to be complex. However, by 5 p.m. on February 29, 1980, five development groups had submitted proposals. Two eventually emerged as leading contenders.

Bunker Hill Associates proposed a $700 million California Center: three spectacular office towers, three residential high rises whose base would include the required museums, a luxury hotel, and a four-block-long park. The proposal included the Museum of Contemporary Art, a 12-theater "cineplex," and land for a freestanding theater for the Bella Lewitzky Dance Company, as well as an outdoor performance plaza to showcase local performing arts groups.

Maguire Partners' proposal featured bold geometry—the museum cantilevering out over Grand Avenue, a wedge-shaped hotel, a residential tower, and two office towers. For the Lewitzky Dance Company, it offered a multipurpose space to be shared with other performers. A notable aspect of the Maguire proposal was Angel's Flats, 400 apartments for tenants with moderate incomes, to be subsidized by downtown employers rather than by government. In an attempt to create a project with diverse architectural styles, Maguire Partners proposed a team of ten architects whose buildings, while relating to a single site plan, might together create a special stylistic complexity and richness.

For four-and-one-half months following the receipt of the proposals, the agency's task force and real estate consultants evaluated each proposal. In an unprecedented move, the agency gave the museum committee a copy of each proposal on the day it was submitted.

On July 14 the task force presented its recommendations to the agency's board. Alan Goldstein and Everett Welmers favored Bunker Hill Associates; Marilyn Hudson and the agency's administrator, Edward Helfeld, preferred Maguire. The seven-member board voted to award Bunker Hill Associates the 180-day exclusive right to negotiate.

In their report, Goldstein and Welmers praised the Bunker Hill Associates proposal for the marketing flexibility of its three office towers, for its handling of mass, and for its variety of open spaces. The idea of placing the museum near the entertainment center, the functional center of the development, was singled out in particular. Goldstein and Welmers were impressed by Bunker Hill Associates' lead architect, Arthur Erickson, by the innovation apparent in earlier work by member firms of the organization, and by Bunker Hill Associates' financial capacity to make this "extraordinary upfront commitment . . . for nonrevenue producing facilities. Only a developer with large resources could handle this type of equity commitment in the first phase in order to set the tone, create the image and

the market, and have the staying power to wait for development of subsequent, more profitable phases."

The Arts Partners Strike Their Deals

Both Maguire Partners and Bunker Hill Associates had been careful to woo the museum committee during the long review process. And with good reason: not only was the museum a major requirement of the Request for Proposals, but the group that was selected would be entering into a close working relationship with the museum committee.

Four days before the agency's July 14 decision, the museum committee signed agreements with both Bunker Hill Associates and Maguire Partners, defining the cost, total space to be provided, and so on, and stipulating site and design matters that would be subject to the approval of the museum board. The agency had delegated a staff member to be present at the committee's meetings with the prospective developers, but the museum committee itself acted to conclude these agreements prior to the agency's final selection.

By this time the committee was reflecting the rapid institutional coming-of-age of the Museum of Contemporary Art. In the spring of 1979, following two large meetings of local artists, an artists advisory council had been formed to study issues relevant to designing, administering, and funding a museum, aiming to make recommendations to the mayor's committee regarding developer selection. Both the artists advisory council and the mayor's committee decided there should be *two* museum directors: Pontus Hulten, then director of the Centre National d'Art Contemporain Georges Pompidou (the Beauborg) in Paris, and Richard Koshalek, then director of the Hudson River Museum outside New York City. The two candidates met and decided that they could work together, and in July the museum trustees voted to appoint Hulten director and Koshalek deputy director and chief curator.

Also in July the trustees decided to change the working name of the museum, which had been the Los Angeles Museum of Modern Art, to the Museum of Contemporary Art, signifying that it would present art from an international rather than regional perspective and that its exhibition program (including performances and media) would be devoted to the art of the recent past and the present (from 1940 onward) rather than to the entire 20th century.

With two new directors noted throughout the museum world, with the personal support of Mayor Tom Bradley, and with the momentum of an exceptionally successful fundraising drive led by Willam Norris and businessman Eli Broad, the museum quickly raised the $10 million required by its agreement with Bunker Hill Associates, and it was incorporated into the California Plaza project from the start.

Both Maguire Partners and Bunker Hill Associates had asked the Lewitzky Dance Company to recommend their designs to the redevelopment agency. Lewitzky liked Erickson's designs for Bunker Hill Associates in particular and told the agency so, speaking publicly on their behalf along with others from her organization at the final hearing. Yet little of the understanding between Bunker Hill Associates and Lewitzky was put down in writing, since there was no legal relationship between the parties at the time. The construction of the Dance Gallery was not officially included in the amenities package for determining fair reuse value of the entire California Plaza site. However, Lewitzky requested that Bunker Hill Associates insert an addendum into their technical plan indicating the developer's interest in including the gallery in the project.

After much preliminary delay, while the parties disagreed over promises made to Lewitzky about a freestanding site as well as about lighting, landscaping, and security, Bunker Hill Associates eventually made space available for the Dance Gallery, and architectural planning proceeded. Nagging disagreements, however, continued to arise over the Dance Gallery's budget, construction costs, and fundraising potential. In January 1981 Bunker Hill Associates announced that Lewitzky had to raise $4 million by March 31—less than three months away—to continue to be assured a place in the project. The Lewitzky board came up with $3.5 million in that time and was able to move the deadline back.

Meanwhile, Bunker Hill Associates was encountering difficulty finding sufficient financing for the project's first phase. The market for housing also had softened considerably, leading to an agreement with the redevelopment agency to postpone construction of the condominium that was to house the Dance Gallery and replacing it with a hotel that had been scheduled to be built in the second construction phase. This decision meant that the Dance Gallery had to be relocated to avoid being reassigned to a later phase of construction. Bunker Hill Associates actually preferred rescheduling it for Phase III, but Lewitzky, who by now had gathered an effective board and strong community support, insisted on remaining in Phase I. A relocation acceptable to all parties was made by moving the Dance Gallery to the corner of Fourth and Grand, where the project will proceed at its own speed with no direct impact on other construction.

Beginning with a dream and a national reputation but little fundraising or political experience, Lewitzky had managed to form an influential board of directors, gain the backing of the mayor, and secure substantial donations: $300,000 each from the Atlantic Richfield Foundation and the National Endowment for the Arts, and $2 million from the Andrew Norman Charitable Trust.

Public-Benefits Package
Subsidizes Arts Components

The partnership that has evolved at Bunker Hill differs from traditional real estate developments and from the ways in which arts organizations have built facilities in two important ways:

1) The site's program was defined by a public agency and its arts partner before the developer was selected.

2) The public-benefits package was expanded from traditional benefits (increased taxes, jobs, minority business enterprise participation, affirmative action) to include construction of and subsidy for arts facilities and programs.

The uniqueness of the Bunker Hill project's mix of uses, its cumulative costs (currently projected at $1.2 billion), the high cost of construction loans, and the intricate leasing details for the various parcels all forced extensions of the negotiations with Bunker Hill Associates. It was September 1981 before the agency and the developer signed a disposition and development agreement, which called for a three-phased construction schedule. The Museum of Contemporary Art still was to be included in Phase I.

To decide the terms of the developer's lease, which was to be based on the principle of fair reuse value, the agency and its economic consultants assembled a list of uses that would *not* have been required had Bunker Hill Associates acquired the site from a private party. These "extraordinary developer obligations and development characteristics" included the following sums:

$22,500,000—Museum of Contemporary Art, to be paid for by the developer at cost of $23 million ($14 million in construction costs plus $9 million in additional costs). The developer will partially subsidize the ongoing operation of the 100,000-square-foot museum, based on a formula tied to attendance. [It should be noted that in the event the museum did not proceed, the developer agreed to pay the redevelopment agency $20 million in cash at the start of Phase I.] Bella Lewitzky Dance Gallery, to be paid for by a nonprofit corporation organized for the purpose of constructing, owning, and operating the facility, at cost of $10 million. The developer is obligated to provide a location and design for the facility.

$2,300,000—Central Performance Plaza, to be paid for by the developer, on a 1.5-acre site. The outdoor park/theater needs a supporting infrastructure of light and sound technologies. The plaza will provide a public forum for civic festivals, concerts, dance, theater, and televised shows.

$1,000,000—Angel's Flight Cultural Museum, to be paid for by the developer, will be an integral part of the hillside terraces on the eastern side of the site.

$800,000—Reconstruction of Angel's Flight funicular, to be paid for by the redevelopment agency, will result in integration of a historic inclined railway as a major internal circulation feature. The developer must provide a location and the environmental features that create the setting, and it must operate and maintain the facility.

$10,400,000—Open space, to be paid for by the developer, will consist of 5.5 acres, providing major areas of landscaping, area enhancement, and open-space relief. The area is to include a system of gardens, terraces, sculpture courts, plazas, and water elements.

$2,800,000—Construction of Olive Street Bridge.

$6,800,000—Minority business enterprise and women's business enterprise programs.

$4,000,000—Timing and transferability requirements and restrictions.

The developer's commitments thus were estimated at $50.6 million in 1981 dollars. Of this total burden, it was estimated that the developer would receive some benefit from the museum and the other cultural and open-space uses, due to more rapid absorption of the income uses and higher rents. An adjusted cost burden of about $30.8 million was assigned. The total land value, before these burdens, was estimated at $89.1 million; less the burdens, the remaining land value was set at $58.3 million.

The agency's approach in negotiating this deal was as follows:

■ Some developer costs would be treated as in-lieu payments for land.

■ Since most of the costs occurred at the front end (Phase 1) of a multiphased development, the agency would forgo an upfront payment for land, in order to enhance the attractiveness of the package to the developer and to lenders.

California Plaza
Project Data

Physical Configuration (in sq. ft.)

Component— Income Generating	Phase I	Phase II	Phase III	Total
Office gross	1,013,231	1,500,000	1,100,000	3,613,231
(net)	(936,864)	(1,300,000)	(953,000)	(3,189,864)
Residential				750 units
Retail/Other				
Commercial	36,000	80,000	60,000	176,000
Hotel		450 rooms		450 rooms
Multiplex Cinema		25,000		12 theaters

Component—Arts/ Culture/Open Space				
Museum of Contemporary Art	100,000			100,000
The Dance Gallery		72,284		72,284
Park and Open Space	2.1 acres	2.0 acres	1.4 acres	5.5 acres
Performance Plaza				
Angel's Flight Funicular				
Angel's Flight Museum				

Other				
Parking	1,170 spaces			4,650 spaces
Metro Station				
Acreage				11.5 acres
Gross Building Area	1,217,000			4,700,000
Floor/Area Ratio (FAR)	10.2			8.2
Development Period	1983–85			early 1990

Master Developer: Bunker Hill Associates, a general partnership consisting of Metropolitan Structures and Cadillac Fairview/California, Inc. The limited partners are Shapell Industries, Inc., and Goldrich Kest & Associates. Metropolitan Structures is the managing partner.

Estimated Total Development Costs (1984 dollars)	$205 million			$1.02 billion

California Plaza
Order of Magnitude Development Cost Summary
(1984 dollars)

Development Costs— Income Generating Uses	Total
Office	$720,000,000
Residential	110,000,000
Retail/Other Commercial	10,000,000
Hotel	50,000,000
Parking	90,000,000
Subtotal	$980,000,000

Development Costs— Arts/Culture/Open Space	
Museum of Contemporary Art	$ 23,000,000
Central Performance Plaza	5,000,000
Angel's Flight Cultural Museum	2,000,000
Urban Park/Open Space	10,000,000
Subtotal	$ 40,000,000
TOTAL DEVELOPMENT COST BY DEVELOPER	$1,020,000,000
Bella Lewitzky Dance Gallery	$ 12,000,000
TOTAL DEVELOPMENT COST	$1,032,000,000

Source: Keyser Marston Associates
Bunker Hill Associates

■ As compensation for the land, and as a reflection of both the agency's cash-flow position and its status as a virtual partner of the developer, the agency would ground-lease the commercial portions of the site in a manner that would generate a relatively modest flow of dollars, but with significant future profit potential to the agency.

■ The agency would sell air-rights parcels in fee to Bunker Hill Associates for the residential uses; few benefits to any of the parties to the transaction could be realized by a land lease for the residential parcels.

During all the negotiations, Bunker Hill Associates downplayed the significance of the museum to the marketing success of the project—particularly to its 3.2 million square feet of office space. But "after our contract was signed and construction started," agency administrator Helfeld reports, "they have produced a marketing brochure which highlights with great enthusiasm the proximity of the museum and other cultural institutions to the office buildings."

The Land-Lease Transaction

The cultural and open-space uses were reflected in the final transaction in three ways. First, the land value was reduced by the developer's obligation to provide the public-benefits package, and the reduction in land value was reflected in the negotiated base rent. Second, the inclusion of the public benefits reduced the participation rent payable to the agency as follows: The developer will receive a 20 percent preferred return on equity that will be deducted from the cash flow before payment of participation rent. The museum and other uses that do not generate net revenue may not increase the amount the lender will finance; therefore, their inclusion will result in an increase in the equity that receives a preferred return. Third, the developer's costs for maintaining open space and for subsidizing the museum's operations costs will be deducted from the cash flow and also reduce the amount of participation rent.

The agency will receive the following payments of land rent for all the commercial phases of the project:

■ Holding rent of $500,000 per phase will

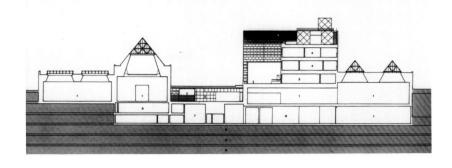

be paid for each of the three commercial office phases. This rent, commencing on stipulated dates for the first 42 months of each lease, will be paid during the development phase.

■ Base rent of from $400,000 to $1,500,000 per year for each phase of commercial development will commence after the holding rent period and will remain constant for the term of the lease. It will not be subordinated to debt service.

■ Escalation rent will be the mechanism by which base rent will be adjusted over time. It will reflect the cash-flow performance of the project and be calculated by comparing the increase in net operating income for two sets of averaging years, with a readjustment of rent every ten years, the first occurring no later than 20 years from commencement of Phase I. Escalation rent is subordinated to debt service, except after refinancing.

■ Participation rent will be the agency's share of the project's net cash flow (after debt service), and after a 20 percent preferred return on equity. (Equity is defined as the difference between total development costs and the mortgage, and applies to both the developer's and the lender's equity.) The agency's share of net cash flow is 10 percent until about the twentieth year of each commercial lease, and 15 percent thereafter.

The terms of the California Plaza lease/sale agreement specified that Bunker Hill Associates must make annual payments to the museum reflective of the economic benefits, if any, derived from the museum's location within the development. Finally, the developer was obligated to provide evidence of financial commitment ($205 million for Phase 1) by July 1, 1982, to draw on the financing by September 1, and to begin construction by September 30.

The Los Angeles City Council approved the development agreement on January 21, 1982. On February 5 the agency executed the agreement, and schematic drawings for the entire site were given preliminary approval in April. Bunker Hill Associates was given 90 additional days to return with finished drawings.

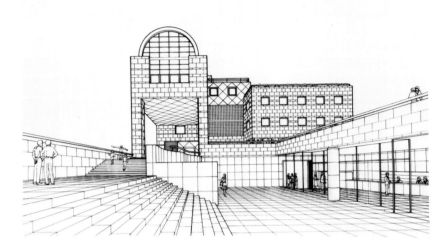

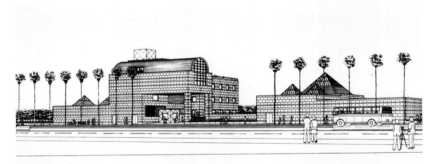

Bunker Hill Associates
Seeks Capital, Finds New Partner

In spite of these positive events, Bunker Hill Associates proved unable to meet its July 1 deadline to secure the required construction funds. The loan market was experiencing severe turbulence, with few forward commitments available on any terms. The magnitude of the project and the public-benefits costs further reduced the project's appeal in a weakened market.

Under the contract, an additional year to secure financing and the addition of partners to obtain permanent financing was established. On July 6, the agency approved a restructuring of Bunker Hill Associates so that new sources of dollars could be attracted to the project.

Harold Jensen of Metropolitan Structures, a joint venture partner of Metropoli-

Section of the Museum of Contemporary Art.

Museum Court. The Museum of Contemporary Art.

The Museum of Contemporary Art. Arata Isozaki, Architect.

Project Data: Museum of Contemporary Art

Location	East side of Grand Avenue between Second Street and Third Street California Plaza on Bunker Hill, Los Angeles
Projected Opening	Early 1986
Architects	Arata Isozaki, Tokyo, Japan, in association with Gruen Associates, Los Angeles
Consultants	John A. Martin & Associates, Structural Engineer Syska & Hennessy, Mechanical/Electrical Engineer Gage-Babcock & Associates, Fire Protection Jules Fisher & Paul Marantz, Inc., Lighting Bolt, Beranek & Newman, Acoustical and Audio-Visual G. E. Evans, Library ABM Security Consulting, Security Chermayeff, Geismar & Associates, Graphics
Contractor	HCB Contractors
Building Cost	$23 million
Gross Area	98,000 sq. ft. on 7 levels, consisting of galleries, auditorium, bookstore, sculpture court, staff offices and library, support services, and permanent collection storage. Building height ranges from 4 stories at its apex, to 18 ft. above street level or less, to a sunken courtyard area.

Breakdown of Interior Area			
	Galleries and Circulation	42,000 sq. ft.	
	Auditorium	7,000 sq. ft.	
	Bookstore	2,500 sq. ft.	
	Subtotal Public Area		51,500 sq. ft.
	Office and Library	11,500 sq. ft.	
	Service Area	35,000 sq. ft.	
	TOTAL AREA		98,000 sq. ft.

Exterior Features	Indian red sandstone walls, natural and honed finished at galleries; copper-clad, barrel-vaulted roof at library; copper-clad, pyramidal skylight base at gallery; painted aluminum panel and glass block walls at offices; granite paving and crystallized glass walls at entrance court.
Interior Features	1) 42,000 sq. ft. of galleries and circulation space. 2 of 7,300 sq. ft. with 18-foot to 20-foot ceiling and skylights. 1 of 2,000 sq. ft. with 23-foot ceiling and skylight (base of skylight is 45 ft. above the floor). 1 of 1,100 sq. ft. with 18-ft. ceiling and twin pyramidal skylights. 3 ranging in size from 1,500 sq. ft. to 4,200 sq. ft. with ceiling heights of 10 ft. to 15 ft. 6,000-sq.-ft. entrance court and lobby containing grand stair, cafe, information, membership, and sales desk. 2) 240-seat auditorium equipped for film and slide projection, closed-circuit television, lectures, and performance. 3) 2,500-square-foot bookstore on the plaza level, serving museumgoers and the general public. 4) Two levels of staff offices connected by an open stair and overlooking the galleries and other public areas. Library containing space for approximately 15,000 volumes, 30,000 slides, and 300 items in flat files. 5) Meeting room with barrel-vaulted ceiling and roof terrace. 6) Support services including secured off-street loading dock, photo studio, permanent collection storage, workshops, registrar's facility for control of incoming and outgoing art shipments, and mechanical, electrical, life safety, and security systems.

tan Life Insurance (one of the original candidates for the project), soon approached Cadillac Fairview (one of Bunker Hill Associates' principal partners) to investigate the potential for general partnership. In light of the difficult financial market, Cadillac Fairview decided to welcome Metropolitan Structures as a general partner, contingent upon its obtaining a satisfactory financial commitment for Phase I construction. In December 1982, Metropolitan Life Insurance's board voted to invest $190 million in California Plaza in return for having Metropolitan Structures named a general partner of Bunker Hill Associates, for only the initial commercial phase. By April 1983 negotiations between the agency and Bunker Hill Associates had produced an amendment to the development agreement that increased the ownership and managerial responsibilities of Metropolitan Structures. The phasing schedule was changed to allow greater flexibility, and the project was segmented into eight distinct phases that could be financed separately, although the agency retained approval of a developer-prepared master plan and of design plans for the entire project.

On May 18 the city council approved the amended development agreement. The groundbreaking for the museum and Phase I occurred on October 12, 1983—three years after Bunker Hill Associates had won the developer selection process.

The Museum/Bunker Hill Associates Agreement

On July 10, 1980, the Museum of Contemporary Art and Bunker Hill Associates had signed a contract outlining the expectations of each party, should Bunker Hill Associates be chosen by the redevelopment agency. The terms of that agreement were later incorporated into the development agreement between the agency and Bunker Hill Associates. The contract stipulates that:

1) The museum corporation will either possess fee title to the museum premises or sublease the premises at a rate of $1 per year for so long as the space is used as a museum.

2) During the first phase of construction, the developer will construct a fully finished museum, to be delivered to the museum

corporation on a turnkey basis (including all fixtures, built-in equipment, and floor and wall coverings).

3) The building will be freestanding and occupy at least 100,000 square feet of interior floor area.

4) The museum may select and engage its own architect, who will be responsible for the museum's design. Such selection will be made in consultation with Arthur Erickson, subject to the approval of the developer and the redevelopment agency.

5) The total museum cost will be $22.5 million in 1984 dollars. The developer has approved a building design that, as jointly estimated by the developer and museum, does not entail a financial liability to Bunker Hill Associates in excess of $19,324,000 including a contingency fund of $1.4 million. To the extent that Bunker Hill Associates' exposure is less than $19,324,000, the cost savings shall be paid by the developer to the museum.

[Points 6 and 7 promised the museum water, heat, and cooling at cost, and a free electronic security system.]

8) The developer will consult with the museum corporation on the design, construction, and management of exterior spaces and will make such spaces available on a nonexclusive basis, at no cost to the museum, for sculptural exhibitions and other appropriate uses.

9) The developer's obligation to construct the building and exterior improvements is subject to the condition that the museum corporation will have raised endowment funds of at least $10 million by July 1981.

By December 1980 a site on Grand Avenue for the museum had been set; in January 1981 the museum's design and architecture committee chose Japanese architect Arata Isozaki. By July 1982 Isozaki's second design for a building of pink Indian sandstone won approval from both the artists advisory council and the museum's trustees. When opened in early 1986, the museum will encompass approximately 98,000 square feet, with 50,000 for gallery space. It will include an auditorium, library, cafe, bookstore, staff offices, storage facilities, and a sculpture court integrated with the project's plazas.

Project Data: The Dance Gallery

Location	Fourth and Grand, Bunker Hill
Projected Opening	1987
Architects	Arthur Erickson Architects Newell Taylor Reynolds, associate architect acting as liaison between Erickson and the Dance Gallery
Consultant	Newell Taylor Reynolds

Building Cost		
	Land	$2,000,000
	Building	9,700,000
	Equipment	1,000,000
	Arch. Design, Permits, etc.	1,000,000
	Fundraising/Administration	1,000,000

Gross Area 72,284 sq. ft.

Breakdown of Interior Area (in sq. ft.)

	Institute	Theater	Shared	Total Floor Area
Below Stage	3,738	6,130		9,868
Stage/Founders *(library, conference, choreographer)		13,805	2,520*	16,325
Orchestra (excludes fly tower area, 4,465 sq. ft.)*	4,750	11,590		16,340*
Lower Balcony	4,486	7,004		11,490
Upper Balcony	4,100	8,260		12,360
Dance Court (*includes lobby, entrance overhand, mechanical)	768*	5,133		5,901
TOTAL	17,842	51,922	2,520	72,284

Exterior Features		
	Gridiron	3,600 sq. ft.
	Institute Roof	4,018 sq. ft.
	Fly Tower Roof	3,936 sq. ft.
	Dance Court & Entrance	4,871 sq. ft.
	Roof over Mechanical	2,438 sq. ft.
	Skylight & Roof over Lobby	2,695 sq. ft.
	Loading Dock Drive	1,200 sq. ft.

Interior Features	1,000-seat dance theater (650 at orchestra level, 350 in balcony) with resilient dance stage and full fly loft; proscenium stage with seats steeply raked. Library Four Studios Scene and Costume Shops Foyer/Exhibit Area

The museum board also approved the concept of an interim gallery, so that it could begin its programs before the California Plaza facility opened. In this way, the trustees planned for the museum to become a gradually functioning cultural institution and provided a clear focus for fundraising for ongoing exhibition and operating costs.

The fledgling museum rented from the city, at a cost of $1 per year, two single-story warehouses near Little Tokyo that had been used as repair shops for police vehicles. Frank O. Gehry designed a 55,000-square-foot "Temporary Contemporary," as it is called, at a cost of $1 million, raised from individuals, corporations, and foundations. It opened in November 1983 with a first exhibition called "The First Show: Painting and Sculpture from Eight Collections 1940–1980."

Lewitzky Secures a Dance Complex

The Lewitzky Foundation, having heard of attorney Fred Nicholas's success in working for the museum as a negotiator with Bunker Hill Associates and the agency, asked him if he would help the dance company as well. Nicholas agreed, and he helped conclude negotiations with the developer. Bunker Hill Associates agreed to donate a $2 million site, provided that the Lewitzky board raised $12 million total—$10 million for construction and another $2 million for its endowment. (This relatively low endowment goal was based on the expectation that, as in the past, 70 percent of the dance company's operating expenses could be met by earned income.) By June 1984, the Dance Gallery had raised $6.9 million. It anticipates groundbreaking in spring 1986 and completion 18 months thereafter. The Erickson office has served as the facility's architect. Newell Taylor Reynolds, Lewitzky's husband and a Los Angeles architect long associated with dance architecture, is an associate architect, responsible for the building's interior and acting as a liaison between the Dance Gallery and Erickson's staff.

When completed, the 70,000-square-foot Dance Gallery will be the first performance theater in the United States to be built specifically and solely for the needs of dance. Within the facility, the Andrew Norman Dance Theater (650 seats at the orchestra level, 350 in the balcony) will have a resilient stage and full fly loft. A proscenium theater, it will offer nearly 100 percent visibility and a balcony that can be shut off for a more intimate space.

Because the Dance Gallery will be more than a theater, it is expected to draw active daytime participants to California Plaza. Its institute will offer professional dance and choreography courses, dance and physical-fitness classes, and seminars in dance man-

agement, education, and costume, light, and set design. A library, "to document the undocumented Western dance tradition," will house an extensive collection of books, periodicals, articles, reviews, letters, costume sketches, films, and photographs. Scenery and costume shops and foyer exhibit areas, along with four rehearsal and student performance studios, will be included.

The gallery plans short, reasonably priced dance concerts at 5:05 p.m. to lure downtown workers, and informal dance performances in the outdoor performance area approximately six weeks each year. More than 200 performances by more than 75 local and touring dance companies are planned for 1987–88. Once California Plaza is completed, the residential density, working population, and nearby mass transit should guarantee the future stability of the Dance Gallery.

Management by the "Operator"

By early 1983 the museum and the Dance Gallery occupied firm niches in the California Plaza plans. Metropolitan Structures had joined the development team, and construction was scheduled to begin in September 1983. Now Bunker Hill Associates and the redevelopment agency turned their attention to the task of making sure that the parks, gardens, and plazas would be well used and maintained.

On August 23, 1983, a construction, operation, and reciprocal easement agreement was signed between the agency and Bunker Hill Associates. In addition to providing for such routine activities as common-area maintenance, repair, and utility easements, the agreement created a special nonprofit corporation called "the Operator." Financed by allocable tenant shares, the Operator would be responsible for the operation of the Angel's Flight funicular, the Angel's Flight museum, and the performance plaza.

The Operator will be responsible for securing quality retail and restaurant tenants, whose services will appeal to on-site office workers, residents, and visitors. It also will work to ensure that the museum operates in a "world-class manner, that its food, beverages, and shops do not conflict with other similar uses on the project site." Other provisions of the Operator agreement establish formulas by which a subsidy based on attendance is to be paid to the art museum by Bunker Hill Associates. The amount of the subsidy will be based on the annual patronage times an amount per patron, in the early years, followed by payment of three-fifths to three-quarters of 1 percent of the participation rent cash flow from the project once participation rent is due to the agency, depending on patronage. At that time, the operating subsidy will be further capped by the amount of the museum's deficit in any one year. The developer's exposure thus will run about $50,000–$100,000 per year from 1985 to 1990, and about $100,000–$200,000 per year through the middle to late 1990s.

In exchange for this subsidy—and to fulfill the intentions of integrating the museum into the mixed-use project—the museum will be given the opportunity each year to place artworks in the project's public areas. Its hours are required to coincide with the busy hours for shops and restaurants—from 11 a.m. to 9 p.m. The agreement also offers the prospect of a review panel that can be invoked to evaluate the museum's program, collections, and staff, should the museum fail to attain a position of international prominence.

The Operator will program and manage the outdoor performance plaza, located on the new bridge spanning Olive Street and containing audience seating and a stage that can accommodate a variety of performances. To ensure the liveliness of this facility, Bunker Hill Associates has engaged the services of programming and technical consultants. They have projected major events with controlled admission access, programs by lesser-known artists and amateurs, temporary exhibitions, and community functions ranging from fashion shows to film showings on an outdoor screen. The plaza will serve as a focal point for three indoor/outdoor restaurants and will be available for brown-bagging, casual meetings, and shaded and sunny sitting and people-watching. The operating costs of the performance plaza will be treated as part of the common area costs to be shared by all tenants.

Interior of "the Temporary Contemporary" facility before renovation, March 1983.

Exterior view at night of "the Temporary Contemporary."

While the presence of the performance plaza should increase the chances for California Plaza to become a downtown focal point, the project as a whole will be linked with the city through an additional network of plazas and terraces. These pedestrian centers will set restaurants and shops in an urban streetscape rather than a mall environment.

Construction Begins

Model of the Dance Gallery's interior.

Model of the proposed entry to the Dance Gallery.

The lobby/foyer area of the Dance Gallery, featuring an unconventional performing space for informal presentation and viewing.

Construction of California Plaza's Phase I office tower and art museum is well underway, with completion of the tower anticipated in fall 1985, and the museum in early 1986. The hotel, the Dance Gallery, the first of three apartment buildings, and retail development will begin in fall 1985, while plans for the second office building are still pending. Under the terms of the development agreement, subsequent commercial phases will commence when market conditions can support them and the developer has obtained a permanent financing commitment. The final residential phase (250 units) must commence no later than August 26, 1987. The Angel's Flight funicular and museum and a third office tower will be constructed in Phase III. A metro station (one of three downtown stations of the Los Angeles subway system) may play a role in the final stages of the project.

The overriding real estate factors making this partnership possible have been the long-term potentials of the site; the conveyance to the developer of approvals for phased construction in a regulatory environment in which approvals have become increasingly difficult to secure; and a flexible, realistic lease structure. These factors overcame the fact that the site was not in a fully established commercial location, and compensated for the heavy front-end burdens on the developer for the public-benefits package.

The redevelopment agency's objectives for downtown Los Angeles have also been important ingredients: it has advocated not only office buildings, hotels, shops, and restaurants, but also a range of arts and amenities that would create a true popular center. The agency therefore treated its arts partners as almost equal participants in the developer selection and negotiation phases. This full participation enabled first the museum and then the Lewitzky Foundation to generate enough contributions from corporate and individual donors to fulfill their capital needs for the project. Sheri Geldin, administrator of the Museum of Contemporary Art, underlines the significance of the Bunker Hill location for corporate giving:

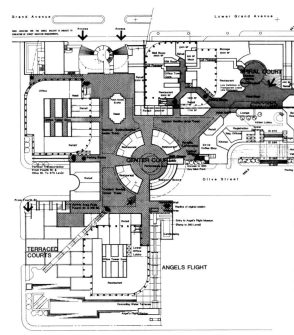

ARCO, Security Pacific, Times Mirror, and numerous other downtown companies made generous commitments to an as-yet nonexistent institution. Many did not even have a particular interest in contemporary art; yet they viewed the museum as a cultural drawing card in a section of the city that boasted very few such attractions apart from the Music Center. They may not have known a Rothko from a Rauschenberg, but they responded to the opportunity to enhance and enrich their community. Though initially reserved and largely adopting a cautious wait-and-see attitude, many corporations were persuaded to join us by the early and generous example set by [the first donors].

Los Angeles's corporations and philanthropists will have contributed well over $25 million to the museum and the Dance Gallery, plus persistent creative leadership and board support. This outpouring of support proved essential in convincing the agency and the developer that the cultural components could be genuine partners in the success of California Plaza.

The project offers a lesson in negotiation and planning. From the beginning the participants have had to make concessions and come to mutual agreements to achieve as a unit what no single partner could hope to accomplish alone. Although the process has been longer and more complicated than the negotiation process for MXDs of more limited scale, the redevelopment agency has set a model for other public agencies in continuing to play a critical role in the project after the developer was selected. By leasing the land rather than selling it outright, the agency ensured its oversight role in all programmatic and design aspects of the project, as well as its share in revenues derived from increased property values.

At California Plaza the agency also will have fulfilled other municipal priorities. New jobs will be created by California Plaza, and additional real estate tax revenues will be produced. A portion of this tax money will be used to help address social concerns such as the needs of nearby Skid Row. Another portion will go to build low- and moderate-income housing throughout the city. The future rental income will provide additional funds to assist in revitalization efforts elsewhere.

During the long negotiations, the agency nurtured a working relationship with the developer that permitted it to support the construction of Phase I of the project while the final operation and design of other parts of the project remained less specific. The emergence of this trusting, collaborative relationship between a public agency and a developer is noteworthy. Without it, the wide range of goals for the project could not be realized.

Most important, the museum, dance theater, outdoor performance plaza, shopping street, and open spaces have been designed to throng with people. California Plaza may, in fact, create the Rockefeller Center–style heart Los Angeles has so long desired.

South Coast Plaza and Town Center

Twenty years ago, South Coast Plaza was farmland bordering Costa Mesa, California. Today it serves as the center of a metropolitan area of 2.25 million people and the emerging hub of Orange County. This mixed-use development of just over 200 acres contains 2.2 million square feet of commercial office space, a 400-room Westin Hotel, a 1.7-million-square-foot retail center, the South Coast Repertory Theater, the nearly completed Orange County Performing Arts Center, parks, cinemas, and restaurants. It also includes a critically acclaimed Isamu Noguchi sculpture garden. The cost of the project's development between 1967 and 1984 has totaled more than $400 million, exclusive of land costs.

Developed under the guidance of C. J. Segerstrom & Sons with some joint venture partners, South Coast Plaza and Town Center are located at the juncture of two major freeways, with Los Angeles 40 miles to the north, San Diego 80 miles to the south, Newport Beach and the Pacific Ocean 5 miles away, and Disneyland 10 miles to the north.

The plaza is emerging as Orange County's most profitable and upscale retail center. When new department stores and retail businesses are added to the complex, it will offer nearly three million square feet of gross building area. A pervasive arts and entertainment presence attracts people who work and live near the area.

South Coast also lies at the heart of a larger geographic region that has been given the name "South Coast Metro" by an alliance of major developers that is promoting the area and working on a variety of issues such as traffic management and redesign of freeway entrances and exits. The consortium aims to provide the kind of coordinated urban planning that will give the region a stronger identity.

"It is important to recognize that in southern California Orange County has not had a recognizable focus," explains Henry T. Segerstrom, managing partner of C. J. Segerstrom & Sons. He is confident that South Coast Metro is becoming that focus. In this sense, South Coast Plaza is reversing the usual process of mixed-use developments: Rather than locating in the midst of a city with an existing central focus, Segerstrom and other developers are creating an urban focus around their MXD.

South Coast Plaza represents a deliberate effort on the part of a private developer to provide art and cultural amenities as major components in a mixed-use setting and metropolitan area center. As the county has evolved from a suburban bedroom community to a cohesive metropolitan area in which work and residence have been integrated, its increasingly affluent and highly educated families now welcome the arts and other urban amenities.

Orange County Moves from Rural to Suburban to Urban in Thirty Years

In 1950 the population of Orange County was 200,000. By 1980 it had reached nearly two million and was still growing. Located south of Los Angeles County, the 786-square-mile county today has 26 incorporated cities, its own airport, a median family income close to $40,000, a regional economy of $55 billion, aerospace and electronics corporate headquarters, major league baseball and football teams, and several art museums.

A critical factor in southern Orange County's growth over the past 15 years has been the San Diego Freeway, completed in 1968, which extends the length of the county and connects Los Angeles with San Diego. In Costa Mesa, with a population of 86,000, the San Diego Freeway crosses the Costa Mesa Freeway, which runs from Newport Beach on the southern coast to Orange and other communities in the northern part of the county. Here, on the northern boundary of Costa Mesa, the Segerstrom family began lima bean farming at the turn of the century.

Their fortunes and those of Costa Mesa were suddenly changed in December 1962 when Sears, Roebuck & Company came to the Segerstrom family to discuss acquiring land on which to build a Sears store adjacent to the proposed San Diego Freeway. At the suggestion of a Los Angeles architect, Sears approached Henry Segerstrom, grandson of the original settlers, who had combined his family's appreciation for the land with the business acumen of a Stanford MBA. In a short time, the May Company joined the negotiations and proposed a shopping center center. The Segerstroms enlisted architect Victor Gruen of Gruen Associates and the real estate consulting firms of Larry Smith & Company and Wimar Realty Development Company in designing a 1.2-million-square-foot shopping center with the May Company at one end and Sears at the other. Thus C. J. Segerstrom & Sons, at one time the largest independent producers of lima beans in the nation, began a new venture as shopping center developers, and by the time the San Diego Freeway opened in 1968, South Coast Plaza had been operating for a year.

The plaza was immediately successful for three reasons: its location was superb; it was the area's first enclosed mall; and it opened after an extensive, year-long promotional program. It was not, however, the only formerly rural area under development in Orange County. In Newport Beach, the Irvine Company was planning and building Newport Center, which was to include the Fashion Island shopping center and office buildings on part of an 86,000-acre Irvine Ranch property. Newport Center was vigorously promoted as the new financial center for Orange County. But a limited-growth community sentiment in Newport Beach and a restricted market area thwarted the Irvine Company's dream of creating the county's prime office and retail center. Robert E. Witherspoon and his colleagues observed in *Mixed-Use Developments: New Ways of Land Use* that Newport

The South Coast area, looking north toward Los Angeles. The major intersection in the foreground joins the San Diego Freeway (running north–south) and the Costa Mesa Freeway (running east–west). South Coast Plaza and Town Center appear in the foreground.

The Arts Operate Out of Station Wagons and High School Auditoriums

The South Coast Repertory Theater was already an arts presence in southern Orange County when South Coast Plaza was being planned in the early sixties. However, this 12-member touring group had few financial resources. Led by two idealistic and talented directors, David Emmes and Martin Benson, it operated out of a station wagon. A year later, the group found its first stationary home—a converted store among the canneries on the Newport Beach waterfront. The dressing room was located in an apartment over the 75-seat theater, and actors reached the stage via an outside staircase—a problem on rainy nights. The audiences did not seem to mind. Cecil Smith, *Los Angeles Times* theater critic, wrote:

A couple of weeks ago we came out of a ramshackle little theater in Newport Beach and the air had the fresh, fishy smell of the sea in it and there was tackle piled on a rotting dock and some small fishing boats moored beyond and the stars were incredibly bright. My wife gave a long, low whistle. "I was thinking," she said, "of those seven Broadway plays we saw in New York in six days—and not one compares with this."

South Coast Plaza's Jewel Court is located at the apex of this 2.1-million-square-foot retail center.

Center lacked physical integration. Its office buildings sprawled over a nine-block area, ringing the open shopping mall. Its distances were great, and cars were necessary to travel between most buildings.

The city of Newport Beach stalled the Irvine Company's plans for further expansion, and the Newport Center office district lost momentum. According to a *Los Angeles Times* report, the Irvine Company's plans began to slow down just as Segerstrom's began to accelerate:

Five months after the groundbreaking for Town Center's first phase, the Newport Beach city council rejected Prudential's plan for a hotel and 16-story office tower on land to be purchased from the Irvine Company in Newport Center. With that action, virtually all Newport Center development ground to a halt—and one of Segerstrom's biggest obstacles vanished.

Mrs. Smith's "this" was Harold Pinter's *The Birthday Party,* one of four plays South Coast Repertory produced that season.

By 1967 the company had outgrown its 75 seats and moved to Costa Mesa, two miles inland. Its new home was a 190-seat former variety store. In this location, South Coast Repertory received its first Los Angeles Drama Critics Circle Award in 1971, and the Rockefeller Foundation and National Endowment for the Arts began to underwrite partial production costs.

By its tenth anniversary in 1975, South Coast Repertory boasted a $250,000 operating budget, 4,000 subscribers, and an average 92 percent attendance. It had developed a Living Theater Project, inviting Orange County schoolchildren to live productions, and it maintained an ongoing theater workshop for adults. Equally important, South Coast Repertory had assembled a board of trustees including Orange County community leaders who began fundraising to help bridge the gap between

Charles Perry's sculpture, *The Ram*, stands guard between Town Center Park and the Imperial Bank Building.

the theater's earned income and its operating expenses. But also, ten years after its first theater opened, South Coast Repertory knew it was time to move once again.

The Orange County Performing Arts Center

In 1973 a countywide organization was formed to plan, build, operate, and endow a regional performing arts center that could present world-class professional companies and artists as well as local performing groups. Nineteen sites were considered in several county locations. Fullerton, the city of Orange, Santa Ana, Newport Beach, and the University of California at Irvine were discussed as possibilities and rejected for various reasons.

Before the mid-seventies, no cultural organization in Orange County attempted raising millions of dollars at any one time. The Orange County Philharmonic Society, formed in 1954, performed in the Santa Ana High School auditorium or in a multi-purpose gymnasium at the University of California's Irvine campus. Ballet Pacifica performed *The Nutcracker* at high school auditoriums and college theaters. The Orange County Master Chorale used local churches, hotels, and shopping centers for its concerts.

Yet Orange County wanted a major cultural and entertainment presence. A *Los Angeles Times* poll found that, in the absence of adequate facilities, only 16 percent of the county's residents would visit a local museum and only 28 percent would attend a live performance. The *Times* concluded:

In general . . . the survey suggested that if there is an area of daily life that Orange County residents think is lacking locally, it would be entertainment, particularly live entertainment.

The Developer Adds Office Buildings, a Hotel, and Park to Complement Retail Business

Once their initial retail components in South Coast Plaza were completed and successful, the Segerstrom family asked their architects, Gruen Associates, to prepare a master plan for the remaining property they owned adjacent to the mall. "The proposal was imaginative, but at the time we could not implement it because the market wasn't strong enough to support the plan," says Henry Segerstrom:

It was more a dream and a forecast than it was a pragmatic program of development. But we accepted the plan and it guided us in making leases with several institutions: banks and a savings and loan and a movie theater. Those buildings followed the opening of South Coast Plaza within two or three years and they became the beginnings of South Coast Plaza Town Center.

In 1968 C. J. Segerstrom & Sons began negotiating for a hotel. Five years later, Westin Hotels agreed to construct a 400-room hotel on the Town Center side of the retail complex, developed in joint venture with Connecticut General Life Insurance Company. Skidmore, Owings & Merrill were chosen as architects. The 17-story hotel, which opened in 1975, was oriented away from the street, to create both a feeling of seclusion and a "sense of arrival."

To assemble the hotel site, it was necessary for Segerstrom to construct a $3 million underground culvert for a flood control channel that bisected the property. The covered channel influenced the configuration of a park Segerstrom had chosen to create in front of the hotel, because the culvert surface could take only a limited weight-bearing load. Eventually a road, Park Center Drive, was placed over part of the culvert, tennis courts over another section, and the park over the rest. Peter Walker, then with the landscape design firm of SWA, planned the three-acre park. Earth fill was brought in to create a series of 12-foot mounds with lawns, trees, and pathways. In certain areas, the landscaped mounds were formed with polystyrene plastic, rather than dirt, to lessen the weight on an underground loading dock. According to Segerstrom:

Now an interesting thing happened. In constructing the park, we wanted to have mounding . . . to give perspective from the hotel entrance. But we had to limit the amount of fill we could put on the flood control channel. So the decision was made to plan some heavy mounding on the other side of the channel to give us the visual focus we desired. The construction of the park commenced and one of our [C. J. Segerstrom & Sons] people was in charge of building these mounds. I went on a vacation at this time, and when I came back, they had gone substantially beyond the flood control channel with the fill, which was not anticipated. Construction had taken some of the land that we really hadn't intended to put in the park. Placing the fill had created an isolated piece of land beyond the flood control channel.

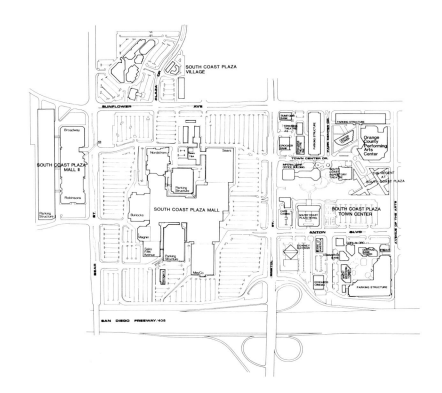

This site was too small for another office building, yet to redo the mounding in the park would be an expensive solution. With Segerstrom land now valued by the square foot rather than by the acre, a perplexing problem had been created.

The isolated-site problem remained unresolved as C. J. Segerstrom & Sons responded to other opportunities in their growing mixed-use development. While visiting cities abroad, Henry Segerstrom observed that a key ingredient that characterized successful urban centers was cultural activity. He decided that South Coast Plaza would be a major metropolitan development only if public art and amenities were included.

Thus the Westin Hotel, the office buildings, and the park became sites for the beginning of South Coast Plaza's art collection. Segerstrom personally chose the artists and works, beginning in the late seventies with Charles Perry's *The Ram,* a 20-foot, 7-ton steel sculpture, painted brilliant yellow. *The Ram* was placed between Town Center park and the Imperial Bank building. A second large sculptural work, Jim Huntington's *Night Shift,* a 10-foot-by-9-foot Sierra white granite rock split by a stainless steel plate, was installed in the park between the Imperial Bank and the Westin Hotel. An Alexander Calder mobile, *Pekin,* found a home in an office building in Town Center, and Jean Dubuffet's *Tour aux Jambes,* an epoxy and polyurethane

Site plan for South Coast Plaza and Town Center.

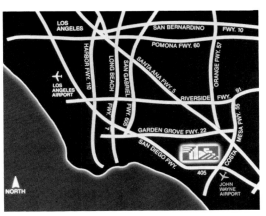

sculpture, became a focal point in the lobby of another.

The developer was working toward the goal of creating an environment that was warm and welcoming. According to Segerstrom, "It was becoming apparent that the pleasant sense of a pedestrian environment was taking precedence over the traditional dominance of the automobile. The Town Center became a place where people wanted to walk and to linger. Sculpture had a humanizing effect on architecture."

South Coast Metro is bordered by the San Diego, Costa Mesa, and Garden Grove freeways. The city of Costa Mesa lies to the east of the South Coast area.

Land Gifts Become Catalysts for Arts Facilities

In 1975 two members of the South Coast Repertory's board of trustees, Tom Peckenpaugh and Herb Kendall, approached Henry Segerstrom with a bold request. Would the Segerstrom family donate land so that South Coast Repertory could build a new theater in the South Coast Plaza and Town Center area? As Segerstrom recalls:

It was something we had never been involved in, nor had we originally had it as part of our plan to have a live theater here. For one thing, live theater is not always available in emerging metropolitan areas and the chance to locate a repertory theater in the Town Center Park became a unique opportunity.

Because South Coast Repertory was successful and had broad-based community support, Segerstrom took the request to his family, where all such decisions were made collectively. They elected to give South Coast Repertory the acre of land that had been isolated by the over-zealous mounder of Town Center Park. The Segerstroms also provided parking facilities and pledged a cash gift of $50,000 to start planning a new building. The family's gift became the catalyst for a building campaign for the new theater. A fundraising feasibility study indicated that perhaps $1.5 million could be raised to build the theater.

In a first concept, the South Coast Repertory projected a facility that would seat 350 people and cost about $1 million. Further

planning determined that 350 seats were not sufficient to cover the costs of operating the theater. Following a programming recommendation by the National Endowment for the Arts, the theater decided to design and build a 507-seat performance space and a smaller 161-seat experimental theater in a single building.

While these early planning studies got underway, new board members were recruited with expertise in construction, development, and technical matters. Simultaneously, a fundraising committee began to solicit contributions on a countywide basis. The county of Orange gave $250,000 from its revenue-sharing reserves and the city of Costa Mesa matched that with an additional $250,000. The firm of Ladd, Kelsey & Woodard was chosen as architects.

Two auditoriums totaling 28,000 square feet were to be provided in the new theater. The larger auditorium (507 seats) would feature a modified thrust stage, fly gallery and facilities for set construction, wardrobe and dressing rooms, green room, and administrative offices. The second auditorium, with 161 seats, would offer a platform stage surrounded by seating on three sides.

As the design for the playhouse evolved, the board increased the fundraising goal until the figure reached $3.5 million—a total well beyond any previous arts group's campaign in Orange County. The drive proved successful, however, and in November 1978 the South Coast Repertory Theater opened.

South Coast Repertory helped to establish the plaza as more than a place to shop and to work. Rather than heading for the freeways at 5 p.m., workers found there was now a reason to stay into the evening— live, high-quality drama. Restaurants began to serve theater patrons and hotel guests in the evening. Meanwhile, C. J. Segerstrom & Sons continued to expand the mall to include high-fashion retail stores and an additional 200,000 square feet of boutiques. Specialty retail included Saks Fifth Avenue, Nordstroms, and I. Magnin. Across a city boundary to the north in Santa Ana, the Segerstroms opened a 160,000-square-foot specialty theme center, South Coast Plaza Village, in 1973.

Town Center Park, looking past mounding to South Coast Plaza on the right. Jim Huntington's sculpture, *Night Shift*, sits in the foreground.

Between 1972 and 1982, 1.7 million square feet of commercial office space was built in South Coast Plaza Town Center, representing an estimated investment of $140 million in office buildings alone. Some of the new space was constructed in joint venture with the Prudential Life Insurance Company of America. Tenants, wooed by the urban feeling of Town Center, included branches of national accounting firms and several prominent law firms. To accommodate this rapid growth, several of the smaller buildings in Town Center, which were less than ten years old, were demolished. Combining a cultural facility with retail and commercial growth and striking sculpture and landscaping had established South Coast Plaza as the county's premier professional office center.

In early 1979, after several years of fruitless searching for an appropriate location for a countywide performing arts center, Jim Nagamatsu and Elaine Redfield, chairman and president of the Orange County Performing Arts Center's board of directors, requested the Segerstrom family to consider a donation: a prime, five-acre parcel of land at the edge of Town Center. Henry Segerstrom recalls the family's response:

Our family has been part of this community for nearly 90 years. The request presented an opportunity for us to make a contribution of lasting value, representing our family over several generations, and it was significant for the future of Orange County. It was something which obviously would coalesce cultural groups and would establish a central focal point in a metropolitan area, causing it to be an attractive "people place."

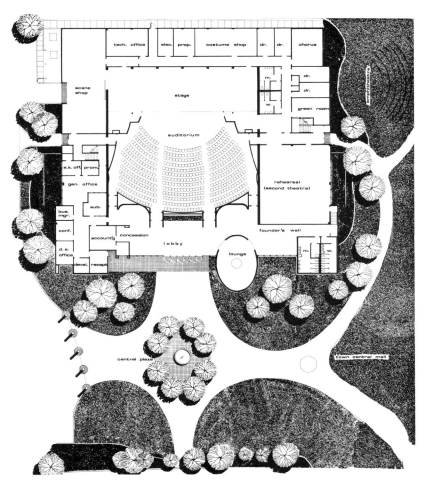

This plan shows South Coast Repertory Theater's interior design, as well as an outside amphitheater used for children's productions in the summer.

The family therefore agreed. In addition, remembering the difference a large cash gift had made for launching the South Coast Repertory's fundraising campaign, the Segerstroms pledged $1 million in cash toward a building fund.

The Segerstrom family believed that an arts center and the fundraising campaign to build it could unite disparate geographic, social, and business forces in Orange County; permanently boost the region's level of philanthropy; and help the arts—and South Coast Plaza—establish a position of prominence in the county's consciousness.

The South Coast Repertory Theater houses two theaters, rehearsal halls, acting conservatory facilities, dressing rooms, scenery and costume shops, and administrative offices.

The Developer, "Entertainment Entrepreneurs," and an Artist Create Space for the Arts

During the campaign for South Coast Repertory Theater, pledges had not always materialized at the time funds were needed for construction. Interest rates also had climbed during the building phase, and short-term borrowing to cover resulting construction costs amounted to an $800,000 loan over and above the $3.5 million eventually raised. That loan was finally retired in 1984. South Coast Repertory fundraisers believe they should have set their sights even higher and raised $4 million for the theater to avoid this additional burden. Also, neither staff nor board members foresaw how much more it would cost to operate a 507-seat theater than South Coast Repertory's previous 190-seat house. Looking back, they concluded that an endowment fund should have been included in the initial campaign. Many of those same fundraisers, later called "entertainment entrepreneurs" by the *Los Angeles Times,* remembered these two lessons when they were given a second opportunity to raise arts dollars.

The Performing Arts Center board commissioned Gary W. Phillips & Associates, a Los Angeles development consulting firm, to study the need, conceptual design, estimated costs, and funding potential for the Orange County Performing Arts Center. Phillips's principal findings were:

The Need. In Orange County there are no theater facilities with sufficient size, acoustical quality, staging accommodations, and accessibility to host international major performing artists and companies. This absence of facilities is further identified as the single most serious constraint to the growth and enhancement of the local performing arts organizations.

Attract Major Artists. The center would attract national and international artists and performing companies by providing the opportunity to expand their audiences in the western United States.

A Two-Theater Complex. A facility with a main theater of approximately 3,000 seats and a second theater with approximately 1,000 seats would best serve the documented needs of audiences and performing groups.

The Site. The site is geographically central for residents of the entire county, is easily accessible by major freeways, and is enhanced by the proximity of fine restaurants, shopping centers, hotels, and the South Coast Repertory Theater.

Funding Potential. In early samplings of more than 300 potential major donors, 75 percent stated that the project should be undertaken and further indicated they would make a financial contribution.

Box Office Support. Cultural interest and population would be more than sufficient to provide the necessary audience for the center.

Economic Stimulus. In addition to creating, both directly and indirectly, up to 2,500 new jobs, the center could generate local taxes of up to $150,000 annually and expend up to $2 million a year into the local economy.

Educational Value. The center's programming would help stimulate the eduational aspects of the performing arts in classrooms throughout the county, and provide new opportunities for people of all ages to enjoy the arts.

Community Pride. This multimillion-dollar project, the largest volunteer effort ever undertaken in Orange County, would unite the 26 communities toward a single goal, create a new spirit of volunteerism, and engender an increased sense of pride in the county.

The capital campaign was set first at $40 million, based on preliminary architectural concepts using comparable per-seat costs. Later that figure rose to $65.5 million. A separate endowment campaign aimed for $20 million.

A group of prominent businessmen and civic leaders joined forces as the arts center's trustees under the chairmanship of Henry Segerstrom. Several guidelines were set forth. The group was advised that it should not proceed unless it could raise $10 million in six months among the trustees themselves. It raised more than $12 million, resulting from an additional gift of $5 million from the Segerstrom family, $2 million from the Fluor Foundation, $2 million from Mr. and Mrs. James Bentley, $1 million from Mr. and Mrs. James K. Nagamatsu, $1 million from the Hoag Foundation, and two anonymous gifts of $500,000 each.

With these large financial commitments and its strong leadership, the board decided neither to solicit nor to accept public funds but to raise the capital and endowment dollars entirely from private funds and contributions. *Variety* called this action "bizarre," but board members found it to be an important motivating factor in attracting major gifts. According to Segerstrom:

People said "That's a wonderful way to go. They're not going to use tax dollars, and instead of giving $100,000, we'll give $300,000." I think everybody sensed that if we were going to accomplish our goal in a timely manner and do it the way we wanted to do it, we had to be independent.

In Orange County, where self-reliance and individualism remain proud traditions, the fundraisers hit a responsive chord. Major new contributions included $3 million from the Irvine Foundation, $3 million from the Harry C. Steele Foundation, $1 million from the Times Mirror Foundation, and $750,000 from the Freedom Newspapers.

This strategy did not mean that local government was uninvolved. The City of Costa Mesa helped in four ways:

1) It approved guaranteed tax-exempt bonds to finance a parking structure to serve the center.

2) It participated in relocating a major street to give the center a strong visual identity.

3) It waived building fees that would have added to planning and construction costs.

4) It allowed the square footage for the center to be exempted from the total square footage authorized for South Coast Plaza Town Center.

Meanwhile, once larger private gifts had been donated, additional community leaders were approached for donations in the $50,000 and over range. Next, the board organized an areawide campaign using 300 volunteers to solicit 2,000 potential donors throughout the county. Finally, a public campaign was planned for the spring of 1986, shortly before the arts center's opening. This campaign will use the media to inform the general public about the center, thus giving all the citizens of the area an opportunity to participate in its funding and alerting them to its imminent opening.

As of early 1985, $45 million of the $65.5 million capital campaign had been raised in addition to the site contribution, and $17 million of the $20 million endowment campaign had been pledged. Several factors contributed to the success of this fundraising effort:

■ The prestige of the project has made it attractive to potential donors. The fact that this will be Orange County's *own* performing arts center is a source of pride for county residents.

■ Because there have been few major fundraising campaigns in Orange County and none on this scale, the leadership was willing to accept the challenge.

■ Timing was fortuitous. Solicitation of major gifts began prior to the 1981–82 recession. The public campaign should benefit from the results of the recovery of 1984–85.

Bricks and Mortar

By 1981 the time had come to select an architect and hire a staff for the arts center. After an extensive search, the Houston firm of Caudill Rowlett Scott was selected, in joint venture with the local Blurock Partnership of Newport Beach. Caudill Rowlett Scott had designed performing arts centers in Houston and in Louisville.

Simultaneously, on the advice of experienced professionals, the board hired an accoustical design team that included A. Harold Marshall of Auckland, New Zealand. Marshall, a professor of acoustical engineering, has developed a new theory of acoustics based on "early lateral reflection of sound." The center's main hall has been designed to his specifications.

In March 1981 the board added an executive director, Len Bedsow, to its growing team of experts. Bedsow had served as general manager of the Los Angeles Civic Light Opera for 17 years. He had to be persuaded to forgo plans for early retirement, and he told the *Los Angeles Times:*

I said to these people, "Why are you doing this? Why are you taking on this monster? You have no idea what you are getting into." Well, they said they did, and I asked again, "Well, why?" expecting to hear, "Our purpose is to uplift the cultural level of the community." That sort of thing. That would have been the end of the discussion. But what they said was, "We want a fa-

South Coast Plaza
Project Data

Physical Configuration Component—Income Generating	Completed as of 1984	Profile at Build-Out (1987)
Office	1,700,000 sq. ft.	2,200,000 sq. ft.
Retail	1,860,000 sq. ft.	2,700,000 sq. ft.
Hotel	375,000 sq. ft. (405 rooms)	743,000 sq. ft. (745 rooms)
Cinemas (two locations)	47,120 sq. ft.	
Component—Arts/Culture/ Open Space		
South Coast Repertory		
Main Stage	507 seats	
Second Stage	161 seats	
Orange County Performing Arts Center		
Main Theater		3,000 seats
Small Theater		1,000 seats
Black Box Theater		300 seats
Noguchi Sculpture Garden	1.6 acres	
Town Center Park	3.0 acres	
Other		
Parking	6,432 spaces	
Acreage	200+ acres	
Gross Building Area	4,339,640 sq. ft.	5,034,640 sq. ft.
Floor/Area Ratio	61	65
Location	Costa Mesa, Calif.	
Master Developer	C. J. Segerstrom & Sons	
Development Period	1967–87	
Estimated Total Development Costs	In excess of $400,000,000 (exclusive of land costs)	

cility here of world-class quality that will bring to us the events we want to see, here in our community. We don't want to drive 100 miles round-trip to the L.A. Music Center." I said, "That's a reason for building this." Now, the natural result of that will be an uplifting of the community. But the *reason* for raising all this money and doing all this work is that they want world-class attractions here.

Thus, by the end of 1981, an advisory group knowledgeable in fundraising and building construction had been assembled and an architectural team was at work with input from acousticians, a theater director, and consultants. Plans were finalized, fundraising continued, and in the summer of 1983, the Orange County Performing Arts Center broke ground.

Noguchi's Space
In 1980, across Anton Boulevard and south of the South Coast Repertory Theater and the future site of the arts center, C. J. Segerstrom & Sons, together with the Pru-

dential Insurance Company, began to erect twin office towers. The two 266,200-square-foot buildings would be coupled with an L-shaped, above-ground parking structure. Into a 1.6-acre open space, created and surrounded by these structures, Segerstrom wished to place a park:

I thought there were some elements it should have. It should be a wonderful people place. It should have a certain amount of green and landscaping. It should have plenty of seating for people, and it should be a magnetic kind of development that would attract people not only from the immediate site, but also from great distances.

With these ideas in mind, the developer was attracted to artist Isamu Noguchi's work. He met with Noguchi and described the space between the parking structure and the two office buildings. Initially, Noguchi was not interested in the project, but Segerstrom persisted in his attempt to work with him.

A few months later, Noguchi came to Costa Mesa, looked at the area, and decided to create a design for the open space. Four months later, Noguchi returned with a model for the garden. Segerstrom recalls:

He brought with him a small valise and a board about 24 inches by 24 inches. He had several maquettes of each element of his garden. He put it all together and then said, "Now, this is an abstract representation of the geology and geography of the state of California." Then he described how the forms would work together. I just loved it. I told him, "I think it's absolutely perfect." He was very delighted. I felt that it was a great achievement and that Isamu Noguchi would create an exemplary garden here because it was his first commission in the state where he was born. He had been educated in Indiana and New York, studied in Paris with Brancusi, and had done the UNESCO gardens. He had done work all over the world but never in California, so it was very important to him.

Besides the garden design, Noguchi also created a sculpture for *California Scenario,* as the garden was named. Originally the work was titled *Source of Life.* It was created in Takamatsu, Japan, using decomposed granite boulders. While the sculpture garden was under construction, Noguchi changed the name of this work to *The Spirit of the Lima Bean.* Segerstrom explains:

At first I thought he was teasing me because, of course, our family had farmed lima beans on that land for over 50 years. As it turned out it was a recognition of the land and its use. I think he changed the name out of respect for our friendship and our ability to work together.

The garden's two fountains, wildflowers, forest and desert plantings, sculptures, meandering stream, and benches all were assembled from natural materials—granites, sandstone, and native plants. On two sides of *California Scenario,* the office building lobbies open onto the garden. On the other two sides, high, stark white walls enclose the parking structures. These walls were plastered to reflect the California sun by day, and moonglow and reflected artificial light at night.

The experience of creating *California Scenario* proved memorable for Noguchi. It benefited from a positive and productive relationship with a patron who understood his artistic vision. Noguchi described this way of working together in a November 1984 letter to one of the Town Center's architects:

It all started with a suggestion that I might design something, possibly a fountain for the wooded area where the earth was to cover the garage walls facing two glass office buildings.

That Henry Segerstrom went along with its transformation into what is there now attests to his immediate response to my own proposal for something entirely different: For a cubic volume of clear California air, not earth. The revealed beauty of garage walls. A sculpture of great proportion to give weight and meaning. *The Spirit of the Lima Bean* gives continuity to the history of the spot, its previous use, a sense of time and place. Water flow directs us from one awareness to another, from *Water Source* to *Water Use.* The *Fountain* becomes energy. Redwood trees become sculpture. Memory recognizes *Land Use,* a passage of life and a testament to those who made America.

Isamu Noguchi's sculpture garden, *California Scenario*, in South Coast Town Center, features six major elements representing the state's environment. Three are shown: in the left foreground is *Desert Land*; behind is *Water Source*; in the right background is *Land Use*.

Noguchi's *California Scenario* includes *The Spirit of the Lima Bean*. Made of Japanese granite, the sculpture pays homage to the former agricultural use of the South Coast Plaza and Town Center area.
Credit: Ron Hummer

Project Data: Orange County Performing Arts Center

Location	Costa Mesa, Calif.
Projected Opening	October 1986 for main 3,000-seat theater; one year later for 1,000-seat theater
Architects	Caudill, Rowlett, Scott of Houston The Blurock Partnership of Newport Beach, Calif.
Consultants	Theater—John von Szeliski; Len Bedsow Acoustics—Paoletti/Lewitz Associates; Jerald R. Hyde; A. Harold Marshall Structural Engineering—Martin Tranbarger Mechanical Engineering—Nack & Sunderland Electrical Engineering—Frederick Brown Associates
Contractor	C. L. Peck, Inc.
Building Cost	$65.5 million
Gross Area	250,000 sq. ft.

Breakdown of Interior Area

Main Theater

	Grid Height	110 ft. with 90 rigging lines available
	Proscenium Height	30 ft. adjustable to 42 ft.
	Proscenium Width	52 ft. adjustable to 68 ft.
	Stage Depth from Apron	65 ft.
	Stage Width	129 ft.
	Orchestra Length (apron to back wall)	115 ft. at deepest section (asymmetrical configuration)
	Max. Orchestra Height	15 ft. below stage to stage level
	Max. Orchestra Width	65 ft.
	Dressing Rooms	5 star plus 5 two-person and 5 chorus dressing rooms
	Pit	2 pits: one holds 35; the other up to 120
	Seating	3,000; Orchestra: 1,260; 1st Tier: 660; 1st Balcony: 480; 2nd Balcony: 600; in an asymmetrical configuration
Small Theater	Seating	1,000 seats. Orchestra: 600; Mezzanine: 400
Black Box Theater	Seating	Up to 300 non-fixed; flexible format seating.

Exterior Features	Front of theater features a heroic arch grand portal. Arrivals garden allows easy access from street level to plaza level for pedestrians or handicapped. Convenient carriage circle for passenger drop-off area under the grand portal. Indoor–outdoor lobbies allow patrons to step out onto exterior balconies on each level.
Interior Features	Main Theater: Both orchestra pits on elevators that come up to stage level, which in effect extends the stage into the auditorium for symphony concerts. Symphony shell breaks down for storage. Four technical offices, two visiting company offices, two large musicians' changing rooms. Main rehearsal room (doubles as black box theater) that is larger than acting area onstage, plus three smaller rehearsal rooms approximately 1,400 sq. ft. each, all equipped with cushioned dance floors and mirrors.

Town Center Business, Arts, and Open Space Complement Plaza Retail

South Coast Plaza Mall and South Coast Plaza Village, across the street from one another, have become vital retail centers, bustling with shoppers from early in the morning until late at night. Nearby Town Center features quite different uses on its 65 acres. *California Scenario* offers a contemplative space enclosed by two office towers and parking structures. Town Center Park is a garden spot one encounters while walking from meeting to meeting during the business day.

The South Coast Repertory Theater sits on the edge of the park, and the Performing Arts Center is being constructed adjacent to the Avenue of the Arts across from the theater. Next to the arts center, at the end of the Avenue of the Arts, will be a planned 340-room luxury hotel, the Regent of South Coast Plaza, designed by I. M. Pei. On the other side of the arts center looms a new 21-story, 464,000-square-foot office tower, Center Tower, the county's largest and tallest office building to date. Center Tower was designed by Caudill Rowlett Scott, the same firm that has designed the arts center. The two buildings were carefully coordinated visually and functionally, so that circulation will flow smoothly between the two structures. Besides sharing an adjacent 1,200-car parking garage, the two buildings will share common sculptural gardens, designed by Peter Walker.

The parking structure was built by a privately owned partnership, Center Tower Associates. Thus the arts center was not required to provide capital investment in the parking structure. The city of Costa Mesa agreed that tax-exempt bonds could be used to finance the structure if a private guarantor for the bonds could be found. C. J. Segerstrom & Sons provided that financial guarantee. The garage will be used by the occupants of Center Tower during the day and by arts center patrons in the evening. All users will contribute toward paying for the structure.

Center Tower and the parking structure will be completed in July 1985. The arts center itself is scheduled to open in October 1986; its board believes the area should be occupied and functioning smoothly before it opens. The new hotel is projected to open in April 1987.

In the middle of Town Center Drive, between South Coast Repertory and the arts center, will lie an open plaza. C. J. Segerstrom & Sons anticipates creating a unified management and assessment plan for this area, and it is examining prototypes from the Dallas Arts District, Bunker Hill in Los Angeles, and Tulsa's central pedestrian system, where two main streets have been closed off and made into a mall. The developer is studying these models to determine how best to:

■ amend and upgrade the improvements in the street right-of-way;

■ integrate the street with the surrounding uses, creating a common plaza area;

■ provide for common management and maintenance of the plaza area; and

■ provide for the allocation of the costs of management and maintenance among the parties.

Inside the arts center patrons will find theaters of state-of-the-art design. The facility will include a 3,000-seat multipurpose hall suitable for the performance of full-scale opera, ballet, symphony, and musical productions. It will have an adjustable proscenium arch, and its asymmetrical design should provide near-perfect acoustics. A second theater of 1,000 seats will be able to be reduced to 600 seats by closing off the 400-seat mezzanine. A "black box" rehearsal hall—30 percent larger than the rehearsal space at the Los Angeles Music Center—also will be provided. This space also can be used as a 300-seat theater or as a television studio. The 1,000-seat theater is scheduled to open approximately eighteen months after the major hall is completed; it will be used by the nearly 250 local performing arts groups in Orange County.

Project Data: South Coast Arts Components

Project	**South Coast Repertory Theater**
Location	Costa Mesa, Calif.
Completed	November 1978 (main stage) November 1979 (second stage)
Architect	Steward Woodard of Ladd, Kelsey, Woodard, Newport Beach, Calif.
Contractor	C. L. Peck, Inc.
Building Cost	$3.5 million
Gross Area	28,000 sq. ft.

Breakdown of Interior Area
Mainstage Auditorium
507 seats
Modified thrust stage with fly gallery
Facilities for set construction, wardrobe, dressing rooms, green room, and administrative offices
Second Stage Auditorium
161 seats
Platform stage surrounded on three sides by seating

Exterior Features	A natural amphitheater used for children's theater productions in the summer

Project	**Laguna Museum of Art Storefront Museum**
Location	South Coast Plaza, Costa Mesa, Calif.
Completed	November 1984
Architects	Interior by Paddock & Flair, Architects
Contractor	Renovation of store interior by Equidon Companies
Building Cost	Renovation work donated at cost; architectural services donated; rent is free for one year
Gross Area	3,000 sq. ft.
Breakdown of Interior Area	1,800 sq. ft. exhibition space (two galleries) 1,200 sq. ft. reception, bookstore, office, lavatories
Exterior Features	Museum is located on the ground-floor level in South Coast Plaza retail center

Project	**California Scenario**
Location	Costa Mesa, Calif.
Completed	1982
Sculptor	Isamu Noguchi
Building Cost	approximately $1 million
Gross Area	1.6 acres
Features	*California Scenario* is composed of six major elements representing the state's environment, and a sculpture by the artist, *The Spirit of the Lima Bean*, which represents the 50 years the land was under bean field cultivation. The abstraction of the California region includes: 1) *The Forest Walk*, featuring giant redwoods, a horseshoe-shaped path, wildflowers, and native grasses 2) *Energy Fountain*, combining granite, a stainless steel cone, and water 3) *Land Use*, using an eight-foot honeysuckle mound as a podium for a rectangular granite form 4) *Water Source*, a sandstone triangle serving as the source of a water stream which flows throughout the sculpture garden 5) *The Desert Land*, featuring a symmetrical mound covered with desert plants 6) *Water Use*, a triangular granite form receiving the water stream at the end of its course through California Scenario

Arts Enhance an Urban Center

The South Coast Repertory Theater currently ranks as the leading attendance-generator among Orange County's performing arts organizations. It attracts between 150,000 and 160,000 people each season for an average occupancy of 92 percent. Eighty percent of ticket sales for its main stage and its experimental stage are season subscriptions (17,929 main stage subscriptions; 4,255 second stage subscriptions). Attendance support is reportedly strongest in the county's southern and coastal communities, reflecting South Coast Repertory's roots, but its productions draw patrons from all areas of the county, as well as from Los Angeles, Riverside, San Bernadino, and San Diego counties. Its budget is currently $3.4 million, 73 percent met through earned income and 27 percent through contributions.

The theater enjoys a national reputation as a forum for new plays, which it frequently commissions. In 1969, it began the Living Theater Project (now the Theater Discovery Project) in which junior high and high school students study a play's text in their classrooms before attending a production and a post-performance discussion with South Coast Repertory artists. The theater's educational touring program has become the foremost children's theater producer in southern California, with 230 performances delivered each year to more than 70,000 young people. Finally, South Coast Repertory's Acting Conservatory provides a training program for children and adults.

South Coast Repertory maintains a cooperative relationship with its South Coast Plaza neighbors. In 1983, several actors and set designers worked with South Coast Plaza's marketing staff to produce *Santasfaction* in South Coast Plaza's mall at Christmas. Its lighting staff designed new outdoor lighting for a local restaurant. The theater received assistance in turn when the South Coast Plaza ground crew brought in their heavy equipment to reshape an outdoor amphitheater South Coast Repertory uses for children's productions.

Says South Coast Repertory director David Emmes:

It's a wonderful relationship that we have with South Coast Plaza. We enhance the Town Center area. We draw people in for nighttime usage and continue to be one of the elements that make this area more desirable. What we get from South Coast Plaza is financial support, help in marketing, and leadership.

The Arts Center's Plans

The Orange County Center for the Performing Arts already is planning a world-class first season for its 3,000-seat hall beginning in the fall of 1986. Plans call for 25 percent orchestral programming, 25 percent opera and ballet, and 50 percent musicals. Negotiations are underway with the Los Angeles Philharmonic and soloists including pianist Andre Watts and violinists Itzhak Perlman and Isaac Stern. The center hopes that John Williams will compose a new work to be performed by the Orange County Master Chorale or the Pacific Chorale and the Los Angeles Philharmonic. It expects to book such nationally known

Section of the Orange County Performing Arts Center, showing the 3,000-seat main theater and stage, backstage area, and five lobbies.

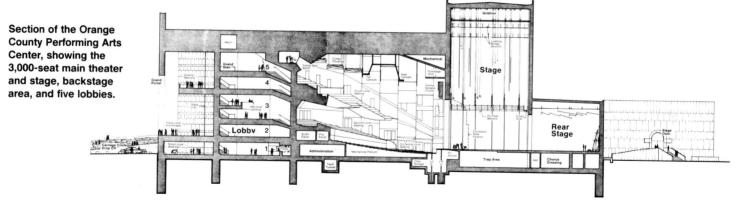

The Regent Hotel, designed by I. M. Pei, will be built in South Coast Town Center between the Orange County Performing Arts Center (on the left) and the South Coast Repertory Theater (on the right). The open plaza in the middle may become a performance area for both cultural institutions.

groups as the American Ballet Theatre and the New York City Opera, as well as international artists.

The center's executives anticipate their main auditorium to offer performances only 50 percent of the time the first year, but to be operating to capacity within three to five years. In 1984 ticket prices were projected to range from $30 per ticket for ballet to $35 for musicals and orchestras and to $40 for opera.

When the 1,000-seat theater opens, one of its expected attractions will be South Coast Repertory. The company has developed an audience potential well beyond its 507-seat main stage for its annual production of *A Christmas Carol,* and it looks forward to using the theater across the street for that show.

A Storefront Museum

This catalyzing effect already is happening. In the summer of 1984, C. J. Segerstrom & Sons learned that the Laguna Beach Museum of Art was closing for expansion of its facilities, and the Segerstrom company offered to donate exhibit space rent-free for one year in South Coast Plaza. The museum found an architecture firm and contracting company willing to donate their services, and it opened its 3,000-square-foot storefront museum in November 1984 with an exhibition of traditional and contemporary quilts. The space also includes a museum shop in the plaza's outreach location.

While the museum originally saw the new location as a temporary move, the staff now is rethinking this decision. Nancy Carlson, assistant director, says:

We now recognize the long-term as well as the short-term potential of the mall site and its benefits to our museum program. The site provides magnificent exposure in a quality mall location. It provides additional space to exhibit our permanent collection. It will be a catalyst for the interfacing of arts and business connections and provides an exceptionally suitable space to bring the aware and unaware to a new experience with the arts.

Entrance to the Laguna Beach Museum of Art's storefront location at South Coast Plaza.

An office building, Center Tower, sits to the left while the Orange County Performing Arts Center occupies the right, with the parking structure in the background. The white building in the foreground is South Coast Repertory Theater, completed in 1978.

The storefront location currently is funded through regular museum operating funds. The staff plans, however, to seek new funding sources so that the storefront museum can continue at South Coast Plaza beyond the fall of 1985.

South Coast Metro

Only time will reveal the full impact the multifaceted arts presence in South Coast Plaza and Town Center will make on the surrounding metropolitan area. A regional investment consortium called South Coast Metro is collaborating on a range of projects that will further urbanize Orange County.

The Metro consortium includes such developers as C. J. Segerstrom & Sons, Trammell Crow Company, Transpacific Development Company, California Pacific Properties, Arnell, and the Prudential Insurance Company of America. The 3.5-square-mile area it is developing first is bounded by the Costa Mesa Freeway, MacArthur Boulevard, the Santa Ana River, and the San Diego Freeway. This area currently contains 3.7 million square feet of office space, 1.5 million square feet of advanced-technology industry, 2.5 million square feet of retail businesses, 690 hotel rooms, and 5,042 units of housing. South Coast Metro thus

represents more than $2 billion in real estate developments.

The consortium intends to define the South Coast as the urban center of Orange County. Certainly South Coast Repertory, Noguchi's *California Scenario,* and the nearly completed arts center give South Coast Metro a substantial cultural edge over other developments. Together they represent a bold experiment to see whether the creation of arts activities can fashion a genuine downtown out of a suburban region.

Since 1975 Orange County and Costa Mesa have experienced significant transformations. Manufacturing, farming, and blue-collar employment have been edged out by professional firms, real estate development, and advanced-technology plants. The county has moved quickly toward an urban lifestyle—a journey accomplished in most areas of the nation only over several generations.

Several factors have contributed to the relative ease of this transformation:
■ Municipal governments have recognized the employment, financial, and social benefits to be derived from cooperating with private real estate developers who have developed multimillion-dollar complexes with office buildings, retail spaces, and hotels.

When completed in late 1985, the Orange County Performing Arts Center will feature outdoor balconies and a 120-foot Grand Portal entrance of flame-finished granite.

■ The county's business and philanthropic leaders have recognized the importance of supporting cultural institutions and have provided extraordinary contributions to capital fund campaigns.

■ The leadership in the public, private, and arts sectors has demonstrated an ability to act quickly and confidently so that opportunities do not bog down in planning or funding delays.

This continuing effort to create an urban center rich in amenities seems likely to succeed, because it remains consistent with goals expressed by the residential and business communities as well as by the county's public officials. Mark Baldessarie, associate professor of social ecology at the University of California at Irvine, has described the transformation of the county and of the South Coast region as follows:

In Orange County's early stages . . . a series of small towns developed into cities. Today no one city dominates the landscape, as I believe is true in the newly emerging metropolitan form. While the downtowns of older urban cities may represent an extinct form, there is a continuing need for centers of commercial, retail, and cultural activity. South Coast Metro represents one such hub of major activity in Orange County and a prototype for development of the new urban form elsewhere.

Model of the interior of the 3,000-seat theater of the Orange County Performing Center, showing an asymmetrical seating plan developed by acousticians.

Yerba Buena Gardens

Just south of Market Street in downtown San Francisco, Yerba Buena Gardens will connect the Union Square shopping and hotel district and the Montgomery Street financial district—both north of Market—with the new Moscone Convention Center, site of the 1984 Democratic convention. The project will encompass three city blocks—from Market to Folsom between Third and Fourth streets—containing a European-style market plaza, a square block of fountained gardens surrounding a Center for Arts and Culture, and a Tivoli-style entertainment park on the roof of the underground convention center. More than half of the 21 acres will be open space. The development, expected to cost $1 billion, is targeted for completion in 1989.

Yerba Buena Gardens is a project of the San Francisco Redevelopment Agency and a joint venture team consisting of Olympia & York, the Marriott Corporation, and Willis & Associates, Architects, Inc. Groundbreaking is scheduled for 1985.

On its block fronting Market Street, the development will contain an office building, 40 condominium apartments to be sold at market rates, a 1,500-room convention hotel connected by underground passage to the convention center, and stores and restaurants developed around a market plaza anchored by the Victorian-era St. Patrick's Church and a historic electric power station renovated as a farmer's market. The Rouse Company has contracted to develop and manage the specialty retail complex.

Featuring newly planted trees and flowers, terraces, pools, lawns, and children's play spaces, the central block's gardens will serve as an esplanade from the market plaza to a large fountain, which will play against a backdrop of the convention center's flags. The garden's open spaces will be able to host a variety of arts programs and community activities and festivals. A skating rink, cafes, and shops will edge the garden on the west.

The Center for Arts and Culture, on the east side of the central block, will give San Francisco's artists and their audiences a museum-quality gallery and exhibition space; a theater for performances of drama, music, and dance; a video/film theater; and a multipurpose forum suitable for many special events. The center has been planned in collaboration with the full breadth of San Francisco's eclectic and sophisticated arts community, but the programs and works presented will represent small organizations and independent artists rather than the city's orchestra, opera, ballet, or established art museums.

Beginning with an undefined requirement that land be set aside within the project for unspecified cultural purposes, a three-year planning process produced a well-defined programming concept, a list of facilities needed to support the programming, and models for the financing and management required to make the plan a reality. More than 200 representatives from the arts community volunteered extensive amounts of time and work to a series of community meetings, workshops, and task forces that were part of the planning effort managed by the redevelopment agency.

South-of-Market Is
Marked for Renewal

The gold rush, the rebuilding after its earthquake, the founding of the United Nations, two world-class bridges, and a renowned opera company—among other events and accomplishments—have given San Francisco an international standing unusual for an American city of its size—707,000—and furnished some justification for its self-description as "the city that knows how." Its cable cars, sourdough bread, ethnic and cultural diversity, climate, views of bay and sea, and a host of other natural and human amenities and eccentricities reinforce boosters' claims that San Francisco is "everybody's favorite city."

Surrounded by water on three sides and by a county line on the south, the city cannot expand physically, so its boom since World War II has created enormous population growth in the counties to the south, north, and east. More than five million people live in the metropolitan San Francisco Bay Area, making it the sixth largest metropolitan region in the nation. For all of them, San Francisco is "the city."

The South-of-Market area was one of the first neighborhoods to be settled in the city, and although elegant shops and prosperous financial towers remain only a five-minute walk away, it has long been considered the "wrong" side of Market Street. Planning for South-of-Market renewal began in 1961, when the city and county board of supervisors funded a redevelopment agency study that certified the area as blighted. This finding triggered clearing and combining many land parcels by condemnation.

The initial redevelopment project outlined in 1966 for the area was named Yerba Buena Center—recalling San Francisco's earlier name—and its boundaries stretched from Market Street southeast to Harrison and from Second Street southwest to Fourth Street. The neighborhood's 87 acres contained a hodgepodge of decaying two- and three-story houses and flats, occupied by low-income people and families of all races; seedy old hotels that served as rooming houses for retired single people (including many seamen) and for the down-and-out; pawnshops; bars; skid-row missions; and deteriorating commercial and industrial buildings. On most blocks, family dwellings were crowded next to factories, warehouses, and garages. Narrow internal alleys and streets with heavy truck traffic presented severe circulation and safety hazards. Recreational and community service facilities were almost completely lacking, and the nearest green space was South Park, a tiny open area separated from the neighborhood by a freeway. The only structures of architectural merit were the venerable red-brick St. Patrick's Catholic Church and the Beaux Arts–style Jessie Street Substation of the Pacific Gas & Electric Company, no longer in use but landmarked for preservation.

City planners believed that clearing the area would remove unhealthy living conditions and develop new and beneficial commercial uses. The 1966 plan to redevelop the area was supported widely by local newspapers and citizen groups such as San Francisco Planning and Urban Research (SPUR), which viewed it as a positive effort to change dangerous slums into an attractive, profitable commercial area. Initial costs for this transformation were projected at $7.9 million, with the city financing $2.6 million and the federal government subsidizing the rest.

The plan was vigorously resisted, however, by neighborhood residents and property owners, low-cost housing advocates, poverty lawyers, and antidevelopment activists. They argued that even though the area's buildings were run-down, they remained serviceable, affordable, and appropriate in scale; that even though the people who lived and worked there were poor, they were mainly self-respecting and, in their diversity and tolerance, more typical of San Francisco than the suburbanites who jammed the bridges, streets, and highrises of a "Manhattanized" downtown.

Multiculturalism Gives Rise to Lively but Crowded Arts

San Francisco's reputation as an international city was gained not only by its resemblance in ambience to some European cities and by its location at the gateway to Pacific trade and travel, but also by its multicultural population and its vibrant arts community.

Many San Franciscans believe that the city's mixture of cultures produces artistic activity richer than that of more homogeneous communities, and that San Francisco's enthusiasm for diversity and personal expression encourages additional creativity. San Francisco arts supporters also believe that the arts help diverse peoples to communicate with each other, cementing the community and providing focal points for shared experiences.

The city's established arts organizations—the opera, orchestra, fine arts museums, and, more recently, the ballet and the American Conservatory Theater—have been balanced by the growth, beginning in the sixties, of a host of smaller grassroots groups. San Francisco now boasts 80 operating theaters, large and small; 120 dance organizations and choreographers, constituting a dance community probably second only to New York's; an exceptionally active music scene; a booming film industry; nationally renowned visual artists, poets, and writers; and a host of galleries and other arts-related organizations.

In 1966, San Francisco created a Neighborhood Arts Program, which became a model for similar programs throughout the nation. The city created the first Comprehensive Employment and Training Act (CETA) program for artists. A San Francisco Foundation study revealed that the arts business expended more than $87 million in the six-county San Francisco Bay Area during the year ending in June 1981, and took in slightly more: $87,785,000.

San Francisco's hotel tax of 9.75 percent on hotel bills contributed $3.6 million to 104 nonprofit cultural groups in 1983–84, but nearly $2 million of that went to the orchestra, opera, ballet, museums, and repertory theater. The smaller organizations received grants ranging from $2,000 to $30,000 for reimbursement of operating expenditures such as salaries and space rentals.

Festival Plaza, looking toward St. Patrick's Church. Immediately behind it lies the Olympia & York office tower.

Thus the state of the arts in San Francisco, while diverse and thriving, has become one of intense competition among hundreds of small organizations for financial support and for adequate space in which to perform and exhibit. In considering a cultural component for Yerba Buena Center that would meet the needs of the arts community and add status and vitality to the project, the redevelopment agency therefore saw the city's established organizations amply housed, with plans for new buildings, or unwilling to move, but the grassroots groups struggling to find places to show their work.

Market Analysis Recommends MXD with Culture

Early on, the planning effort for Yerba Buena narrowed its focus to the Market Street block adjoining the retail district and to the two blocks behind it stretching southeast to Howard Street. Simultaneously the concept emerged that these three blocks should contain a mixture of uses that would include the arts.

In May 1969 Development Research Associates (now Environmental Research Associates) completed an agency-sponsored market analysis that recommended mixed-use development with a strong public component. The private uses envisioned for the Yerba Buena Center included offices, hotels, and stores. The public uses suggested by the analysis included a commercial theater, a sports arena, an exhibit hall, and possibly an ethnically oriented cultural/trade center similar to the Japan Center, already built in San Francisco's Western Addition redevelopment project. Such public facilities were seen as a way to create "a fresh, new urban environment" that would stimulate a variety of private land uses. The theater was projected as particularly beneficial, because it could make a positive architectural impact on the area and because it could draw significant nighttime activity and encourage quality restaurants.

The researchers concluded that Yerba Buena Center's central blocks had two major advantages—their proximity to downtown stores and the financial district, and their convenient access to both San Francisco's Muni transit system and the Bay Area Rapid Transit light-rail system then being built to connect the city with the East Bay. But the area still had to overcome its skid-row image. That goal could be achieved with cultural and recreational uses and the specialty retail and restaurants they attract. Such uses, the report pointed out, "do not develop spontaneously—they must be planned for and promoted."

The consultants also suggested malls and plazas to encourage a flow of pedestrians from the financial and retail districts north of Market Street into Yerba Buena's interior blocks; placement of a 2,200-seat theater, a public plaza, and parking garages on the middle block; and a large sports arena and an exhibit hall for trade shows on the third block.

The report concluded with recommendations to proceed with a collaborative planning process that would involve the redevelopment agency with the city's full range of arts and community groups. It also argued that cultural facilities would be valuable not just for themselves but as a strengthening ingredient for the entire project, and it suggested that the arts facilities be integrated into a viable and attractive program concept.

Site plan of Yerba Buena, showing existing and proposed development.

☐ New Housing
☐ New Development
☐ Mixed-Use Development
☐ Rehabilitation

1. Jessie St. Substation
2. Downtown Community College
3. St. Patrick's Church
4. Mercantile Building
5. Meridien Hotel
6. 5th & Mission St. Garage
7. Yerba Buena West Building
8. Clementina Towers
9. Woolf House
10. Ceatrice Polite Housing
11. Convention Plaza Building
12. Moscone Parking Garage
13. Planters Hotel
14. Silvercrest Residence
15. Dimas-Alang Housing
16. Proposed Housing
17. Fourth Street Associates

A Tivoli on the Roof and Midblock Gardens

The Yerba Buena project remained deadlocked, however by multiple lawsuits over relocation of residents, financing difficulties, and environmental disputes. In 1976 then-Mayor George Moscone appointed a citizens' select committee to make recommendations on the future course of the area. Chaired by Judge Leland Lazarus, the committee included prominent business leaders, public activists, neighborhood representatives, planners, and architects. After hearing months of testimony, it proposed a development of truly mixed uses, with market-rate and subsidized housing in addition to the commercial uses and public facilities envisioned ten years earlier. The committee also advocated the preservation of St. Patrick's Church and Jessie Street Substation.

The committee's most significant contribution, however, was its proposal for an underground convention center with a unique urban theme park on its roof, extending north into the adjoining block. This park concept, inspired by Copenhagen's Tivoli Gardens, was generated by local architect and planner Richard Gryziec. The theme park proved a key factor in generating broad public support, and voters passed a bond issue to build the proposed convention center on Yerba Buena Center's southernmost block.

Once the convention center was approved, the city redevelopment agency engaged the architectural and planning firm of Skidmore, Owings & Merrill (SOM) in 1977 to provide guidance in shaping the rest of the project. Reviewing the problems that the project had encountered in the past, the SOM team felt that what was needed now was a more flexible development plan that could accommodate changes as necessary. They created an "urban design framework" that provided a comprehensive physical design and planning context for the public and private improvements within the project area.

The SOM study evaluated the feasibility of alternative land uses from the standpoint of design rather than from financial return or highest and best use. It set out certain organizational principles for the project that could lead to a variety of land use solutions. The principles included:

- the use of the convention center roof for a variety of recreational and cultural purposes;
- the creation of ample open space within the project, including gardens in the central blocks linking the convention center with Market Street;
- subdivision of the site that would permit multiple developers to be brought into the project;
- height and bulk limits and floor/area ratios for new development that would be compatible with the existing buildings, including the historic ones, and that would minimize shadows on the gardens and open spaces; and
- the use of the land for suitable purposes, with possible and preferred sites indicated for a hotel, offices, "commercial recreation" (including specialty retail), regional retail, housing, and parking.

To suggest how these design guidelines might work in practice, the consultants provided four alternative land use plans that would be consistent with the historic fabric, would provide a share of housing appropriate for childless professionals, would contribute to the area's nighttime liveliness, and, "since the redevelopment process represents vast amounts of public monies," would serve recognized public needs.

With one exception, these principles SOM set forth guided the redevelopment agency's subsequent thinking as it developed its Request for Qualifications (RFQ), issued to the development community in 1980. The exception was the concept of subdividing the parcel and making parts of it available to different developers; the agency believed that the unusual urban gardens program suggested by Richard Gryziec and endorsed by Mayor Moscone's select committee only could be achieved in a large-scale project involving a single developer and architect.

Otherwise, the agency reiterated SOM's design principles, and it incorporated SOM's renderings into the RFQ, thus establishing a guiding image of low-scaled, finely detailed, pedestrian-oriented uses.

Agency and Developer Accept
Arts Community as Partners

By the winter of 1980 the basic design approach for Yerba Buena seemed settled, but its economics remained uncertain. The response to the redevelopment agency's preliminary RFQ indicated insufficient income-producing space in the program to secure developer interest. The agency's new director of development, Judy Hopkinson, therefore brought on a real estate consultant, Keyser Marston Associates, Inc., to work with the agency to revise the project in such a way as to stay within the spirit of the mayor's select committee but to enhance the potential commercial uses. A key Keyser Marston recommendation was to include in the commercial package a major piece of property near the Market Street "window" to Union Square and the financial district. One such property, known as the GSA parcel and suitable for a major hotel, seemed ideal for this purpose. But since there was a possibility the GSA parcel could not be acquired and delivered to the Yerba Buena project developer, a fallback parcel was included in the developer offering. The agency issued a revised RFQ in April 1980, calling for:

...an imaginatively conceived mix of...uses that will be a major attraction in San Francisco for residents and visitors alike. In both business and creative fields, San Francisco is a unique city with a great diversity of talented people. This development will provide the opportunity for San Franciscans to contribute their talents...creating a uniquely exciting and viable place in the city. It is desired that the developer utilize the local reservoir of available talent to operate theaters, unusual fairs, restaurants, and shops, and to conduct special exhibits and performances....The objective is to achieve an "urban garden," to create something uniquely San Francisco...to have places for people to dine, relax, and enjoy the city in a casual atmosphere in a garden setting.

Office and hotel uses were limited to the block fronting on Market Street. The middle blocks and the convention center roof were designated for the gardens and for specialty retail, amusement, recreation and entertainment, and cultural uses. This plan still meant that the total site would be de-veloped at a level well below its full financial potential, although it would provide many significant amenities.

The precise nature of many uses was left undefined, especially in the case of the cultural component. In setting out the obligations of the developer, the RFQ stated:

The developer must, as a minimum, reserve...a total of 50,000 square feet of land...for future use by cultural institutions such as museums, exhibits, and theaters. These locations are to be fully landscaped by the developer until the cultural use is developed.

To provide an incentive, the RFQ specified:

Additional commitment [from the developer] for construction or operating funds for cultural activities is encouraged and will be negotiated as part of the overall Agreement for Disposition of Land between the agency and developer. Any such additional contribution will be a factor in determining land price.

The agency received ten responses to this developer solicitation package, including some of the most prestigious U.S. and Canadian firms. From these strong developer teams, two emerged as finalists: Olympia & York and Cadillac Fairview. Both offered substantial financial capacity and experience with large-scale MXDs. They also included cultural consultants on their teams.

Before selecting the developer, the redevelopment agency's project director, Helen L. Sause, began to formulate a planning process for Yerba Buena's cultural component. It was important to begin this planning process before entering negotiations with the developer, to ensure that the cultural program, its required space, and the financial mechanisms necessary for its construction and operation could be articulated and considered before crucial design and financing decisions for the total project were finalized.

In July 1980 the agency hired a full-time cultural consultant, Harold Snedcof, a former New Yorker who had developed and administered programs in both visual and performing arts. He participated on the team that selected the developer. His principal assignment, however, was to produce an arts program concept that would justify setting aside 50,000 square feet and would enliven and distinguish the entire project.

Snedcof knew that San Francisco's established arts organizations could not be lured to Yerba Buena. The San Francisco Museum of Modern Art, which needed more space, did not want to move from the Civic Center, next to the Opera House. The San Francisco Symphony had just built a new hall. The Asian Art Museum might be persuaded, but it had reservations. Moreover, the arts concept would have to be realistic in its capital and subsidy requirements, and it would have to represent a significant consensus among the entire arts community to gain approval from the mayor and the board of supervisors. Snedcof says:

I didn't know how to do this, so I went to my friend David Straus of the Center for Collaborative Problem Solving, and we decided to see what would bubble up from the community. We thought that was a way to make the arts program authentically San Franciscan and also to show that there was consensus. I really thought that we could somehow provide homes for the smaller organizations which do make San Francisco unique, and at the same time convince the developer and the city that it was a good idea, since it was arrived at by consensus.

In the late summer of 1980 Snedcof talked with more than 50 members of the San Francisco cultural community, ranging from individual artists and neighborhood-based theater groups to the powerful established arts organizations. Almost all said they did not want to be treated as "advisors" to yet another public process in which final decisions would be made behind closed doors. They wanted a planning process that would obtain significant input from the entire arts community and not only from the largest groups.

The redevelopment agency therefore sought and received a $17,500 grant from the National Endowment for the Arts—as well as funds from several corporations and foundations—to facilitate genuine community participation in the planning. Help was obtained from consultants with expertise in

Yerba Buena Gardens
Project Data

Physical Configuration	First Phase 1988 Completion	Profile at Build-Out
Component—Income Generating		
Office	750,000 sq. ft.	1,250,000 sq. ft.
Residential	40 DUs	340–540 DUs
Retail	190,000 sq. ft.	200,00 sq. ft.
Amusement/Recreation/Entertainment	170,000 sq. ft.	170,000 sq. ft.
Ice Rink		
San Francisco Pavilion		
Cinema Center		
Children's Learning Garden		
Hotel	1,500 rooms	1,500 rooms
Component—Arts/Culture/Open Space		
Gallery/Exhibit Space	20,000 sq. ft.	20,000 sq. ft.
Theater	600 seats	600 seats
Video/Film Facility	100 seats	100 seats
Forum	10,000 sq. ft.	10,000 sq. ft.
Admin./Box Office	5,400 sq. ft.	5,400 sq. ft.
Plazas/Gardens		
Market Street Plaza		
St. Patrick's Square		
Festival Plaza		
Classical Chinese Garden		
Children's Garden		
Other		
Parking	1,650 spaces	2,250 spaces
Acreage	21.37 acres	23.99 acres
Gross Building Area	2,400,000 sq. ft. (plus cultural)	3,390,000 sq. ft.
Floor/Area Ratio	2.58	3.24
Location	Downtown San Francisco	
Master Developer	YBG Associates:	Olympia & York California Equities Corp. Marriott Corp.
Development Period	1985–88	Early 1990s
Estimated Total Development Costs	$525 million	$685 million

Source: Keyser Marston Associates

Yerba Buena Gardens
Development Cost Summary

	Private	Public
Office	$220 million	
Retail (including Galleria)	30 million	
Amusement/Recreation/Entertainment	25 million	
Hotel	225 million	
Residential	65 million	
Parking	40 million	
Site Costs		$25 million
Gardens/Public Area		25 million
Cultural Facilities		25 million
Housing Fund		5 million
Total	$605 million	$80 million

Source: Based on data provided by San Francisco Redevelopment Agency and by Adamson Associates (cost consultants) and on estimates by Keyser Marston Associates

planning for arts-inclusive MXDs, and from the Center for Collaborative Problem Solving, a San Francisco–based nonprofit organization experienced in managing large-group decision-making processes.

Arts Groups Plan
Specifies "Showcasing"

The arts community's first general meeting took place on November 11, 1980, in the board room of the San Francisco Museum of Modern Art. More than 70 people attended, representing a wide range of arts disciplines and organizations. The participants were thoroughly briefed on Yerba Buena's history, the RFQ requirements for cultural uses, and the developer selection process. During November and early December, these representatives met weekly to plan a public process responsive to the agency's needs and schedule.

Their first event was a one-and-a-half day conference in February 1981 for nearly 150 artists and representatives of arts groups. The agency outlined several criteria that had been developed for the cultural component of Yerba Buena Gardens: The programs should be comprehensive; should be active 12 to 18 hours a day, seven days a week; should appeal to a wide range of groups; should not duplicate existing arts programs in the city; and should be dynamic and ever-changing.

The participants split into four task forces to examine the image and theme of the cultural component, its programming and facilities, its management, and its finance. At the end of the day, the task forces selected chairpersons, reported back to the larger group, and then set dates for weekly meetings to develop ideas more fully. The task forces met throughout the month of March, and at a community meeting in early April issued their recommendations.

Consultants William Morrish and William Fleissig of CITYWEST, an urban planning and design firm, developed a "cultural planning workbook" that outlined more than 100 separate options and programming decisions that had to be made. In a meeting on May 13, 1981, more than 100 members of the cultural community voted on each of these items.

The task force reports and the voting results then were synthesized by CITYWEST into a "YBC Cultural Plan Design Scenario," which was ratified by the arts community at a meeting on June 22. This document, with various community responses appended, was the principal product of the first phase of community planning. It was nicknamed the Blue Book for the color of its cover.

The Blue Book included the following recommendations:

■ There should be a commitment to the concept of "showcasing"; that is, cultural facilities and programs of the highest quality should be used to highlight the full range of artistic talents and events. National and international programming should be featured, but the emphasis should be on the local arts community. Ethnic, cultural, and intergenerational diversity should be emphasized.

■ To maximize the opportunities in Yerba Buena for performance, presentation, and exhibition under the showcasing concept, there should be no resident companies and artists.

■ Existing facilities in the Bay Area should not be duplicated.

■ The facilities should have a strong, independent management structure and a firm financing plan to make the facilities available for a broad range of programs and audiences. The development should support the cultural programs entirely so that the organizations using the facilities would not have to compete with one another for scarce funds.

Nine facilities were recommended to house and support the showcasing concept:
■ a museum-quality gallery/exhibition space;
■ a large and a small theater;
■ A video/film screening room;
■ an arts library;
■ education space;
■ arts studios or workspaces;
■ a central box office; and
■ administrative offices.

The report emphasized the need for state-of-the-art facilities with individual spaces designed to meet the quite separate needs of film, theater, dance, visual arts, and other disciplines.

The showcasing concept, which would aim to make Yerba Buena's cultural center an ongoing festival of Bay Area arts, was the single most important contribution to the planning. It became the arts community's guiding principle, and it influenced all future decisions about the arts component.

In a policy statement issued on August 11, 1981, the redevelopment agency endorsed the showcasing model and the facilities recommended by the arts community, and it authorized the agency's staff to work toward their implementation. The agency confirmed that the proposal would satisfy the obligation to set aside 50,000 square feet for cultural uses, and it promised to seek from the development a significant contribution for the capital and operating costs of the showcasing effort.

Olympia & York Plans
Culture and Recreation

In November 1980 the redevelopment agency had selected the development team of Olympia & York for exclusive negotiations. Olympia & York Equity Corporation's headquarters were in Toronto. Associated with them for the Yerba Buena project were the Marriott Corporation; the Rouse Company; Beverly Willis, principal of a San Francisco architecture firm that had brought the team together; Zeidler-Roberts, an architecture firm; and Lawrence Halprin, a noted San Francisco landscape architect.

This team engaged another Toronto organization, Harbourfront, as its cultural consultants. Harbourfront, a mixed-use development project on the shore of Lake Erie, houses a variety of small-scale visual and performing arts organizations in rehabilitated factory buildings. The presence of Harbourfront's general manager Howard Cohen and director of programming Ann Tindall on the development team indicated that Olympia & York was indeed committed to helping define an appropriate range of arts uses for Yerba Buena.

The Harbourfront team was invited to the arts planning meetings, and they participated fully. They reviewed drafts of all documents as the planning proceeded, and they shared valuable information on how uses could interrelate in a mixed-use project.

At the arts community's general meeting in April 1981, Harbourfront presented a draft program concept for what they called "The Yerba Buena Center of Culture and Recreation." The proposed center would aim to attract the San Francisco population with a dynamic range of visual and performing arts programs, including film, with provision for children, ethnic groups, hobbyists, and senior citizens. These programs would be anchored in specialized arts facilities, but there would be no resident companies or groups. Managed by a single nonprofit organization created for that purpose, the arts facilities could, Harbourfront believed, serve as a community center for San Francisco and a major draw for the total project.

The Harbourfront consultants proposed four kinds of physical spaces for the center:

1) informal indoor and outdoor spaces lined by shops and restaurants, in which a variety of arts events could take place;

2) multipurpose spaces that could be modified to accommodate everything from visual arts exhibitions to educational programs to small performances;

3) specialized or more structured facilities, such as a 500–1,000-seat performance space with a proscenium stage and a spring floor, especially suited to dance; and

4) an outdoor performance area that could act as a downtown amphitheater for full-scale music and staged performances.

In many ways the Harbourfront suggestions coincided with those of the redevelopment agency and the arts community. However, their concept report opened up two issues that sparked sharp debate. The first issue was whether the cultural facilities should be single-use spaces specially designed to house particular disciplines, or multipurpose spaces adaptable for a variety of programs and events. Both the arts community and the agency believed that the high quality of professional programming envisioned for the cultural center could not be achieved without first-rate facilities, specifically designed to meet the unique needs of a given arts discipline. Olympia & York's team, on the other hand, argued that the mandate of the center would be met best by facilities that could accommodate the broadest possible range of activities.

This issue led to the second debate, concerning the proper definition of "cultural." The arts community and the redevelopment agency wanted professional-level programming in the visual and performing arts. The developer, however, advocated that the cultural uses include fairs, festivals, community meetings, and other "non-arts" events. Such activities, countered the arts leaders, should be considered as recreation, amusement or entertainment. These distinctions were crucial, because how such activities were defined would determine what budget they would come under, who would be responsible for them, and how costs would be allocated.

In September 1981 Olympia & York presented three alternative design concepts for review by the mayor, the general public, and the redevelopment commission. All three scenarios prominently included the kind of cultural complex envisioned by the agency and its arts advisors—drama, dance, and music theaters; exhibition space for visual arts and crafts; and studios to serve as working and teaching spaces. Olympia & York made two additions— a flexible, multipurpose forum space, which it still advocated strongly, and active programming of cultural activities in the plaza.

The proposals treated the cultural facilities as "destination uses . . . having high visibility" and the capacity to "draw large numbers of people to the site." Endorsing the arts community's programming concept, the developer's document stated: "The gardens will be designed to give the cultural community the opportunity to showcase their work, along with that of visiting artists, in a program format that is creative and stimulating for San Francisco audiences."

Olympia & York also submitted a proposal called the Esplanade for commercial development and a marketplace on the first block; an esplanade or mall from block one to the convention center; and, on the roof of Moscone Center, a cinema center that would include a film archive and screening rooms, and a pavilion devoted to San Francisco history. This complex on the convention center roof was designed primarily for nighttime entertainment.

During 1982 the developer continued conducting studies toward a comprehensive arts and culture program for Yerba Buena. Olympia & York expanded its cultural consultant team to include specialists in theater design and programming, visual arts, and community arts programs. The plan this team presented in October 1982 again recommended the showcasing concept for the cultural center's programming, a nonprofit management entity with a strong staff and community-based board, and a multipurpose festival or forum space for general community use, charged to the cultural component's capital and operations cost. The developer clearly was convinced that the arts alone would not draw sufficient numbers of people to Yerba Buena.

The Agency Studies Costs and Needs
Comparing Olympia & York's list of proposed cultural facilities with the arts community's Blue Book recommendations, Peat, Marwick, Mitchell & Company reported that 116,000 square feet of theaters, galleries, studios, and administrative offices had been proposed by the arts groups and the agency, and 90,000 by the developer. Included within its square footage, Olympia & York had proposed the multipurpose facility or forum, and it omitted the arts library and video studio requested by the arts groups.

To help resolve these differences, Peat, Marwick, Mitchell recommended that the redevelopment agency conduct an extensive survey of arts organizations to determine whether each proposed facility was genuinely needed and wanted and whether similar facilities already were available. They pointed out that the capital costs of building the 116,100 square feet of facilities listed in the Blue Book would be $30.6 million in 1982 dollars, and they formulated a summary of operating costs and earned revenues for a 10-year period from 1982 to 1992 that showed projected annual deficits ranging from $111,000 in the initial years to more than $5 million by 1992.

The size of the cultural component and its need for an ongoing subsidy already were beginning to affect financial negotiations for the total project. Olympia & York's assumptions and conclusions differed somewhat from the agency's and Peat,

The Agency Retains the Gardens and Arts Center

Marwick, Mitchell's, but all parties agreed that capital costs would exceed $10 million and projected deficits would run over $1 million per year.

Two issues thus became apparent:

1) That whatever the final configuration of the cultural complex, the developer would seek a trade-off in lower land costs, increased densities, or both.

2) That the issue of management and control of the cultural complex, which was just beginning to be studied and discussed, would be equally as important as the physical characteristics.

Studying the situation, Mayor Dianne Feinstein's staff noted that these managerial issues would be harder to solve than the physical ones and that "the wrong management of the facilities could turn them into an unmitigated disaster artistically, financially, and politically, no matter how fine the buildings."

The agency staff decided, however, to keep the full Blue Book program on the negotiating table and to proceed with the proposed survey of groups that would use the arts center. A questionnaire developed by arts consultant Virginia Hubbell & Associates aimed to determine the arts community's ability to use the proposed facilities. Replies to 256 detailed questions and 249 personal interviews confirmed a severe shortage of well-equipped, high-quality performance and exhibition spaces in San Francisco and found strong support among potential users for all the proposed facilities—including the developer's festival space—except the studio workshops and the education space. The study further noted:

The Yerba Buena Center is looked on by the community as something of far greater importance than merely a central location where business and culture happen to reside. It is perceived as a true center, a place for the presentation of works, but also, and more importantly, a place where the creative process can be shared by the artists with the public and with each other. It is perceived as a focal point for the city, a space in which the finest quality, and the most exciting, creative, contemporary, and traditional cultural activities from around the entire world may be experienced.

In late 1981, to continue its collaborative planning process, the agency had formed a technical assistance committee that represented the full range of arts disciplines and brought expertise in the financing, management, and administration of arts programs. Chaired by Michaela Cassidy, president of the Bay Area Dance Coalition, the committee was charged with keeping the larger arts community informed as the agency and the developer considered plans for the cultural center and advising the agency and its consultants on financing and management strategies.

During the course of negotiations with Olympia & York in 1982, the redevelopment agency set $20.6 million as a feasible and affordable budget for the construction of the cultural facilities. The technical assistance committee then was asked to identify the "critical mass" of facilities—those that would be most essential to the success of the center and that could be built within this budget. In May 1983 the committee designated the facilities it deemed essential: the exhibition gallery; the large 1,800–

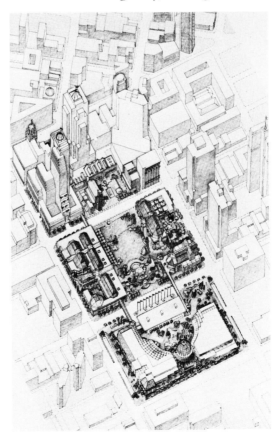

Rendering of Yerba Buena Gardens, with Moscone Convention Center in the foreground.

2,000-seat theater; the 400-seat theater; the video screening room; the arts library; the administrative offices; and the central box office.

The committee agreed that Olympia & York's multipurpose forum was appropriate, but it recommended that its costs not be included in the cultural component's construction budget but rather charged as part of the separately budgeted amusement/recreation/entertainment package.

Even with the list of facilities reduced to this critical mass, the costs were still $5 million over the agency's budget. Further negotiations raised the capital budget to nearly $22.5 million with the multipurpose festival space included. Reluctantly, the redevelopment agency concluded that the large 1,800–2,000-seat theater would have to be dropped. Although estimates varied widely on how much it would cost to build, it was clear that this single facility would require half to all the available budget. The other casualty was the arts library; though strongly supported in the survey, it did not offer the direct showcasing opportunities of the other facilities.

By the summer of 1983 the cultural program for Yerba Buena finally appeared to meet most of the needs of the arts community, the agency, and the developer at feasible costs. As now constituted, it would include a visual arts exhibition gallery of museum quality, a 600-seat proscenium-stage theater, a video and film screening theater, a multipurpose forum, and support facilities including administrative offices and a central box office. These facilities would be arranged in two buildings. The first building, totaling 36,000 square feet, would include the visual arts gallery, the video/film theater, the 10,000-square-foot forum, the administrative and box offices, and building support space. The proscenium theater, with its lobbies, backstage areas, and support spaces, would occupy the second building, a 49,000-square-foot structure. Financial analysts concluded that this revised center could indeed be constructed within the proposed $23 million budget, based on 1983 dollars.

After studying other cities that own and operate cultural complexes, the agency concluded that the most successful man-

agement occurs where an independent nonprofit organization handles operations under contract with the city. Under this model, a 501(c)(3) nonprofit corporation would be established to manage the Yerba Buena arts center. The operating agreement with the agency would set forth the center's operations principles, establish performance standards that the operator must meet, and provide for financial reporting and operations audits. The corporation would be set up as a membership organization, with a board composed of representatives of the agency, the developer, the arts community, and the general San Francisco public.

The negotiations of the business terms between Olympia & York and the redevelopment agency had continued throughout the arts planning process, since 1981. The negotiations proved so protracted because many complex, interrelated issues had to be resolved: What would be the nature and extent of the public-benefits package at Yerba Buena and how would their value be determined? Was responsibility for these benefits to be assigned to the agency or to the developer, or should it be shared between them? If they were to be shared, how were they to be divided? How would these public amenities be financed? If providing them was primarily the developer's responsibility, how would financial arrangements for the project be adjusted to compensate for these costs:
- By adjusting the land costs downward?
- By permitting higher densities for the income-generating parts of the project?
- By some other mechanism?

Other questions needed to be addressed. What revenue-producing uses would be allowed? At what densities? In what configuration on the site? How much real estate was to be included in the transaction? Which parcels would be sold and which leased? How was their value to be determined? How was payment to be structured?

The agency established a core negotiating team, composed of the agency's executive director, Wilbur Hamilton; its special counsel, Joseph E. Coomes, Jr.; and its real estate consultant, Michael Marston of Keyser Marston Associates, Inc. Crucial decision points involved direct intervention by Mayor Feinstein, who had appointed an unofficial emissary to monitor the progress of the negotiations.

The agency's 1980 RFQ had allowed an adjustment of the land costs based on the developer's contribution to the cultural uses. It became clear during the course of negotiations, however, that the agency and the developer disagreed about which amenities qualified as "cultural." Should the term apply only to the arts center or should it be broadened to include the gardens, which could be used as settings for a broad range of festivals and community events? The two parties also could not reach agreement on the dollar value that should be assigned to the public amenities or on how that value should be reflected in land costs.

The negotiating team proposed that the developer pay fair market value for all the property that would be sold or leased; in exchange, the agency would take upon itself the responsibility for providing all public benefits, including the cultural center and the gardens.

A key element of this approach was that the capital costs for the public uses were to be generated by the sale of office and residential land in the project and by the sale of other city-owned real estate. Lease of the hotel, retail, and amusement/recreation/ entertainment land would provide the income to operate the public facilities.

Throughout the negotiations, Keyser Marston Associates provided the agency with value estimates and cash-flow projections to ensure both that the agency received full market value for its property and that its proposals would be economically feasible for the developer. In addition, the firm monitored trends in the financing market, to ensure feasible leasing arrangements. Sensitive to the commitment that the staff had made to Yerba Buena, it recommended that the agency continue to avail itself of such top-flight consultants as Adamson Associates and Barton-Aschman Associates.

The agency and Olympia & York announced the final terms of their agreement in April 1984, nearly three and a half years after the developer had been selected.

The land disposition was structured as follows:

■ The sites for the office building and residential building on the first block, owned by the redevelopment agency, were to be sold to the developer. The office building site was to be sold at $43.33 per square foot of gross building area (GBA)— $32,497,500 escalated from July 1, 1983. In addition, the office developer will pay an annual participation fee of 8 percent of net cash flow after a 15 percent preferred return. The residential site was to be sold at $36,900 per unit, similarly escalated, against 30 percent of the net profit (whichever is higher).

The sites for the hotel and the retail and open-space uses on that block will be leased, and the developer will rehabilitate, for commercial and cultural uses, the historic Pacific Gas & Electric Company substation building that occupies part of the leased site. The hotel is leased for 60 years with two 15-year options that can be exercised separately or together. The hotel pays 4 percent of the gross income from rooms and 2 percent of the gross income from other sales, against the minimum rent.

■ On the middle block, the sites for retail, amusement, recreation, and entertainment uses will be leased, and the sites for the gardens and the cultural center will be retained by the agency.

The retail space is leased for 60 years with two fifteen-year options. There is a minimum retail rental of $1 per square foot, plus a percentage rent based on net cash flow after: (a) a developer preferred return on actual equity of 20 percent, (b) mortgage payments, and (c) operating expenses. The percentage rent is escalated from 15 percent to 49 percent on net cash flow per square foot; for example, 15 percent on $15 or less; 30 percent on $30, and 49 percent on $49 or more.

The amusement/recreation/entertainment is leased for 60 years at the same rental as the retail except there is no minimum rent. The parking on Central Block Two is leased for 60 years at 50 percent of net cash flow.

■ The third block is already occupied underground by the convention center, completed in 1983 and named for the late Mayor George Moscone. The city leases Central Block Three to the agency (minus the area for the convention center meeting rooms) for 50 years at 6 percent of the agency's net income from Yerba Buena Gardens after agency commitments for the project have been satisfied. The cinema center and other uses above the convention center will be leased, with the agency retaining the areas designated for the gardens.

■ East Block Two will be sold at the appraised market value for a 500,000-square-foot office building and 300–500 residential units. An option remains for a site being retained for a major museum or large theater.

According to this agreement, Olympia & York is responsible for building, operating, and maintaining the commercial uses throughout the project, including retail, amusement, recreation, and entertainment facilities, as well as the open-space plazas in the first block. The redevelopment agency is responsible for building, operating, and maintaining the extensive gardens on the middle block and on the Moscone Center roof, along with the cultural center on the middle block, with the developer contributing 20 percent of the operations costs for the public spaces on these blocks. This agreement places the burden of financing the cultural uses on the redevelopment agency rather than on the developer, as was originally intended.

The proceeds from the sale of the office building and residential sites in the first block have been committed by the agency to finance the construction of the gardens and half of the cultural center. The funds have been deposited into a special capital account to be drawn on by the agency for those purposes. Other funding available to the agency will be used to complete the cultural center and to construct the gardens above the convention center.

An annual operating budget is to be established for the operations, maintenance, and security of the cultural center and the gardens. These costs will be funded by the agency from the rents and participation fees paid by the development's commercial uses.

Thus, the revenue-producing portions of the project will be supporting the public amenities. The agency has committed itself to the construction and successful operation of the cultural center and the gardens, both because of the essential role they will play in the economic viability of the total development and because of the enormous public benefits they promise to provide.

As part of the decision to charge Olympia & York for the full market value of the land, the agency assumed the costs of maintaining all the amenities in Yerba Buena Gardens beyond the open-space and pedestrian improvements on Block One. There the developer agreed to construct a two-level retail galleria accessible to the public as a passageway into the project from Market Street, and to provide several large plazas in this most densely developed block. The basis for this commitment was that the amenities on this block would convey major economic benefits to Olympia & York's office building and Marriott's hotel and would have been required by the agency even without the multiblock disposition agreement.

Michael Marston, chairman of the board of Keyser Marston Associates, Inc., sums up the negotiating process:

The Yerba Buena Gardens project is clearly the largest real estate transaction in the history of San Francisco, and one of the most complex. Seven land uses, each with their own particular market and financial characteristics, had to be interrelated physically, functionally, and financially. Capital costs and operating budgets for the cultural facilities and gardens—a $50 million package—had to be carefully analyzed and tied directly to the business terms negotiated on the real estate. Further, the negotiations were, of necessity, done in the context of a city charter that favors checks and balances over effectiveness, and results in a political climate that is more used to stopping projects than making them happen. The fact that the project was put together and approved is a minor miracle and a testament to the vision and commitment on both sides of the table, private and public.

Groundbreaking Set for 1985

On November 26, 1984, San Francisco Redevelopment Agency Executive Director Wilbur Hamilton presented the final Yerba Buena Gardens plans to the San Francisco Board of Supervisors, and they approved those actions requiring their consideration, such as street vacations and lease of the Moscone Convention Center rooftop. They also passed a resolution memorializing their intent that all the gardens and cultural facilities specified in the plan should be completed, using the agency funds set aside for those purposes. Groundbreaking was scheduled for 1985. The agency and city expect the entire project to be complete by 1989.

The projected development can be described in block-by-block detail as follows:

On the block fronting Market Street, a forecourt highlighted by a fountain and framed with columns will provide the entrance to Yerba Buena Gardens from Market Street. Pedestrians will pass into a galleria of shops and cafes on two levels under a 120-foot domed roof. Here also will be entrances to the BART and Muni subways under Market Street and to parking. To the east of the forecourt and retail promenade will be Olympia & York's new office building, containing 750,000 square feet of commercial space. To the west on the block will be the 1,500-room Marriott Convention Hotel, connected below ground to the Moscone Convention Center. The galleria will lead to the market square, where the old Jessie Street Substation will resume businesss as a Rouse Company food marketplace. A 40-unit residential condominium building will front on the plaza, with underground parking.

The middle block, lying between the market plaza and the convention center, will contain eight acres of gardens around a spectacular central esplanade rising to a baroque fountain designed to serve as a setting for major outdoor events. The block also will contain a contemplative garden, designed in cooperation with representatives from San Francisco's sister city, Shanghai, and play areas for children. West of the esplanade will be two levels of shops and cafes and an Olympic-size indoor ice skating rink, as well as cabarets and a "learning garden" with educational games for children.

East of the esplanade, in the Center for Arts and Culture, a local nonprofit corporation will showcase San Francisco artists in a 600-seat proscenium theater; a museum-quality, 20,000-square-foot gallery for visual arts exhibitions; a 10,000-square-foot performance space for recitals, workshops, and meetings; and a 100-seat theater for video and film art viewings.

The Market Street Forecourt Plaza as viewed from Grant Avenue. Serving as the main entrance to Yerba Buena Gardens from Market Street, the plaza will provide access to the office building, the hotel, and the Grant Avenue Concourse, a retail space with a 120-foot-high glazed roof.

Central Block Two contains the Festival Plaza, where outdoor public events such as seasonal festivals, pageants, concerts, and other performances will take place. The cultural facilities—theater and gallery space—are shown in the center background.

157

The restored Jessie Street Substation, designed by Willis Polk and developed by the Rouse Company, will house a food market featuring gourmet groceries, fresh California produce, fine wines, and quality crafted merchandise. The second level will contain a restaurant and space for cultural activities.

In the third block, atop the Moscone Convention Center, will lie a complex of film theaters and screening rooms, an amusement pavilion with historic San Francisco themes, restaurants and retail stores, and meeting rooms. They all will be set in a park called Starlight Gardens, with winding walkways, landscaping, and a small lake. The park will be connected to the middle block by pedestrian bridges.

The first buildings to go up will be the office building and hotel on Block One. At the same time, the Rouse Company will be striving to design a marketplace that is not just uniquely San Franciscan, but unique within San Francisco. Mathias DeVito, chief executive officer at Rouse, suggest how formidable this assignment will be:

San Francisco doesn't need anything. It's chock-a-block with small, high-quality stores. So when we do that project, it's not going to be a replica of what's already there. It will have to be a very careful market decision.

Construction of all of the components of the Center for Arts and Culture and the gardens awaits the agency's sale of the office building site on Central Block One. The developer is legally required to purchase this site by the end of July 1986. Before then, the agency will create a nonprofit or-ganization that will work with the agency in the design of the facilities and the construction of the building. The nonprofit also will create a specific program, budget, and management approach for the center. The agency has proposed to provide an annual subsidy of between $2 million and $3 million for the center's projected operations. Activities over and above this operational level, such as presenting and underwriting productions, will have to be generated through donations.

The economic agreement struck by the agency and Olympia & York is flexible and should be able to stand the test of changing market conditions. It provides latitude to the developer in taking down parcels, and it calculates the method of payment—an escalating percentage of net cash flow—in a way that reflects the developer's risks.

San Francisco Planning and Urban Research (SPUR), a nonprofit organization, has pointed out that the cultural center remains the project's unique element, potentially enabling Yerba Buena Gardens to be something more than "a very spacious, nicely landscaped, elegantly designed . . . shopping center." But its management will have to cope with a "somewhat contradictory mandate":

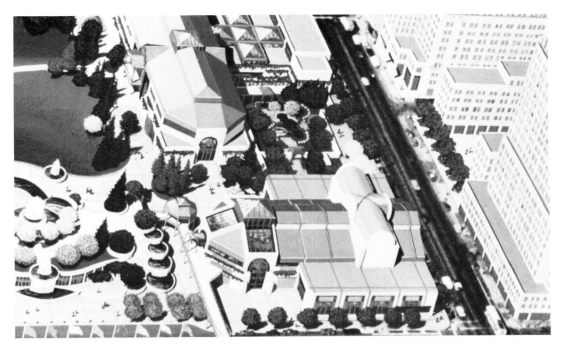

The concept is being praised as a truly innovative means of activating Yerba Buena Gardens, which means that it must succeed in drawing large crowds to the development. It is simultaneously being praised as a means for nurturing aspiring artists and performers in San Francisco. By their very nature, aspiring artists do not have a large following, and using publicly subsidized facilities at Yerba Buena Gardens to nurture them may not draw large crowds to the development.

It is imperative that the nonprofit corporation have in its charter a statement of purpose that emphasizes that it is to manage the cultural complex in such a way that maximizes the number of people visiting Yerba Buena Gardens while at the same time promoting a high quality of artistic merit.

SPUR recommended that an inspired manager be hired as soon as possible to determine how to meet this contradictory mandate. The history of the arts in San Francisco suggests, however, that something more complicated and imponderable probably is necessary, if Yerba Buena Gardens is to convey the city's unique cultural flavor. Perhaps that enlivening ingredient is already at work throughout the arts community, like the yeast in a batch of San Francisco sourdough bread.

Now the hopes and dreams that have sustained the arts community and the re-

development agency must be institutionalized in a capable nonprofit intermediary organization that will make sure that Yerba Buena's arts are neither window dressing for the revenue-producing uses nor simply new venues for performances and exhibitions that already occur in less accessible sites throughout the city. Showcasing is an untested idea in this city that is said to welcome challenge. Yet Yerba Buena's planners have amply demonstrated their commitment to the broad arts community of San Francisco, and the project's potential impact remains remarkable.

South Street Seaport

South Street Seaport and Seaport Marketplace, Inc., occupy a complex of renovated historic buildings and historically compatible new structures within a national historic district just south of the Brooklyn Bridge in Manhattan. The combined museum and commercial development preserve and revive the last vestiges of a 19th-century port that made New York City a world center of commerce. The four-block complex, located between the East River and Water Street and Beekman and John streets, lies about a ten-minute walk south from City Hall.

The project's total budget—$350.55 million—and its sources of funding—$289.5 million from the private sector and $61.05 million from the public—reflect its strategy of mixing commercial with cultural uses to preserve the buildings and operate the surrounding neighborhood as a museum of history.

The South Street Seaport Museum was chartered by the state of New York as a nonprofit educational institution in 1967. Since then, it has been acquiring and restoring landmark warehouses, shops, countinghouses, and sailing ships to create a major maritime museum. Its intent has not been to freeze the district into a replica of the 19th century, but to recreate the ambience of South Street as "a street of ships."

Seaport Marketplace, Inc., created by the Rouse Company, has developed and operates the Fulton Market and Pier 17 Pavilion, new structures devoted to retailing and restaurants that dovetail with the museum's historic buildings across the street and its ships on neighboring piers. Developer Jack R. Resnick & Sons operates a new 35-story office building, One Seaport Plaza, at the Water Street entrance to the historic district. Both enterprises generate income to benefit the museum, whose financial vitality also is enhanced by its own real estate and retail operations in the historic buildings.

The land on which the museum and the commercial projects have been developed was acquired by the museum with the assistance of both the city and state. A series of intricate transactions in 1973 among the museum, the city, and several New York banks resulted in the museum's ownership of the historic buildings in return for the banks' receipt of the air rights above them, along with permission to transfer the air rights to other locations in Lower Manhattan and to sell them when the market for commercial development improved.

The city and the state also obtained a series of federal grants to underwrite various aspects of the design, construction, and restoration of many of the buildings and the enhancement of the pedestrian walkways between them. Few projects have received as much public and private commitment on the basis of a comparatively small amount of private philanthropic investment. This investment has enabled the Seaport Museum to plan for its commercial affiliations with the Rouse Company and to survive until its retail income reaches substantial levels.

The museum enjoys the support of about 10,000 members, who participate in tours of the ships and seaport streets and buildings, special events such as sails in the New York harbor, and concerts on the pier.

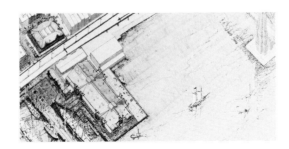

Urban Renewal Threatens
Historic Waterfront

During the late fifties and the sixties, New York City experienced a boom in speculative office development. Many areas of the city came under development pressure, and entire 19th-century districts were demolished for new construction. Lower Manhattan, which had always grown by the replacement of older and smaller buildings with newer and larger ones and by landfill, proved no exception. In 1965, an interim report to the city planning commission recommended that landfill be extended out to the federally defined pierhead line, all the way around Lower Manhattan from Battery Park to the Brooklyn Bridge, and that housing and office buildings be built. The housing, for up to 60,000 residents, would offer some of the 500,000 downtown workers a chance to live within walking distance of their offices, the report declared, and it could add life to an area of the city that essentially shut down after working hours.

To an observer subscribing to that definition of "improvement," the South Street blocks along the river seemed merely a shabby backwater of dilapidated city-owned piers and tumble-down brick buildings that were privately owned but occupied by marginal enterprises or by "squatters" paying no rent. In 1968, a Brooklyn Bridge Southeast urban renewal district was formed, including the entire East River waterfront from the Battery to the Brooklyn Bridge. Block after block of New York's history began to be demolished. Water Street, for instance, once a two-lane, Belgian-block-paved thoroughfare lined with five-story vintage buildings, was turned into a six-lane freeway.

At the same time, however, New York City was creating zoning regulations and incentives to encourage preservation of historic districts and neighborhoods with special characteristics. The first such action, the 1967 theater district legislation, provided a legal framework for negotiation between real estate developers and the city planning commission. Within the boundaries of 40th Street to 57th Street and Sixth Avenue to Eighth Avenue, developers could apply for permits to increase the floor area of their buildings, in exchange for including a legitimate theater inside

them. Following that, a Lincoln Square special zoning district was created in the neighborhood of Lincoln Center to encourage pedestrian uses, and a Fifth Avenue special zoning district aimed to conserve department stores and other retail shops threatened by office and residential tower construction. In Lower Manhattan, a variety of special zoning districts attempted to control new development on the landfill areas and to ensure that large additions would respect and extend the geometry of already existing streets and buildings.

In May 1968 the South Street neighborhood received designation as a special urban renewal district within the larger Brooklyn Bridge Southeast district, and the new South Street Seaport Museum was named the "unassisted" sponsor of the area. This arrangement meant that the museum could acquire properties that the city condemned with its power of eminent domain. The rationale appeared to be a switch: the city would use urban renewal to preserve rather than to clear an area.

Meanwhile, Mayor John Lindsay established the Lower Manhattan Development Office under the chairmanship of Donald H. Elliott (chairman of the city planning commission), to enable the city to participate effectively in the planning and development of this sensitive area. Architect Richard S. Weinstein headed this office. He had supervised the creation of an integrated plan for Manhattan south of Canal Street, projecting residential development and a pedestrian esplanade along the East River at South Street, with commercial development inland.

The city's plan for the South Street district therefore was to preserve the historic buildings and revitalize them with appropriate dense commercial activities, as well as a seaport museum. The Lindsay administration believed that commercial development, controlled by and integrated with seaport restoration, would meet multiple objectives of economic growth, urban design, quality of life, and preservation.

Sea Buffs Save "Old Salt" Structures

Buying and selling have been the life-blood of the South Street waterfront from the time it emerged as Manhattan's principal port in the 18th century, and the dynamics of the marketplace have determined its fate ever since. Until the Civil War, the district remained the center of the city's flourishing maritime commerce. Merchants directed their empires from countinghouses such as the Schermerhorn Row on Fulton Street, and tall ships from around the world lined the South Street wharves. Ferry service to Brooklyn's Fulton Street commenced in 1814, and the first Fulton Market, a general emporium for provisions and dry goods, opened in 1822; it became New York's central source of both food from Long Island farmers and spices from China traders. The port's prosperity began to wane in the 1860s as steamships replaced clippers, but its gradual decline preserved a rare assemblage of low-rise 18th- and 19th-century buildings.

What survived into the 1960s—despite severe rot and dilapidation—were some streets lined with simple warehouses, countinghouses, and places of business built of brick and granite in an agreeable scale of four to six stories. After a century of abuse, many of them still survived with their original beams, walls, commercial paint, and the undisturbed patina of time.

As these old buildings were threatened with demolition, a small group of concerned citizens mounted an effort to save the waterfront blocks, approximately from John Street northward to the Brooklyn Bridge. This group was led by Peter Stanford, an advertising executive with an affinity for old ships and shipping environs. In 1967, after the group formed the South Street Seaport Museum and received a charter as a nonprofit organization, he became the organization's president.

The museum moved immediately to obtain city landmark status for Schermerhorn Row, twelve red brick buildings along the south side of Fulton Street built as warehouses between 1810 and 1812. The size, age, and architectural quality of this row made it a site of national importance as well, and it was designated a national historic landmark in 1969.

Even before the museum had been formed, a number of the row buildings had been occupied by artists who lived rent-free in spaces they converted to studios and residences. The work they did on the buildings probably helped to preserve them, and they proved sympathetic to the Seaport Museum's plans. Also contributing to the area's vitality was the Fulton Fish Market. The oldest continuously operating wholesale market in the United States, located in the district since 1823, it was no relic but one of the largest and busiest wholesale fish markets in the world.

Stanford and his growing band of ardent volunteers did not envision their museum merely as buildings in which collections would be displayed. Instead they wanted to preserve an entire neighborhood within

South Street from Maiden Lane in 1828.

South Street area in 1949. Fallen into disrepair after most of its clientele moved uptown, the Fulton Market was torn down and replaced in 1953 with a one-story storage garage that also housed vendors from the wholesale fish market across the street.

Museum and City Bank Air-Rights "Futures" to Buy Buildings

which people who appreciated its character would live and work—artists, craftspersons, and shopkeepers catering to all income levels. The plan also aimed to assemble a rare combination of restored historic ships, berthed in the East River next to the buildings that once served such vessels. The museum already owned the *Wavertree*, an 1885 full-rigged sailing ship built for the jute trade between India and Europe; the *Pioneer*, a 102-foot schooner built as a coastal sloop in 1885, restored in 1970, and used for public sails around the harbor during the summer; the *Lettie G. Howard*, an 1893 Gloucester fishing schooner, typical of the vessels that brought their catch to the Fulton Fish Market; and the *Maj. Gen. William H. Hart*, a 1925 steam ferryboat, a survivor of the last generation of East River ferries. However, the museum increasingly was hard-pressed simply to maintain the ships, let alone to restore them and open them to the public.

The museum's leaders believed that some new commercial structures could be built to fill in gaps in the South Street Seaport streetscape, but they were determined that these buildings should respect the character and scale of the neighborhood. To acquire the Schermerhorn Row buildings, Stanford developed a scheme with the Lower Manhattan Development Office. Although preserving the low-rise buildings would mean that the rights to develop the air space above them would go unused, precedents existed for transferring such rights. The museum intended to stretch those precedents and pool the air rights pertaining to *all* the old buildings and the closed streets in the district, "bank" their development rights, sell them to developers of other sites in Lower Manhattan designated by the planning commission, and use the proceeds to buy the historic properties. This plan envisioned that the row buildings then would be restored one by one by the artists, craftspersons, and shopkeepers who would occupy them.

When the South Street Seaport Museum was founded in 1967, Schermerhorn Row was owned by Atlas-McGrath, Inc., a development company that intended to demolish the buildings to build a large commercial tower. To prevent their destruction, a business corporation called Seaport Holdings, Inc., was created by Jakob Isbrandtsen, a prominent shipper who served as chairman of the museum board. Seaport Holdings bought 155 John Street, behind Schermerhorn Row, in January 1969, thus disrupting the Atlas-McGrath assemblage. It also purchased the blocks north of Schermerhorn Row, with the intent to hold the buildings in escrow until the museum could buy them. These Seaport Holdings purchases were financed almost entirely by bank loans secured by mortgages on the acquired properties.

Meanwhile, the museum had been designated by the city as an entity that could benefit from urban renewal powers to condemn and could purchase the Schermerhorn Row buildings at fair market value. The Lower Manhattan Development Office and the city planning department worked out special zoning district legislation that would allow for the transfer of the buildings' air rights to seven sites elsewhere in Lower Manhattan, so that these development rights could subsidize the preservation of the buildings.

By the early seventies, however, the market for office buildings in Lower Manhattan had begun to decline, and while Atlas-McGrath could not move to demolish, neither could the museum move to preserve, since there were no purchasers for the air rights. Seaport Holdings fell in arrears on both its taxes and on interest payments on its mortgages, which the banks moved to foreclose.

To save its plan for a pedestrian-oriented historic district, the Lower Manhattan Development Office orchestrated a complicated plan. The city paid $8 million to purchase four blocks on Fulton Street, including the Atlas-McGrath properties, Schermerhorn Row, and piers 15 and 18, and to pay off $2.8 million of the mortgages on Seaport Holdings' properties in the two blocks across from the row. The rest of the money owed by Seaport Holdings was paid in the form of 1,200,000 square feet of transferred air rights given to a consortium of the banks, who received permission to hold them until improved market conditions enabled their sale. Richard Weinstein of the development office termed this transaction "a kind of air-rights futures commodity exchange."

The plan to rescue Seaport Holdings from its obligations was completed in June 1973. Subsequently, the banks made sales of a portion of the development rights at prices significantly above their 1973 values. The city immediately leased to the museum three of the blocks it had bought, as well as the piers and other properties it owned in the district. Thus the museum acquired a 99-year lease on the Schermerhorn Row block (which became known as the museum block) bounded by Fulton, Beekman, Water, and Front streets, and on the Fulton Market block bounded by Fulton, Beekman, Front, and South streets. The city leased an empty lot at the Water Street entrance to the seaport district to the telephone company, which intended to build a switching tower on top of a retail complex. The $8 million lease payments paid to the city equaled the debt service paid by the city on bonds it issued to purchase the seaport blocks. Thus the private sector and the museum held the city free from any actual costs. In the end, the telephone company did not pick up its option to buy the block at the end of its lease, and the city sold the block for $13 million to a developer who has built an office building. So the city eventually made $5 million on the property it rescued.

In July 1974 the Schermerhorn Row block was removed from the 99-year lease and sold to the Seaport Museum, which then immediately sold it to the state of New York to house the seven-year-old, financially strapped New York State Maritime Museum. The $300,000 profit realized by this transaction was set aside to be used to relocate the Schermerhorn residents.

The Maritime Museum set up shop in Schermerhorn Row, believing that the two museums could complement each other. As negotiations developed with the Rouse Company, however, and the South Street Seaport Museum sought as much space as possible to offer Rouse for commercial uses, it became clear that the two museums had differing long-term objectives, and that they would compete adversely for the same private funds. In 1979 the Maritime Museum lost its battle to stay open at the seaport. Before it closed, it supported the work of a team of restorationists who documented the entire row for the purpose of restoring the facades.

The Seaport Museum, meanwhile, had launched its own program of restoration and education. The *Wavertree* and the *Peking*, a four-masted steel bark it received in 1974, were restored. The museum presented musical and dramatic performances on the piers and published a popular magazine. It also managed the commercial prop-

Warehouses related to the Fulton Fish Market along Beekman Street, circa 1970. These were characteristic of the utilitarian structures that surrounded the more important Market House of the 19th century. Cable-hung tin canopies were a typical addition.

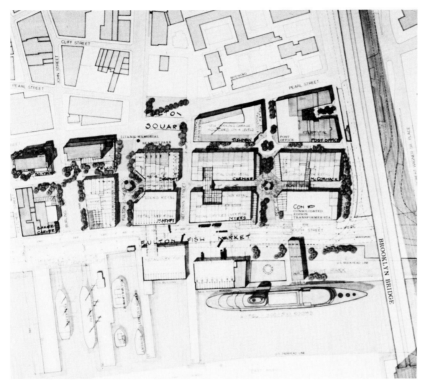

erties in the museum block, Fulton Market block, and Piers 15–18. In 1976, the seaport became a focal point of Bicentennial activity when the tall ships sailed into its harbor on the Fourth of July. In 1977, the New York City Landmarks Preservation Commission designated the entire existing urban renewal district—from John Street to the Brooklyn Bridge—as the South Street Seaport Historic District.

Several years followed of search and struggle to produce income sufficient to create an authentic historic setting. Dissension reigned on the board; disheartened staff members and volunteers left, eventually including even Peter Stanford. Board members whose interest lay more in yachting and the maritime trades than in preservation argued that the only way to save the buildings was to consider them as business investments. These board members believed that the incremental, building-by-building approach to the district's development would be too complicated, too costly, and too long. They advocated fewer developers—or possibly only one—who through the economics and efficiencies of scale could start money flowing into the museum.

Management problems further complicated the situation. Between 1974 and 1977, four different executive directors—and much of the rest of the staff—came and went without maintaining continuity in program or financial planning. In 1977 the New York City Comptroller's Office issued a report criticizing the museum's financial management. The museum had not paid its rent to the city for two years; it had negotiated unprofitable concession leases; and it had taken the $300,000 special fund for the relocation of the Schermerhorn Row artist "squatters" and spent it on administrative matters.

There was even dissatisfaction within the preservation community concerning the museum's care of its collection. The museum had received a $4 million federal public works grant for the restoration of Pier 16 and the entire neighboring block, but some of the restorations were deemed unsatisfactory and had to be redone. Relationships with neighbors, who at first had enthusiastically welcomed the museum, soured; the museum staff supported an effort to relocate the fish market to the Bronx (as a way to get more commercial space), and it even attempted to evict the Schermerhorn Row artist tenants. As a result, it was accused by other property owners in the area of throwing its urban-renewal weight around.

Early in 1977 John Hightower, former director of the Museum of Modern Art, was appointed president of the museum, and James Shepley, president of Time, Inc., assumed the position of chairman of the board. After examining the museum's spotty financial record, they began exploring retail development of the seaport district, within a historic seaport theme.

Rouse's Marketplace Joins
Street and Sea, Past and Present

In 1976, Seaport Museum officials had begun talking with staff at the Rouse Company of Columbia, Maryland. The success of Rouse's Faneuil Hall Marketplace in Boston gave the museum board hope that the company could develop a similar complex of retail shops and eating places that could be at once historic and contemporary, and would stabilize and save the district.

This notion provoked a spirited debate among New York's preservation community. Could such development truly preserve the seaport's earthy vitality and history and at the same time generate sufficient dollars for cultural and restoration programs? Considering the museum's financial, management, and preservation problems, there was some question as to whether it could negotiate a contract that would be to the advantage of its ships and buildings. Several other questions emerged that would recur as the development evolved: How could the variety and surprise found in the old buildings be preserved as they were rehabilitated and as new restaurants, food shops, and boutiques were placed next to them? Would the seaport's drawing power, springing from its long-established identity as a wholesale fish market, be compromised by trendy boutiques or fast-food eateries? What mixture of retail uses could attract sophisticated New Yorkers in sufficient numbers to cover costs and make a profit? Would a place remain for maritime-oriented arts, crafts, and workshops as originally envisioned? Would the infill buildings visually or physically overwhelm the seaport and hinder access to the river? Would this new development escalate the real estate values in the area and thus change the scale and use of the surrounding neighborhood?

Even proponents of the idea that the museum should develop the property itself were impressed, however, by Rouse's track record and level of taste. "Rouse makes a point of balancing uses," the Municipal Art Society's Margot Wellington told *Historic Preservation* magazine. "They're able to go out and get what's missing in a project. They're comfortable in encouraging local entrepreneurs. And they have the credibility to put the package together."

The museum decided to go ahead. To conduct a feasibility study, it put up $100,000 from a gift by the Astor Foundation, and the Rouse Company contributed an equal share in time by its employees and consultants. The museum hired Christopher Lowery, who had served in the New York City planning department and development office, to head the museum's real estate effort, and it retained Webster & Sheffield to be its special counsel for the project.

The feasibility study aimed to test the original vision of the seaport as a magnet for visitors who would patronize both the museum and a marketplace. The Rouse Company relied on Benjamin Thompson & Associates, architects and planners of Faneuil Hall Marketplace, to find a commercially viable site within the historic blocks between the Brooklyn Bridge and Fulton Street or Burling Slip and John Street. Which streets and properties could be assembled and unified to make a coherent development core with convenient circulation, consistent environment, and ample public space?

Three inland blocks west of Franklin Delano Roosevelt Drive and oriented to Front Street were controlled by the museum, but they did not provide sufficient area for commercial development and they lacked complexity and historic impact. The museum's principal exhibits—the tall ships *Peking* and *Wavertree*—were docked along the river east of Franklin Delano Roosevelt Drive, yet the pedestrian connections to them along Fulton Street and across South Street—both heavily trafficked—remained difficult and at times dangerous.

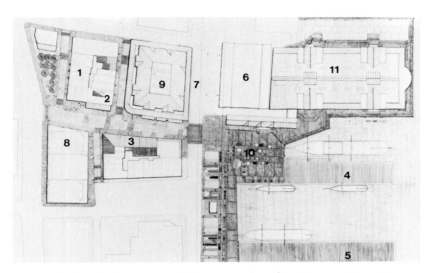

Master plan for development of the South Street Seaport historic district, including (1) museum block; (2) Bogardus Building; (3) Schermerhorn Row; (4,5) Piers 15 and 16; (6) Fulton Fish Market; (7) fish stall annex; (8) Seaport Plaza; (9) Seaport Marketplace; (10) plaza; and (11) Pier 17 Pavilion.

After extensive planning studies of the north–south Front Street locale, Benjamin Thompson & Associates made a strong recommendation that the east–west Fulton Street—which, controlled by the city, was technically out of bounds—be transformed into a central walking street that would tie the district together. It would lead from the financial district to the river's edge where, on a reconstructed pier, a new building could be constructed to contain 150,000 square feet of commercial space adjacent to the tall ships. This plan called for a new market on the site of two previous market buildings at the corner of Fulton and South streets, and it left the Fulton Fish Market undisturbed. The two new buildings—at the market and on the pier—would solve the Rouse Company's space needs while providing pedestrian access to the water and to the museum's exhibition ships.

Assessing the commercial feasibility of this proposal, the Rouse Company believed the seaport would be supported by a clientele comparable to that of Boston's Faneuil Hall Marketplace. It therefore would have three constituencies—residents, workers, and visitors—each with a different point of origin but with a similar perception of the retail center as a source of entertainment and as a unique offering of food and specialty items in a single urban complex.

While part of the ultimate success would depend on an increased number of workers in new offices to be built around the site, visitors would provide the largest initial potential source of buyers at South Street Sea-

port. Rouse projected annual sales at $724 per square foot by 1987, when all phases of the marketplace would be operating. To achieve this goal, the seaport would need to maintain a strong historical atmosphere to attract a high volume of tourists. But besides visitors, the seaport's success also would depend on area residents patronizing grocery stores, butchers, and bakeries, and on office workers lunching and shopping in the neighborhood.

Rouse proposed to create a marketplace setting that, although not similar in function to the wholesale trading markets of the 19th century, would be similar in flavor to the markets of that time. The museum agreed with this concept. "It was never the intention of the original seaport supporters," said museum director Ellen Fletcher, "to create a district like historic Williamsburg—perfectly preserved at a certain point in time. Instead, supporters intended South Street Seaport to be a continually usable living area."

A report on these ideas resulted in a letter of intent signed in 1979 by Governor Hugh Carey; Mayor Edward Koch; James Shepley, chairman of the board of the museum; and Mathias DeVito, president of the Rouse Company.

Museum, City, State, and Rouse Decide Who Does What

The feasibility study and the letter of intent set in motion a formal land use plan that required approval by the city planning commission and the New York City Board of Estimate.

The letter of intent also defined the roles of each of the participants. The museum was to be responsible for presenting the historical exhibits and programs in the restored ships, including the *Wavertree* and the *Peking*; for carrying out exhibitions on the piers, in Schermerhorn Row, and in the museum block buildings; and for maintaining the public spaces on the piers and streets in the district. It also was to develop approximately 100,000 square feet of commercial office space itself, enabling it to restore other historic buildings and to complete various parts of Schermerhorn Row and the museum block. Finally, it would eventually launch a multimillion-dollar capital fund drive to prepare the interior spaces of its buildings and to complete all ship restorations.

The Rouse Company was to develop approximately 100,000 square feet of festival marketplace space by constructing a building facing South and Fulton streets, using property leased from the museum on the ground floor of Schermerhorn Row and in the museum block. As the city completed its construction of a new Pier 17, Rouse was to build the second stage—a new retail-and-restaurant pavilion on the pier and other new and renovated properties, bringing its total retail space to approximately 300,000 square feet and its cost to $90 million.

An Urban Development Action Grant of $20.4 million from the U.S. Department of Housing and Urban Development was awarded to the city in January 1981 to construct Pier 17. To obtain the UDAG grant, the city and a private developer, Jack R. Resnick & Sons, agreed to construct a $100 million office tower with first- and second-floor retailing on Fulton and Water streets at the entranceway to the seaport. The city also was responsible for making infrastructure improvements in the 14-block area, including street improvements, lighting, and pedestrian promenades along the river.

The state of New York, through its Urban Development Corporation, was to restore

Detailed model of Fulton Market demonstrates use of vernacular forms in hipped roof, canvas canopies, and cable-hung canopy, which wraps around the building for weather shelter.
Credit: Steve Rosenthal

Schermerhorn Row and its block and to build a new building on the corner of South Street and Burling Slip, all at an estimated cost of $10.5 million. The finished space would be part of the lease of the museum, which in turn would sublease most of the ground floor to the Rouse Company. The residential tenants in the Schermerhorn buildings would be permitted to stay and would have an opportunity to purchase their units at much below their market value.

The Board of Estimate approved these land use plans in November 1980. The museum and the city renegotiated their lease to accommodate a museum sublease to the Rouse Company. The negotiations proved extended, but they were successfully completed and unanimously approved by the Board of Estimate in October 1981.

The Seaport Becomes a Living Timeline

The approval of Benjamin Thompson & Associates' plan to make Fulton Street the pedestrian spine for the seaport meant that, once again, a food market building would become the center of the district, and that Fulton Street would provide the major commercial frontage. The scheme moved the critical mass of new retailing space out of the preservation blocks to the riverfront, where it could provide dramatic new experiences and pleasures.

For nearly 200 years South Street had been the heart of the wholesale fish business in New York City, and from midnight until dawn the area still was alive with trucks delivering and picking up fish and with individual fish filleting and processing businesses. Half of the 39,000-square-foot block reserved for Rouse's new Fulton Market was occupied by one-story fish stalls fronting on South Street. The market therefore was designed to be built over them, allowing new ground-level retailing only on the upland side facing Front Street. Like the 1823 and 1882 markets that preceded it, the new four-level Fulton Market for groceries, specialty foods, and restaurants took a shed-like form and structure, as open as possible on all sides to emphasize the historic link with the sea from which goods flowed to the city. It aimed for "shirtsleeves" character, achieved with materials traditional to the Seaport district—granite, brick, corrugated steel, tile, and stone—and elements such as a hipped roof, dormers, and cable-hung canopy that convey authenticity while serving a tight functional plan and exacting contemporary code requirements.

The old Tin Building, which houses the main portion of the wholesale fish market, would remain across South Street under Franklin Delano Roosevelt Drive. Thus, the district could enjoy a daytime and a nighttime population—tourists, office workers, and residents by day, and the fish market by night.

The designers projected the new Rouse building on Pier 17 as a great hall of commerce that would be alive with stores and restaurants, providing a much-needed public gathering and viewing place on the waterfront. Precursors of this pier could be found in New York's 19th-century "recreation piers," which had provided city dwellers with large, parklike, open-air structures on the upper decks of shipping docks. People could stroll, dance, and play games while enjoying the breezes of the riverfront. The Pier 17 Pavilion would be a three-story shed with some 40,000 square feet on each floor. On each level, arcades, corridors, and crossings beneath large lightwells would give restaurants, cafes, and retail areas maximum waterfront exposure and views up and down the river. It would be constructed of steel and glass, with the steel siding painted the red color of the nearby *Ambrose* lightship.

The pavilion will call attention to the museum's exhibition ships. Walkways will connect the pier and the ships, the Fulton market, and the museum block and Schermerhorn Row museum spaces and shops. In designing the two new Rouse buildings, Benjamin Thompson & Associates hoped to respond to the museum's needs, to fulfill current city codes and laws, and to create a place where culture and commerce could blend. As the architects put it:

The challenge was to design two new buildings that might have grown on their sites, that would feel right as the festive centerpiece of a revitalized neighborhood, that would feel at home with the past but not historical. . . . We wanted to create buildings that belonged to a neighborhood without donning a costume of any kind.

Fulton Market's east–west building sections show escalator connection that rises over the existing fish stalls on South Street.
Credit: Benjamin Thompson & Associates

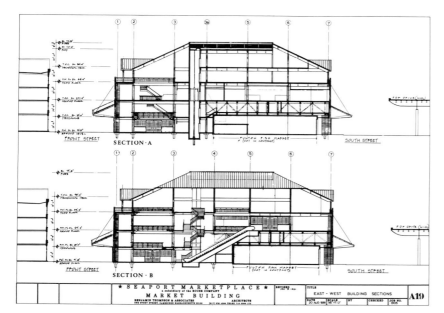

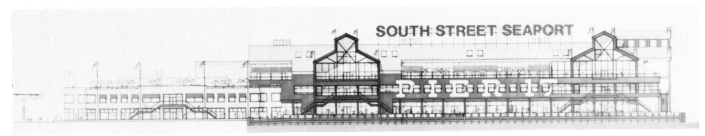

SOUTH STREET SEAPORT

Being sensitive to the buildings' attractive patina of age was different from being nostalgic, they said:

Buildings, like people, must be allowed to develop, change, and be superseded by new generations. . . . We have the chance to restore "forward," to join successive periods and forms in elegant and compatible ways. . . . Cumulatively, [new buildings] express the depth of a timeline in the life of a . . . city. That timeline is one of architecture's most important contributions to historic understanding, and understanding of history's many dimensions is what museums are all about.

Expansion of Cultural/Interpretive Functions

When negotiations over the basic construction, lease, and operations of the expanded district were concluded in early 1982, the South Street Seaport Museum staff turned its attention to an expanded exhibitions program, making use of historic vessels, galleries, shops, and interpretive and educational tours to bring visitors into contact with New York City's roots as a center of international maritime trade.

By the spring and summer of 1984, the museum's staff had formulated an interpretive concept that would stimulate seaport visitors to examine four major historic forces that shaped the seaport and the city: the physical relationship between the waterfront and commercial development; the economic process by which New York rose to the status of the largest port in the world by World War I; New York's contribution to maritime technology; and the social aspects of life at sea and on shore.

The museum plans to make its new building at 90 South Street an orientation center where it can present a short slide show on the history of trade in New York City. A series of permanent exhibits will cover the city's maritime and commercial history. They will include both traditional exhibits and restored spaces on the first floors of the Low Building and in the A. A. Low Countinghouse. Since printers and stationers were a mainstay of the waterfront community throughout the 19th century, a major exhibit in the Seaport Gallery on Water Street will create a historical context for Bowne & Co. Stationers located next door. Changing temporary exhibits will aim to keep visitors coming back. The ship restoration program continues as a priority.

Given the district's mix of museum, retail, and office uses, the museum will need to call increased attention to itself as a major presence, identifying its own facilities and providing some introductory historical information about the streets, ships, and buildings. An outdoor signage program will include large wall signs at entrances to the district: logotype signs to identify the galleries, installations, and shops that are components of the museum; labels to provide basic information about ships and selected historic buildings; and a series of replaceable posters presenting information about historic businesses and people.

This ambitious interpretive program, funded by earned income from the museum's stores, restaurants, and offices, will aim to fulfill the purpose of the museum, inscribed on a sign near its entrance:

This Museum is a neighborhood. It is streets, piers, ships, shops, markets, galleries, people. New York City's history and great mercantile tradition began here and await your discovery.

The financing to realize these efforts has come from a variety of sources, and little of it would have been either directly or immediately available to the museum without the participation of the Rouse Company.

South Street Seaport
Project Data

Component—Income Generating	Phase I	Profile at Build-Out (1985)
Retail		
Schermerhorn Row	29,000 sq. ft.	29,000 sq. ft.
Fulton Market	60,000 sq. ft.	60,000 sq. ft.
Museum Block	20,000 sq. ft.	20,000 sq. ft.
Seaport Plaza	23,500 sq. ft.	23,500 sq. ft.
Pier 17 Pavilion		125,000 sq. ft.
Subtotal	132,500 sq. ft.	257,500 sq. ft.
Office		
Seaport Plaza	1,000,000 sq. ft.	1,000,000 sq. ft.
Museum Block	35,000 sq. ft.	35,000 sq. ft.
Schermerhorn Row		25,000 sq. ft.
Subtotal	1,035,000 sq. ft.	1,060,000 sq. ft.

Component—Arts/Culture/ Open Space		
South Street Seaport Museum		
Museum Block (incl. Visitor Center)		
Exhibit Space	3,050 sq. ft.	5,570 sq. ft.
Office	9,675 sq. ft.	9,675 sq. ft.
Support	11,575 sq. ft.	9,050 sq. ft.
Schermerhorn Row		
Exhibit Space	2,500 sq. ft.	34,650 sq. ft.
Support	11,050 sq. ft.	4,400 sq. ft.
Two Piers		
Subtotal	37,850 sq. ft.	63,345 sq. ft.

Other		
Parking	400 spaces	400 spaces
Residential		30,900 sq. ft.

Acreage		
Land	13.1 acres	13.1 acres
Water	4.8 acres	4.8 acres
Gross Building Area	1,167,500 sq. ft. (plus cultural)	1,317,500 sq. ft.
Floor/Area Ratio	2.07	2.32
Location	Manhattan, south of Brooklyn Bridge	
Master Developer	The Rouse Company	
Development Period	1967–83	1985
Estimated Total	$350.55 million	

Source: South Street Seaport Museum

Each portion of the commercial development at Rouse's Marketplace is designed to generate substantial income for the museum. The Rouse Company will pay as rent to the museum the greater of $3.50 per square foot or 15 percent of its gross rental income from its subtenants. Then, by a complex formula and after deducting operating and nonreimbursable expenses and allowing for a return on the company's investment, the commercial revenues will, in effect, be shared equally with the museum.

In addition, the Rouse Company has agreed to pay 50 percent of the cost of maintaining much of the seaport's outdoor public spaces, with the remainder of the costs being paid by the museum. In turn, the museum will share its rental income from the project with the city and the state, who are the actual owners of the property. The museum will pay them $2.40 per square foot of space leased to Rouse. Revenue in excess of this amount will be shared, with 80 percent going to the museum and 20 percent to the city and state.

It is estimated that in 1985, when the first full year of the development project is complete, the city and the state will collectively receive $972,000. The museum expects to earn $1,582,000, with which it must meet its daily area maintenance obligations. It is projected to increase its development revenues by 1990 to just over $1.9 million. By 1991, estimates predict that the museum's earned income will be 80 percent of its budget; membership and contributions will be 20 percent. This ratio contrasts with 1981 figures, in which only 40 percent of the museum's budget was earned and 60 percent was contributed, and with a 1984 estimate of 55 percent earned and 45 percent contributed.

The maintenance/management approach that has been taken for the district's outside areas is equally complex. The museum was concerned about maintaining an appropriate historical setting in which new retail and commercial uses would support rather than overwhelm the historic buildings and exhibition program. The Rouse Company, while endorsing these goals, wanted to ensure that its retail tenants would be supported in *their* objectives of achieving a commercial environment that would attract workers, residents, and visitors.

In the 1981 lease agreement between the city and the museum, the museum assumed responsibility for overall maintenance and security of the streets and common areas within the district. It also retained the power to decide on the appropriateness of all retail and festival activities in the public open spaces, on the basis of consistency with the historical mission. This operating partnership—a first for the Rouse Company—presents a significant benefit: Because the museum is a nonprofit corporation, it can contract for maintenance and security more cheaply than can Rouse.

This arrangement also required a lengthy series of negotiations between the museum and Rouse on the nature and extent of activities within the site, technically called the "joint maintenance area." Rouse must obtain approval from the museum on street vendors, outdoor entertainment, and seasonal decorations. In planning for and in advertising these activities, Rouse will pursue its primary goal of bringing large numbers of people to its project to eat and shop. The museum, while respecting the need of the Rouse Company and its tenants (many of them local merchants without independent reputations) for high sales volume, will aim to maintain a sense of historic integrity for the district as a whole. To resolve potential conflicts and to develop a common understanding of how these differing objectives can be met, representatives from each sector meet weekly to develop a streetscape program that will make the streets festive but respect the neighborhood's historic integrity.

During the years when the commercial development of the seaport was being planned and coming into operation, the museum expanded its administration by creating three new corporations to handle the commercial restoration, real estate, and curatorial tasks. In 1982 the nonprofit South Street Seaport Corporation was established to help insulate the museum from those duties more appropriate to a real estate corporation and to ensure that the museum could remain in possession of its own buildings and interpretive materials in the remote possibility that it would default on its lease with the city. A majority of its

South Street Seaport
Development Cost Summary

	Public	Private
Seaport Plaza (office building)		$176.0 million
Development of Market block, Pier Pavilion, and retail improvements in Schermerhorn Row, Museum and Telco blocks plus tenant construction		102.5 million
Development of multiscreen theater		3.0 million
Development of rental office space in Museum and Schermerhorn Row block		8.0 million
Restoration of Museum block	$4.3 million	
Fulton Fish Market improvements	3.3 million	
Design, construction, and management fees for structural stabilization and rehabilitation of Schermerhorn Row	10.0 million	
Design and construction of waterfront streetscape, South Street, and related improvements (sewer and waterworks)	23.0 million	
Construction of pier platform and pedestrian infrastructure improvements; loan to SSSM for facility renovation and construction	20.45 million	
TOTAL	$61.05 million	$289.5 million

Source: South Street Seaport Museum

15-member board is nominated by and must be members of the museum board.

Since income derived from the restoration and development functions of this corporation is to be exempt from taxation, it was important to preserve its nonprofit status from legal challenge. Two additional subsidiaries therefore were created to engage in profitable ventures. South Street Seaport Properties manages the offices on the upper floors of the museum's properties and the retail spaces at ground level. It collaborates with outside investors in the development of these sites and manages them when they are leased. The South Street Seaport Museum Shops operates a range of galleries and shops scattered throughout the district, including a stationery store, a book and chart store, a model shop, and a children's store.

By organizing itself into these separate nonprofit and business sectors, the museum has expanded its traditional historical and interpretive functions and directly involved itself in the real estate opportunities of the entire mixed-use district.

Historic Preservation Coexists with a Shopping/Dining Extravaganza

In a November 1984 newsletter to cardmembers of a national credit card company, South Street Seaport was featured as one of a half-dozen festival-marketing shopping centers around the country: Come for Christmas—and bring your credit card!

Charles Dickens would love New York's South Street Seaport. In fact, during the holiday season, this restored 18th-century seaport-turned-shopping/dining-extravaganza will have many authentic trappings of Dickens' day, featuring horse-drawn carriages that carry shoppers down cobblestone streets, outdoor market vendors offering roasting chestnuts, hot apple cider, and fresh-cut wreaths. There will be daily performances by Victorian-garbed Dickens characters and a special reading of *A Christmas Carol* by New York celebrities.

Whether preservation purists would approve of this come-on by the Rouse Company's Marketplace is perhaps not so much to the point as whether the visitor who is lured by Dickensiana will at least get a whiff and a glimpse of some authentic seaport history in between buying and eating. Here is what South Street Seaport offers current visitors:

■ *The Museum Block.* Fourteen buildings have been restored by the museum for its exhibits and offices, as well as for commercial retail (22,000 square feet) and office space (35,000). The oldest building in this block dates from 1797. Besides the museum's maritime library and a theater presenting a multimedia show about the area's history, there are history-oriented commercial establishments—the Seaport Gallery, the Edmund M. Blunt Book & Chart Store, Bowne & Co. Stationers (founded on the site in 1775), and the like.

■ *Schermerhorn Row.* With their structures stabilized and the storefronts restored, the twelve buildings on Fulton Street are truly living landmarks. In these buildings and in the warehouses and countinghouses behind them are 29,000 square feet of stores, 50,000 square feet of museum galleries, 25,000 square feet of offices, and 31,500 square feet of loft residences.

■ *Historic Ships.* Restored, berthed, and exhibited at Piers 15 and 16 are the *Ambrose*

lightship (1908); the *Maj. Gen. William H. Hart*, an East River ferryboat (1925), the *Lettie G. Howard*, a fishing schooner (1893); the *Peking*, a four-masted steel bark (1911); the *Pioneer*, a coastal sloop now used for summer sails in the harbor (1885); and the *Wavertree*, the last full-rigged sailing ship on the east coast (1885).

■ *Fulton Market.* This centerpiece of the Rouse Company's Seaport Marketplace, Inc., opened in 1983. Its four stories contain 60,000 square feet of leasable area for restaurants, specialty food stalls, and a market hall offering fresh groceries.

■ *Pier 17 Pavilion.* Also operated by the Marketplace, this new, three-story, steel-and-glass structure is built on top of piers in the East River. Scheduled to open during the summer of 1985, it will house 110,000 square feet of shops and restaurants, plus public promenades and sitting places with views of the museum's exhibit ships to the south and the Brooklyn Bridge to the north.

■ *One Seaport Plaza.* This 35-story office building was developed by Jack Resnick & Sons at the Water Street entrance to the district, on the block the city leased and then took back from the phone company. Stores on its lower levels are leased and managed by the Marketplace.

With the opening of the Rouse Company's Marketplace and its own growing success in leasing stores and offices, the museum has the potential to generate more earned income from commerce than it receives from memberships and contributions. For museum staff members responsible for operating and shaping the historic district's public spaces, authenticity is no longer a question of making the fewest possible compromises in order for the museum to survive, but rather of how to maintain original purposes in the face of possibly spectacular commercial success. In January 1981 a *New York Times* editorial warned that a sophisticated 20th-century commercial complex would not be compatible in the long term with the district's historic character: "The present concept is more dependent on the spirit of retailing than on any older spirit of time or place."

The museum staff has certainly accepted the challenge to disprove that judgment, as it develops a multifaceted program to make visitors aware of the seaport as far more than a backdrop for shopping. There are exhibits and tours of the ships at the piers, historic collections and interpretive exhibits on view in the museum galleries in the old buildings, dramatic presentations of seaport history, and a host of guided tours—from visiting the Fulton Fish Market at dawn to seeing the long-abandoned but still haunting hotel spaces in the upper floors of the Schermerhorn Row block.

The Rouse Company shows every indication of remaining in sympathy with the museum's priorities, for the very good reason that the museum improves business. In 1984, Rouse chairman and president Mathias DeVito explained that "The Rouse Company would be very reluctant to do a Faneuil Hall or a Harborplace or a Seaport if there wasn't already strong evidence of people being interested in and drawn to that location. Retail cannot be the pioneer." He acknowledged "tugging and hauling" with the museum staff over what the Marketplace can do within the seaport's historic setting:

We have to work very closely with them. Their buildings and our shops are very interrelated. . . . We both have the same objective—that the buildings should represent a contemporary use, at the same time preserving their historic sense. . . . When that project is finished it will reflect the best interrelationship between a cultural institution and a private developer that you will be able to find in America.

Critics of the museum's tug toward upscale commercialism—through its own enterprises as well as through its lease with Rouse—also must remind themselves that no urban neighborhood can be expected to exist apart from its social and economic context and populace. For the seaport, that context is Lower Manhattan adjoining Wall Street, a fast-changing, ever-more-fashionable area. In 1981, before the Marketplace and One Seaport Plaza had been built, New York preservationists Barry Lewis and Virginia Dajani lamented in *The Livable City* the inevitable encroachment of out-of-scale skyscrapers and out-of-character "boutiques and spinach-salad cafes" upon the old sea-

Crowds of spectators jam Fulton Street on opening day, July 28, 1983. The corner adjacent to Fulton Street (left), part of the block restored by the South Street Seaport Museum, was rebuilt by Beyer Blinder Belle, Architects, in the style of 19th-century cast-iron architecture.
Credit: Steve Rosenthal

port streetscape. But they acknowledged the realities the South Street Seaport Museum had to accept as the price of survival:

We should not fault the museum for being born in one age and having to live with the realities of another. If, as seems inevitable, future buildings in the seaport district are to be luxury loft apartments and mammoth office towers, perhaps this is all the more reason to throw united support to the Seaport Museum. There's got to be someone to look after what little is left of the past.

In the final analysis, it is hard to fault the museum for its commercialism. Commercialism is inlaid in every brick and dollop of mortar of the old seaport buildings, in every original timber or bolt of the tall ships. It does seem that 19th-century commerce was less crass, less ostentatious, more human in scale, less passive, more involving—because that buying and selling existed in a kindlier, slower, sweatier, handmade age. But maybe this, too, is romantic delusion. As preservation consultant James Marston Fitch commented, "Old Man Schermerhorn was a developer. He had monumental ambitions—a palatial place in mind. Why, the Rouse Company isn't that much different from Peter Schermerhorn; it's just bigger and more powerful."

These continuing questions about the seaport-present's relationship with seaport-past will not be answered definitively for many years. Meanwhile, they spur New Yorkers and tourists to seek out this long-overlooked section of Lower Manhattan and discover its history for themselves.

Dallas Arts District

The Dallas Arts District encompasses 17 blocks (61.7 acres) targeted for revitalization at the northeastern edge of Dallas's central business district. The total private and public costs for completing the district are projected to be $2.6 billion. When it is fully functioning at about the turn of the century the district will include the Dallas Museum of Art, the Dallas Symphony's Morton H. Meyerson Symphony Center, a playhouse for the Dallas Theater Center, LTV Center, and other office buildings and residences. Side by side with the new buildings will stand a number of renovated structures, among them a high school for the arts, St. Paul's United Methodist Church (the second oldest black church in the city), the Cathedral Santuario de Guadalupe, and the historic Belo Mansion, now used by the Dallas Bar Foundation. Flora Street, running down the center of the district, will become a European-style boulevard lined with shops and restaurants, shaded by hundreds of trees, and punctuated by parks, fountains, exhibit kiosks, and spaces for outdoor performances. The district is expected to be used by as many as 55,000 pedestrians each day.

Different parcels of land within the arts district's boundaries are being developed individually by different landowners, including the city of Dallas, the museum, the orchestra, the Trammell Crow Company (developer of the LTV office tower), and others. Each property owner voluntarily has joined a Dallas Arts District Consortium to realize from their different agendas and needs a comprehensive master plan—the Sasaki Plan—for a mixed-use district with memorable visual themes and a carefully orchestrated pedestrian environment. Strong zoning regulations and equally strong central management practices will govern the district, even though it is not a single mixed-use project designed and built by one developer. Within agreed-upon constraints, the members of the consortium will plan their own buildings and programs. But they have agreed upon common zoning and design controls and areawide management mechanisms to achieve synergy.

No Focal Point

Dallas, whose current population amounts to just under one million, enjoys a vital economy and a history of strong entrepreneurship. Its downtown remains the largest employment center in the metropolitan area, with more than 120,000 workers. In 1983, the property tax base accounted for more than 20 percent of the overall city revenues. New construction proceeds at record rates and presents both opportunities and obligations in accommodating a projected 50 percent increase in downtown workers over the next ten years. The central business district, which includes the designated arts district area, encompasses 998 acres (1.56 square miles). For 1981, it contributed city taxes of $12 million and reported retail sales of approximately $397 million.

The city has undergone tremendous growth in the past quarter century. As the

The Dallas Museum of Art's entrance on Flora Street and courtyard.
Architect: Edward Larrabee Barnes.

New York Times described it in an article about Dallas's new mayor in 1983, "The city rocketed through the 1960s and 1970s to become one of the brightest stars in the Sunbelt sky." In the sixties, Mayor Eric Jonsson launched a program called Goals for Dallas. The goals, drawn up by citizens and organizations, outlined what Dallas needed to do to become a world-class city. With regard to the arts, Goals for Dallas suggested that the city "provide beautiful, functional, conveniently located physical facilities for each art form and use tax funds to supplement only—not replace—private subscription. The city of Dallas should provide some tax funds to sustain and support cultural pursuits when clearly justified." In the seventies, the city joined with Fort Worth to construct the huge, modern Dallas–Fort Worth airport—to assure the northeast Texas region's future as an international business center.

The hard work of the sixties and seventies has paid off. According to Victor Suhm, an assistant city manager, "Dallas is now seen as one of the most attractive business environments in the world." Downtown Dallas reflects this success. In 1982 the city planning and development department reported that "Dallas's central business district is experiencing the greatest boom in its history."

That boom played mainly on one note, however: offices. Between 1980 and 1983, developers constructed 11,948,000 square feet of office space. The rapid office growth has exacerbated a long-standing deficiency: Dallas lacks a central downtown focal point. It has no "corner of Main and Main," as one observer has put it. The workers who fill the office buildings by day drive or ride home to the outlying residential areas at night. "People are proud of Dallas because it's a good business climate, a pleasant place to live," explains Victor Suhm, "but it doesn't have an exciting center that you'd bring your out-of-town visitors to. There's no central focus. The city that is the seventh largest in the United States ought to have a more vibrant downtown area. It has a long way to go toward that."

Pinched for Space

Dallas launched a fledgling symphony orchestra in 1900 and its Museum of Fine Arts just three years later. This early start made the Dallas Symphony one of the six oldest orchestras in the United States, yet by the late seventies it still had no permanent home of its own. The Dallas Museum of Fine Arts had spent most of its 70-odd years concentrating on art of the American West. Both institutions had nevertheless built modest national reputations. The city also had a ballet, a critically esteemed opera company, and a number of theater groups, as well as historical and science museums. While studies showed attendance figures for all of these groups rising, most of them faced shortages of space and financial support.

By the mid-seventies both the Dallas Symphony and the Dallas Museum of Fine Arts had outgrown their facilities and were suffering as a result. Both were located in Fair Park, a district two miles east of downtown that drew too few patrons most of the time and then would be swamped when the Texas State Fair was produced for two weeks every year.

The museum was seriously cramped in a 1936 building, built by the city, that did not provide enough space to exhibit most of its own collection, much less host important traveling exhibitions. In the sixties it had gained a whole new specialty when it merged with the Museum for Contemporary Arts, and in the years following it dramatically expanded its collection into entirely new areas, including Asian, African, and pre-Columbian art. By the seventies, its overcrowded condition had made it an unlikely recipient for future bequests.

The Dallas Symphony was feeling even more pinched in the Fair Park Music Hall, which accommodated a great number of other tenants. Sometimes the orchestra had no space in which to rehearse. For more than half the year it was obliged to find other quarters for its concerts. For these reasons and others, in 1974 its finances were in such disarray that it had to suspend operations for nine months while its trustees debated its future.

That year, however, both the museum and the symphony hired new leaders. Lloyd Haldeman, a new manager at the orchestra, quickly brought it back from the brink of financial disaster. At the museum, Harry S. Parker III, whom the trustees hired away from the Metropolitan Museum of Art in New York City, enthusiastically undertook a campaign to find new quarters.

The Dallas Arts District site plan.

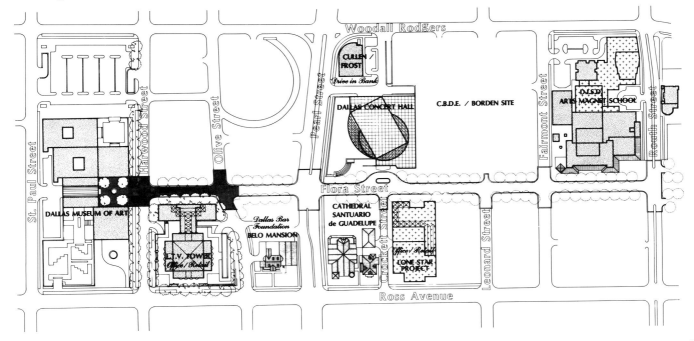

The Museum Looks for a Place to Grow

Carr, Lynch Proposes an Arts District

Frustration at the Dallas Museum of Fine Arts deepened into pain when rival Fort Worth opened three art museums attracting record crowds. In the spring of 1976, urged on by board chairman Margaret McDermott, the museum established a study committee to seek possible sites for a much larger building.

The study committee evaluated the possibility of the museum raising the $12 million to $15 million that such a move would require. Although that amount of money had never previously been raised for an arts group in Dallas, committee members' early discussions with likely patrons proved encouraging.

Mayor Robert Folsom made it clear that the city, already committed through the Goals for Dallas program to supporting the arts, would be interested in helping the museum solve its problem. He raised the possibility of the city's floating a bond issue to help buy land for a new museum, if a suitable location could not be found on city-owned property.

By the fall of 1976 the study committee had found nearly nine acres on Harwood Street between Ross Avenue and Woodall Rogers Freeway. The site had the advantage of proximity to the city's center, offering the museum the hope of attracting people already in the vicinity and not just those willing to make a special trip. Furthermore, nine acres would provide all the elbow room the museum needed.

The Harwood Street site lay right in the path of likely downtown development, which was clearly moving northeast, but this prospect had not yet touched the market. Prices for the various parcels in the nine-acre site ranged from $8 to $25 a square foot. At those rates, the land could be acquired for roughly $5.5 million. By May 1977 the museum's board had acquired options to 40 percent of the needed land and had selected Edward Larrabee Barnes as the architect for its new building. Barnes, pleased with the extent of the proposed site, proposed building a horizontal rather than vertical structure.

In September 1976, under the leadership of Mayor Robert Folsom and City Manager George Schrader, the museum and eight other local cultural institutions were invited to meet with city representatives and discuss their needs for new space. Besides the museum and the orchestra, the participants included the Dallas Ballet, the Dallas Civic Opera, the Dallas Health and Science Museum, the Shakespeare Festival, Dallas Summer Musicals, the Dallas Theater Center, and Theater Three. The city suggested hiring a consulting firm to assess the situation for all these groups and to propose ways the city could help them meet their needs, and the nine arts groups agreed to halve the cost of this undertaking with the city. In the spring of 1977 Carr, Lynch Associates of Cambridge, Massachusetts, was retained to work with representatives from all nine organizations, with Weiming Lu, a member of the city planning department, and with a local architect, E. G. Hamilton, to recommend a plan for arts facilities.

The report that Carr, Lynch presented in October 1977 summarized the results of its survey:

With many important variations in technical detail, certain existing physical problems are often repeated: a house that is too small or too heavily committed for the present stage of growth, a location difficult to reach for some important segment of their audience, a lack of parking and an appropriate setting. All express a desire for supporting activities such as restaurants, hotels, safe, active streets, and a pleasant setting.

Out of these first surveys of the cultural institutions of Dallas have come the first list of desired new facilities: a new fine arts museum, a new outdoor theater, a new 600-seat indoor theater and another of 200 seats, a hall of intermediate size (1,500–2,000 seats), and a new concert hall for the symphony, or perhaps a new multipurpose music hall for opera and symphony together. . . . A site for a future music conservatory should be provided in relation to the symphony. In addition to these rather definite, major facilities, there are needs for a number of smaller or supplementary ones, such as storage, rehearsal, and office space, plus all the supporting private uses whose absence is so keenly felt.

After considering nine examples of new arts facilities in other cities around the United States, Carr, Lynch offered Dallas the bold suggestion that would one day remake the face of the city: that the cultural institutions that needed new space all relocate to a single area.

Different propositions were considered as to where this area ought to be and how closely the institutions should be grouped. A massive single complex such as Lincoln Center was rejected as too monumental as well as impractical, because it would cost too much and would straitjacket its constituents into a single plan and relocation schedule. Randomly scattered sites also were rejected because they would not "allow for mutual support, nor would they create any identity for the city." The best arrangement, Carr, Lynch said, would be a grouping in a single arts district. This district should not be located at Fair Park, with which most arts groups were dissatisfied, but downtown:

. . . a territory which belongs to all [population] groups in the city, and which has excellent automobile access and the best public transportation in the city (99 of the city's 101 bus routes pass through it). Over 100,000 people who work in the CBD are a large potential daytime audience, to which may be added a heavy flow of convention visitors. Conversely, the arts institutions will help to balance the present office and shopping use of downtown with leisure-time and nighttime events, benefiting workers and shoppers in the core, reviving the old Dallas tradition of going downtown for entertainment, and supporting further private development there. If the major arts institutions cluster downtown, they will in themselves provide an important tourist attraction and help to strengthen convention activity.

Another reason to cluster the arts institutions was that, alone, any one of them might feel overwhelmed:

Downtown is a rather harsh landscape of office towers, surrounded by parking lots and ringed by expressways. Special efforts will be necessary to create a more humane setting in this location —one suited to the arts and to the Texas climate.

The way to do that, Carr, Lynch suggested, would be through design standards enforced throughout the district and strong zoning controls. There should be generous open space and some commercial undertakings. The basic aim should be to make the area attractive for pedestrians day and night.

The particular area that Carr, Lynch suggested for the arts district was northeast of the central business district—exactly where the Dallas Museum of Fine Arts was acquiring options to buy property.

Claes Oldenburg's *Stake Hitch*, 1984. Work made of painted epoxied aluminum, urethane foam, polyester resin, and fiberglass, and installed at Dallas Museum of Art. Commissioned to honor John Dabney Murchison, Sr., for his contributions to the arts and presented by his family.

Museum, Orchestra Buy Land, Preserve District Momentum

As an outgrowth of a collaborative process in which nine arts institutions and the city all had had a voice, the Carr, Lynch recommendations represented a consensus of what most parties wanted to see happen, and the city government moved swiftly to act on the recommendations. The report had urged that the city initiate a general policy of predictable financial support for the arts—especially support for creating a "setting"—while the planning and actual management of structures would remain with the arts institutions themselves.

In December 1977 the city council established a generous formula of support for the arts. Facilities built with city support would be constructed, owned, and maintained by the city. The city would bear 75 percent of the cost of acquiring and clearing sites, while the cultural institution(s) would raise the remaining 25 percent. For construction costs, the city would pay 60 percent, the arts organization(s), 40. This kind of backing would be available to all prominent cultural institutions that had proven their ability to survive and to raise funds.

With the Carr, Lynch report in hand, the city and several of the arts institutions planned a bond issue to launch the arts district. The voters were asked to authorize bond sales of $45 million as the city's contribution toward building a museum, constructing a new concert hall for the orchestra, acquiring a site for a new opera house, and supporting various other capital undertakings for the arts. On June 10, 1978—less than a week after disgruntled voters in California clamped a lid on public expenditures with Proposition 13—the bond measure that would have launched the Dallas Arts District went down to defeat.

With the defeat of the bond program, the museum lost its existing options to buy the land on Harwood Street. The museum reassessed its position: Landowners in the proposed arts district had started raising their sights as developers began inspecting the area. The impending completion of the Woodall Rogers Expressway would further increase property values. The museum board already had raised $12.5 million dollars toward its new home; it had joined with an architect to commit ideas to paper; and it had interested private collectors in the museum's future. It decided it had no time to lose.

Museum director Harry Parker and the board of trustees therefore launched a sophisticated $250,000 public relations campaign to persuade city residents that funding to build a new Dallas Museum of Fine Arts would be a worthwhile investment. They hired Philip Seib, a writer, political scientist, and television commentator, to run the campaign. They bought time on radio, ran telephone banks, and plastered Dallas with signs and bumper stickers. They displayed a handsome model of the proposed new museum and made sure that all their visitors passed directly by it.

The city wrote a new $31 million bond program gauged more realistically: $24.8 million to build the museum; $2.25 million to buy a site for a concert hall; and $4 million to renovate the Majestic, an old downtown movie theater.

In November 1979 the voters agreed to give the museum $24.8 million, nearly half its building fund. As a sign of a future that was now assured, the museum decided to change its name from the Dallas Museum of Fine Arts to the more encompassing Dallas Museum of Art, effective upon the opening of the new facility in 1984.

With the passage of the second bond election, the idea of the arts district revived as well. The city reopened discussions with

Cross section of the Morton H. Meyerson Symphony Center.

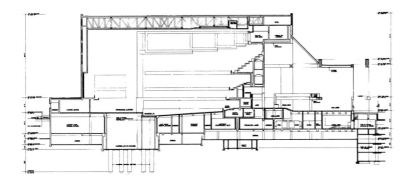

the arts institutions originally involved in the Carr, Lynch study to explore how they would use land in the district and what the area should look like. The orchestra, for its part, had won a first step toward a new home—funds with which to purchase land.

Finding Land for the Symphony

The foremost quality the Dallas Symphony sought in a new home was not a downtown location or proximity to the art museum, or the questionable support from a still-nebulous arts district. What the orchestra wanted most was superior acoustics. "With a proper hall," its music director, Eduardo Mata, declared, "the Dallas Symphony could attain its goal of being recognized as one of the great orchestras of the world."

Accordingly, the orchestra chose its acoustical engineer, Russell Johnson of Artec Consultants, with care. And since it was hoping to put its musicians onto the world stage, the orchestra's board could hardly remain indifferent when one of the architects bidding for the job, the renowned I. M. Pei, said at his final interview, "I've never designed a concert hall in my life, but before I die, I must design a great one."

In January 1981 Pei got the commission. The orchestra's search committee found a site only two blocks from the art museum, at the corner of Pearl and Flora streets, which would put the concert hall roughly at the center of the arts district. This location seemed to meet the needs of both the city and the orchestra. It would create a balancing focus for the arts district on acreage that easily could be assembled.

The planning and design process, however, revealed that the new site posed serious traffic problems and that more square footage would be required than projected in the bond plan to improve flow and allow an open plaza. Inflation and the real estate market also were complicating matters. When the orchestra had begun planning for its move in 1978, land in the arts district area was selling for $15 to $20 a square foot. In 1981, the same land was bringing more than $100 per square foot. The orchestra now could not afford to buy even half the land it needed if it was to remain in the vicinity of the museum. Cha-

Model of the Morton H. Meyerson Symphony Center.

grined, the Dallas Symphony told Mayor Jack Evans in the summer of 1981 that it would have to build its home outside the arts district and south of the central business district.

The mayor was appalled. He knew the city couldn't plan an arts district with only one arts institution in it, and he saw the Carr, Lynch vision in peril, all for the price of a tract of land. He urged the orchestra not to abandon the district, and he instructed his staff to find an alternative site.

They didn't need to look far. Right across the street at Pearl and Flora was a five-acre parcel of land occupied by a Borden's Dairy processing plant. Since Borden's already had plans to move from the site within a few years, the corporation was persuaded by the mayor to donate a 25,000-square-foot portion of the site to the orchestra—a gift then worth at least $2.5

million. The mayor's staff then brokered land purchases and swaps among the city, Triland Development Corporation, and a holding company of the Central Business District Association, thus completing the land assemblage for the orchestra. To help the orchestra past the financial burden that locating in the arts district would create, the city council agreed to shoulder the complete costs of building the concert hall's garage with a combination tax and revenue certificate of obligation.

While time had made land prices soar, it also gave the orchestra a valuable opportunity to plan an effective bond-issue campaign when the time came to raise funds for the I. M. Pei concert hall. To build voter interest and support for the August 1982 bond election, in March the orchestra released the results of an economic impact study it had commissioned from LWFW Inc., asserting that construction of the new hall would generate nearly $133 million in new economic activity, and that regular concerts would yield the Dallas economy more than $26 million a year in increased spending. The hall would speed further building activity in the arts district, the report argued, bringing the city an extra $25 million in taxes. A newspaper editorial shortly before the election endorsed "the sweet sounds of culture"—regardless of whether or not the voters liked classical music:

Dallas voters need to understand that a viable symphony is a significant element in the decision-making process of executives who move their companies here, and the continued influx of those quality companies into Dallas is the very thing which makes the city's tax rate one of the lowest among major cities in the country. The real threat several years ago when the symphony collapsed was not that we wouldn't have the sweet sounds of culture; the real threat was bottom-line economics. Without the symphony, Dallas stands to lose millions in increased taxes because of thousands of jobs that will not be moved into the economy by executives of relocating companies who consider a city without a symphony to be culturally deprived.

To the relief of all arts district supporters, 57 percent of the voters pulled the "yes"

lever for a new concert hall. The orchestra now had $28.6 million for its building; the city had a green light to proceed with its dream. In the fall of 1984 H. Ross Perot, founder and chairman of Electronic Data Systems Corporation, Inc., made a gift of $10 million toward the construction costs of the new concert hall in honor of his partner, Morton H. Meyerson, for whom the building will now be named. Construction began in the spring of 1985 and the hall is scheduled to open in 1988.

Property Owners Create a Consortium
The orchestra's difficulties, which had endangered the arts district, made the city's leaders realize just how much this extraordinary idea was likely to benefit them. Private developers began to see its advantages. One of them, Webb Wallace of Tishman Realty, told the *Dallas Morning News* that the special character of the district would allow developers to charge higher rents; in turn, they would lean over backwards to build "very high quality" buildings. "We would stretch a lot farther to put in the right kind of retail and amenities," he said. "We would be willing to do a lot more in an arts district—as kind of a community amenity—than we would in just another downtown area."

The perils of the orchestra also had made it clear that an arts district was not going to create itself if all property owners went their own way and simply left it to the city to do modest coordinating. Shortly after Borden's gift, the district's property owners decided that they should form a group to consider their common interests. Only eight owners were involved at the time—the city, the museum, the orchestra, and five private developers: Triland, Trammell Crow Company, Tishman Realty Corporation, Young-Gentek Company, and Luedtke, Aldredge, Pendleton. Coordinating their efforts, they felt, would prevent them from pursuing eight different directions and leaving the district idea behind. In October 1981 they created the Dallas Arts District Consortium, a voluntary unincorporated association without written bylaws but able by the strength of its participants to govern many aspects of the district's development.

The consortium met a strongly felt need. By its second and third meetings, members were considering design issues central to the district—questions such as what to do with the district's main artery, Flora Street, and how to handle parking. The members demonstrated their joint commitment to the district by each contributing $20,000 for planning studies. They also reviewed how to make decisions among themselves, and they quickly agreed that the consortium needed the guidance of a person who represented the district idea in itself rather than any of the owners' particular viewpoints. The city council should nominate such a person, they agreed, and once the consortium members approved, the mayor could officially name a Dallas Arts District coordinator.

Although the consortium members wanted someone to steer the ship, they did not want a full-fledged independent authority. The first candidate the city council suggested therefore was rejected as too "authoritarian" for the loose, cooperative arrangement that the consortium preferred. By February 1982 they had found an ideal candidate: Dr. Philip O'Bryan Montgomery, Jr., professor of pathology at the University of Texas Health Science Center, who was officially appointed by Mayor Evans and the city council that month.

Dr. Montgomery had overseen millions of dollars' worth of construction at the University of Texas and was willing to serve as the arts district coordinator on a voluntary basis. He was clearly a facilitator with a flair for mediating within a large group and for making sure that every point was heard and considered. He took a great interest in the district and quickly became almost synonymous with its promotion. He also agreed to serve as unpaid coordinator until the late 1990s, when the district should be mostly built and in full operation. Staff assistance was provided to Dr. Montgomery by the city and the Central Business District Association.

In March 1982 the consortium members hired a consulting firm, DeShazo, Starek & Tang, to study the district's parking needs. Their next concern was design. Even with two sizable arts institutions located in it, the arts district streetscape would differ little from the remainder of the central business district unless it had unifying design elements and perhaps some coordinated management. The consortium members decided that they needed a comprehensive design strategy proposed by a firm not already working on any building in the district, and each member was invited to propose two candidates for drawing up such a master plan. In the end, twelve firms from around the nation—many of them distinguished by long experience in urban planning, design, and landscaping—were invited to submit proposals.

The memo soliciting proposals for this $116,000 contract quoted the Carr, Lynch report in defining the district as a loosely knit concentration of arts organizations located in a mixed-use area where "parking and other facilities could be commonly used, and an active street life would be encouraged both day and night. Public art and open space, as well as special planting, climate protection, lighting, and street furniture, would combine for the comfort and delight of the person in the street."

The request for proposals asked that the main artery, Flora Street, be developed with a distinct character emphasizing the safety, comfort, and pleasure of pedestrians rather than the accommodation of automobiles. Proposals were asked, among other things, to suggest places for artists to work and show their work, to create areas for outdoor performances, and to assure that ground-floor space be devoted to shops and restaurants.

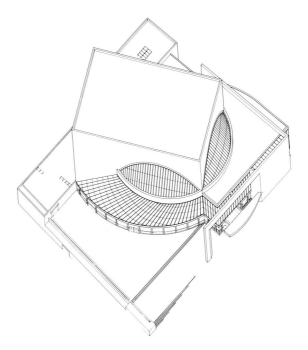

Axonometric rendering of the Morton H. Meyerson Symphony Center.

Sasaki Makes Arts Depend on Retail, Which Depends on Offices

In May 1982 the consortium devoted two days to evaluating nine proposals and the firms that had submitted them. By unanimous vote the winner was Sasaki Associates, Inc., of Watertown, Massachusetts, a firm that had worked on urban design plans for the Kentucky Cultural Complex in Louisville, the Downtown Cultural District in Rochester, and the Theater District and Urban Cultural Park in Buffalo. The Sasaki proposal identified the programming of restaurant and retail activity as the first task to address, because of the support these could give to the district's arts organizations. Halcyon Ltd., retail development analysts participating in the Sasaki proposal, suggested establishing three arts-related "theme areas" to help define commercial groupings of retail activity and restaurants.

Suggesting that extensive space be allotted to retail operations was a risky stand for a proposal in Dallas, since local developers generally do not regard retailing as a high-income use—especially when a project is being built on land as expensive as the arts district's acreage. But Halcyon projected a large proportion of high-volume (and therefore high-income) retail operations

because of the downtown's high-density daytime population. The office buildings already planned for the arts district by various developers would bring tens of thousands of potential consumers into the arts district every day. The Sasaki project manager told the consortium members that their projected office developments would be crucial to retail operations, just as retail would be crucial to the development of viable arts uses.

For the next three months Sasaki representatives and Dr. Montgomery met individually with all primary members of the consortium as well as with a number of other interested parties: the Old City Park, the Dallas County Community College District (which was invited to provide a number of arts-related education programs in the district), the Dallas Bar Foundation (which owned and occupied the historic Belo Mansion), the bodies that owned the historic Cathedral Shrine of Guadalupe and St. Paul's United Methodist Church, the Dallas Independent School District, and a number of arts groups besides the two already planning their arts district buildings. Sasaki offered workshop sessions for all consortium members and made presentations to the Dallas Institute of Humanities and Culture, city staff, the park and recreation board, and the city planning commission. It also made a public presentation at the Dallas Museum of Fine Arts in Fair Park. Finally, Sasaki analyzed the results of a survey that the city's department of health and human services had conducted among 29 cultural organizations regarding their interest in the arts district.

In short, creating the district master plan became a group process, and what emerged was a document that represented the consortium's objectives, community input, and Sasaki's and Halcyon's expertise. In August 1982 Sasaki presented a final report that set forth a series of design plans for the public areas, general guidelines for developers in their own projects, and extensive suggestions on how to handle food and retail operations.

Building massing concept proposed for the Dallas Arts District by Sasaki Associates.

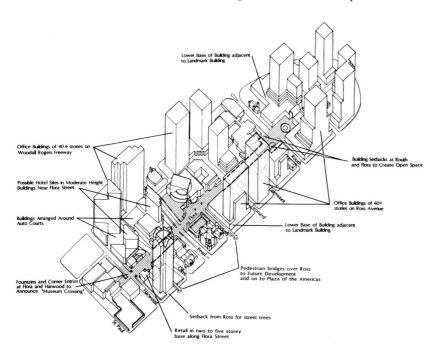

Lower Base of Building adjacent to Landmark Building

Office Buildings of 40+ stories on Woodall Rogers Freeway

Possible Hotel Sites in Moderate Height Buildings Near Flora Street

Buildings Arranged Around Auto Courts

Fountains and Corner Entries at Flora and Harwood to Announce "Museum Crossing"

Building Setbacks at Routh and Flora to Create Open Space

Office Buildings of 40+ stories on Ross Avenue

Lower Base of Building adjacent to Landmark Building

Pedestrian bridges over Ross to Future Development and on to Plaza of the Americas

Setback from Ross for street trees

Retail in two to five storey base along Flora Street

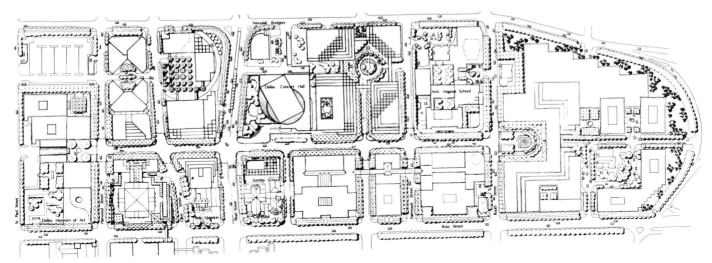

Let the People Walk!

The Sasaki design plan emphasized natural landscaping and creating a pedestrian environment where:

... artists, performers, visitors, workers, residents, and patrons of the arts may attend "hands-on" pottery workshops, negotiate a business deal, savor Texas chili or coquilles St. Jacques, muse over the meaning of a contemporary dance performance or an African sculpture, purchase Dallas souvenirs or additions to an art collection, or meander through trees along the street exchanging pleasantries with patrons of a sidewalk cafe.

Flora Street's diverse attractions would aim to draw people of many nationalities and all walks of life—people who wanted to walk, not ride. The street, as Sasaki envisioned it, would accommodate automobiles but keep them to a minimum. The plan called for all parking to be contained either below ground or in buildings with facades exactly matching non-parking buildings.

After it is improved according to Sasaki's master plan, Flora Street should be instantly recognizable for its distinctive paving, lavish canopy of trees, and attractive soft lighting that emphasizes specific features rather than casting general illumination over everything. The paving will designate moving traffic lanes, drop-off lanes, and pedestrian areas with large, medium-sized, and small paving stones, respectively. All buildings fronting on Flora are to open onto it, with

entrances clearly distinguished. Those that will reach great heights are to be set back from the street, with frontage directly on Flora not exceeding 50 feet in height. Building massing will show the same respect for scale where the landmark structures are concerned, setting back high-rise buildings that might go up on adjacent properties to give the low buildings air and light. Public improvements on the six-block central boulevard, which runs about 2,000 feet long, will cost close to $19 million, Sasaki estimated; sprucing up the adjacent streets will bring the total for the whole district to $21 million. These figures covered general items such as paving, plantings, and water and sewage lines, plus the cost of special features such as fountains.

Sasaki posited a district with three distinct centers of arts activity: the museum at the southwestern end, the concert hall in the middle, and another cluster—still to be defined—at the far end of Flora Street. A park was projected in the vicinity of each; at the museum, it will be the museum's own sculpture garden.

Sasaki's plan showed an extensive concern with retailing and with design and management concepts to help promote it. It divided Flora Street into three distinctive sections, relating food and retail outlets to the major arts organization in each. Because Museum Crossing will be the first area of the arts district to be completed, the Sasaki report went into particular detail on the retail possibilities there, suggesting

Sasaki Associates' 1982 plan for the Dallas Arts District.

Dallas Arts District
Project Data

Component—Income Generating	First Phase 1984 Completion	Profile at Build-Out
Office	1,300,000 sq. ft.	12,800,000 sq. ft.
Hotel		1,250 rooms
Restaurants		207,000 sq. ft.
Retail		294,000 sq. ft.
Component—Arts/Culture/ Open Space		
Dallas Art Museum	210,000 sq. ft.	210,000 sq. ft.
Morton H. Meyerson Symphony Center		260,000 sq. ft.
Dallas Theater Center	20,000 sq. ft.	20,000 sq. ft.
Other		
Public Parking		1,651 spaces
Acreage		61.7 acres
Gross Building Area	1,520,000 sq. ft.	14,971,000 sq. ft.
Location	Downtown Dallas	
Master Developer	Various/separate ownerships	
Master Planner/Urban Designer	Sasaki Associates, Inc., Watertown, Mass.	
Development Period		Through 2000
Estimated Total Development Costs (1984 dollars)		$1.6 billion

where to place specific services for museum patrons and hotel residents. (The Trammell Crow Company plan for the ground-floor uses of the LTV Tower will realize many of these goals.) Fifteen to 20 percent of the retail operations in each section, the plan recommended, should relate to the arts theme.

To encourage retail and food outlets, the plan called for planting trees three abreast in staggered rows, leaving sidewalk areas available for street cafes and street performances. Design guidelines for buildings along Flora Street suggested requiring that 50 percent of the lower two stories be made of glass and 75 percent be devoted to retail uses or exhibits. The plan also addressed a subject that shortly would become a major concern of the consortium: management issues such as the phasing of construction, developing a sophisticated leasing plan, and skillful public relations. These efforts would require a commitment of $350,000 a year in the early stages, Sasaki estimated.

Ordinance Defines Boundaries, Design Specifications, Cost Sharing

Strong support was voiced for the Sasaki master plan, since all consortium members had helped to formulate it. Early in 1983 Dr. Montgomery, city staff, and lawyers representing the property owners prepared a district-creating ordinance that met with all parties' approval. On February 16, 1983, the city council adopted it as law, defining the arts district as "generally bounded by Woodall Rogers Freeway, Routh Street, Ross Avenue, and St. Paul Street."

Ordinance no. 17710 stated that the Sasaki plan would serve as a guideline for development in the arts district and formalized the specific requirements of the plan. Any owner planning to develop property in the district first would have to consult with the city's director of planning and development to make sure that what was proposed was consistent with the Sasaki plan and met the ordinance's formal requirements.

The city council also authorized a new $440,000 contract with Sasaki Associates to develop schematic design drawings for the public improvements in the district and detailed design and construction documents for a prototype block of Flora Street. It also passed a resolution on cost-sharing for the streetscape improvements.

The consortium had agreed that all its members would bear part of the cost of transforming the public areas in the district. The formula for sharing was based on a division of costs where public and private developments meet or overlap. Basically, the city would unilaterally undertake the items considered standard city responsibilities (street paving, the main water and sewer lines, and the like), while special arts district amenities would be paid for jointly. On Flora Street, the city would construct the street paving within 40 feet of the right-of-way and would be responsible for installing drainage, curbs and gutters, bollards, and street lights. After the street was finished and prior to development, the city would install temporary 10-foot-wide sidewalks.

New owners of particular parcels in the district would pay only for improvements made directly along their own frontage. These would include paving of 30-foot-wide sidewalks, planting of three rows of trees (one row to be planted when the temporary 10-foot sidewalk is constructed), tree drainage, irrigation, grates and guards, and street furniture such as benches, kiosks, and waste containers. The city's work along the center of Flora could be accomplished before the adjacent improvements, with property owners fulfilling their part of the bargain when their own developments were being built.

A similar division of costs would occur on the side and peripheral streets, with the city bearing the general costs and individual owners paying for the installation of trees and any special paving called for in the master plan. Special features classed as public amenities, such as the large fountain at Fountain Plaza, it was agreed, would be funded on a basis to be worked out individually for each feature.

Management Plans Ensure Marketing, Security, Upkeep, Programming

In prospect, at least, the arts district was shaping up as an attractive location for arts and for business, but Sasaki's report cautioned that the atmosphere the master plan was intended to create depended not just on installing amenities but also on maintaining them. If successful, the district would attract heavy use day and night, probably much more than the city sanitation department's manpower and equipment could keep pace with. Other cities, Sasaki warned, had erred by creating high-quality public spaces without funds to maintain them in first-rate condition. "The consultant team's national experience over the past 20 years," the Sasaki report stated, "clearly indicates that the degree of success of public open spaces depends largely on the quality of the maintenance program." A related concern was that the high-traffic district also would need superior security arrangements to keep its reputation intact.

Sasaki pinpointed several other management issues critical to the arts district's future. The district should be marketed like any other product or service in the consumer economy: programming an interesting variety of public events would be one important strategy; orchestrating an effective media campaign while the district was

Dallas Arts District
Development Cost Summary

Development Costs*— Income Generating	Total	Private	Public
Office	$1,280,000,000	$1,280,000,000	
Hotel (1,250 rooms)	168,800,000	168,800,000	
Restaurants	20,700,000	20,700,000	
Retail	29,400,000	29,400,000	
Subtotal	$1,498,900,000	$1,498,900,000	
Development Costs— **Arts/Culture/Open Space**			
Dallas Museum of Art	$ 52,400,000	27,600,000	$ 24,800,000
Morton H. Myerson Symphony Center	75,000,000	39,000,000	36,000,000
Dallas Theater Center	1,300,000	1,300,000	
Street Improvements	42,900,000	9,600,000	33,300,000
Subtotal	$ 171,600,000	$ 77,500,000	$ 94,100,000
Other			
Parking 1,651 public spaces	$ 20,400,000		$ 20,400,000
TOTAL	$1,690,900,000	$1,576,400,000	$114,500,000
Other Possibilities			
Residential	$ 162,500,000	$ 162,500,000	
Performing Arts (opera, theater)	106,800,000	39,500,000	$ 67,300,000

*Projected as of 1982 by Halcyon, Ltd.

Source: Dallas Central Business District Association
Keyser Marston Associates

being built would be another. The district's success also would rest on choosing appropriate retail services, on grouping them properly, and on attracting high-quality tenants—all matters that would require the consortium to develop a sophisticated leasing policy.

None of these complicated tasks, Sasaki cautioned, could be accomplished by one volunteer coordinator with no staff or office. Advertising, publicity, and general promotion alone, with a staff to handle them, could cost $350,000 a year to start. Proper maintenance could run more than half a million dollars annually just for Flora Street. To succeed, the arts district needed expert management, and the consortium needed to determine how to pay for it and how to provide it.

Over the winter of 1982–83, members of the consortium debated these points. That spring, using a grant from the National En-

Project Data: Dallas Museum of Art

Location	Downtown Dallas
Completed	January 1984
Architects	Edward Larrabee Barnes Associates
Consultants	Pratt Box Henderson & Associates, consulting architect Kiley-Walker Farms in conjunction with Myrick, Newman, Dahlberg & Partners, landscape architect
Contractor	J. W. Bateson Company
Building Cost	$50 million for land acquisition, construction, fees, and equipment
Gross Area	210,000 sq. ft.

Breakdown of Interior Area	*Exhibition Areas*	
	Contemporary art	12,000 sq. ft.
	Traditional European & American art	15,300 sq. ft.
	Non-Western art	18,400 sq. ft.
	Temporary Exhibition Galleries	9,500 sq. ft.
	Expansion Galleries	15,000 sq. ft.
	Sculpture Garden	1.2 acres
	Public Education Facilities	
	Gateway Gallery	8,500 sq. ft.
	Education Courtyard	13,225 sq. ft.
	Orientation Room	1,500 sq. ft.
	Curatorial and Professional	14,740 sq. ft.
	Restoration and Conservation	1,000 sq. ft.
	Library	50,000 volumes
	Art Storage and Services	34,500 sq. ft.
	Administration	6,000 sq. ft.
	Auditorium	5,000 sq. ft. 360 people
	Gallery Buffet	5,200 sq. ft.
	Museum Shops	2,500 sq. ft.

Exterior Features	Structural steel frame with concrete floor slabs; exterior walls of Indiana limestone
Interior Features	Interior floors of limestone pavers, oak, and carpet, with wall surfaces of limestone and painted gypsum

Project Data: Dallas Theater Center Arts District Theater (temporary)

Location	Dallas Arts District
Completed	February 14, 1984
Architects	Eugene Lee and Art Rogers
Building Cost	$1.3 million
Gross Area	20,000 sq. ft.
Breakdown of Interior Area	400–500 seats possible
Exterior Features	Barnlike metal structure, with finished lobby and service facilities
Interior Features	Flexible stage area and seating arrangement; finished lobby, box office, rest rooms, and coat check area

dowment for the Arts plus matching funds, the city issued a request for proposals "to establish a management structure necessary to implement and maintain the design concept for the arts district." The contract was won by a New York City firm, the Project for Public Spaces, which submitted its final report in October 1983.

The report warmly seconded Sasaki's recommendations. "In the Project for Public Spaces' experience," it said, "a strong management organization can be the single most important factor in the success of a downtown district or public area." Comprehensive management, it noted, pointing to the experience of other cities, "is becoming increasingly popular in downtowns, as downtowns attempt to compete with suburban malls for business." Dallas especially needed good management because the arts district would be so large and diverse and because anything attractive to pedestrians was relatively untested in the city. Finally, the Project for Public Spaces stressed, good management would be essential to protect the role of a potentially neglected participant in this vast downtown development—the arts.

A great deal of the Project for Public Spaces report was devoted to suggestions for how artists and the arts could share in the space, the programming, and the management of the arts district. The management, the report urged, should focus on every aspect of promoting arts in the district. It should give grants to artists and arrange outdoor exhibits and performances. Its leasing arm should lure galleries and other arts-oriented outlets as tenants. It should encourage temporary arts spaces as well. It should negotiate arrangements for artists-in-residence working in public view. It should program performances in all public spaces, not just in those facilities specifically developed for such uses.

The Project for Public Spaces proposed a two-part management structure, one side of which would be constituted as a trade association—that is, structured under section 501(c)(6) of the Internal Revenue Code—to handle maintenance, security, and questions affecting commercial vitality. The other side would be structured as a 501(c)(3) nonprofit organization with the

Renderings of the floor plan for the Dallas Museum of Art.

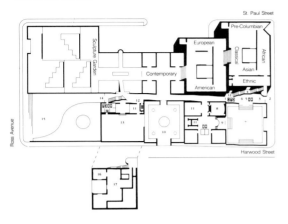

1 Study Gallery for Prints, Drawings, Photography, Textiles
2 Parking Lot Entrance
3 Library
4 Museum Offices
5 Auditorium
6 Information Desk
7 Education Courtyard
8 Orientation Theater
9 Education Wing
10 Flora Street Courtyard
11 Museum Shops
12 Handicapped Access
13 Temporary Exhibitions Galleries
14 Ross Avenue Entrance
15 Museum Plaza
16 Founders Room
17 Gallery Buffet Restaurant

responsibility of promoting arts activities.

The consortium decided on the arts district's management structures during the spring of 1984. The city's legal staff drew up articles of incorporation and bylaws for three separate organizations:

■ one to handle business matters, such as maintenance and leasing, as well as to guide relations among the principal owners and lessees in the district;
■ a second to make and implement policy, promote the district and its activities, and to receive grants; and
■ a third, constituted as a membership organization, that will provide a forum where all elements of the public can be heard on arts district issues. This last organization will provide a sizable group of interested people to help mount special events.

On June 5, 1984, all three organizations were chartered as Texas nonprofit corporations. A common staff for the three organizations currently is provided by the Central Business District Association, pending the consortium's decision on how to budget and pay for them.

Project Data: Morton H. Meyerson Symphony Center

Location	Site bounded by Pearl, Munger, Crockett, and Flora streets, Dallas	
Projected Opening	Fall 1988	
Architect	I. M. Pei, I. M. Pei & Partners, New York	
Consultants	Acoustician:	Russell Johnson, Artec Consultants Inc., New York
	Cost:	Hanscomb Consultants, Inc., Toronto
	Mechanical and Electrical:	Skilling, Helle, Christiansen, Robertson, Inc., New York
	Life Safety:	Rolf Jensen & Associates, Springfield, Va.
	Security:	Joseph M. Chapman, Inc., Wilton, Conn.
	Organ:	C. B. Fisk, Inc., Gloucester, Mass.
Construction Management	J. W. Bateson Company, Inc., Dallas	
Building Cost	Estimated at $75 million, which includes basic building construction, performance equipment, and fees.	
Gross Area	260,000 sq. ft.	

Breakdown of Interior Area

Performance Platform Depth from Apron	36 ft.
Performance Platform Width	60 ft. downstage 41 ft. upstage
Orchestra Level Length (apron to back wall)	94 ft. at main floor level
Maximum Orchestra Height	85 ft.
Maximum Orchestra Width	84 ft. at main floor level
Seating	2,179 seats
Dressing Rooms	7 small private, 4 large locker-room style
Lobby Dimensions	Approx. 43,000 sq. ft. on 3 levels
Rehearsal Rooms	1 ensemble warmup; several multipurpose smaller rooms

Exterior Features	The basic plan is a combination of overlapping geometric forms: a masonry rectangle (the "shoe-box" concert room) set at an angle within a glass and masonry square (the overall shape of the building) containing public and backstage areas, enveloped on three sides at the roofline with a circle of glass lenses. The entire building is angled on its site.
	To the west of the Symphony Center is a pocket park featuring trees, shrubs, water works, tables, and seating and sculpture.
Interior Features	The primary access is from an enclosed underground parking garage. This leads to the building's functional lobby entrance with box office, coat check, public telephones, rest rooms, and four large meeting/reception rooms. Elevators and broad staircases lead to spacious main floor and first-tier lobbies. A full-service restaurant is at the main-floor lobby level. The green room and access to backstage is also at this level.

The concert room, named the Eugene McDermott Concert Room, is the result of close collaboration between architect I. M. Pei and acoustician Russell Johnson. The focus of the concert room, behind the performance platform, will be an organ and organ case designed both for performance with the orchestra as a concerto instrument, and as a recital instrument. Four rows of chorus/audience seating appear behind the performance platform. The performance platform itself is terraced. Above the concert room is a main acoustical canopy with 3 flanking canopies whose positions can be mechanically altered to enhance the production of the orchestra's sound. Audience seating is arranged in 5 areas: (1) main floor, (2) main floor terrace, (3) first tier, (4) second tier, and (5) third tier. A sixth area of seating appears behind the performance platform. All seats will have unobstructed sightlines.

The backstage area contains a musicians' lounge, a music library, guest artists' dressing rooms, the music director's suite, instrument storage, musicians' warmup areas, building maintenance storage areas. The back, eastern corner of the building contains administrative offices on two floors.

Getting Off the Ground

A project on the scale of the Dallas arts district takes years of planning, as its history already makes clear. Dallas citizens, who have already voted it $101.6 million in bonds and who ultimately must provide more if the district is to achieve its promise, have been sold a dream, heard it described for years, and in effect have been asked to be patient. It will be at least another 15 years before all the elements planned for the district are built and functioning. So the question is, How deep is that patience? The answer will depend in part upon the payment the public receives against the promises.

The initial player on the stage of the arts district has been the first to take its bow. In October 1983 the Dallas Museum of Art opened its sculpture garden to the public. This debut was an important symbol—for the museum, which now has 1.2 acres in which to display its sculpture collection—and for the arts district, whose first park is now functioning. The sculpture garden contains limestone water walls, canals, oak trees, wisteria—and works by Henry Moore, Tony Smith, Barbara Hepworth, Ellsworth Kelly, and others.

Just three and a half months later, in late January 1984, the $50-million museum itself opened to national acclaim. Critic Paul Goldberger wrote in the *New York Times*:

The new building of the Dallas Museum of Art . . . looks like the sort of museum that a secure, well-established city might build. It is an immense, sprawling building of limestone, with a great vaulted space at its center, and it bespeaks a kind of self-assurance that is altogether different from the image most Easterners have of Dallas. This is not a nouveau-riche museum, or a pushy one, or a glittery one. It is a museum built by people who know about art and who know about monumentality, and who have shown respect for both.

Its galleries give the new Dallas Museum of Art more than twice the exhibition space the museum had in Fair Park, not counting the sculpture garden outside. Just as the trustees and staff had hoped, the building program has indeed inspired generous donations of money and art.

The first set of figures for the museum—from February to May 1984—indicates that attendance was 338,389, compared to 73,721 during the same period a year earlier at the Fair Park site. Purchases by visitors rose significantly in the museum's shops and restaurants. Membership income nearly doubled, from $471,135 in February through May 1983 to $828,755 in early 1984. These statistics clearly suggest that the move downtown will have a dramatic effect in increasing the museum's revenues and in widening its audience.

The Dallas Museum of Art's sculpture garden, featuring *Untitled* by Richard Serra (1971), funded by matching grants from the National Endowment for the Arts and The 500, Inc.
Credit: Daniel Barsotti

In August 1984, when the Republican National Convention came to Dallas, a two-day arts festival sponsored by the 500 Inc., a local arts support group, was held in the arts district, showcasing visual and performing artists and food concessions from local restaurants. Thousands of residents and visitors attended this first celebration, entitled Montage, suggesting that the arts district could indeed become the "people place" its founders desired.

The District Gets a Playhouse

In February 1984, following the successful opening of the art museum, the Dallas Theater Center, one of the nation's finest regional repertory companies, opened a temporary playhouse in the arts district. The facility, a barn-like metal structure occupying nearly 15,000 square feet, includes a flexible stage, lobby, and support spaces. Its cost was approximately $1.3 million, provided by private donations.

This new theater gave the Dallas Theater Center an opportunity to alternate productions between its original building on Turtle Creek and its new, more experimental theater on Flora Street. While younger audiences responded to the new theater more enthusiastically than older ones, the group believes that the arts district will be the place where it can continue to grow and become a truly prominent force in the regional theater movement.

The LTV Center

At the close of 1984, the LTV Center opened, providing the first commercial focal point for the arts district. The building, designed by Skidmore, Owings & Merrill, rises 50 stories high and encompasses some 1.4 million square feet of office space. Described as "the campanile of the arts district," it constitutes a dramatic marker and a symbol of quality and excitement.

The center's classical form is sheathed with polished brown granite and energy-efficient reflective glass. Its two-story, glass-topped, ground-floor pavilion will house a variety of restaurants and shops. A full-service bank will serve the business environment of the tower and of the arts district.

Viewed purely from an economic perspective, it would have been less expensive to provide one million square feet of office space in two smaller towers. Two towers would have met Dallas standard building codes but would not necessarily have enhanced the arts district's design or program objectives. To support the district's long-term objectives, the Trammell Crow Company instead decided to build its office building in the form of a tall clock tower. This design resulted in a taller, more compact shape that provides maximum ground space for such amenities as landscaping, plazas, walkways, gardens, and fountains.

The LTV Center, located at the northeast corner of Olive Street and Ross Avenue, opened in November 1984 with 1.7 million gross square feet of office, retail, and parking space. Bay windows clad with gray-brown granite rise 44 floors to a multistoried, sloping glass pyramid defining the tower as a 50-story "campanile." Around the base of the building are 20 bronze sculptures by Rodin, Maillol, Bourdelle, and other French artists.

To further promote and support an artistic climate, the Trammell Crow Company acquired a major collection of French sculpture focusing on the human figure. Including works by such noted sculptors as Auguste Rodin, Emile-Antoine Bourdelle, and Aristide Maillol, the seventeen bronzes stand among the terraced walkways, plazas, and fountains adjacent to the LTV Center and the Dallas Museum of Art. They provide a minihistory of French sculpture from Rodin's masterpiece, the *Burghers of Calais,* to a recently commissioned lifesize figure by Jean Carton.

While the executives of the Trammell Crow Company are reluctant to correlate the display of art in a commercial building to leasing sucess, they have felt that the use of art sets a tone of quality for the project:

If we can make these commercial developments a more pleasant place in which people can work, then, subjectively, this should enhance our building and hopefully keep it full and at higher rental rates.

Dallas's commercial rents have related more closely to the costs of development than to what the market will bear. New buildings with amenities, such as the LTV Center, therefore, are likely to enjoy rental rates 5 or 10 percent higher than buildings constructed in past years.

Trammel Crow intends to make the LTV Center a full partner in the arts district, moving beyond a passive display of sculpture to include a seasonal special events program and a program of lunchtime entertainment called Noonfest, in which musicians, dancers, and singers will perform in a professionally designed and equipped performance space in the pavilion fronting on Flora Street. In good weather these performances will extend outdoors, where light and sound systems have been installed.

The LTV Center thus is contributing significantly to the goals and aims of the arts district. The personal involvement of Harlan Crow in the planning of the district, as well as the commitment that the company has made to the visual and performing arts, have enhanced the district's attractions as a business location.

More Arts for the District?

The 1983 Project for Public Spaces study stressed that the arts would need sustained attention to survive in the arts district. The city's planners—and many of the institutions whose space needs triggered the idea of an arts district—remain keenly aware that the district's blueprint allocated no space for theater, opera, or dance. Although seven theater groups, two dance companies, the opera company, and a classical guitar society surveyed by the city all felt favorably disposed toward the arts district, most of them also wondered if they would ever be able to afford to perform there.

To serve these organizations and to increase the diversity of the arts in the district, the city has kept watch for locations that could house one or more additional facilities. Such an opportunity presented itself in early 1983 when a private developer decided not to exercise his option for a five-plus-acre property owned by the Borden Corporation on Flora Street, immediately adjacent to the orchestra's site.

Though given the opportunity to acquire the land directly, the city was not in a position to make such a financial commitment quickly. At the request of the mayor and city manager, the Central Business District Association, through its newly formed companion organization, Dallas CBD Enterprises, acquired the Borden property for a reported $26 million on September 1, 1983.

According to the association and CBD Enterprises Chairman John T. Stuart, the purchase was made to ensure the land's availability for new arts facilities and for reserving an additional small tract of land needed for the orchestra's concert hall. Financing for the purchase was arranged for two years through the prompt and cooperative efforts of Republic Bank Dallas, InterFirst Bank Dallas, and Mercantile Bank Dallas. Lease income from Borden's remaining on the site until 1985 partially offset the interest charges. The intent was for the association to hold the property for two years while the city staff developed a case for the use of the site and, it was hoped, floated a successful new bond issue to buy it. If the city purchases the property, its use will be restricted by contract to arts and culture for ten years.

The association's purchase of the site also helped keep the general arts district development on schedule. Now the challenge became projecting an appropriate mixture of uses so that a public bond campaign, intended for 1985, will garner sufficient public support to be passed. With funds raised from a variety of arts and non-profit organizations hoping to have facilities provided for them on the Borden site, Theatre Projects, Inc., was contracted to propose a use plan for the site.

In May 1984 the consultants' preliminary report suggested that a further comprehensive plan be formulated for arts uses in the district, including facilities for the performing arts, education, historical exhibition and library spaces, media studios, and necessary parking and administration spaces. The report urged that private developers throughout the district be encouraged to incorporate commercially viable arts and entertainment facilities into their projects—in the manner of the LTV Center.

For the Borden site, the consultants suggested that a new opera/ballet theater hall, seating more than 2,000, would provide an ideal performing environment for the Dallas Ballet and the Dallas Civic Opera, allowing them to expand their seasons and their performance goals. Such a hall also could accommodate touring Broadway shows. Its cost was estimated at $86 million. A smaller playhouse seating 750 also could be constructed on the site to replace the Dallas Theater Center's temporary facility in the arts district. Besides these two theaters, the consultants recommended that space be set aside for an outdoor or courtyard theater seating 450. The consultants concluded by urging that the city's opportunity to purchase the site for arts uses be exercised through the passage of a bond issue and through a collaborative partnership with private developers who could combine arts, office, and residential uses on the site.

The Arts District Consortium worked diligently throughout 1984 to define a range of arts, educational, and commercial development uses that could win widespread public support. The bond campaign for the Borden site, when it occurs, will provide the first real public referendum on the arts

Exterior view of the Dallas Theater Center's temporary facility.
Credit: Linda Blase

district itself. Assistant City Manager Victor Suhm explains that the art museum bond passed in 1979 on its own merits, and three years later the concert hall bond was viewed essentially as a matter of support for the Dallas Symphony. "Now," Suhm observes, "to go further—to have an opera house, a multipurpose performing area—is going to require a real endorsement by the people of the arts district itself. They will need to perceive it as a valuable and important amenity for the community—a place to be proud of."

James Cloar, former president of the Dallas Central Business District Association, adds:

From the beginning, the Dallas arts district has been a true partnership in every sense of the word. The private sector has been an active participant in the planning, a vocal advocate for the solution, and a financial leader in the implementation. As in Tulsa, it's a Dallas tradition.

Playhouse Square

The Playhouse Square Theater Project aims to create a cultural district in downtown Cleveland by restoring and modernizing a group of three 1920s vaudeville theaters and movie palaces on the city's principal shopping street, Euclid Avenue.

When completed in 1986, this integrated arts center, operating under a single management entity, will seat in aggregate approximately 7,000 people. Playhouse Square thus constitutes the largest theater restoration project ever undertaken in the nation. Expenditures are currently projected at $27 million for the restorations, carrying costs, and financing.

The district is being completed in stages. The 1,035-seat Ohio Theatre opened in July 1982; the 3,095-seat State Theatre, with its new $7 million stagehouse, in June 1984. They are serving as homes for three resident companies—the Cleveland Ballet and the Cleveland Opera in the State, and the Great Lakes Shakespeare Festival in the Ohio. With the Palace, they will produce or host a variety of events: opera, ballet, symphony, local repertory theater, and touring plays and musicals. Playhouse Square will draw audiences from a large area of northern Ohio, expecting as many as a million patrons a year by 1988. It aims to become one of the Midwest's most important regional cultural centers.

From the start of the Playhouse Square project in 1970, its proponents believed that restoring the theaters and renewing the surrounding area could not be accomplished without attracting people back from the suburbs to the downtown. They therefore encouraged the adaptive use of surrounding buildings in a 60-acre superblock bounded by Euclid and Chester avenues, from East 13th to East 17th streets.

Playhouse Square is noteworthy because its initial impetus was restoration rather than new development, and because its re-development has been guided jointly by an arts organization and a community philanthropy—the Playhouse Square Foundation and the Cleveland Foundation—with significant participation from Cuyahoga County and the city of Cleveland.

Substantial private investment in the area is still to come. But a pattern for private development has been set: An architecturally significant building that once housed the Bonwit Teller store has been rehabilitated into a new home for Cleveland's largest in-vestment banking and brokerage firm, Prescott, Ball & Turben. The old Halle's Department Store is being renovated into offices. The Cleveland Foundation has purchased the Bulkley complex with the intent to use revenues from its commercial, restaurant, and retail uses to help support the theaters and their resident companies.

In the spring of 1984, just before the State Theatre's gala re-opening, the Cleveland Foundation moved its headquarters to the Hanna Building across the street from the Bulkley complex and the theaters. Its relocation, plus the recent moves of some corporate headquarters into Playhouse Square, appears to ensure continuing financial support, staffing, and board participation in charting Playhouse Square's future as an entertainment and shop-ping district.

From Showplace to Slum

Located on the southern edge of Lake Erie, Cleveland's current population totals 574,000. The four counties that comprise the greater Cleveland Standard Metropolitan Statistical Area have 1.9 million residents, making it the nation's 19th largest metropolitan area. In the sixties Cleveland's economy suffered rising foreign competition in the steel and automobile industries. During the seventies, with an eroded tax base and high unemployment, the city government could meet its yearly budget only with a combination of borrowed money and cuts in basic services. In December 1978, with banks holding $15 million in overdue notes that could not be paid, Cleveland became the first American city since the Great Depression to go into default.

The fiscal crisis sobered Cleveland voters, who responded with actions to put the city government on a sounder basis. In 1979 they elected a reform-minded mayor, George Voinovich, who had previously been a county commissioner. In 1980 they extended the terms of the mayor and city council from two to four years and reduced the size of the city council from 33 to 21 members. Since 1980 Voinovich has revamped the city's administration. By late 1981 Standard and Poor's had moved Cleveland's bond rating up from suspen-

sion to investment grade, and in 1983 the city successfully reentered the bond market. It continues a gradual return to fiscal health.

The fortunes of the Playhouse Square area have reflected the city's ups and downs. Euclid Avenue, the square's main artery, was once a glittering center for popular entertainment and elegant retail business. Two department stores, Bonwit Teller and Halle Brothers, plus a host of carriage-trade specialty stores, attracted daytime crowds all year long and made Christmas shopping trips a major event, while theaters, restaurants, and supper clubs drew lively customers every evening.

Built in the twenties with an abundance of chandeliers, gold leaf, and red carpeting, the State, the Ohio, and the Palace theaters were designed by leading theater architects. The State, a vaudeville/movie palace, and the Ohio, a legitimate theater for road companies, were designed by Thomas Lamb for the Loew's chain. The Palace Theatre was designed for vaudeville and films by C. W. and George Rapp as a flagship for the Keith chain. All three are listed today on the National Register of Historic Places.

When television began remaking the entertainment market, the Playhouse Square theaters converted to movies, and in the late sixties they went out of business altogether. The county government unintentionally sped the area's decline when it decided in the late fifties not to connect the outlying area's rapid rail system with Playhouse Square. In the sixties the city cleared vast tracts of land between downtown and the lake, encouraging subsequent office development nearer the lakefront and further isolating Playhouse Square. In the seventies the leading retail establishments along Euclid Avenue closed up shop. Blight set in.

Palace Theatre Auditorium.
Credit: Foto Arts Inc.

Cleveland Arts Groups
Don't Play a Lone Hand

At the turn of the century, Cleveland's booming vitality produced rapid growth in population, wealth, and influence. Wealthy Clevelanders thought of themselves as cosmopolitans, and they expressed their civic enthusiasm by supporting new cultural institutions—the Cleveland Museum of Art, opened in 1916; the Cleveland Orchestra (1918); Karamu House (1915), a settlement house that launched the nation's first interracial and black theater company; the Cleveland Music School Settlement (1912); and the Cleveland Play House (1915), the nation's oldest professional resident theater company.

These institutions reflected a strong spirit of cooperation among patrons and arts institutions. As R. L. Duffus wrote in his 1928 book *The American Renaissance*, "The Cleveland Museum of Art is Cleveland to the core, especially in matters of organization and cooperation. It dovetails with nearly everything else in the city . . . it does not play a lone hand—no one can do that in Cleveland—but is part of what may be designated as the 'Cleveland Movement.'"

In spite of Cleveland's decline in the sixties and seventies, the community's performing arts continued to grow. The Cleveland Ballet and the Cleveland Opera came into being and quickly established strong regional identities, as did the Great Lakes Shakespeare Festival. Other new or expanding groups included a chamber orchestra, small modern dance companies, and several small theater groups. Many of these organizations lacked suitable performance spaces that would foster their artistic growth and build their audiences. Even the Cleveland Orchestra, which had both a winter and a summer home, grew intrigued by the prospect of a downtown setting for a new type of festival concert that could attract a broad audience.

As all these groups had become substantial beneficiaries of the Cleveland Foundation, they were ready to suspend skepticism when it broached the notion that they consider the Playhouse Square theaters as permanent homes or additional performance spaces.

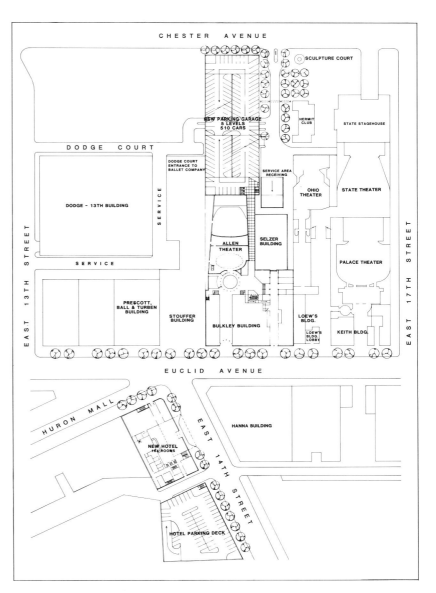

Overall Playhouse Square site plan, including proposed commercial development.
Credit: Landmark Design Associates

"Jacques Brel" Stimulates Vision of Downtown Theater Complex

Rendering of proposed Tower of Light museum.
Credit: Dalton, van Dijk, Johnson & Partners, Architects

In 1970, when the theaters of Playhouse Square had been boarded up and Euclid Avenue was sinking into decline, Ray Shepardson, a young employee of Cleveland's Board of Education, hit upon the notion of using one of the empty theaters for a teachers' meeting. Looking at the lobbies and stages gave him an altogether different idea: a vision of lights, crowds, music, and movement. Soon Shepardson resigned from his job and, along with a small group of other interested citizens, formed the Playhouse Square Association, a nonprofit organization to work toward the theaters' restoration.

In 1971 the association began experimenting with performances in the theaters and in cabarets created out of their lobby spaces to see if audiences actually would come downtown. The answer was yes. Playhouse Square brought in traveling companies such as the Budapest Symphony and a dance troupe from Sierra Leone. In the State Theatre's lobby, the association produced its own cabaret show, *Jacques Brel Is Alive and Well and Living in Paris.* The planned three-week appearance turned into two-and-one-half years, the longest run for any show in Cleveland's history. On the State's stage, the group also produced a local musical revue, *The All Night Strut!,* which ran for a year and a half. In 1976 Shepardson tried another experiment to broaden his audience—free theater. Some observers felt this conveyed an inappropriate "experimental" image, but Robert Sweeney, president of the Cuyahoga County commissioners at the time, was impressed:

Shepardson . . . got himself a foothold in there, sort of winging it without a buck. He got a group of volunteers to participate. I think *Jacques Brel* was one of the first things he did. He put this thing out in the lobby and he got people coming down. I'll never forget one day he came out and said he was going to institute a thing called free theater. He said, "Come down, see the show free, all we'll charge you for is the food." Well, they came out of the woodwork! He just astounded everyone with the fact that he had punched the right button and all of a sudden the response was there. People *couldn't* afford to pay $11 a seat and $5 to park the car and $8 for a babysitter. When Shepardson [offered free theater], he got the interest of people at the second level, who said, "Maybe the Playhouse Square idea can work."

Playhouse Square needed public support in far greater measure, however, than simply people who were willing to go downtown for a performance. It needed capital for restoring the theaters, and it needed political skill. The issue of the theaters themselves, not just the performances in them, had to be placed firmly on the public agenda.

Two actions helped start this process. In May 1972 the owners of the Loew's building, which contained both the State and the Ohio theaters, announced plans to raze it and install a parking lot. The Junior League of Cleveland pledged $25,000 to help save the theaters (by far the largest single donation the Playhouse Square effort had yet seen), and the city planning commission agreed to block the demolition at the last minute by denying the permit for a curb cut the wrecker needed to get his equipment onto the site. In 1973 the Playhouse Square Foundation was incorporated as a nonprofit organization to raise monies for the rescue, restoration, and management of the old theaters.

An Architect Suggests Connecting the Theaters and Creating a Square

Playhouse Square's next assist came from a Cleveland architect, Peter van Dijk, who was retained by the new foundation in 1973 to assess the renovation costs for the three theater interiors. Van Dijk actually produced a compelling vision for all of Playhouse Square. He understood the area's strategic location, one-half mile east of Public Square, to which many stores had migrated from Euclid Avenue over the years. It also was only a block west of Cleveland State University and its 19,000 students, and immediately southeast of the only downtown residential concentration, with about 4,000 persons living in high-rise apartments.

Van Dijk's concept concentrated on the district's central 60-acre superblock, built largely in the early twenties. It contained four theaters, several office buildings, retail shops, and parking concentrated on the rear half of the block. Reviving a design scheme characteristic of Cleveland's turn-of-the-century building boom, van Dijk proposed interior arcades to shelter office workers and shoppers from harsh weather. He suggested that breakthroughs could be made in the walls separating the theater lobbies, enabling the facilities to be transformed into a single cultural center. He proposed another breakthrough into the Bulkley/Selzer buildings to the west, where

he envisioned uncovering old skylights to create an atrium of boutiques and dining places, with more retail spilling over into an alley known as Dodge Court to the rear, and joined by a new parking structure. Patrons would be able to walk from car to shops to the theater without feeling a drop of Cleveland's rain or snow.

On Euclid Avenue, around the open space that gives Playhouse Square its name, he proposed a hotel, an office/condominium building, and a "tower of light" and museum commemorating Thomas Edison's work and many subsequent advances in the technology of light that have occurred in Cleveland. As van Dijk has said:

We were really hired to restore the theaters, not to do master planning. But as architects, we said: This is quite a nice collection of buildings from the 1920s. Also, there's a nice mix of uses here, as opposed to the Erieview Urban Renewal Project [a 1960s project along East Ninth Street, designed by I. M. Pei], which was an office ghetto. Here you have the makings of a much more healthy renewal. The Playhouse Square area has a university, retail, banking, entertainment, the Union Club—and, most important, it has housing nearby. Also, most people didn't realize how these theater buildings nested. They could be interconnected and you could create a superblock.

Dodge Alley today and sketch for the future of Dodge Court.

Cleveland Foundation, City, and County Keep the Concept Alive

The scale and complexity of the Playhouse Square ideas sketched by van Dijk would make sense only when they could be set in the context of broader downtown redevelopment. The programs already operating in the unrestored theaters clearly were stimulating revenue in the form of new restaurants and retail. Some came too early and failed, but they provided a convincing argument that full-scale restoration could contribute to the city's overall economic health.

County Government
Rescues the Theaters

In the early seventies, while the Playhouse Square project was taking its first tentative steps, Cleveland's city government lacked an economic development division, and its planning department—struggling with mammoth social problems—showed scant concern for real estate matters. Eventually, however, the city and county were able to perform some essential services that supported the Playhouse Square Foundation's ambitions.

In November 1977 the Playhouse Square Foundation found itself short of the funds necessary to exercise its option to purchase the Loew's Theater Building when its owners again threatened its demolition. The Playhouse Square Foundation persuaded Cuyahoga County to invest $1.7 million to acquire the building and to renovate its office spaces for a federally funded court program. The county then leased the theaters back to the foundation. Payments on the 40-year lease were waived during the early years of construction and renovation. The foundation secured a long-term lease on the Palace Theatre from its private owners in January 1978, thereby bringing all three theaters under the management of a single entity for the first time.

The county's dramatic action gave the project such a boost in credibility that the city of Cleveland released to the county, in August 1979, a $3.147 million public works grant from the U.S. Department of Commerce's Economic Development Administration. The county in turn applied the money toward the renovation of the State Theatre auditorium.

In 1980 another publicly supported contribution was made by Prescott, Ball & Turben, an investment banking firm that had purchased the nearby Bonwit Teller building to renovate as its headquarters. The purchase and renovation were financed largely with low-cost loans received through the city and county, including $500,000 in federal Urban Development Action Grant (UDAG) money. The U.S. Department of Housing and Urban Development agreed that repayment and interest on the UDAG loan, as it was paid, could be turned over to the Playhouse Square Foundation; the foundation in turn was able to use this pledge as partial collateral for industrial development revenue bonds to finance the Ohio Theatre renovation. In addition, Prescott, Ball & Turben underwrote and guaranteed the bonds for retail placement.

In the fall of 1980 the mayor, the city council president, and the three county commissioners declared that Playhouse Square had "priority status" for any new federal funding that might come to Cleveland. Shortly thereafter, a $3.5 million Economic Development Administration grant was awarded to the county for the construction of a new stagehouse for the State Theatre.

Cleveland Foundation
Provides Venture Capital

The Cleveland Foundation has awarded grants totaling nearly $2 million directly to the Playhouse Square Foundation over the past dozen years. Its support of resident arts organizations now performing in the district, and its purchase of commercial real estate in the area, represents an additional investment of many times that amount.

Founded in 1914 as the nation's first community trust, the Cleveland Foundation's assets now exceed $300 million. When Homer C. Wadsworth became director in 1974 after 25 years of philanthropic leadership in Kansas City, Missouri, he brought a new entrepreneurial spirit, stressing "the need for venture capital in philanthropy as in business." In January 1975 the foundation created a position for a program officer for cultural affairs.

	Source	Amount
1979	National Endowment for the Arts and Cleveland Foundation (challenge grant)	$ 500,000
1980	Economic Development Administration (withdrawn and later reinstated)	3,500,000
	UDAG #1 (Prescott, Ball & Turben)	500,000
	Cuyahoga County cultural arts subsidy	5,000
1981	UDAG #2	750,000
	Cuyahoga County	3,500,000
	Ohio Arts Council	7,216
	Cuyahoga County cultural arts subsidy	15,000
1982	National Endowment for the Arts (for Museum/Tower of Light feasibility study)	25,000
	Ohio Arts Council	3,654
	Ohio Arts Council	250
	Cuyahoga County Cultural Council	13,000
1983	Ohio Arts Council	55,398
	Ohio Arts Council	3,000
	Cuyahoga County Cultural Council	13,000
1984	State of Ohio budget appropriation (for purchase and renovation of Palace)	3,750,000
	National Endowment for the Arts	25,000
	Cuyahoga County Cultural Council	13,000
Total		$12,678,518

The timing was right: Cleveland's arts renaissance was in full swing. Both the Cleveland Ballet and the Cleveland Opera launched their first professional seasons in 1976–77, and both received major support from the Cleveland Foundation. The foundation also nurtured the growth of the Great Lakes Shakespeare Festival.

The foundation had been one of the first supporters of Playhouse Square activities. Yet it found its enthusiasm wavering in the mid-seventies while the fledgling Playhouse Square Foundation experienced a crisis of mission. The new organization found it difficult to raise money for three abandoned theaters that for most Clevelanders lived only in memory. And there remained much skepticism as to whether arts patrons would throng to downtown Cleveland at night.

In 1974 Playhouse Square decided to produce an original musical, *Alice*, based on *Alice in Wonderland*, in the lobby of the unrenovated Palace Theatre, with underwriting from the Cleveland Foundation. The musical touched off some excitement but closed before it could earn any profit. Entertainment moved tentatively onto the stages of the unrenovated State and Palace theaters: first, free theater featuring little-known performers and then bargain-priced entertainment featuring such artists as Mel Tormé and Sarah Vaughan. The financial results were not sufficient to sustain the original interest in the theaters as a home for the fine arts as well as popular entertainment, and the "people's theater" programming nearly bankrupted the fragile organization as its deficits mounted to about $1 million. Furthermore, few substantial private contributions had materialized, and doubts grew as to the likelihood of the Playhouse Square Foundation ever being able to exercise its option to buy the State and Ohio theaters.

"Fortunately there existed a vision that was more compelling than the reality," recalls Patricia Jansen Doyle, program officer for cultural affairs at the Cleveland Foundation. "That vision came from van Dijk's master plan and remained alive over the years with key leadership at both the Cleveland Foundation and the Playhouse Square Foundation."

When the Cleveland Foundation resumed its funding of Playhouse Square in late 1976, it therefore focused on three priorities:

■ enabling van Dijk to refine his master plan, develop a slide show, and prepare

Playhouse Square
Project Data

Physical Configuration
Component—Income Generating

Bulkley Building/Retail/ Other Commercial	Feasibility study for specialty retail adjacent to theater center
Office	Rehab of architecturally significant structure
Residential	Uncertain/under study
Hotel	Proposed/under study
Mixed Use	The configuration around the cultural uses (theaters) creates possibilities for mixed-use commercial development on a superblock
Bulkley Building	213,408 sq. ft. net leasable area (NLA)
Office	97,567 sq. ft. NLA
Ground Floor Retail	19,523 sq. ft. NLA*
Second Floor Retail/Office	20,699 sq. ft. NLA*
Basement (most used as business school)	12,919 sq. ft. NLA
Selzer Building—office	36,000 sq. ft.
Allen Theatre	
Auditorium	13,700 sq. ft.
Lobby and Rotunda (now a restaurant)	13,000 sq. ft. NLA*
Replacement Garage	510 spaces
Proposed Hotel	164 rooms
Hotel Parking Deck	100 spaces

Entry court to Bulkley garage
and retail center

*Bulkley Arcade, second floor, and Allen lobby and rotunda leasable space to be reduced to 49,000 sq. ft. of retail/restaurants

Component—Arts/Culture/Open Space

State Theatre	3,095 seats
Ohio Theatre	1,035 seats
Palace Theatre	2,700–3,000 seats
Acreage	69 acres Playhouse Square District 6 acres—theaters 2 acres—Bulkley Building
Location	Downtown Cleveland
Master Developer	Playhouse Square Foundation for theaters Cranston Development Company of Pittsburgh is completing feasibility analysis, under auspices of Cleveland Foundation for Bulkley Building
Master Planner	Peter van Dijk, Dalton, van Dijk, Johnson & Partners
Estimated Total Development Costs (1984 dollars)	$27 million (theater acquisition, rehabilitation, and new stagehouse) $3.8 million (Bulkley Building purchase price) $31.5 million (retail/commercial development improvements for Bulkley Building)

Source: Playhouse Square Foundation
Cleveland Foundation

more detailed design recommendations for the theaters;

■ enabling the Playhouse Square Foundation to hire its first paid director and other administrative staff; and

■ validating the economic feasibility of the area's development plan, especially involving the Bulkley/Selzer complex, through a study by the American City Corporation, a research arm of the Rouse Company.

In November 1977 the Cleveland Foundation invited six of the city's arts organizations and the Playhouse Square Foundation to engage in a collaborative long-range planning process. Each organization would develop its own five-year plan, considering such variables as artistic and management strength, audience, financial and facility needs, and the staffs and boards that would be necessary to achieve momentum.

The foundation's initiative stemmed from its concern that all these organizations, some of them young and fragile, would need to find new and larger sources of income to sustain their programs. None of the groups except the Cleveland Orchestra had built any significant corporate support. The foundation therefore created an advisory committee that included the chief executives of several multinational corporations as well as legal and accounting firms. This strategy sparked the first significant corporate awareness of the potential impact of the Playhouse Square development on the city's downtown.

At the first joint meeting in November 1977, it became clear both that every arts organization was looking either for a new home or for additional performance space and that Playhouse Square had more space than it knew what to do with. Consequently, a facilities planning council was formed, and each group was encouraged to inspect the Ohio, State, and Palace theaters and suggest what specifications would be required to make them suitable for their performances.

A serious facilities planning effort ensued, sustained by grants from the National Endowment for the Arts and the Cleveland Foundation. These enabled the continued involvement of architect van Dijk, theater/ lighting designer Roger Morgan, and acoustician Christopher Jaffe.

The long-range planning process culminated in six of the participants asking the Cleveland Foundation to submit a challenge grant application to the National Endowment for the Arts under the banner of the "Cleveland Consortium for the Performing Arts." Of the groups participating in this consortium application, four—the Cleveland Ballet, the Cleveland Opera, the Great Lakes Shakespeare Festival, and the Playhouse Square Foundation—all would make their homes in the Playhouse Square Center that eventually emerged.

In October 1979 the National Endowment for the Arts announced the award of a $1.75 million challenge grant on behalf of the consortium. The Cleveland Foundation added $250,000 to raise the total to $2 million. Of this amount, $500,000 was allocated to the Playhouse Square Foundation to eliminate its accumulated deficit and to support construction costs for performance spaces for resident and touring performing arts.

In the months following the award, the Playhouse Square Foundation engaged national consultants to assess the project's fundraising potential and to develop operational plans for the center. Changes occurred in management, and the board of trustees was expanded and strengthened. Several members of the Cleveland Foundation's corporate advisory committee agreed to serve on the steering committee for the capital campaign and ultimately joined the board.

The Cleveland Foundation provided a leadership gift of $710,000—the largest single grant from unrestricted funds in its history—to launch a $20 million campaign effort in 1980, and it awarded $500,000 to launch the second phase of the campaign in 1983. The first grant subsidized architectural work and operating support during the period when the theaters would be generating little income. The second supported marketing for the Playhouse Square Center and the booking of noted touring groups.

Meanwhile, Playhouse Square attempted unsuccessfully to buy the Bulkley/Selzer buildings, a complex that included two parcels of land needed to construct a stagehouse for the State Theatre. The Bulkley

Playhouse Square
Capital Cost Summary

Loew's Building Purchase	$ 700,000
Ohio Theatre	3,800,000
State Theatre	
Auditorium	3,600,000
Stagehouse	7,000,000
Lobbies and finishes	1,050,000
Palace Theatre	
Tower suites	600,000
Purchase	600,000
Renovation	7,900,000
Computer Center/Central Box Office	750,000
Contingency	1,000,000
TOTAL CAPITAL COSTS	$27,000,000

Bulkley Complex

	Public/philantropic subsidy funds (incl. some federal funds)	Private	Public development funds (industrial revenue bonds)
Income Source	$11,384,000	$12,950,000	$7,172,000
Development Costs			
Hotel	$14,399,000		
Retail	9,307,000		
Parking			7,172,000
Entry	628,000		
TOTAL DEVELOPMENT COSTS	$31,506,000		

owners refused to sell the land separately, thereby delaying the Playhouse Square Center for two additional years.

In 1981 the Playhouse Square Foundation finally negotiated an option to buy the Bulkley complex for $3.8 million. The organization requested and received funding from both the Cleveland Foundation and the George Gund Foundation, the largest private foundation in Cleveland, to pay for the option and to complete architectural work that would be needed for submission of a UDAG application. When the deadline for exercising the option approached, Playhouse Square leaders returned to the Cleveland Foundation and asked for either a grant or a low-interest loan to consummate the purchase. Mayor Voinovich added his plea in a personal address to the foundation's distribution committee. The committee concurred that the properties should come into friendly hands but concluded that the owners should possess greater resources than those of the Playhouse Square Foundation. The distribution committee eventually decided to create a nonprofit corporation, Foundation Properties, Inc., and authorized grants of $3.9 million to the new corporation—about three-fourths from principal assets and one-fourth from grant money. Five committee members were named as trustees of the new corporation.

The Cleveland Foundation thus became the nation's first community foundation to make a major program-related investment (PRI) with its assets. The Tax Reform Act of 1969 had permitted private foundations to invest in such for-profit ventures, as long as those ventures supported the programmatic interests of the philanthropic organizations.

Subsequent to the foundation's investment in the Bulkley/Selzer buildings, a search for a developer began with the assistance of the Playhouse Square Foundation and the city of Cleveland. The latter funded an economic update of the van Dijk master plan by Halcyon Ltd., a development consultant firm.

Playhouse Square Foundation Gains Fiscal and Management Strength

During the first five months of 1980, the Playhouse Square Foundation redefined its program and management plans. Joseph H. Keller, the chief operating officer of Ernest & Whinney, a worldwide accounting firm based in Cleveland, agreed to chair a steering committee of corporate chief executive officers to advise and to assist the Playhouse Square staff and trustees in their $20 million capital campaign. With sophisticated cash flow projections now provided, a line of revolving credit was promised by the Clearinghouse of Cleveland Banks to help finance cash imbalances during the upcoming construction period.

In July 1982 the Ohio Theatre reopened as the fully restored home of the Great Lakes Shakespeare Festival, whose eight-and-one-half-hour production of *Nicholas Nickleby* won national critical acclaim during the opening season. That same month, Lawrence J. Wilker became the new president of the Playhouse Square Foundation. He had formerly served as director of properties of the Shubert Theater Organization's Broadway theaters and its real estate holdings in six other cities.

During the final quarter of 1982, Playhouse Square Foundation staff and trustees

reassessed their capital campaign goals and timetable against increased cost projections caused by delays and changes in renovation specifications. They decided to close out the first phase of the campaign December 31, 1982, at $16 million and to mount an $11 million Phase II campaign to cover the additional renovation costs and to begin creating operating mechanisms such as a central box office, passages between the theaters, and staff for their operations.

As of December 1984 the Phase II capital campaign had achieved 89 percent of its goal. Toward the combined goal of $27 million, more than $24 million had been raised, more than $12.7 million from government sources, more than $6 million from foundations and individuals, and $5.3 million from business.

A Small Theater District Rather Than Festival Marketing

While the Cleveland Foundation moved with dispatch in the purchase of the Bulkley complex, it proceeded more cautiously in its unaccustomed role of landlord and developer. The foundation sold the parcels of land needed for the State Theatre expansion to Cuyahoga County, thereby reducing its purchase cost by $330,136. It engaged the city's leading commercial real estate firm, Ostendorf-Morris, to manage the complex, and began long-deferred maintenance. Occupancy (exclusive of the complex's unused Allen Theatre auditorium) rose from 84 to 95 percent in two years. In the second year, the property was providing a net return of 8 percent and in the third year 12 percent, exclusive of capital appreciation. Even if nothing else happened, the foundation clearly had made a sound investment.

Meanwhile, Halcyon Ltd. had updated the economic feasibility study for the Playhouse Square cultural district and had contacted about forty potential developers throughout the nation. Of those who expressed an interest, Halcyon recommended two firms for careful consideration: a local firm beginning to achieve national recognition and Cranston Development Company of Pittsburgh. Representatives of the Cleveland Foundation and the Playhouse Square Foundation interviewed the candidates. Cranston was favored because of the success its president, Arthur Ziegler, had achieved with Station Square in Pittsburgh.

Ziegler and his partner, Robert Cranston Kanuth, were convinced that, although Cleveland's downtown remained generally deserted on weeknights and weekends, "with the investment that already has been made in Playhouse Square, you have the possibility of filling the vacuum right there. The theaters provide the sizzle. They can be the anchors for a specialty retail center in the heart of the city." He was familiar with the ideas of Peter van Dijk, including his suggestion for creating a "tower of light."

While Ziegler regarded the project as potentially successful, his firm nonetheless saw it as a high-risk venture. Therefore, Cranston would make only a limited investment at the outset; it would contribute the initial time of its partners but wanted to re-

Project Data: State Theatre

Location	1519 Euclid Avenue, Playhouse Square, Cleveland
Originally Built	1921, Thomas Lamb, architect
Completed	Auditorium: 1980
	Stagehouse: June 9, 1984
Stagehouse Architects	Schematic design and design development: Dalton, van Dijk, Johnson & Partners
	Contract administration and construction documents: Hoag-Wismer Partnership

Stagehouse Consultants

Mechanical and Electrical Engineers:	Byers Engineering Company
Structural Engineers:	Barber & Hoffman, Inc.
Site Planning Consultants:	Knight & Stolar, Inc.
Acoustical:	Jaffe Acoustics, Inc., Norwalk, Conn.
Theater:	Roger Morgan Studio, Inc., New York City
Contractor	Hausman & Johnson, Cleveland

Building Cost	$3.6 million—Auditorium renovation
	$ .7 million—Loew's Building
	$7.0 million—Stagehouse
	$ .5 million—Furniture and equipment
Gross Area	Loew's Building—127,594 sq. ft.

Breakdown of Interior Area
Stage

Grid Height	80 ft. & 82 rigging line sets
Proscenium Height	28 ft.
Proscenium Width	52 ft.
Stage Width	128 ft.
Stage Depth from Apron	65 ft.

Auditorium

Orchestra Length (apron to back wall)	135 ft.
Max. Orchestra Height	60 ft.
Max. Orchestra Width	109 ft.
Dressing Rooms	Space for 100 performers
Pit	75 musicians (1,200 sq. ft.)
Seating	3,095 seats
Lobby	320 ft. long × 37 ft. wide (11,840 sq. ft.)
Rehearsal Rooms	(2) 44 ft. wide × 52 ft. long; (1) 20 ft. × 30 ft.
Exterior Features	Facade: Original Beaux Arts exterior facing materials of limestone, granite, and marble have been replaced with patterned brick terra cotta.
	Stagehouse: Case in place concrete; insulated, white metal panels with baked-on finish; white brick base; black curtain wall with tinted gray glass windows.
Interior Features	Shares Loew's Building with Ohio Theatre.
	The State Theatre is known for its spacious house, magnificently appointed with Roman, Greek, and European baroque design motifs. Tiffany style, backlit glass exit signs are scattered throughout the theater. Ascending to the mezzanine level are two elegantly curved marble staircases. The 320-foot lobby is the longest in the world. Ornamentation is provided by the richly coffered ceiling and a series of outstanding murals painted by the early American modernist James Dougherty. There are eight colossal mahogany columns; floors are white Vermont marble and terrazzo; staircases are Vermont marble and terra cotta.

Project Data: Palace Theatre

Location	1625 Euclid Avenue, Playhouse Square, Cleveland
Originally Built	1922, C. W. and George Rapp, architect
Projected Opening	Summer 1986
Restoration Architect	Dalton, van Dijk, Johnson & Partners
Building Cost	Purchase: $ 600,000 Renovation: 7,900,000 Tower: 600,000
Gross Area	46,944 sq. ft.

Breakdown of Interior Area
Stage

Grid Height	79 ft., 3 in., 67 rigging lines
Proscenium Height	37 ft.
Proscenium Width	56 ft.
Stage Width	73 ft., 5 in.
Stage Depth from Apron	43 ft., 6 in.

Auditorium

Orchestra Length (apron to back wall)	126 ft.
Max. Orchestra Height	69 ft.
Max. Orchestra Width	119 ft.
Dressing Rooms	70 rooms
Pit	35 musicians
Seating	2,700–3,200 seats

Exterior Features Outer lobby has brass box offices; bronze doors

Interior Features Grand Hall: 154 Czechoslovakian cut crystal chandeliers throughout theater; marble from Carrara, Italy; all of the Promenade done in plaster with Scaglia glaze finish; Empire bronze railings from Nüremberg were 189 years old when installed.

Auditorium was designed after a palace garden near Beijing (Peking).

cover its costs for the rest of the preconstruction activities. This requirement meant that the Cleveland Foundation had to authorize yet another grant, this time up to $378,208—an amount that might be recovered when the project was implemented. A substantial part of this money would subsidize architectural and engineering work and would obtain a guaranteed construction cost from a contractor.

The development contract was executed on November 29, 1983. It named Cranston as the developer; Dalton, van Dijk, Johnson & Partners of Cleveland and Landmarks Design Associates of Pittsburgh as the architects, and Navarro Corporation of Pittsburgh as the contractor—all at least through the preconstruction activities. Ziegler proposed and the Cleveland Foundation agreed that at the outset the largest possible forms of development should be explored. This arrangement meant that:

■ The potential project site would encompass the entire superblock area and some key yet underutilized parcels across Euclid Avenue and surrounding the district.

■ The potential project would include a hotel and possibly apartments and condominiums as well as a specialty retail/dining complex with connecting parking garage.

Among the issues explored over the next several months were the following:

■ Could the developers afford to transform the Selzer building, a turn-of-the-century brick structure, into a four-story atrium surrounded by shops, as envisioned in the original van Dijk plan?

■ Should the Selzer building instead be razed, as well as the decaying Bulkley garage, and these facilities be replaced with a one-story food court and retail mall that would wrap around two sides of the Allen Theatre?

■ Could the retail uses wrap around the third side by extending into a building to the west owned by another party?

■ Could the auditorium of the Allen Theatre be transformed into retail space or some other use?

■ Could a hotel be built at the west end of the superblock and connected to the retail/theater area by an enclosed walkway?

■ Should a hotel instead be built across Euclid Avenue on a site geographically closer but separated by traffic?

■ Could a new parking garage be sited in such a way as to leave room for an entry court—a second front door to the complex—and also for future development of an apartment or condominium building?

In December 1984 Cranston Development Company released a detailed proposal with costs guaranteed by a contractor. The plan called for a large entry court or park, a 155-space parking garage, a 164-room hotel, and 90,000 square feet of leasable retail space in the Bulkley building, with a food court and retail mall replacing the Selzer building. The cost was projected at $39 million. However, projections for private funding, industrial revenue bonds, and government subsidy still left a funding gap of several million dollars.

The Cranston team set to work on ways to reduce costs. On February 1, 1985, they returned with a modified plan estimated to cost $31.5 million, with a much smaller funding gap. The financing plan assumed a supportable UDAG of $5.2 million based upon a 2.5:1 private-to-public ratio, the use of industrial revenue bonds for the Bulkley garage (if private financing appeared less advantageous), and investment tax credits, currently threatened by federal tax reform proposals. It also assumed generous participation by the city and county in writing down land acquisition costs and construction loans, defraying working capital allowances, and developing the entry court and hotel parking deck. The costs projected that the retail space would be leased from the Cleveland Foundation, but Cranston also expressed a willingness to consider buying the Bulkley complex outright. The financing remained difficult but closer to realization.

The plan currently consists of the following:

■ A total of 49,000 square feet of leasable retail space, to be concentrated on the first and second floors of the existing Bulkley building. About 60 percent would be in food and beverage services and 40 percent in nonfood retail.

■ The Selzer building would be retained as an office building but would be available for retail expansion at a later date.

■ A 510-space parking facility would be built, running from Chester Avenue to the rear of the Allen Theatre. This would require razing the existing Bulkley garage. The new parking structure would be connected to the Bulkley retail center by an enclosed elevated walkway to be built between the Selzer building and the Allen Theatre.

■ A small entry park and landscaped driveway would be created on Chester Avenue in front of the Hermit Club and along the east side of the parking garage. The Hermit Club, a handsome, red-brick, Tudor building nestled at the rear of the theaters, is a dining club where businesspeople enjoy amateur theatrical and musical productions.

■ A 164-room hotel would be built across Euclid Avenue at a point where East 14th Street and Huron Road converge into Playhouse Square. The site now houses a restaurant, a vacant store, and surface parking, with most of the site owned by the Playhouse Square Foundation. The hotel would

provide limited dining, meeting rooms, a health club, and its own parking deck.

The retail complex would take its tone from the embellished brass elegance of the Bulkley Arcade and the movie-palace environment of the Allen Theatre. An estimated 25 retail shops could be created in the arcade and in the lobby of the abandoned theater, with many opening onto a U-shaped interior mall. The featured open space would be the theater's rotunda. The

Project Data: Ohio Theatre

Location	1511 Euclid Avenue, Playhouse Square, Cleveland
Originally Built	1921, Thomas Lamb, architect
Restoration Completed	July 1982
Restoration Architect	Peter van Dijk; Dalton, van Dijk, Johnson & Partners
Consultants	Mechanical/Electrical Engineers: Byers Engineering Company, Cleveland Structural Engineers: Barber & Hoffman, Inc., Cleveland Theater: Roger Morgan Studios, Inc., New York City Acoustical: Jaffe Acoustics, Norwalk, Conn. Plaster Work: Acme Arsena
Contractor	Dunbar Construction Company—restoration
Building Cost	$3.8 million—renovation and construction
Gross Area	Loew's Building—127,594 sq. ft.

Breakdown of Interior Area
Stage

Grid Height	64 ft., 9 in.
Proscenium Height	28 ft.
Proscenium Width	41 ft., 3 in.
Stage Width	74 ft.
Stage Depth from Apron	44 ft.

Auditorium

Orchestra Length (apron to back wall)	81 ft.
Max. Orchestra Height	42 ft. (off the stage)
Max. Orchestra Width	77 ft.
Dressing Rooms	5 floors, 33 stations for actors
Pit	25 musicians
Seating	1,035 seats
Exterior Features	Shares the Loew's Building with the State Theatre. The original Beaux Arts exterior facing materials of limestone, granite, and marble have been replaced with patterned brick terra cotta.
Interior Features	As much as possible, existing original ornamentation was retained and restored. Lobby, originally Italian Renaissance, was completely destroyed by fire; ceiling restored to recall original in texture and form. Coffered ceiling and plaster medallions; elaborate crystal chandelier, saved from the old Hippodrome, is suspended from the restored dome; small brass and crystal sconces illuminate the walls; pale green plush seats match the rich-looking stage curtain; new concrete floor was placed over original wood floor to increase the rake of the auditorium and improve sightlines; movable chairs in orchestra-level boxes can be removed or adjusted for handicapped patrons. Top-quality computerized lighting system.

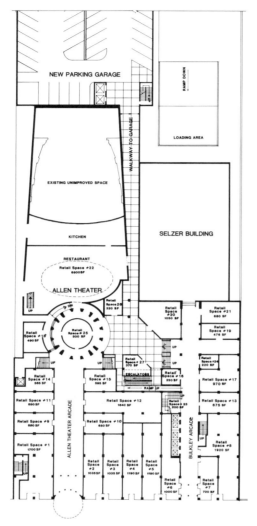

Bulkley Building floor plan, showing proposed retail space.
Credit: Landmark Design Associates

theater's auditorium would be divided. The section under the balcony would be transformed into a spacious restaurant embellished by another dome and by its own ring of balconies. The theater balcony itself could be divided into two small cinemas and, while there are no immediate plans for the main auditorium of the former movie theater, it has been suggested that it might be used for a nightclub or a ballroom.

The Cranston Development report expressed a firm belief that a wide range of restaurant facilities and entertainment spots, combining eating and drinking with jazz, folk, bluegrass, and popular music, would be eagerly patronized by theatergoers. The challenge for Playhouse Square will be to find the right blend of specialty shops and restaurants that fill a void in the

shopping opportunities both downtown and in the suburbs. While downtown Cleveland still has two strong department stores and a variety of specialty and discount stores, there are no first-rate specialty shops dealing in such items as books, recordings, toys and games, posters and prints, children's clothing, and American arts and crafts.

Plans for parking also will have to arrive at realistic solutions. While representatives of the Playhouse Square Foundation had urged construction of a 1,000-space garage, research has indicated that a garage in the 400-car range would be more easily financed. The original plan called for the garage to be oriented east to west in the western end of the superblock between Dodge Court and Chester Avenue, leaving room for a large entry park behind the Bulkley/Selzer buildings. But the cost of land has become prohibitive, so the garage site has been rotated by 90 degrees and moved behind the Bulkley building, reducing the size of the proposed entry court and creating the need to vacate a section of Dodge Court.

The Playhouse Square Foundation had been pursued by a parking syndicate for endorsement of construction of a garage in the block immediately to the east of the theaters. This possibility held considerable appeal, since the Playhouse Square Foundation was continuing to experience financial strains in operating theaters whose expenses were vastly exceeding their income. It hoped to obtain an income stream from commercial developments in the neighborhood, including parking facilities.

The Cleveland Foundation diverted the time of its developer, architects, and other planners into exploring whether this unforeseen garage could be constructed without compromising the rest of the Bulkley development. Consultants explored developing a limited retail plan in the Bulkley Arcade and creating a breakthrough into the theater center at the same time, but concluded that the entire retail configuration had to be determined before a garage could be sited. The garage proposal collapsed.

This episode served to bring a wider number of participants into an understanding of the complicated issues involved in development planning. It also accelerated two other activities. First, it led to an independent parking study by Wilbur Smith & Associates of Alliance, Ohio, which tended to dispel the belief that a parking garage could provide a quick revenue stream for the Playhouse Square Foundation. Second, it spurred further land acquisition by the Cleveland Foundation. By the spring of 1985 most of the marginal buildings in the rear portion of the superblock had been razed and converted to surface parking.

Cooperation and interaction with local government also began to accelerate after a Playhouse Square Working Committee was created in mid-1984. The group includes the city economic development director, the city planning director, the county administrator, the project developer, the Playhouse Square Foundation president and area development director, and the director, cultural affairs program officer, and administrative officer of the Cleveland Foundation. Peter van Dijk and the Cleveland Foundation's attorney are also frequently involved.

It is within this group that infrastructure needs first have been discussed—especially the need for improved street lighting and other street amenities. It is here that the idea was broached of the city or county paying for the entry court. City officials told the working committee that it was time to put a Playhouse Square community development plan through the city council for approval. Such a plan and accompanying blight and traffic studies had been completed in 1983 but were awaiting a realistic financing package for implementation. Council approval will be a necessary step, however, if the city is to use its condemnation powers to acquire any remaining parcels needed for the garage and entry court.

City officials have been working in other ways as well. The economic development department is helping Greyhound Bus Lines find a new location for its terminal, currently located on the north side of Chester Avenue immediately across from the proposed garage site. The departure of Greyhound would free land for apartment or condominium development and remove a clientele not viewed as compatible with

theater and retail patronage. When Trailways Bus System decided to move its terminal from the south side of Chester Avenue, Mayor Voinovich helped the Cleveland Foundation secure Trailways' key parcel at a favorable price.

Perhaps most important of all, city and county officials as well as board and staff representatives of the Playhouse Square Foundation and the Cleveland Foundation have attended each meeting when the Cranston Development Company has presented various development plans and financing alternatives. "It is still a very difficult and complex project," says Gary Conley, the city's economic development director, "but Cranston has been very beneficial in helping us identify our development opportunities and how best to go about exploiting them."

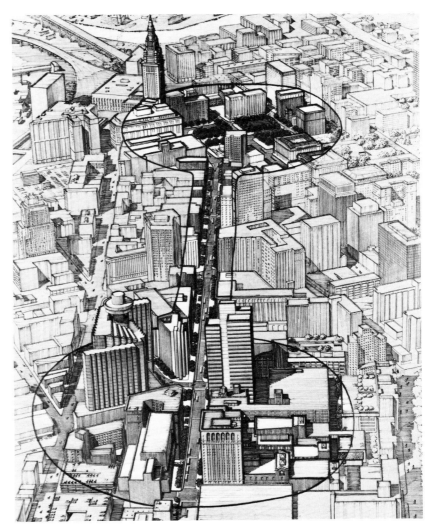

Euclid Avenue corridor from Public Square and Terminal Tower at the top to Playhouse Square with proposed hotel and office development at bottom.
Credit: Dalton, van Dijk, Johnson & Partners, Architects

Reopened Theaters Bring Arts Downtown, Spur Private Investment

State Theatre's grand stair and chandelier.
Credit: Dalton, van Dijk, Johnson & Partners, Architects

State Theatre section with new stagehouse.
Credit: Dalton, van Dijk, Johnson & Partners, Architects

Much of Playhouse Square as a cultural center is now a reality. Two of the three theaters slated for rehabilitation, the State and the Ohio, are fully renovated and functioning at a sophisticated level, with advanced lighting and stage equipment. All three theaters have been united into a single, integrated performing arts and entertainment center by the opening of corridors in the common walls of their lobbies and through the installation of a central box office.

The 3,095-seat State Theatre, which reopened in June 1984, now has a massive stage, large orchestra pit, dressing rooms, backstage area, and loading docks that give it the versatility to handle touring shows with large casts, full orchestras, and many scene changes. In addition, the $7 million stagehouse provides two large studios, each the exact size of the stage, for use by its resident ballet and the opera companies, who presented their 1984–85 seasons in the facility. The Metropolitan Opera used the theater during its 1984 and 1985 spring tours, and the Cleveland Orchestra presented three weeks of concerts at the State in the spring of 1985.

The 1,035-seat Ohio Theatre, which reopened in July 1982, houses the Great Lakes Shakespeare Festival for five to six months of the year. During the remaining weeks, it becomes a community showcase for ethnic and cultural productions, Off-Broadway shows, lectures, and chamber ensembles. Its 1984–85 season was heavily booked by many of northern Ohio's lead-

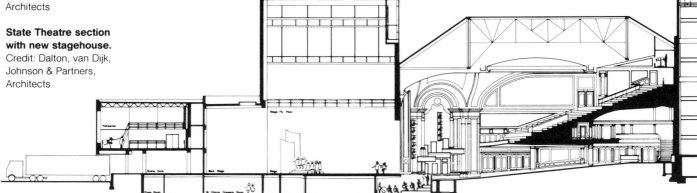

ing community, neighborhood, and minority arts groups. On the scarce dates available for its own use, the Playhouse Square Foundation presents a limited schedule of small productions, ensembles, soloists, and lectures, as well as a children's theater series cosponsored with the Junior League of Cleveland.

Playhouse Square is creating its own version of Times Square with a Cleveland Ballet New Year's Eve production of *The Nutcracker* in the State, complete with glittery hats, balloons, noisemakers, and three bands, plus fireworks and a nutcracker (instead of a Times Square ball) to mark midnight. A total of 1,800 paying patrons were joined by throngs of revelers in the square as 1984 turned into 1985.

Attendance figures for both theaters indicated that they would draw 650,000 persons during 1984–85 and reaffirmed projections that the center would draw a million patrons a year when all three theaters are fully operational.

In the spring of 1984 a lifetime lease was obtained for the 3,000-seat Palace Theatre from its private owners, and a purchase price has been set pending the day when the Playhouse Square Foundation has the financial resources to buy the facility. The foundation received $3.75 million from the state of Ohio toward the Palace's restoration from a grant made through the Cuyahoga Community College. This arrangement will enable the college to enjoy rent-free use of the center for a number of events each year.

State Theatre Auditorium.
Credit: David Thum

State Theatre's new stagehouse.
Credit: Dalton, van Dijk, Johnson & Partners, Architects

**Lobby of the Palace
Theatre.**
Credit: Foto Arts Inc.

Also in 1984 the Playhouse Square Foundation engaged a local market research firm, Tactical Decisions Group, to conduct focused group interviews with various audience segments, while in early 1985 an arts marketing survey commissioned by the Cleveland Foundation neared completion. It involved telephone interviews with committed patrons, occasional visitors, and nonusers of 18 cultural institutions concentrated in University Circle and Playhouse Square. The Cleveland Foundation survey and its analysis are being provided by two nationally recognized firms, Ziff Marketing and Clar, Martire, Bartolomeo of New York City.

The same week the State Theatre opened, a lively new restaurant debuted in Playhouse Square with a varied, unconventional menu and singing waiters. The restaurant, with more than 200 seats, has been jammed before and after theater performances and is even busy on Monday evenings when the theaters are almost always dark. Another fine restaurant opened across the street six months later.

Significant private investment in Playhouse Square began with the 1980 purchase and renovation of the long-empty Bonwit Teller building by brokers Prescott, Ball & Turben. The former Halle's Department Store is being converted into a series of shops and offices by Tower City Development Corporation. Seven corporations, the Cleveland Foundation, and the Greater Cleveland Hospital Association all have moved their headquarters to Playhouse Square, bringing 891 new employees to the area.

Palace Theatre section.
Credit: Dalton, van Dijk,
Johnson & Partners,
Architects

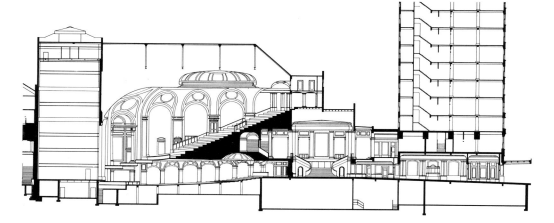

Ten existing buildings have been purchased and upgraded, representing an investment of $55.75 million. Improvements totaling $2 million have been made to the Hanna Building and the Keith Building. Nine new restaurants have opened, bringing 223 employees to the area and representing an investment of $2,225,000.

Some individuals continue to question the wisdom of bringing downtown the performing arts organizations that had been serving local audiences at significantly lower costs than must be met at Playhouse Square. However, all agree that the move now represents the future of the performing arts in Cleveland. As Dennis Dooley summarized in *Northern Ohio Live*:

. . . the question of whether the [Cleveland] Foundation's grand scheme (pulling together under one multimillion-dollar roof so many diverse groups at such different stages in their development and nearly all with their own internal problems at a time when federal monies have dried up and corporate funding is growing harder to get) should ever have been undertaken is now, say these critics, beside the point.

"It's too late now to ask that question," says a fellow philanthropist, who asked not to be named. "The only question now is how to make it work. Because it *has* to work now." The revival of downtown Cleveland, to say nothing of the continuing health of a large part of the area's most glittering asset, its rich cultural life—and hence the very image of Cleveland in the eyes of outside businesses and other groups the city hopes to attract here either as visitors or on a permanent basis—depends in very large part on the success of Playhouse Square.

Ohio Theatre before and after restoration.
Credit: Dalton, van Dijk, Johnson & Partners, Architects

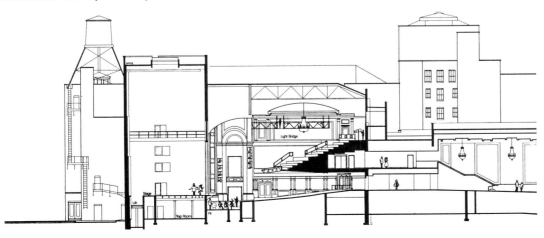

Ohio Theatre section.
Credit: Dalton, van Dijk, Johnson & Partners, Architects

Downtown Cultural District

A public/private venture, spearheaded by the Howard Heinz Endowment and reinforced by the city of Pittsburgh and Allegheny County, has stimulated commercial and cultural development in an old downtown area adjacent to the central office core. The new corporate headquarters for Allegheny International—two 34-story buildings containing 1.3 million square feet of commercial and office space—will adjoin Heinz Hall, the home of the Pittsburgh Symphony Orchestra, on the block between Liberty and Penn avenues and Sixth and Seventh streets. Across Seventh Street, the new 2,800-seat Benedum Center for the Performing Arts, a renovation of the 60-year-old Stanley Theatre, will complement Heinz Hall and provide a new home for the Pittsburgh Opera, Ballet Theatre, Civic Light Opera, and Dance Council, as well as for touring Broadway shows.

These two related developments are expected to initiate a full-fledged cultural and entertainment district that eventually will contain more than 7,800 seats in five or more theaters. The district will extend along Liberty Avenue from Heinz Hall and Allegheny International to the new David L. Lawrence Convention Center and convention hotel, creating an "opportunity district" for more commercial, entertainment, and residential development. Benedum Center and the other theaters will receive funding from the area's commercial office development through a new public/private institution, the Pittsburgh Trust for Cultural Resources.

Both the Benedum Center and Phase I of the Allegheny International complex are scheduled to be completed in 1987. Land and financing for each project are in place, with a total estimated project cost of more than $140 million. Neither the center nor the complex would have occurred without the other. The identification and documentation of a strong market for increased performing arts activity in Pittsburgh complemented the public and private objective of bolstering downtown development. Not only has the private real estate project provided the financial leverage for public and philanthropic funding to renovate the theater: For the next 60 years, a portion of the office building's annual income will serve as an endowment providing seed money for cultural development of the surrounding area.

The success of the project to date has hinged on two factors: the identification of a common vision that was shared by business leaders and local government; and the definition of a feasible first project that had size and program impact, momentum based on a wide range of participants, and funding credibility. The establishment of the common vision began with acceptance of two interdependent goals: to enhance the city's quality of life through increased cultural activity; and to continue Pittsburgh's economic development, by retaining existing corporations and by attracting new employment and growth.

Government and Business Resume Activist Stance to Stimulate Growth

Exterior detail, Stanley Theatre.

The Pittsburgh metropolitan area—which includes 2.23 million residents—began an economic transition in the late seventies from steel and manufacturing to finance, health, computer science, and robotics.

Thirty years before, the administration of Mayor David L. Lawrence had found that the local business community shared many of its goals for the revitalization of what was then aptly known as the "Smoky City." The private sector organized the Allegheny Conference on Community Development in 1943 to conceive and implement a series of revitalization efforts in partnership with the city government. In addition to the successful reduction of air pollution, these efforts also included the construction of Gateway Center, one of America's first urban renewal successes.

The effects of these undertakings were dramatic: The clean new image of the city revolutionized national as well as local attitudes toward Pittsburgh, and additional downtown development followed throughout the sixties, including office buildings and amenities such as a new sports stadium and the renovation of Heinz Hall for the Pittsburgh Symphony.

This era of development drew to a close in the early seventies, owing to a series of changes in the city's economic and political structure. Economic pressures resulted from setbacks in the steel and heavy industries. Reform mayor Peter Flaherty made a sharp break with the development-oriented policies that had preceded his tenure, focusing instead on community-based social issues.

Since the mid-seventies the city therefore has faced the need both to retain as much as possible of its old economic base (especially to protect its position as the third-ranked location for corporate headquarters) and to attract new employment, particularly in fast-growing white-collar service industries. Thus Pittsburgh's current administration, under Mayor Richard Caliguiri (in office from 1977 to the present), has joined again with local business institutions to promote downtown development, with the mayor advocating public investments that can hasten the growth of Pittsburgh's economy.

In the mid-seventies, several key businesses made commitments to stay in Pittsburgh and create new headquarters buildings and real estate developments, among them Oxford Plaza, PPG Place, and the Mellon Bank Center. Local governments played an important role in encouraging these projects. For instance, Allegheny County made land available and sponsored a developer competition that resulted in Oxford Plaza. Pittsburgh's Urban Redevelopment Authority helped assemble the site for the Philip Johnson–designed PPG Place multiblock complex. For the Mellon Bank Center, the city coordinated negotiation of a complex four-party agreement that combined as a single development parcel several city streets, properties condemned by the Urban Redevelopment Authority, a new Port Authority subway station, and U.S. Steel–owned land.

An innovative downtown development strategy prepared by the city planning department and its urban design consultant, Jonathan Barnett, set the public framework for these private improvements. And the Allegheny Conference established an economic development committee, a blue-ribbon advisory panel that has defined objectives (from developing advanced technology capabilities to improving the area's quality of life) for diversifying the region's economic base.

With Pittsburgh's public, private, and nonprofit sectors agreeing to resume their activist roles, the stage was set for dynamic initiatives. Each sector was prepared to invest time, energy, and money for the realization of common goals.

A Culture Boom
Outgrows Its Facilities

Pittsburgh's performing and visual arts play an important part in the region's quality of life and contribute both directly and indirectly to its economic strength. A 1982 study by the Pittsburgh/Allegheny County Cultural Alliance found that Pittsburgh's 20 leading cultural institutions contributed more direct expenditures to the area's economy than did a similar quantity and quality of groups in the combined areas of Minneapolis/St. Paul and St. Louis. (These two areas combined represent twice the population of the Pittsburgh Standard Metropolitan Statistical Area.)

The city's 200-plus cultural organizations are primarily concerned with the creative and performing arts. Although many of them are small, locally based groups, serving only one segment of the region such as the South Side or the East End, a wide variety of groups have built constituencies from throughout the city or region. But with the exception of the orchestra, opera, ballet, and Civic Light Opera—all of which currently perform in Heinz Hall—few of these organizations have a downtown base. Many are headquartered in the Oakland/Shadyside area to the east of downtown, clustered about the Carnegie Institute for Art, or based on nearby campuses of the University of Pittsburgh or Carnegie-Mellon University. The Pittsburgh Public Theater, a

popular and respected professional company, occupies space in a city-owned facility on the north side of the Allegheny River. If these groups were able to present performances or exhibitions downtown, they could gradually expand their market to include the larger region.

During the early half of the century, Pittsburgh had supported a vibrant cultural life. Seven legitimate theaters once flourished downtown, hosting traveling musicals, plays, and vaudeville, as well as fostering a thriving local community of actors, producers, musicians, and artists. These theaters were cultural catalysts of Pittsburgh's early growth as a major urban center. Some of the theaters are gone—the Nixon Theatre was the latest to close—and some, like the Fulton, the Gateway, or the Warner, have been converted to movie houses, health clubs, or retail centers.

The creation of Heinz Hall suggested a possible reversal to this trend of disappearing performance space. Refurbished in 1969–70, its sparkle and success provided a major incentive for the construction of new downtown headquarters as well as restaurants and other improvements. Formerly the Loew's Penn movie house, the theater was purchased and renovated by the Howard Heinz Endowment, a foundation chaired by H. J. Heinz II, one of Pitts-

Heinz Hall.
Credit: Ben Spiegel

The Heinz Hall garden plaza.

Exterior view of Heinz Hall's garden plaza, an open-space component of the arts district.

burgh's leading businessmen and philanthropists. A new backstage was built, allowing additional rehearsal room and dressing room space.

In 1979 the adjacent Heinz Hall Plaza was created, not only as an adjunct space to the hall but also—when not used by the Pittsburgh Symphony—as a landscaped urban oasis for the general public. A major portion of the total capital cost of these improvements, approximately $20 million, was donated by the Heinz Endowment as a gift to the city. The return on this investment has been an immeasurable positive impact on Pittsburgh's downtown cultural and economic environment. With a capacity of 2,867 seats, Heinz Hall is now the fully booked home of the Pittsburgh Symphony as well as the Pittsburgh Opera, Ballet Theatre, Civic Light Opera, Dance Council, and a host of touring shows.

It has also become, in a sense, a victim of its own success. The artistic and economic potential of the groups it houses have become constrained by the hall's space limitations and attendant scheduling conflicts. The hall has had a less than successful experience with traveling Broadway shows; its stage facilities are inadequate for the large-cast, large-set productions characteristic of first-run shows; Pittsburgh has only been able to support older, reduced-cast versions of these shows. Although the market for such attractions exists, part of the problem is the necessary short run of the shows compared to the large investment required in publicity and front-end expenses.

The adjacent unrenovated Stanley Theatre has long presented a potential resource for dealing with these problems. It had a larger house capacity (more than 3,000 seats) and the ability to schedule longer runs, but it was similarly constrained by the size of its stage facilities, which restricted its programs to rock concerts and small-cast traveling shows similar to those presented in Heinz Hall. However, a parking lot to the rear of its stagehouse and the availability of adjacent property increased its renovation potential in the late seventies. The need to control these crucial adjacent properties, as well as to tackle maintenance problems that were beginning to threaten the Stanley's splendid interior, lent a sense of urgency to defining the feasibility of its reuse.

The Heinz Endowment
Assembles a Planning Team

In 1979 the Allegheny Conference on Community Development sponsored the Penn/Liberty Urban Design Study, a major planning and design analysis of a neglected area of downtown. A mixed-use zone situated on the Allegheny riverfront adjacent to the Inner Triangle office district, the Penn/Liberty area contains both historically significant 19th- and early 20th-century loft buildings and less valuable commercial structures and surface parking lots. Some of these buildings are occupied by stable businesses, while others—especially along Liberty Avenue, one of the city's main thoroughfares—house adult bookstores, pornographic theaters, and other undesirable uses. The area also contains, at one end of Liberty Avenue, Pittsburgh's new convention center and, near the other end, Heinz Hall and several other older theaters identified for potential renovation.

Assisted by close cooperation with city planning officials, the Penn/Liberty study advocated streetscape improvements, historic preservation, riverfront amenities, and residential development. Two of its principal recommendations were to propose a performing arts district in the area around Heinz Hall and to reinforce city proposals for a new hotel and associated development adjacent to the convention center. These two projects were conceived as incentives for the revitalization of the connecting Liberty Avenue spine. The city of Pittsburgh, which owned the hotel site, sponsored a competition in 1980 to choose design and development partners. The winning project design, an office/hotel complex proposed by the Grant-Liberty Development Group, a consortium of locally and nationally based architects and developers, was awarded a $21 million federal Urban Development Action Grant in October 1983 and broke ground in December 1984.

In the summer of 1980 the Allegheny Conference asked Buckhurst Fish Hutton Katz, a New York planning and urban design firm whose partners directed the Penn/Liberty study, to spearhead implementation of the recommendations for a downtown performing arts district. As part of this effort, the firm was retained by the Howard Heinz Endowment, a major con-

tributor to the Penn/Liberty study, to help define its potential role in future development. To assist his firm in this work, Ernest Hutton, partner of Buckhurst Fish Hutton Katz, established a consultant team with William Conway of the Conway Company, Inc., real estate consultants, and Donald Elliott, partner of Webster & Sheffield, legal and implementation advisors. This initial team also included New York City architect Richard Weinstein, who, with Donald Elliott, had conceived plans for the Museum of Modern Art project, in which private residential development provided the leverage for a doubling of the museum's gallery space.

The Howard Heinz Endowment, in supporting these consultants' studies, recognized its own vested interest in protecting its investment in Heinz Hall and the adjacent plaza. From this interest grew two corollary objectives:

- to find the best way to satisfy the expanding space needs of both the organizations performing in Heinz Hall as well as other performing arts groups, and
- to define the best way to improve the area's physical appearance and to make it an attractive pedestrian-oriented environment.

Although these were philanthropic objectives, the endowment had an economic objective as well: to earn a fair return on

Renovated and expanded, the Stanley Theatre will house the Pittsburgh Opera, Ballet, and Civic Light Opera companies. At the same time, it will provide a facility suited for full-cast, first-run Broadway musicals and popular concerts.

Office Tower Revenues Initiate Cultural District Developments

Model shows the 34-story headquarters for Allegheny International, designed by Kohn Pedersen Fox.

funds invested in the project, thus making additional revenue available for philanthropic purposes. Before involving the project team, the endowment already had taken initial actions to advance its philanthropic objectives. It had begun the acquisition, as sites became available, of individual properties on the block adjacent to Heinz Hall, although without a long-term consolidation or development plan other than to protect the hall's immediate environment.

The primary role of the project team was to work with the endowment's trustees—in essence, as a project-related staff—to define and implement an approach to achieve both the cultural and physical objectives.

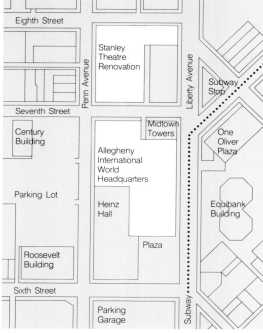

Cultural district site plan.

The Howard Heinz Endowment had commissioned studies that suggested that not only the organizations that played in Heinz Hall, but other Pittsburgh groups as well, needed more performance space—and that if they could get it they would draw larger audiences and grow artistically. It became apparent that the Penn/Liberty area could become an opportunity zone for new entertainment, commercial, and residential development: a downtown cultural district featuring multiple theater and performance spaces, related restaurants, shops and galleries, park and streetscape improvements, and renewed attention to the riverfront. The development of this new district would:

■ encourage new cultural facilities that would aid the operation of existing or emerging performing arts groups;

■ enliven downtown by encouraging a mix of uses and amenities that would help clean up Liberty Avenue and provide incentives for office and future residential development;

■ support the convention center and the planned adjacent hotel by providing an attractive nearby area for visitors to stroll, eat, shop, or enjoy a performance; and

■ create a new and highly visible regional asset to attract and retain jobs and businesses in the Pittsburgh region.

The district, corresponding to the Penn/Liberty area, would be a 12-block zone stretching from the Gateway Center renewal area to the convention center and from Liberty Avenue north to the Allegheny riverfront. It would contain not only Heinz Hall and the proposed renovated Stanley but also other theater resources, buildings suitable for renovation, and potential development sites. Only a portion of the area was under urban renewal jurisdiction, and the Heinz Endowment's consultants therefore projected that future growth of the area should take place within the private marketplace. Their proposed market-driven development, occurring within the framework of public-sector improvements and development controls, would be prompted by strategically planned "catalyst developments" in which both public and private sectors would participate.

Beyond performance space, this proposed district offered the potential to support two to three million square feet of new residential, hotel, office, parking, and open-space development by the year 2000. Its amenities would include streetscape improvements such as new trees, paving, and lighting; new market housing overlooking riverfront parks and walkways; and new eating places, clubs, theaters, and shops in renovated buildings along Liberty and Penn avenues.

To implement such a comprehensive vision would require a communitywide effort: unlike Heinz Hall, it could not be accomplished by a single foundation—or even a consortium of philanthropic sources. The city of Pittsburgh, through its department of planning and its Urban Redevelopment Authority, had jurisdictions and powers that could be enlisted. Allegheny County, because of its common objective with the city of fostering economic and cultural growth for the region, could contribute funding and technical assistance. The state of Pennsylvania had programs and agencies available. And with help from all, the potential for federal participation was a further possible resource.

But to enlist the participation of these groups, a concrete project that could generate its own momentum and support was required. This need, in turn, required not only philanthropic and public participants, but also the involvement of private, for-profit investors.

The outlines of the initial catalyst project emerged from a series of feasibility studies prepared by the consultant team. Researched over a period of 18 months from October 1981 to April 1983, the studies involved physical analysis of the Heinz block's development potential, economic analysis of the risks and returns associated with its development, and programmatic analysis of the adjacent cultural district idea.

The consultants examined a variety of scenarios for the Heinz Hall block, including a series of physical options, market analyses, program alternatives, and financing schemes. The Howard Heinz Endowment board, however, was a philanthropic

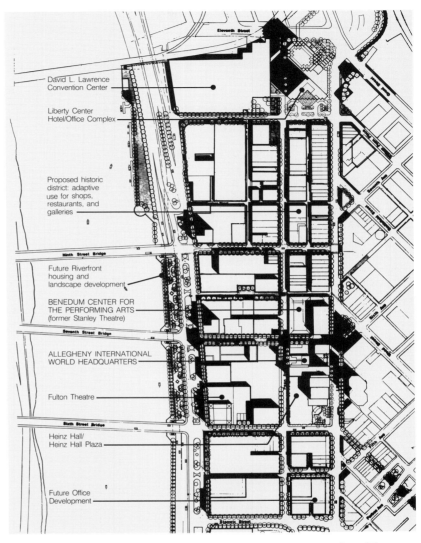

body that met only two to four times a year. Although its individual members represented years of business experience, some in real estate, the endowment as an institution was not experienced in real estate development nor was it prepared to make necessary and rapid development decisions. The consultants' analysis of the endowment's role therefore evolved into an educational process in which the team worked with the board to help it reach consensus on the level of its financial commitment and on courses of action in which the probable returns would justify the potential risks.

Illustrative plan of the proposed cultural district, showing potential development of theater, commercial, office, hotel, and landscape improvements.

Once this consensus was reached, the endowment established an executive committee, chaired by trustee William Rea, which oversaw two separate but related streams of consultant work: one, the commercial real estate development, supervised by Rea and the endowment's finance director Dixon Brown; and the other, the cultural district development, supervised by businessman William Boyd and assisted by the endowment's executive director Alfred W. (Burr) Wishart, Jr. The decision-making problems eased as these committees held regular meetings with the consultant team.

As a result of this intensive analysis, the endowment decided in January 1983 to complete acquisition of all remaining available properties on the block—approximately 30,000 square feet of older, four-story loft buildings. These final transactions doubled the endowment's existing land-holding and more than tripled its financial outlay. The resulting site, through a combination of potential new development or possible renovation of existing structures, would allow, with transfer of excess development rights from adjacent sites, a total of more than one million square feet of commercial space.

This decision to complete the site assembly, which culminated more than two years of intermittent negotiations for individual properties as they came available, committed the Heinz Endowment to a firm and positive course of action. This final decision to proceed was all the more difficult because of the time it took to make it. As the endowment's executive director, Burr Wishart, describes the process:

It took us over two years to acquire the property from the time of our first purchase. This was complicated by a series of leaks and rumors that resulted in inflated prices and stubborn land-owners. In fact, at a certain stage, we foresaw the distinct possibility that a holdout might make the project developmentally infeasible. In mid-1981, for instance, a developer initiated discussions for hotel development on the property. An unauthorized press article prompted by one of the participants immediately doubled the price of certain key parcels on the site.

The Heinz Hall block development scenario initially was based on the approach used in New York City's Museum of Modern Art condominium tower development. Earnings from the commercial project, to be used for publicly oriented cultural purposes, would take two forms: a negotiated participation in the private real estate development, and the allocation to the project sponsor of real estate taxes from the development (which otherwise would flow directly to the public sector). In the New York project, these in-lieu-of-tax payments were used for specific public purposes—the capital construction and continuing operation of expanded gallery spaces for the museum. In Pittsburgh, they would be used for cultural district developments.

The idea was elaborated by using representatives of the Allegheny Conference, who were familiar with both public- and private-sector requirements and possible responses, as a surrogate sounding board for the eventual public and private partners. The initial proposal embodied several themes that, with further refinement, would become key selling points for the project:
■ the definition of an economically feasible private commercial development of more than one million square feet on the Heinz Hall block;
■ the identification of a downtown cultural district as a publicly supportable cultural and commercial development objective; and
■ a way to link the two goals together so that a short-term project could initiate the long-term development process.

At this stage, the project consultants had not identified the Stanley Theatre as the priority first-stage cultural development, tied directly to the commercial project. They simply proposed using the private real estate development's return, over the next 10 to 20 years, to renovate theaters and further develop the cultural district. Nor did the project yet include the specific local or federal financing mechanisms—the city-county bonds or the federal Urban Development Action Grant—that became a major part of the final package. And the commercial complex on the Heinz Hall block was smaller in scope than what finally was proposed once air rights from the

Stanley Theatre were added. These necessary but unanticipated refinements grew out of collaborative planning once the public and private participants were involved.

The Heinz Endowment was aware that it had taken a great risk. Finance Director Dixon Brown comments:

The Howard Heinz Endowment had invested over $12 million in real estate without a developer in hand. There was only the faith that the economic and political rationale for the development was so strong that we could recruit the partners we needed. The trustees were willing to take this risk only for certain reasons: One was their acceptance of the philanthropic goals set for the project, that is, the establishment of the cultural district and the resulting benefits for the Pittsburgh region. The other was their agreement that these goals justified such an innovative and entrepreneurial approach for a foundation.

Arts market studies by Economics Research Associates/Brannigan-Lorelli Associates in 1983 confirmed that the endowment's goals were realistic. A demand by local audiences existed for a wide variety of events, from grand opera to experimental drama. A comparison of Pittsburgh with other metropolitan areas having close demographic similarities (Baltimore, St. Louis, and Cleveland) revealed that on a per-capita basis Pittsburgh had far fewer performances or active companies. One reason was that Pittsburgh had far fewer performing arts facilities, not only for plays but also for music, dance, and traveling Broadway shows. The other cities also had a more complete range of facilities—not only large spaces but also a variety of theaters in the 1,500-, 500-, and 250-seat range. The stage capacities of their large theaters were superior.

A detailed analysis of the Pittsburgh market examined both supply and demand factors. A comprehensive survey of audience preferences evaluated the potential demand for a variety of future types of performances in Pittsburgh. This market survey reached several conclusions:

■ The number of tickets sold to cultural performances in Pittsburgh could increase by almost 50 percent (up to 450,000 new tickets per year) if the proper facilities and events were available.

■ These ticket sales would support up to 5,000 new or renovated theater seats.

■ This market would support a wide variety of events, ranging from popular concerts and touring Broadway shows to expanded seasons for local or touring opera and dance.

■ The most pressing demand for audience development was the availability of Broadway musicals—one of the basic foundations for developing an expanded performing arts market.

The result of this demand survey, together with the comparison of Pittsburgh with theater space distribution in other cities, suggested a long-term scenario for theater facilities:

■ The first priority should be the renovation of the Stanley. In conjunction with Heinz Hall, this new theater would give Pittsburgh two major performance spaces (such as presently supported by Cleveland, St. Louis, and Baltimore, and currently being considered for Philadelphia). The theater could house the opera, ballet, Civic Light Opera, major dance events, and traveling musicals. Heinz Hall would then become a purely orchestral space.

■ An approximately 1,500-seat theater (the future renovation of the Fulton Theater) was needed for smaller or dramatic performances.

■ One to two 200-seat spaces were needed for experimental theater groups.

■ Finally, as a later project, a 500-seat resource theater should be provided for use by local or regional theater groups not based downtown.

What Pittsburgh needed was, therefore, a phased approach to performing arts development that focused concurrently on supply and demand, providing financial and development support for new theater space at the same time as incentive for audience development. As other cities such as Baltimore have found, once a "critical mass" of space, performers, and audience is created, internal growth dynamics in the market will supply the rest of the momentum. Local groups and performers then have an environment in which to grow, and national attractions have access to the local audience.

The Heinz Endowment
Recruits Partners

Establishing the working relationships and finalizing the negotiations for the initial Stanley Theatre/Allegheny International project was accomplished in less than 12 months, a remarkably short time for a project of this magnitude. The time pressure itself, imposed both by external events as well as internal schedule requirements, proved a significant factor in the success of the negotiations. The events and requirements included tenant occupancy schedules, public funding deadlines, and the limited "window of availability" of certain key optioned properties.

The collaboration began once the Howard Heinz Endowment brought in the local public sector and a major tenant and developer. The resulting partnership took the process through transactions that led to local, state, and federal approvals of both the project's physical plans and its required financial package, as well as additional private contributions and participation.

In early April 1983, within a week of final site control of the Heinz Hall block, H. J. Heinz II, chairman of the endowment,

The new 2,800-seat Benedum Center for the Performing Arts will be a careful restoration of the existing Stanley Theatre, preserving ornate detail while expanding backstage support space.

met with Mayor Richard Caliguiri and laid out the project goals and strategy. The mayor's response was immediate and enthusiastic: the scheme fit the city's short- and long-term development goals; it would improve the city's quality of life, enhance its tax base, and strengthen its position as a corporate and commercial center.

However, a number of problems emerged. First was the city's concern that the in-lieu-of-tax approach, by which the cultural district would retain the office building's tax payments (and which would require state as well as local legislative approval), would conflict with existing city revenue policy. The creation of an independent public/private authority to receive and spend these monies, another feature of the Museum of Modern Art model, raised similar policy objections: the city preferred to use existing institutions, and preferably those with a regional base. For its part, the endowment was concerned that, without the proposed authority's potential power of eminent domain, the required site for the Stanley Theatre expansion and renovation might be lost. A potential buyer for one of the key parcels already had begun negotiations with the building's private owner.

After a series of discussions over the next month, the city presented a proposal. David Matter, the mayor's executive secretary, and John Robin, chairman of the city's Urban Redevelopment Authority, met with Ernest Hutton. If the Stanley Theatre site could be privately controlled and its renovation made a condition of the Heinz Hall block commercial development, then the city would support an application to the federal government for an Urban Development Action Grant (UDAG) for the joint commercial/theater development project. Moreover, the city would enlist the assistance of the county to support a joint $7.5 million bond issue by the City/County Auditorium Authority as further support of the theater project. On its part, the endowment pledged to raise an equivalent amount in foundation or individual philanthropic contributions. A following meeting with the mayor and Thomas Foerster, chairman of the Allegheny County Board of Commissioners, confirmed the county's potential interest in participating in the project.

This new approach, relying on the financial and administrative resources of existing agencies and institutions, proved a creative and enabling response by the public sector to the endowment's original proposal. Over the next four weeks, further meetings resulted in an additional series of agreements: on the commitment of the endowment to establish control of the Stanley Theatre site through option or purchase; on the form of a vehicle to implement the project—the new Pittsburgh Trust for Cultural Resources, a private nonprofit institution that would receive and invest the UDAG repayment funds; and on the definition of the allowable long-term use of these funds for continuing development of a downtown cultural district.

This series of agreements was finalized as a written document, a preliminary statement of intent that spelled out the roles and responsibilities of each party. At this stage, however, as far as the city was concerned, the project remained largely theoretical: there was no major tenant, no development partner, no immediate momentum. The existence and identity of these crucial participants were kept closely guarded secrets until the completion of a parallel series of negotiations that were occurring simultaneously between endowment representatives and Allegheny International.

Recruiting Allegheny International

Immediately after its initial successful contact with the city, the Howard Heinz Endowment project team met with Robert Buckley, chairman and chief executive officer of Allegheny International, a Pittsburgh-based company producing consumer items and high-technology industrial specialties. Allegheny International, whose current lease (at Two Oliver Plaza opposite the Heinz Hall block) would expire in 1986, had launched a nationwide search for a new world headquarters site.

The response of Buckley (who was also chairman of the board of the Pittsburgh Symphony Orchestra) to the Heinz Endowment's proposal for a linkage between commercial and cultural development was as positive and unhesitating as that of Mayor Caliguiri. If the deal made economic sense and Allegheny International could occupy office space on schedule, it would act as not only the lead tenant but as a development participant for the office complex—with the understanding that there would be simultaneous renovation of the Stanley Theatre and further rehabilitation of the surrounding neighborhood.

Over the next few months, endowment consultants met with Allegheny International representatives to work out financial arrangements. An agreement to lease, signed in August 1983, established the initial framework for the development, to be elaborated later in the final lease documents and the federal UDAG agreement.

The basic structure was simple: The Howard Heinz Endowment, as owner of the proposed office site, would lease the office property to Allegheny International or its developer for a fixed annual payment. Further, the developer would pay to the Trust for Cultural Resources an additional fixed payment of a minimum $250,000 per year, plus 5 percent of the project's annual net cash flow over an agreed-upon base amount. Allegheny International and its development partners also would support the UDAG grant application, permitting the office development to participate in the theater renovation project. (A second $8.5 million UDAG would be proposed for the theater renovation itself.)

Buckhurst Fish Hutton Katz established basic design criteria for the site development on behalf of the endowment. These standards, describing landowner-required urban design relationships both for the building complex itself and for adjacent buildings, formed part of the site package delivered to Allegheny International. During negotiations with Allegheny International, it was established that Allegheny International would team up with an experienced partner to develop the project, and that it would choose its partner and architect from a preference list compiled by the endowment. Based on these criteria and agreements, Allegheny International selected a managing developer, Urban Investment and Development Company of Chicago, and a project architect, Kohn Pedersen Fox from New York.

Pittsburgh Cultural District
Project Data

Physical Configuration **Component—Income Generating**	Phase I	Profile at Build-out
Allegheny International (total)	650,000 sq. ft.	1,300,000 sq. ft.
Office (net)	530,000 sq. ft.	1,080,000 sq. ft.
Retail/restaurant (floors 1 & 2)	30,000 sq. ft.	60,000 sq. ft.
Future development in district Office/retail/residential/hotel/parking		2,000,000 sq. ft.

Component—Arts/Culture/ Open Space		
Heinz Hall	2,847 seats	2,847 seats
Heinz Hall Plaza	12,000 sq. ft.	12,000 sq. ft.
Benedum Center for the Performing Arts	2,800 seats	2,800 seats
Allegheny International Plaza	10,000 sq. ft.	10,000 sq. ft.
Future development Fulton Theater		1,600 seats
Other Theaters (1–3)		600–1,000 seats
Open Space		12,000 sq. ft.

Other		
Parking	90 spaces	690 spaces
Location	Downtown Pittsburgh	
Floor/Area Ratio	7.5 (with additional transfer of development rights)	
Development Period	Phase I—1984–86 Phase II—1987–89	
Estimated Total Development Costs	Phase I—$130 million Phase II—$100 million Long term—$300 million	
Development Participants	Allegheny International Realty Development Company Lincoln Property Company Howard Heinz Endowment	
Project Architects	Kohn Pedersen Fox Associates—Allegheny International building MacLachlan Cornelius & Filoni—Benedum Center	

Source: Buckhurst Fish Hutton & Katz

The Pieces Come Together

By August 1983 the participants were all assembled. The city and county were informed that the previously theoretical cultural district project had become real: it not only had a real tenant, developer, and architect, but development objectives and project deadlines as well. It was at this point that the public sector's commitment was put to the test—and passed with flying colors. Without leadership, staff assistance, and funding from the city and county, the project could not have proceeded further. The financial risks to the endowment and to Allegheny International were substantial.

But the political risks to city and county officials in making such a large-scale commitment were of equal magnitude. The city already was involved in a UDAG application for the convention center hotel site. This grant had been sought for almost two years and was still delayed, pending further financial agreements. The prospect of applying for a second, possibly competitive, grant was daunting. The offer of $7.5 million in local bonds ($3.75 million each from the city and the county) also constituted a major commitment. In the case of the county, this was an especially delicate situation since its bonding capacity was being reviewed by its underwriters at the time. Each of those worries eventually was resolved.

Until this point, the Allegheny Conference had been serving as a facilitator and conduit through which much public and private communication took place. Now, however, the city established a public/private task force to act as the project's coordination committee. Meeting on a weekly basis under the leadership of the mayor's executive secretary, David Matter, this group included consultants and representatives of the Heinz Endowment and the Allegheny Conference, Allegheny International and its legal advisors, the project's managing developer and architects, and key members of the city administration.

A major issue for the group was the structure of the UDAG grant application. A series of detailed technical agreements between the developer, landowner, city, and federal government helped define the basic UDAG framework. The final grant, for a total of $17 million ($20.1 million had been applied for), was based on an award of $8.5 million to the city for the office complex (primarily to purchase air rights from above the adjacent theater sites) and $8.5 million for the theater renovation. Each grant (actually a low-interest soft loan) will be repaid, through the city as a conduit, to the Trust for Cultural Resources for use in further cultural district development. The theater's repayment will take the form of free or reduced-price tickets to theater events; the office building's repayment will consist of the negotiated fixed payment and percentage participation to be paid an-

Pittsburgh Cultural District
Development Costs Summary

	Total	Public	Private
Allegheny International Office Complex	$200 million	$8.5 million	$191.5 million
Benedum Center for the Performing Arts	37 million	16 million	21 million
Heinz Hall	14 million		14 million
Heinz Hall Garden Plaza	2 million		2 million
Future Theater Development	20 million (est.)		

nually to the Trust for Cultural Resources.

Since the Stanley Theatre renovation provided the major justification for the UDAG grant and public participation, control not only of the theater but of three adjacent properties became mandatory. Options therefore were obtained through the Allegheny Conference (acting as a surrogate for the yet-to-be-incorporated Trust for Cultural Resources), subject to purchase funding once Auditorium Authority bonds and private contributions were in place.

To have a physically and economically feasible site for the office development, while maintaining service access to Heinz Hall, the project architects and developers determined that all on-site buildings should be removed. A major purpose of the office development was to provide the means to rehabilitate the Stanley Theatre to detailed historic preservation standards; yet that required that the old buildings on the office development site be demolished. Particularly problematic was the necessity to remove the Moose Hall, an architecturally significant building with an ornate classic revival facade. A series of negotiations with local, state, and federal historic review boards resulted in a memorandum of agreement that stipulated a variety of mitigating measures to be taken, including preservation of the hall's artifacts as well as assistance in creating an adjacent historic district along Liberty Avenue.

Planning and design approvals for the joint office/theater met the project's tight timetable due to complete cooperation among all partners. Prior to the project's inception, the city already had initiated a major zoning revision for the project area, including several innovative procedures that affected the form of the cultural district plans. These measures included new trans-

fer of development rights criteria (allowing excess air rights from Heinz Hall and the Stanley to be sold to the adjacent office complex, thus raising funds for the theater renovation), and new urban design criteria (including the creation of new height limits, forming an orderly view-oriented transition from tall Inner Triangle office buildings to low-rise riverfront structures.) Based on these new zoning criteria, which significantly affected the size and design of the complex, the city and the developers were able to achieve approval of the office/theater complex as the first project to be submitted under the new regulations.

The project was announced publicly on November 18, 1983. By the end of the month, meetings with Governor Richard Thornburgh and his economic development committee had established state support for the project, and the first local public hearing had been held on the UDAG application. During the month of December an additional public hearing was held before the city council, resulting in a unanimous 9–0 vote in favor of the city's sponsorship of the UDAG and establishing support for the $7.5 million Auditorium Authority bond issue. This progress was matched within three days by a 3–0 vote by the Allegheny County commissioners pledging their share. The final UDAG application was submitted on January 31, 1984. Final planning commission and city council approvals, including agreement on historic preservation measures and site planning issues, come through in February and March, and on March 31, 1984, the announcement was made that the U.S. Department of Housing and Urban Development had awarded the project a $17 million UDAG grant. The project was now reality.

Project Data: Benedum Center for the Performing Arts (Stanley Theatre)

Location	Seventh Street & Penn Avenue, Pittsburgh
Projected Opening	Early 1987
Originally Built	1928, Hoffman Henon Company, architect
Architects	MacLachlan, Cornelius & Filoni—Renovation Architects
Consultants	Buckhurst Fish Hutton Katz—Project Planning Brannigan-Lorelli Associates, Inc.—Theater Consultants Economics Research Associates—Arts Market Consultants Bolt, Beranek & Newman—Acoustical Consultants
Contractor	Not yet selected
Building Cost	$37 million
	Land purchase $12 million
	Renovation 21 million
	Fees/financing/etc. 4 million
Gross Area	107,000 sq. ft.

Breakdown of
Interior Area

Grid Height	80 ft. with 104 rigging line sets
Proscenium Height	36 ft.
Proscenium Width	56 ft.
Stage Depth from Apron	79 ft.
Stage Width	144 ft.
Orchestra Length (apron to back wall)	100 ft.
Max. Orchestra Height	79 ft.
Max. Orchestra Width	144 ft.
Dressing Rooms	21 with accommodations for 225 people
Pit	Space for 80 musicians
Seating	2,800
Lobby Dimensions	Lower—25 ft. × 80 ft.; Main—45 ft. × 88 ft.; Upper—18 ft. × 88 ft.
Rehearsal Halls (size)	2—58 ft. × 56 ft. 1—27 ft. × 18 ft.

Exterior Features	The Benedum Center for the Performing Arts is the renovated Stanley Theatre. Built in 1928 in a classic revival style, the theater will be expanded with a major new 75-foot-deep backstage and a six-story support building permitting rehearsal spaces and dressing rooms. The facade has been designed to blend with the adjacent 19th-century loft buildings as well as the carefully renovated theater exterior.
Interior Features	Renovation will enlarge and improve stage, add dressing rooms and rehearsal facilities, upgrade lighting, heating, air conditioning, and appearance, including new back and side stage areas. Classic revival decor similar to other great movie houses of the 1920s. Richly decorated and gilded interior, domed ceiling, ornate proscenium arch.

Private Philanthropic Support

After additional architectural and financial studies, the budget for the Stanley Theatre renovation was set at $37 million: more than $20 million for construction, $12 million for theater and adjacent land and building acquisitions, and the remainder for miscellaneous fees and financing charges. The venture capital for the overall project financing (in addition to the initial contribution of the land on the Heinz Hall block) was a guarantee by the Howard Heinz Endowment that almost $12 million in additional contributions would be raised. This substantial community-based commitment had leveraged, by the spring of 1984, more than $24 million in public-sector contributions (the $17 million UDAG grant and the $7.5 million in local city/county Auditorium Authority bonds), as well as more than $130 million in private investment for the adjacent office complex.

Twelve million dollars is, of course, too much for any single foundation to donate alone. The intent of the Heinz Endowment was to serve as a catalyst for the project, attracting support from other sources. The effort to establish this community base began in the summer of 1983. Presentations for philanthropic support were made to a variety of Pittsburgh foundations, and three responded with funds sufficient to cover the initial Stanley Theatre option or acquisition costs: $1 million each from the Claude Worthington Benedum Foundation and the Vira I. Heinz Fund of the Pittsburgh Foundation and a $500,000 grant from the Pittsburgh Foundation itself. In June 1984 the trustees of the Benedum Foundation voted an additional grant to the Stanley Theatre project—this time for a further $4 million. As a result of this generous gift, the theater has been renamed the Benedum Center for the Performing Arts.

Although requests and applications for the remaining theater development funds were still outstanding as of early 1985, indications of support had been received for an additional $2 million to $3 million. It is expected that other contributions, including grants from national funding sources and local in-kind services and equipment, will eliminate any remaining gaps in the theater's funding. Preliminary expressions of interest also have been received for future projects in the district, such as the renovation of the 1,500-seat Fulton Theater.

Allegheny International Towers and Benedum Center Catalyze District

The initial project that has emerged from this collaborative effort is a mixed-use development with two interdependent components. The commercial real estate development adjacent to Heinz Hall will provide not only the economic stimulus for the cultural development, but also a major work of architecture for downtown Pittsburgh. The $37 million renovation of the Stanley Theatre will provide a major expansion of the city's performing arts facilities. Each of the projects, now in final design, should be complete in late 1986.

The 34-story Allegheny International world headquarters building has been designed as a twin-tower, two-phase, office/retail complex. Architects Kohn Pedersen Fox, working from guidelines prepared by both the city planning department and Buckhurst Fish Hutton Katz, have created a distinguished design. Each tower will contain 650,000 gross square feet of floor space, for a total of 1.3 million square feet. Current approved plans call for office development in each tower, linked by dramatic ground-level lobby and restaurant/retail space. In a response both to city open-space requirements and to site context, the two towers will face on a new park on Liberty Avenue at the end of the Sixth Avenue view corridor looking toward the site. This park will balance the Heinz Hall Plaza at the opposite side of the site.

When the Stanley Theatre's renovation is complete, it will retain a 2,800-seat capacity but will offer enlarged and improved stage space, dressing rooms, and rehearsal facilities, as well as upgraded lighting, heating, and air conditioning. It will contain a generous new back and side stage area—more than tripling the current stagehouse volume—as well as a new six-story support building on Liberty Avenue. This building will house two stage-sized rehearsal halls, one of which will double as an occasional experimental theater with public access from Liberty Avenue.

The result will be a theater with stage and support facilities equal to most in the nation. It will feature state-of-the-art design for lighting and sound systems and live television presentation, making possible production of up to three different operas

Project Data: Heinz Hall for the Performing Arts

Location	600 Penn Avenue, Pittsburgh
Originally Built	1927, converted to symphony hall in 1968–71
Architects	MacLachlan, Cornelius & Filoni, Renovation Architects (1968–71)
Consultants	Dr. Heinrich Keilholz, Salzburg, Austria, Acoustical Consultant (1968–71)
Contractor	Mellon-Stuart Company
Building Cost	1968–71 renovation: $10 million
Gross Area	137,000 sq. ft.

Breakdown of Interior Area

Grid Height	72 ft. with 46 counterweight sets & 11 motorized sets
Proscenium Height	34 ft.
Proscenium Width	52 ft.
Stage Depth from Apron	32 ft., plus rear stage storage area
Stage Width	82 ft., 6 in.
Orchestra Length (apron to back wall)	100 ft.
Max. Orchestra Height	90 ft.
Max. Orchestra Width	90 ft.
Dressing Rooms	14 with accommodations for 85 people
Pit	Space for 60–70 musicians
Seating	2,847
Lobby Dimensions	150 ft. x 50 ft.
Rehearsal Rooms	3

Exterior Features	The renovation of the old Loew's Penn movie palace offers a handsome classic revival facade, featuring intricate terra cotta detail and a large semicircular window signaling major public lobby space. Adjacent to the theater is Heinz Hall Plaza, a tree-shaded oasis featuring a waterfall, sculpture, and movable seating. The plaza is open to the public when not reserved for the use of the symphony.
Interior Features	Home to Pittsburgh Symphony Orchestra. Breche opal and Lavanto marbles, plush red velvet, shimmering crystal, and brilliant gold leaf dominate the interior of the hall. 264 new chandeliers were imported from Vienna. Two large gallery/lounge areas on the lower level. Wing includes orchestra rehearsal room and two-story choral and dancing rehearsal rooms.

or other full-stage performances in any given week.

Early schematic architectural, functional, and cost studies verified the feasibility of the theater's renovation as approximately half the cost of new theater construction. Detailed financial projections indicate that with professional management and quality events, the Benedum Center will not require outside support to maintain feasible rent levels for potential users. Its availability also will free Heinz Hall for use primarily as a concert facility.

The theater will be managed by the Trust for Cultural Resources, incorporated as a private nonprofit corporation in 1984. Its 12-member governing board includes the mayor, city council president, chairman of the county board of commissioners, and nine citizens named by the Pittsburgh Foundation and the Allegheny Conference on Community Development. Using public and private contributions and revenues from the office building, the trust will:

■ initiate and coordinate a cultural district development process that will stimulate and implement projects in conjunction with the city, arts groups, landowners, and potential developers;

■ provide cultural district services and promotional activities, including coordination with constituent arts groups and regional educational institutions;

■ facilitate broad public access to the district and its resources (including support of reduced-price ticket sales for young people and the elderly, as well as participation in creating an innovative performing arts curriculum for the Pittsburgh public schools); and

■ develop and manage the Benedum Center and plan and implement future theater projects in the district.

An economic impact analysis of the Allegheny International complex and Benedum Center anticipated that downtown food, parking, and retail expenditures will increase by more than $5.8 million per year. Ticket sales are expected to total almost $7.5 million, providing an additional $750,000 in city amusement taxes (much of which will come from audience members from outside the city). Revenues in excess of $2.5 million per year in new real estate, parking, and business privilege taxes for the city, county, and school district are expected when the project is complete.

Future cultural development beyond the Benedum Center is projected to add another 2,000 theater seats to the district and result in more than 300,000 additional tickets sold. This additional theater renovation or construction should result in yet another $425,000 in annual amusement tax revenues to the city.

The district's variety of potential sites, surface parking lots, and areas with dilapidated buildings offers rich opportunities for further renovation or development of office, retail, hotel, residential, and parking facilities. The accelerated rate of development of these sites, as well as preservation and renewal projects made possible by the Trust for Cultural Resources, should provide millions of dollars in additional investment, construction payroll, secondary spending, food and retail expenditures, and local tax revenues.

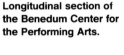

Longitudinal section of the Benedum Center for the Performing Arts.

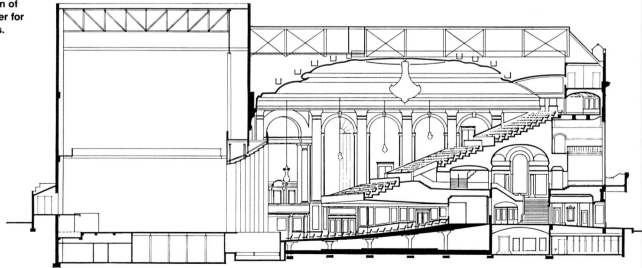

Phase One Gets Underway

Both the first building of the Allegheny International complex and the Benedum Center renovation were expected to break ground in early 1985 for occupancy in early 1987. The Allegheny International project underwent a management shift in summer 1984, in which Allegheny International substituted a new managing developer, Lincoln Property Company of Dallas, an experienced and aggressive land development firm that specializes in mixed-use projects. Kohn Pedersen Fox continue as architects. The building site has been cleared, with all on-site buildings demolished, utilities relocated, and land brought to grade.

A special theater development subcommittee of the Trust for Cultural Resources—consisting of business advisors, funding participants, and performing group constituents—acts as the ultimate approval body for the Benedum Center renovation. Because the Stanley Theatre is a National Register–eligible historic structure, the renovation is proceeding according to exacting rehabilitation standards. Local, state, and federal review agencies are involved in maintaining the spirit and decor of the original building while the architects solve a variety of acoustical and theatrical problems inherent in adapting a movie house to a legitimate theater.

At the other end of Liberty Avenue, Liberty Center, an office/hotel complex adjacent to the David L. Lawrence Convention Center, began construction in late 1984. The city also has announced plans to formalize a historic district in the area along Liberty Avenue between the convention center and the theater area, providing tax incentives and other programs to help spur sensitive renovation of this important area.

The full dimensions of the cultural district development will emerge as the first projects are completed and provide evidence of the market for expansion. The timing for launching Phase II of the Allegheny International complex will be determined by market supply and demand. Its second tower will be vital to the future of the cultural district, as much of the trust's income is expected to come from its participation in both phases of the Allegheny International project.

As the Benedum Center nears completion, the option on the Fulton Theater will come due. In 1984, acting on behalf of the trust, the Howard Heinz Endowment negotiated a three-year option on the Fulton, which was being used as a cinema. Plans call for the renovation of the Fulton as the third theater in the cultural district, providing space for touring plays, dance, and other events requiring more intimacy than

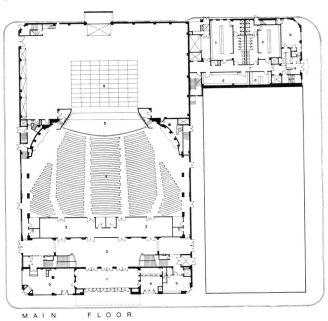

MAIN   FLOOR

Floor plan for the Benedum Center for the Performing Arts.

LEGEND
1 Vestibule
  a Ticket Office
  b Retail Space
2 Lobby
3 Lounge
4 Orchestra Level Seating
5 Orchestra Pit
6 Stage
7 Support Facility
  a Entry
  b Green Room
  c Group Dressing Room
  d Make-Up, Wigs, Wardrobe

Allegheny International complex as seen from Liberty Avenue. Heinz Hall Plaza is in the foreground, with Heinz Hall to the left.

Heinz Hall or the Benedum Center can offer. Its renovation, as well as any construction of further theater spaces, will depend on the future needs of Pittsburgh's performing arts groups and audiences, as well as on continued public and private fundraising support for the trust.

The trust has pledged to support studies and renovation in the adjacent Liberty Avenue historic district. The success of this revitalization effort will, over time, be a function of the market demand for shops, restaurants, and galleries created by the Allegheny International/Benedum project and the convention center's office and hotel. As other hotel, office, residential, parking, and open-space needs emerge, the trust will work with local landowners, public officials, private investors, and philanthropic resources to promote their development on vacant or underused sites.

Initiative, Risk, and Personality

At this stage of having completed the design and development process, Pittsburgh's collaborators cite several lessons they have learned:

■ *Complexity can be a positive factor.* Enlisting a necessarily wide variety of participants requires that a project meet multiple goals. The interrelationship of these goals —that a theater cannot occur without an office building, and vice versa; that private funding cannot occur without matching public contributions—leads to a leveraging strategy based on contingent commitments: pledges dependent on corresponding actions by each participant.

■ *One major participant must take the lead in initiating and implementing the process.* The orchestration of contingent commitments constitutes a major undertaking. Although no one person can fully coordinate such a large project, one organization must devote considerable organizational and financial resources to ensuring that the project succeeds. In Pittsburgh, because of the congruence between its own goals and those of the project, the Howard Heinz Endowment took on this key role. The endowment now has turned much of the coordinating responsibility over to the Trust for Cultural Resources.

■ *The sizable risks to all participants must be counterbalanced by attractive and achievable returns.* The relationship of cultural development to economic development not only has to be stated, it has to be proven—with logic, statistics, and commitments. For the public sector to risk political and economic capital, the public value must be communicated in an uncomplicated, noncontroversial way to voters and the press. For private tenants or developers to risk time and money, the ability to deliver a marketable product must be readily apparent to their stockholders and financial backers.

■ *The role of personalities should not be underestimated.* Organizations are managed by people, and leaders with strong personalities can have a positive impact on the planning and implementation process, from setting goals and project direction to making tough decisions when faced with the necessity for action.

Happily, in the case of the Allegheny International/Benedum Center project, the right mix of objectives and participants could readily be assembled. What it took to make the concept a reality was a catalyst, in the form of a dedicated and persistent foundation, that stimulated the equally important cooperation of a forward-looking local government and an enlightened corporate tenant and partner. As the Allegheny Conference's executive director, Bob Pease, concludes:

Most important, the project was blessed with a multitude of strong leaders. These included H. J. Heinz II, Mayor Richard Caliguiri, the mayor's executive secretary, David Matter, Allegheny County Chairman Thomas Foerster, Allegheny International Chairman Robert Buckley, and Trust Chairman Robert Dickey III. Their continuing participation and key leadership when needed really epitomize Pittsburgh's great success—public/private cooperation, which for many years has provided the momentum for growth of the region's economy and its quality of life.

The success of Charles Center, Baltimore's renowned downtown revitalization project, led to an ambitious series of projects surrounding the Inner Harbor, a U-shaped basin at the head of the port of Baltimore where the city originated. The Inner Harbor renewal constitutes a success on a much larger scale, both in acreage and public use. It encompasses 240 acres and blends major cultural and recreation attractions with commercial and residential construction.

Launched in 1964, the Inner Harbor development program is being completed in seven phases and managed on behalf of the city by the same private nonprofit corporation—Charles Center–Inner Harbor Management, Inc.—that handled the development of Charles Center. Public expenditures totaling $200 million have been made over the years to acquire and clear the land and attract massive private investment. These funds include federal grants amounting to $150 million and city bond issues totaling $50 million, approved by Baltimore citizens between 1964 and 1984. Public improvements to the harbor's shore and piers have transformed the water's edge from an abandoned area of decaying warehouses to playing fields, parks, walkways, and a marina. McKeldin Square forms a gateway to the Inner Harbor.

Nine office buildings have been constructed and five more are under construction. A Hyatt Hotel will be joined by four other luxury hotels and five moderate-rate hotels, all stimulated by the nearby Baltimore Convention Center, completed in 1979. Residential development includes luxury condominiums, townhouses, subsidized housing for the elderly, and the city's Otterbein Homesteading Area, in which 100 houses on a three-block parcel three blocks west of the harbor were sold for $1 to buyers who would move in and bring them up to standard.

The hallmark of the area, however, lies not in its commercial and residential development, but rather in the public and private cultural and entertainment attractions established around the waterfront. These constitute an extraordinarily powerful magnet, bringing Baltimoreans and visitors in record numbers to the once-decrepit Inner Harbor. Most of these facilities have been encouraged, planned, and built under the 12-year leadership of Baltimore's energetic mayor, William Donald Schaefer. The center of these facilities is Harborplace, a Rouse Company development that presents shopping and eating as a form of entertainment in two glass pavilions. This marketplace overlooks the frigate *Constellation*, the U.S. Navy's oldest fighting warship. The Maryland Academy of Science's museum and the National Aquarium at Baltimore also have located on the waterfront. A summer concert pavilion occupies a pier over the water, and an old power plant adjacent to the water is being recycled by Six Flags Company as an indoor historic theme park.

The result of all this investment and imagination is that Baltimore gradually has experienced a civic renaissance—both physical and psychological—and has been discovered by visitors from around the world as a model of revitalization and the value of urban amenities. The Inner Harbor has become a cultural and recreational destination.

Charles Center Creates a Model for Renewal

Baltimore Inner Harbor area in 1956. The area that would become Charles Center is at the upper right.
Credit: M. E. Warren

The Inner Harbor in the early eighties. The Pier 6 Pavilion (white tentlike structure) can be seen in the lower right. The power plant is two piers away. On the pier next to the power plant is the National Aquarium in Baltimore. At the far end of the basin on the right is the U.S. frigate *Constellation*, flanked by the two pavilions of Harborplace. At the left corner of the Inner Harbor basin stands the Maryland Science Center.
Credit: M. E. Warren

Baltimore today is a city with a population of 787,000 and a reputation for a remarkable renaissance of commerce and civic spirit, initiated three decades ago. In the fifties, Baltimore was a grimy obstacle to drive around or through as quickly as traffic jams would allow. It was far from a destination point. Merchants and business and civic leaders watched as families, industry, and downtown retailers moved out of the city and into the suburbs of Baltimore County.

In 1954 business leaders decided something should be done about the city's future. J. Jefferson Miller, executive vice president of a large department store chain, coalesced downtown merchants, bankers, and civic groups into the Committee for Downtown, which began to examine how other American cities in similar situations were attempting to solve their problems. Almost simultaneously, business executives from throughout the metropolitan area formed the Greater Baltimore Committee, with goals closely resembling those of the Committee for Downtown.

In a cooperative effort, the two groups raised $225,000 and the Greater Baltimore Committee formed a planning council, a fully staffed nonprofit professional planning organization, to devise a master plan for the downtown, working outside the structure of the city government. Using privately raised funds, the committee was able to employ several leading professionals headed by David A. Wallace (now of the Philadelphia firm Wallace Roberts & Todd) who were not directly involved in the politics of the city. In March 1958 the committee presented a plan for a 33-acre site to be called Charles Center.

Meanwhile the city had created the Baltimore Urban Renewal and Housing Agency, and by November 1958, less than eight months after the presentation of the Charles Center plan, a bond issue was on the ballot asking Baltimoreans to approve $25 million in working capital for the creation of Charles Center. The bond issue passed, and in March 1959 the city council adopted the Charles Center plan as a full-scale redevelopment priority. Charles Center went on to become a $200 million project that would win numerous architectural, planning, and landscaping awards for its office buildings, restaurants, retail shops, hotels, housing, parking, fountains, sculpture, and system of pedestrian bridges and plazas over a 14-block area.

Adjacent to the southern border of Charles Center, at the Baltimore waterfront, remained a decaying area of old wharves, wholesale produce markets, warehouses, and railroad yards. The area's all-purpose piers had become obsolete once the expansion and modernization of Baltimore's commercial waterfront had provided 42 miles of industrial shoreline to the east and south. The Inner Harbor had sunk into disuse in spite of the attractiveness of its open water within two blocks of the financial district. The land formed a "U" shape—and an unmet challenge to the city and its business community.

Science and Drama
Seek Spaces Downtown

Planning to enliven Baltimore's downtown focused from the beginning on activities other than the visual or musical arts. The city already enjoyed three major art museums—the Baltimore Museum of Art located near Johns Hopkins University to the north of downtown, and the Peale Museum and the Walters Art Gallery, both located in the city's center. None of them was looking in the fifties for new facilities. The Baltimore Symphony Orchestra was ensconced in the somewhat outmoded but still functional Lyric Theater, not far from the Walters Art Gallery.

The plans for Charles Center did call, however, for building a combined performing arts and television center. In 1961 Morris Mechanic, owner of the recently demolished Ford's Theater, Baltimore's only facility for touring Broadway shows, received negotiating priority to build a new theater at the corner of Charles and Baltimore streets.

Mechanic's plan called for a multitiered structure with a parking garage below ground, retail space at ground level, and the theater above. As he pursued it, however, Mechanic realized that he would not be able to break even on the theater if he had to buy the land and also finance the construction. So the city's Charles Center Management corporation appraised the property at $500,000 and gave Mechanic a lease of 6 percent ($30,000) per year, so long as the structure would be used primarily for live theater.

Mechanic sought an award-winning architect to design his theater, and he engaged John Johansen, designer of the Indiana University Theater in Bloomington, Indiana. Johansen proposed a bold structure of cast-in-place concrete rising above the plazas of Charles Center—a 1,600-seat theater costing $4.5 million when completed. In 1964, Mechanic signed the lease with the city and construction began.

Charles Center's revival of downtown also had caught the eye of the Maryland Academy of Sciences, which in 1957 had started looking for a place to build a museum. The academy, which had been founded in 1797 by gentlemen who met to discuss philosophy and natural history, had accumulated a collection of stuffed birds and unusual rocks. These were displayed in a number of locations throughout the city and finally came to rest at an old tobacco warehouse owned by F. A. Davis & Sons, long-time supporters of the academy. Academy members who had been looking for a site in the area north of the city's center, near Johns Hopkins University and the Baltimore Museum of Art, began to think in terms of a downtown location.

And the planners of the new downtown began thinking in terms of culture. M. J. (Jay) Brodie, Baltimore's former housing and community development commissioner, states their rationale:

Arts and culture are an expanding American business. Studies show there's more leisure time—more time for people to be involved—and no matter how many videocassettes or cable TV channels there are, there's a basic desire to go out and mix with other people, to be out in the air, to see and be seen . . . and to try new and different activities, to broaden experiences. . . . These are permanent, authentic human reactions and if you build urban environments on and around them in an exciting way, you will get the benefit.

Project Data: Morris Mechanic Theater

Location	Charles Center, Baltimore	
Completed	1967	
Architect	John M. Johansen	
Consultants	1976 interior renovation by Roger Morgan Associates and Armstrong/Childs Interior Design; 1976 sound system consultants: Theater Technology, Inc., and Otts Munderloh	
Contractor	Jolly Construction Co.	
Building Cost	$1.5 million (1976 renovation)	
Breakdown of Interior Area	Proscenium Width	45 ft.
	Proscenium Height	30 ft.
	Stage Depth from Apron	41 ft.
	Flying Height	62 ft., 6 in.
	Pit	40 musicians
	Dressing Rooms	total capacity 55, including chorus rooms; musicians' room accommodates 42
	Seating	1,601
	Elevator	25 ft. × 6 ft. on center back wall

Charles Center–Inner Harbor Management, Cultural Organizations, and Commerce

Public Hoopla Encourages Diverse Citizens to Claim Downtown

In 1964, spurred on by Mayor Theodore R. McKeldin, the Greater Baltimore Committee recognized the opportunity presented by the Inner Harbor and joined forces with the city planning department and the urban renewal and housing agency to transfer some of Charles Center's momentum toward the blighted area around the harbor basin. In September 1964 an Inner Harbor Plan was announced, projecting a 30-year program for redeveloping a huge 240-acre area with new residential, social, and cultural facilities, as well as hotel and office buildings. The plan also keyed the construction of city government buildings along a stately mall linking City Hall with the Inner Harbor.

Within two months of the announcement, two bond issues for the Inner Harbor project were on the ballot. This time the voters rejected a $4.5 million package for the construction of the city buildings. However, they approved $2 million to start the implementation of the rest of the Inner Harbor plan:

- offices to be built as an extension of Charles Center south and east of it to the Inner Harbor;
- residential development with a broad spectrum of costs in high-rise and low-rise buildings to the east and west; and
- a city park including recreation, cultural, and entertainment facilities around the shoreline of the basin itself.

With the creation of the Inner Harbor site, a new entity also was born that would serve as a prototype for other American cities in redevelopment projects. This body was the nonprofit Charles Center–Inner Harbor Management, Inc., which serves under contract as the city's agent in planning, advocating, negotiating, and managing the redevelopment process.

In the midst of constructing his new theater, Morris Mechanic died. His family managed to get the theater finished and it opened in January 1967, under theatrical management that enrolled 8,000 subscribers and brought in top Broadway shows. Unfortunately, the quality of shows gradually declined, subscriptions dropped, the theater foundered, and in 1975 this cultural showplace on Charles Center's plaza teetered on the brink of becoming a movie house for X-rated films.

Since Baltimore held a land lease requiring the Mechanic's use as a legitimate theater only, the city took over the theater, creating a nonprofit management entity, the Baltimore Center for the Performing Arts. Sandra Hillman, executive director of Baltimore's Office of Promotion and Tourism, became president of the Baltimore Center for the Performing Arts, which, with $720,000 from the city, renovated the theater's interior, improving acoustics and sight lines. The center hired a Broadway producer to book first-rate shows back to Baltimore. Then it staged a large public luncheon, heavily covered by the local media, at which it signed up 2,000 subscribers.

From that time on, the Morris Mechanic Theater has been a success and now operates in the black. Hillman attributes the turnaround to a good product, competent management, fair pricing, the management's credibility for promising a product and delivering it, and a great deal of public hoopla. The Mechanic Theater established a precedent for similar private/public partnerships in the Inner Harbor area.

During the early seventies, while the Mechanic Theater was struggling, the city first attempted another strategy for persuading Baltimoreans to come downtown. Baltimore Fair, Inc., was organized in 1970 to emphasize commonalities among the city's ethnically diverse residents—Italians, Greeks, Poles, Lithuanians, other European nationalities, and blacks.

To get these tightly knit groups "to mix and match and share space with people who were different from themselves"—in the words of Sandra Hillman—the city organized its first public fair. They located it on neutral turf—the plazas of Charles Center—and they designed it to be highly participatory, with much food, cultural color, and local entertainment. Hillman's staff organized a massive volunteer effort and worked hard with the media to build interest and excitement. Over its subsequent 15-year history, the Baltimore City Fair has changed locations every year and now draws more than 1.5 million people.

Partially as an outgrowth of the fair, Hillman led the Office of Promotion and Tourism to initiate a number of other activities in downtown Baltimore. During summer weekends, a series of ethnic festivals enlivened the public spaces that the city was developing around the Inner Harbor. Baltimore's various neighborhoods were encouraged to bring their foods, crafts, dances, and other traditional activities down to the harbor. Concessionaires were told they could keep their profits from the weekends, while Hillman's office would furnish all sound equipment, chairs, tables, scaffolding, and technical staff.

In 1975 Baltimore's Inner Harbor hosted the Tall Ships, the fleet of international sailing vessels celebrating the nation's bicentennial. Virtually the entire city turned out for a week-long party, as Baltimoreans from all neighborhoods and suburbs came down to the Inner Harbor, day after day and night after night, to see the ships decorated with lights and to talk with the sailors. By this time, the bulkheads around the harbor had been rebuilt and many street improvements were in place. Thousands of suburban Baltimoreans making their first visit to the new Inner Harbor were surprised and pleased with what they saw.

Baltimore's city officials have continued to rely on the use of public events to encourage Baltimoreans to visit the Inner Harbor and claim it as their own. As Hillman says, "Now the whole city belongs to everyone. It didn't in 1970."

John Johansen's Morris Mechanic Theater, a 1,600-seat facility designed for Broadway road shows. Restaurants and retail stores occupy the ground floor.
Credit: M. E. Warren

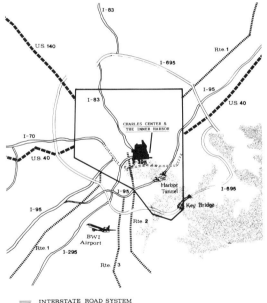

Map of Baltimore showing the location of the Charles Center and Inner Harbor redevelopment areas.

The Collaboration

Charles Center–Inner Harbor Management, Cultural Organizations, and Commerce

Since 1965 the city of Baltimore has used a private nonprofit corporation as its agent in managing its downtown redevelopment projects. The Charles Center Management Office, created to coordinate the Charles Center building effort, had operated under the direction of J. Jefferson Miller, the department store executive who had spearheaded initial redevelopment efforts back in 1954. Persuaded to come out of retirement, Miller took the job at a salary of $1 a year. In 1965 Miller and his deputy, Martin L. Millspaugh, signed a contract with the city establishing Charles Center–Inner Harbor Management, Inc., to continue to manage the completion of Charles Center and to oversee the planning and execution of the Inner Harbor project.

Charles Center–Inner Harbor Management came under the direction of the city's urban renewal and housing commission (forerunner to the department of housing and community development). Since its inception, it has proven an efficient vehicle to move costly development projects rapidly through city government channels.

The city advances the corporation money on a monthly basis, from which the corporation pays its own expenses. The total cost to the city for the management of the Charles Center and Inner Harbor redevelopment projects has amounted to less than 2 percent of the public funds involved.

Charles Center–Inner Harbor Management's job has been made more efficient by the city's charter and its Board of Estimates. Jay Brodie explains:

The great difference between Baltimore and other cities in development terms is a strong mayor and the city Board of Estimates, which the mayor controls. [Mayor Schaefer sits on the board and appoints two of the remaining four

The Baltimore City Fair attracts 1.5 million people annually. It is just one of several public events held in the city each year.

seats.] The Board of Estimates solely approves disposition agreements for the sale or lease of land or buildings to developers; the city council only approves the overall plans for renewal projects. It's fewer people to deal with and a much simpler mechanism. That's very appealing to developers.

Brodie explains that nonprofit organizations like Charles Center–Inner Harbor Management work to a city's benefit because they can take a single-minded focus on a particular area or neighborhood, are not bound by the full range of governmental constraints, and are viewed by the development community as being more understanding of developers' abilities, interests, and limitations—an advantage at the negotiating table.

Millspaugh, still chairman and chief executive officer for Charles Center–Inner Harbor Management, has seen the city's role shift in other ways over a 20-year period. In the Institute for Environmental Action's 1979 handbook, *Learning from Baltimore*, Millspaugh explained that in the fifties and sixties the city's principal role was to work with the business community to plan renewal areas; then developers fit themselves into a planned framework in exchange for support from the public and private sectors. Now that major changes in federal funding have evolved, Charles Center–Inner Harbor Management serves as a more active intermediary, working out the terms of a deal with both the developer and the city.

However, Millspaugh believes the essential development process followed by Charles Center Management in the early sixties still applies today. He outlines it as follows:

1) identifying the opportunity;
2) acquiring and clearing a site, where appropriate, and installing the environment and infrastructure;
3) recruiting the developer—through personal contacts or a competitive selection process;
4) negotiating a deal between the developer and the city;
5) working with the developer's architect for approval of the developer's plans; and
6) coordinating construction between

the developer's contractor and city services (street improvements, power, sewers, and so on).

The Maryland Science Center

Charles Center–Inner Harbor Management followed this general procedure in working with the Maryland Academy of Sciences to build the first new building on the shoreline of the Inner Harbor. At the south end of the basin, bordering Light Street, was a site that offered commanding views of the water and proximity to three other sites for retail pavilions projected by the Inner Harbor master plan. The city offered the academy this site for its science center. An adjacent site to the north, along the basin, was set aside for future expansion.

The academy hired Edward Durell Stone to design the building and in 1965 unveiled its plans. The city signed a final disposition agreement with the academy in 1970, and the state legislature approved the use of state funds for the museum's construction. Unlike city bond issues, the construction costs did not have to be approved by the voters. Groundbreaking therefore occurred in September 1971 almost unnoticed by Baltimoreans.

By the time the footings, pilings, and some of the steel were in place, however, inflation had taken its toll, and the appropriated state funds were not sufficient. Construction stopped for 11 months while the academy returned to the state legislature for more money to complete the building. Finally, with a total of $6 million in state bonds, construction began again in December 1972.

Design problems also emerged. Stone had planned the building to be clad in rope-cast concrete. When funding became an issue, it was decided to change the facade to less expensive red brick. Once completed, however, the museum resembled a walled fortress. James Beek, a reporter for *Forecast* magazine, wrote that "the military bearing of the building is so severe, you get the impression that it could take on any other three buildings in central Maryland and win, with one wing tied behind its back." James Backstrom, who came to the Science Center as director shortly before its opening in June 1976, be-

The Maryland Science Center, located at the edge of the Inner Harbor basin, was designed by Edward Durell Stone. Kenneth Snelson's *Easy Landing* appears in the foreground.
Credit: Sara W. Barnes

lieves that being the first cultural facility in the Inner Harbor posed attendance problems for the Science Center. Backstrom suggests that a psychological barrier also existed at the time the museum opened:

Pratt Street [to the north] was a powerful boundary between the financial district and the grubby, seedy, down-and-out area to the south. [In people's minds] it was the old Columbus idea—you sail out that way too far and you fall off the edge of the earth. There were a lot of people who would never come down here.

That first year totaled only approximately 63,000 paid admissions. Visitor traffic for the center had been projected at about 400,000 per year.

A further problem for the Maryland Science Center was its orientation on the site. The building originally was expected to be a close neighbor to three retail pavilions that would lie parallel to Light Street. But when the Rouse Company made its proposal to develop the retail spaces, the three pavilions were changed to two and their orientation shifted north so that one building paralleled Light Street while the other paralleled Pratt Street. This redesign left an open space of about 1,000 feet—a long walk from the south end of what is now Harborplace to the Science Center. Instead of being an anchor for the retail area, the center appeared as a distant island. Even its entrance, opening on Light Street, seemed in the wrong place.

Though the reorientation of Harborplace isolated the Science Center, the opening of

The balconies of Harborplace's food pavilion provide a place for a brown-bag lunch or people-watching. Harborplace's retail pavilion, the U.S. frigate *Constellation*, and I. M. Pei's World Trade Center are shown in the distance.
Credit: M. E. Warren

The Rouse Company Builds Harborplace

By 1977 Charles Center–Inner Harbor Management and the Office of Promotion and Tourism had succeeded so well in making the Inner Harbor an attractive public area that some reluctance surfaced about permitting a private developer to launch the next phase. Ironically, a major goal of the public sector—to attract private dollars to the Inner Harbor area—was questioned by Baltimoreans because they now felt that the Inner Harbor was "theirs."

When the Rouse Company began negotiating for the specialty retail site that is now Harborplace, opposition was voiced by nearby merchants—particularly restaurant operators fearing competition. Various citizens also expressed fears that the Inner Harbor would become ringed with buildings and less accessible to the general public. According to Millspaugh:

Once site planning was completed, the opposition was in full cry. We knew we had a contest. We all thought it was going to go to a referendum and felt we had to have the design in hand in order to show people what Harborplace was going to be. Otherwise, it would be easy for the opponents to describe [Harborplace] as a great big department store that would block all of the Inner Harbor waterfront. That's when Ben [Thompson, principal architect of Benjamin Thompson & Associates] came in and started working on the design. The model was finished in time for the referendum.

The petition that was ultimately voted on in 1978 was for a provision to be added to the city charter that would prohibit any more buildings along the shoreline of the Inner Harbor. Since referendums in Baltimore can be requested by petition or by the city council, the city council submitted a second charter amendment stating that no more buildings could be built in the open space around the Inner Harbor except on the future Harborplace site and on the future expansion site of the Maryland Science Center. The remaining land, from the Science Center to the World Trade Center, would be for park use. The council's amendment passed.

Today, the views of the water are pre-

the specialty retail center eventually made a positive difference in the number of visitors who came to the museum. Backstrom keeps a chart that chronicles attendence and significant Inner Harbor events over the past eight years. Once Harborplace opened in 1980, the center's attendance jumped dramatically and has grown ever since, even in the winter months. Backstrom concludes:

Harborplace has been the economic engine. We on our own did not have sufficient drawing power. Even if we had been at the level we are now, with good exhibits, programs, and activities, it wouldn't have done it. . . . There's almost an ecological sense to mixed-use districts like this one. They really have to work together. They're like linkages in food chains and those kinds of things in scientific ecology. Structures like the Science Center can only do so much. As soon as Harborplace opened it was literally like someone turned the light on. . . . That light is people.

served and the nearby restaurateurs do more business than they did prior to Harborplace's opening. The first year it opened, Harborplace and its cafes, food markets, and specialty shops attracted 18 million visitors.

The National Aquarium in Baltimore

In 1974 Robert C. Embry, Jr., then commissioner of Baltimore's department of housing and community development, visited Boston's New England Aquarium and suggested to Mayor Schaefer that the Inner Harbor should have an aquarium as one of its main attractions. The mayor visited the New England Aquarium and endorsed the idea. At this point, Charles Center–Inner Harbor Management picked up its role as the delivery system.

According to Millspaugh, "This is sometimes the way these public or nonprofit projects can happen in Baltimore. Somebody will get an idea and take it to the mayor. He'll say, 'yes, let's do it,' and then it will come back to us to do the initial planning, both financial and physical."

The federal government's interest was solicited in granting Baltimore's aquarium status as the national aquarium, replacing one that had been located in the basement of the U.S. Department of Commerce. After much negotiation, Congress decided in 1979 that Baltimore's aquarium could use the term "national" but must add "in Baltimore" to the title. In return, the city agreed not to request federal funds to build or operate the first stage of the project.

Peter Chermayeff, chief architect of Cambridge Seven Associates, Inc., who had designed the New England Aquarium, was retained as the aquarium's architect. Simultaneously, Charles Center–Inner Harbor Management retained Gladstone Associates, an economic consulting firm in Washington, D.C., to complete a development analysis for the facility.

Funding for these design and market studies was approved by the city's Board of Estimates. Contracts with the architect and consulting firm were negotiated first with the mayor and city council, acting through the department of housing and community development. Charles Center–Inner Harbor Management then became the client super-

The National Aquarium in Baltimore, designed by Peter Chermayeff, has a tropical rain forest for a roof.
Credit: Greg Pease

A diver offers shrimp to a rainbow parrotfish in the National Aquarium in Baltimore's Atlantic Coral Reef Exhibit. One of the largest reef exhibits in the United States, the ring-shaped environment houses several thousand tropical reef fish in 325,000 gallons of water.
Credit: Richard Anderson

vising the contract on behalf of the city. All public improvements in Charles Center and the Inner Harbor—the streets, bulkheads, and parks—have been planned with a similar administrative arrangement.

The next step in the aquarium's evolution was the formation of an advisory committee, appointed by the mayor and including local design, development, and construction professionals, as well as experts such as the director of the New England Aquarium. After schematic plans for the aquarium had been developed under the supervision of Charles Center–Inner Harbor Management, the advisory committee assumed a client role with Cambridge Seven and Gladstone Associates, under the housing and community development department's overall authority.

Originally, the land under consideration for the aquarium included the area between the Harborplace site and the Maryland Science Center. As design plans progressed, that site proved problematic because of the building's height (the aquarium, capped with a rain forest atrium, rises to 157 feet). During a design review session, Millspaugh and others suggested moving the aquarium model to Pier 3, and it became apparent that this was a better location for the structure.

The building's costs were estimated at $15 million. The planners expected to finance half the building with a $7.5 million bond issue and to match that with a second $7.5 million available from monies set aside at the time Baltimore sold its airport to the state of Maryland. This funding plan proved not entirely popular. Many Baltimoreans, not realizing that the $7.5 million from the airport sale legally was required to be used for a capital project, argued that the money should be spent on increased salaries for police and firefighters or on neighborhood improvements. But after Mayor Schaefer formed a citizens' committee for public education on the aquarium, the bond issue passed in November 1976.

Jay Brodie believes that the aquarium bond issue was worth the fight:

Public approval of bond issues can be a painful experience, but it's amazing . . . . [A bond issue] makes the city government conscious of having to convince the citizens that these are valid things that they should tax themselves on.

The citizens' committee that had worked to pass the bond issue asked that it be designated the aquarium board of directors. The mayor agreed and appointed Frank A. Gunther, Jr., a local businessman, as chairman of the new nonprofit organization. Gunther had the idea that the aquarium should pay for itself. This goal meant opening to the public free of debt and charging enough at the door to cover operating expenses. It also meant recruiting members and having a marketing staff in place a year prior to the aquarium's opening. Finally, it meant going to Baltimore's corporate community and to foundations to ask for substantial funds. Gunther and his board developed a fundraising campaign so that businesses could fund specific pieces of the aquarium. Corporations signed up to sponsor exhibits or to belong to the "Aquadopt" program, providing funds to acquire, house, and maintain the aquarium's fish and other animals. In-kind services, including legal, architectural, construction, marketing, accounting, and public relations services also were donated.

When bids for Chermayeff's design came in, the lowest was $19 million—$4 million over the planned $15 million cost. When completed, the cost was actually $21.3 million for the building, plus $1.5 million to reinforce the pier on which it stood, work financed by a federal grant. The board made up the $6.3 million difference through innovative corporate giving programs, donations from foundations, financial help from the city, and a preopening membership drive that produced 28,000 memberships. Today Gunther says:

We did not predict the kind of success we actually had. We were just trying to pay our way as we went along so when we opened our doors we would not be in debt. . . . This project was the best example you could find of the public/ private partnership that Baltimore has become famous for, and Mayor Schaefer made it happen. He not only helped and challenged us, but a mutual respect developed and he let us run the show.

Public Spending and Housing Ensure Citizen Approval

When the overall plan for the Inner Harbor was endorsed in the 1964 bond issue referendum, Baltimoreans were not approving the specific cultural components housed in the Inner Harbor today. Instead, the plan provided guidelines for business and residential development alongside an "urban playground" of recreational, cultural, and entertainment facilities centering on the piers and around the shoreline. Nor were the cultural components dependent on the commercial components. Rather both relied on preliminary public development of the area. This strategy proved crucial for attracting private developers.

Mathias J. DeVito, chairman of the board and president of the Rouse Company, confirms the importance of the strategy of starting with the public improvements—new piers, streets, bulkheads, marinas, overhead walkways, promenades, grassy commons, parks, and playing fields, with stands for spectators:

Harborplace is often credited with creating the Inner Harbor and having been the part that got that area off the ground. That really isn't true. We were one of the last to come. When we made the decision to do Harborplace, the Hyatt Regency was under construction, the aquarium had just been approved, the Science Center was here, the World Trade Center was here, the harbor was complete. We were the keystone to visible success. But we would never have gone into Baltimore unless we had seen a great deal of activity and potential interest on the part of the people to be at that location on the harbor.

In 1980, when 400,000 Baltimoreans came for the opening of the two glass-enclosed pavilions flanking an open-air performance space, they could see three other new attractions completed or under construction:

■ Across Light Street to the west, the 500-room Hyatt Hotel's exciting design already was visible.

■ A block further west, Baltimore's new convention center had just been completed.

■ At the end of Pier 3, a short distance to the east, the National Aquarium in Baltimore was due to open in August 1981.

A Greek ship docks beside the Rouse Company's Harborplace food pavilion, designed by Benjamin Thompson & Associates. Across Light Street in the background is the Hyatt Hotel and to its left is the McCormick spice factory, a Baltimore landmark since 1889.
Credit: Sara W. Barnes

The Inner Harbor's water taxi passes the *Constellation* on its way to the cultural and entertainment attractions that ring the Inner Harbor.
Credit: Sara W. Barnes

The Pier 6 Pavilion was built with profits earned by the Morris Mechanic Theater. During the summer as many as 3,200 people gather there for concerts.

The power plant, being recycled, will soon become an urban entertainment center in the Inner Harbor. Mark di Suvero's *Under Sky/One Family* sits in the foreground.
Credit: Sara W. Barnes

In 1981, with profits from the Mechanic Theater, the Baltimore Center for the Performing Arts opened the Pier 6 Pavilion, east of the aquarium. A permanent tent structure designed by William Gillet, it seats 2,000 under cover and an additional 1,200 on a grassy lawn planted on top of the old pier. It hosts a variety of concerts several nights each week from July through Labor Day.

Cooperative efforts among the different cultural, restaurant, and retail entities reinforce their individual strengths. From May through October, a water taxi takes visitors to several different stops within the area—the aquarium, the Science Center, Harborplace, the *Constellation*, the playing fields, the power plant, and Little Italy. Plans are underway to develop a one-price ticketing system covering admission to several Inner Harbor attractions. Harborplace has received several National Endowment for the Arts grants to support musicians and artists "in residence." It also sponsors Sunday evening summer concerts at the water's edge.

The Power Plant

The most recent addition to the Inner Harbor's cultural cornucopia is a three-building power plant that provided coal-fired energy for Baltimore's former trolley system. Bought by Charles Center–Inner Harbor Management for $1.65 million, it was slated for demolition under the plan of 1964. With interest in historic buildings reviving, however, Charles Center–Inner Harbor Management recommended in 1979 that the plant be saved. Plans to recycle the plant as a hotel proved infeasible, and it was decided to offer it for adaptive use as

an entertainment center. Jeff Middlebrooks, director of planning and research for Charles Center–Inner Harbor Management, describes what the agency hoped the power plant could add to the Inner Harbor mix:

We knew we wanted some kind of pure entertainment component, but we weren't sure what would work in that situation. We wanted to continue to attract our current market—a wide mix of older folks, middle-aged couples with children, folks in their twenties and on dates, and young children—but we didn't have a prototype. We put out a prospectus saying what we *didn't* want—not housing, hotel, or office use.

In December 1982 the city accepted a proposal submitted by Six Flags Corporation, a national operator of theme parks. Six Flags' offer to build an indoor, turn-of-the-century adult amusement park was not only unusual, it was sensibly scaled to deal with the practicalities of the old building. Four huge smokestacks shoot up through the center of the structure. Massive iron and concrete foundations protrude into this central space. The cost of demolishing these remnants of the past would have been tremendous. Six Flags proposed instead to plan around such obstacles and use them in the final design. The company also was prepared to take full responsibility for the $25 million to $30 million project development costs, because it saw the Inner Harbor as an ideal location for its concept of "urban entertainment," designed to attract affluent 25- to 40-year-old adults. Six Flags had been seeking an area where new mixed-use development already had begun to draw adults downtown. Important requirements for such an urban location were a crime-free atmosphere, adequate public parking or public transportation, and pedestrian amenities.

A development agreement was signed in December 1983. The city agreed to lease the land and power plant to Six Flags for 20 years, renewable for three more 20-year periods. The agreement recognizes that 650 new parking spaces are scheduled to be built within 1,500 feet of the power plant. After a specified amount of gross revenue is realized by Six Flags, the city will receive 5 percent of any additional gross receipts. Baltimore also will receive 10 percent of all ticket sales (in the form of the city's amusement tax). The project is expected to generate about 200 jobs for city residents.

Larry Miller, Gary Goddard Productions, and Charles Kober Associates—designers and architects—have created a series of shows within the plant's 115,000 square feet and several levels, following a theme of a 19th-century exposition hall housing the inventions of a fictitious character, Professor Phineas Templeton Flagg.

Scheduled to open in the summer of 1985, the power plant is expected to attract approximately 1.45 million people during its first year of operation—about 70 percent adults and 30 percent children. Tickets will be priced at $7.95 for adults and $5.95 for children, with the city amusement tax added. The plant will operate from 10 a.m. until 8 p.m. during the summer months, seven days a week. It will be open from 10 a.m. to 6 p.m., five days a week (closing Mondays and Tuesdays) for the remainder of the year. The building will hold 3,000 people at one time, and the average length of stay is expected to be about three hours. Six Flags will have a reservation system to accommodate large crowds, so that visitors can buy tickets for a time later the same day. Thus, rather than standing in long lines, they can go to other Inner Harbor attractions, returning to the plant at the times designated on their tickets.

In the evenings, after operating hours, the power plant will be available for conventions, local corporations, and other large groups to rent and tour. Its Pratt Street Music Hall will feature live performers, drinks, and light food at night.

According to Middlebrooks, Six Flags and the power plant offer a case of "the right company in the right building at the right time":

I think it will become some kind of a model for other cities. . . . This particular product won't be replicated because of the building, but some of the ideas may be. And it fits our mix. One of the things we're trying to do is to move from a day trip destination to an overnight tourist destination. . . . Tourism into the city is a brand new an-

An interior model of the power plant shows the exposition center's main hall. The new facility is expected to attract 1.45 million visitors annually.

imal and a tremendous one. . . . In the summer of 1983, 9.2 million regional visitors spent about $48 per person in Baltimore. That works out to $500 million in spending and that's not counting the other 4 million visits of city folks and people from local counties. More hotel stock is being built in Baltimore and our job is to fill it. We need to increase the length of stay by programming enough things to do so it makes it worthwhile [for visitors to stay overnight]. The power plant will bring the average [Inner Harbor] stay from four hours up to six hours, which gets up closer to that goal.

With more hotels, additional housing, the power plant, and new cinemas showing first-run films, the city deliberately is structuring a 24-hour activity cycle for the Inner Harbor area.

Baltimore Inner Harbor
Project Data

Physical Configuration Component—Income Generating	Project I Shoreline	Profile at Build-Out— Specifics To Be Determined
Office	1,805,000 sq. ft.	
Residential	683 units	
Retail	551,700 sq. ft.	
Amusement/Recreation/Entertainment		
Inner Harbor Marina	158 slips	
Small Boat Rental		
Submarine *Torsk*		
USF *Constellation*		
Water Stage		
Power Plant	90,000 sq. ft.	
Component—Arts/Culture/Open Space		
International Pavilion	.06 acres	
Baltimore Common	4.36 acres	
Public Wharf	540 linear feet	
Promenade	2.46 acres	
McKeldin Square	7.70 acres	
Finger Piers	.418 acres	
Playing Fields	6.3978 acres	
Maryland Science Center	40,000 sq. ft. exhibits 350-seat planetarium	
National Aquarium in Baltimore	287,000 sq. ft.	
Pier 6 Pavilion	2,000 seats	
Public Works Museum & Streetscape		
Other		
Parking	5,795 spaces	
Acreage	95 acres	300 acres
Gross Building Area	2,356,770 sq. ft.	
Floor/Area Ratio (FAR)	14 (office space) 9 (hotel space) 1.5 (restaurant and retail)	
Location	Harbor Basin, Baltimore	
Master Developer	Charles Center–Inner Harbor Management, Inc.	
Development Period	1967–84	
Estimated Total Development Costs	$647 million	$1.7 billion
Development Costs (1984)	$647 million, including $61.6 million in public site costs	

Source: Charles Center–Inner Harbor Management, Inc.

Inner Harbor

Development Cost Summary	Private	Public
Office	$113.0 million	$21.0 million
Retail	31.6 million	
Amusement/Recreation/Entertainment	39.6 million	36.2 million
Hotel	253.2 million	
Residential	76.1 million	
Site Costs	.5 million	14.2 million
Gardens/Public Area		
Public Facilities		
Housing Fund		
TOTAL DEVELOPMENT COSTS	$514.0 million	$71.4 million

Offices, Hotels, and Residences

After two decades of carefully orchestrated development, Baltimore's office market finally has taken off around the Charles Center–Inner Harbor area and beyond. In a recent article in *Baltimore* magazine, Eric Garland pointed out that "by delivering such attractions as the Convention Center and National Aquarium, the city primed the surrounding land for development. . . . The private market has rushed in." In 1984, 24 office buildings, retail centers, and hotels were being planned, were under construction, or had recently opened downtown. Class A office space rents remain modest compared to many other cities ($20 per square foot); according to Martin Millspaugh, however, rents run about 20 percent higher within a two-block radius of Charles Center and the Inner Harbor.

New housing has been calculated into the Inner Harbor mix. Middle-cost and low-cost high-rise apartments and low-rise townhouses have been built south of Charles Center and west of the harbor area. Some of this building offers housing for the elderly. In the Otterbein homesteading area, the city has sold rundown houses for $1 to residents willing to move in and rehabilitate them. Luxury condominiums are opening beside a hotel and offices at Harbor Court on the west side of Light Street. Walter Sondheim underscores the long-term importance of housing to the Inner Harbor's success.

Charles Center and the Inner Harbor have not been done as a kind of oasis in a desert of blight. I and a lot of other people wouldn't have had anything to do with downtown development if it hadn't been for the fact that this was done in a city which has put more of its effort into residential rehabilitation. . . . One of the reasons we have hordes of people even when nothing is going on in Inner Harbor is because it has not turned its back on the city: Baltimoreans feel the Inner Harbor is part of the city.

Baltimore nevertheless has had to struggle to retain a downtown retail presence. In the last ten years, one major department store has built a new facility downtown between Charles Center and the Inner Harbor. Smaller retail development and reconfiguration of existing stores currently is planned for Charles Center. The Rouse Company is planning "better-quality retail" across Pratt Street from Harborplace. Called the Gallery at Harborplace, this project, scheduled to be completed by 1987, will include approximately 1,200 parking spaces on four underground levels; 140,000 square feet of retail on the next four levels; a 600-room hotel on six levels; and 250,000 to 400,000 square feet of office space on the top 17 floors.

Along the water's edge itself, to the east of the power plant, Charles Center–Inner Harbor Management is planning more attractions, hotels, and perhaps a maritime activity center, with an extension of Eastern Avenue ending in a major plaza on Piers 5 and 6. Beyond that, further east, prospects call for more housing, mixed with other uses.

The principal mechanism used to redevelop the Inner Harbor changed with the 1973 demise of the federal Title I urban renewal program. Under the Community Development Block Grant system that was substituted, the city now allocates for the Inner Harbor only $1 million or $2 million of the $28 million it receives annually. Revenues for expansion and development of new sites may have to come from rents or from participation in ground leases and the trading and sale of property owned or controlled by the city.

Baltimore always has been aggressive in attracting federal dollars and ranks second in the nation for its total of 54 Urban Development Action Grant awards (New York is first with 60). Millspaugh emphasizes that the private development seen today in downtown Baltimore would not have been possible without the availability of substantial public funding in the past. But the heavy capital investment is now in place; future increments of development dollars will rely at least 90 percent on private sources.

Charles Center
Project Data

Physical Configuration Component—Income Generating	Profile at Build-Out
Office	2,000,000 sq. ft.
Residential	656 units
Retail	430,000 sq. ft.
Hotel	700 rooms

Component—Arts/Culture/Open Space	
Three Public Plazas with Fountains, Overhead Walkways, Sculpture, Plantings	8 acres
Morris Mechanic Theater	1,600 seats

Other	
Parking	4,000 spaces
Acreage	33 acres
Gross Building Area	7,000,000 sq. ft.
Floor/Area Ratio (FAR)	Typical FAR: ±18
	Average FAR: 5
Location	Center City CBD, Baltimore
Master Developer	Charles Center–Inner Harbor Management, Inc.
Development Period	1959–85
Estimated Total Development Costs (1983 dollars)	$195 million, including $35 million in public development costs

Source: Charles Center–Inner Harbor Management, Inc.

Charles Center

Development Cost Summary	Private	Public
Office	$78.8 million	$18.80 million
Retail	1.7 million	
Hotel	11.3 million	
Residential	43.5 million	4.28 million
Amusement/Recreation/Entertainment —Morris Mechanic Theater	4.5 million	
Site Costs		42.50 million
Gardens/Public Area		
Public Facilities		
Housing Fund		
TOTAL DEVELOPMENT COSTS	$139.8 million	$65.58 million

A National Destination Point and Model

Baltimore reached a psychological turning point in July 1980, when the Rouse Company opened Harborplace, a $22 million, two-pavilion retail and restaurant center of 145,000 square feet at the water's edge. With national news coverage, multiple magazine articles, and an estimated crowd of 400,000 people converging on the Inner Harbor for its grand opening, Baltimoreans knew that their city had become a national destination point.

When the National Aquarium was being planned in 1976, no one could fully predict the synergy that would occur in the early eighties in the Inner Harbor area. Gladstone Associates based their estimates on the assumption that the Inner Harbor would remain a downtown attraction for Baltimore and its surrounding counties, not a full-fledged national destination. Frank Gunther recalls:

The first real inkling I had that maybe we had underestimated where we were going was in spring 1981, four or five months before we opened. I took Jim Rouse [founder of the Rouse Company] through the building . . . and after the tour we got to talking about it. He asked, "What kind of traffic flow are you predicting?" and I said, "We have the opportunity to attract up to 600,000 people a year." He said, "You're going to double that." Well, hearing that, I knew we had another whole set of problems. How could we handle that many people? So we got hold of people from Marriott and Disney World and they helped us. The first full calendar year we had over one and a half million people.

Once the aquarium opened, those large crowds were a mixed blessing. Swimming in an open tank designed to be viewed from above and below, the aquarium's dolphins could not stand the stress of being in a fishbowl surrounded by so many people. The constant noise of excited viewers gave them stomach ulcers, and eventually they had to be removed from the building. According to director J. Nicholas Brown, the public is disappointed that, with the dolphins' departure, the aquarium no longer exhibits large marine mammals. "We are not a complete aquarium because of this," he laments.

That surprising first year also generated an income surplus of $2 million. The Rouse Company's market studies showed that 11 percent of Harborplace's initial visitors came to the Inner Harbor with the aquarium as their primary destination point.

Today, a single adult ticket to the aquarium is $5.75 and ranges down to $2.25 for a three- to twelve-year-old child who is part of a group of 20 or more. Baltimore school groups are admitted free. Admissions cover 66 to 70 percent of the National Aquarium's annual $4.5 million budget.

Although the building was designed for a staff of 66, the aquarium now houses more than 120 employees, and despite this increase, employee areas have had to be converted to checkrooms and rental stroller storage for visitors. More rest rooms are needed. Interior wear and tear on railings, carpeting, and walls has been intense. Each year since its opening, the aquarium has had to close for ten days.

An interior traffic pattern problem also exists. Designed so that the entrance and exit cross, the building clogs during peak hours. To combat this difficulty, the aquarium has reduced the number of people who can enter during prime hours and has limited after-hour rentals by large groups.

The board and staff now are talking about "Phase II." "The original aquarium was built through a partnership with the private and public sectors," says Gunther. "Now, I'm firmly convinced that we will not have a major Phase II unless the state becomes a full partner." This phase would include new office and research accommodations for staff, a classroom, tanks for marine mammals, and an outdoor amphitheater. Staff and board members are examining a site on Pier 4, adjacent to the existing building. Estimated costs average between $20 million and $40 million. Gunther admits that the aquarium could survive with a much more modest addition providing only staff space. He adds, however:

I think the aquarium as originally conceived by the mayor and other people was a recreational and educational marketing tool for the city. Now it has become a major economic issue for the entire state. Last year, 700,000 people visited the aquarium from out of state. . . . We need a Phase II to continue to be on the cutting edge of the latest aquarium technology.

The aquarium has helped bolster in turn the Maryland Science Center's attendance. "People come down here, go to the aquarium in the morning, have lunch at Harborplace or a picnic at Rash Field [adjacent to the Science Center], and come over here in the afternoon. They make a day of it," says Backstrom. The Science Center has upgraded its exhibits, developed an educational outreach program, and even hosted Girl Scouts who have camped overnight in the building. To let visitors know what it is and that it is indeed open, the museum now hangs large, bright banners on the facade facing Harborplace, announcing current exhibits. The banners also have the effect of softening the building's harsh exterior. A large, airy sculpture, Kenneth Snelson's *Easy Landing*, stands near the museum on the north side, attracting attention and helping to draw people from Harborplace down to the building.

Recent figures show that such outreach is making a difference. During its first year (1976–77), the Science Center earned $104,000 in paid admissions, accounting for 30 percent of its total budget at the time. In just two months—July and August—of 1984, the museum brought in $170,000 in admission fees. It now has a yearly budget of $2 million, of which 70 percent is met through earned income.

A new addition also is planned to help correct the museum's current awkward orientation. This three-story, $2.8 million structure, designed by the Baltimore firm of Cochran, Stephenson & Donkervoet, will be an all-glass building facing toward Harborplace and resembling a giant show window. Balconies on each level will overlook the harbor.

In November 1984 the museum joined the Baltimore Museum of Art, Walters Art Gallery, and Peale Museum in a city bond issue totaling $4.9 million. Its passage provided $1.5 million for the Science Center. An additional $750,000 already has been raised privately to match $750,000 from the state legislature to fund the new addition.

Project Data: National Aquarium in Baltimore

Location	Inner Harbor, Baltimore	
Completed	August 8, 1981	
Architects	Cambridge Seven Associates, Cambridge, Mass. Peter Chermayeff, principal architect	
Consultants	Exhibit Fabrication:	General Exhibits, Inc., Philadelphia
	Habitat Exhibit Construction:	Jerry M. Johnson, Inc., Boston
	Tank Acrylics:	Swedlow, Inc., Garden Grove, Calif.
Contractors	Builder:	Whiting-Turner Construction Co., Towson, Md.
	Electrical:	J. P. Company, Baltimore
	Mechanical:	Poole and Kent, Baltimore
Building Cost	$21.3 million	
Gross Area	115,000 sq. ft. Aquarium tanks hold more than one million gallons of fresh and salt water	

Project Data: Maryland Science Center

Location	South Shore of the Baltimore Inner Harbor	
Completed	June 13, 1976	
Projected Opening	Addition: April 1986	
Architects	Original building:	Edward Durell Stone
	Addition:	Cochran Stephenson & Donkervoet, Baltimore
Consultants	Addition:	Loschky, Marquardt & Nesholm, Seattle
Contractors	Original:	Consolidated Engineering Co.
	Addition:	Harbor Construction, Inc.
Building Cost	Original:	$6 million
	Addition:	$2.8 million
Gross Area	Original:	106,000 sq. ft.
	Addition:	10,000 sq. ft. (net)
Breakdown of Interior Area	Exhibits	32,000 sq. ft.
	Planetarium	20,000 sq. ft.
	Offices	15,000 sq. ft.
	Educational	15,000 sq. ft. (not offices)
	Storage, Workshops	
	Mechanical	24,000 sq. ft.
	New Space	10,000 sq. ft. (lobby/ circulation/exhibits)
Exterior Features	Red-brown brick cavity wall construction with steel frame Large, attractive rooftop terraces	
Interior Features	Eighty percent of public areas are carpeted; very flexible and complete exhibition lighting system; wall surfaces are plaster or exposed brick	

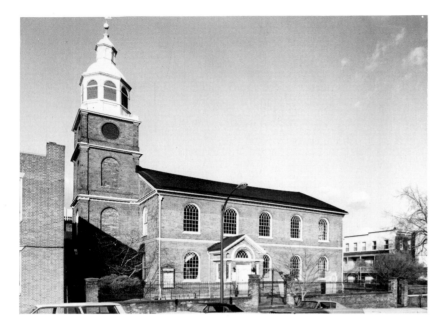

Model for the new addi-
tion to the Maryland Sci-
ence Center. The addition
will add exhibition space
and also reorient the en-
trance from Light Street
to the Inner Harbor itself.

Lessons from Baltimore

Martin Millspaugh attributes the Inner Harbor's success to balance among its attractions:

1) Balance between old people and young people. The Inner Harbor really doesn't appeal to teenagers, except at a time when nobody else is here. . . . The preteens and adults go together as families, and that's the fastest-growing population in the United States. It's the baby boom and their children.

2) Balance between expensive and affordable attractions. The aquarium and Science Center—where you go in and spend a long time and take a family of five—are expensive. But there are also things you can do for practically nothing. In Harborplace, you can spend a lot of money or no money at all.

Baltimore remains a city of comparatively limited means. But with creativity and diligence, its leaders have made genuine economic progress. The city has added enriching new experiences for its citizens, and it has greatly improved its appearance. Several outstanding qualities have contributed to the city's successes:

■ *Strong leadership.* During its postwar redevelopment history and particularly over the past thirteen years encompassing Mayor Schaefer's terms of office, the city has enjoyed strong mayoral leadership. The mayor has steered a course toward development that encourages public/private collaboration. Business leaders and local officials have shown remarkable willingness to spend long hours and to take risks to bring about creative change. The Board of Estimates' approval process enables the city to take decisive action even in the face of opposition.

■ *Continuity of leadership.* A striking majority of the key people involved in Baltimore's renaissance have stayed involved over a long period of time.

■ *A predilection for action.* The leadership in Baltimore has been willing to invent its own prototypes and to take substantial risks.

■ *A realistic assessment of strengths and weaknesses.* Since the fifties, Baltimore has confronted its economic weaknesses, built on its strengths as a port city, and found ways to amplify its existing assets. Built-in features such as water and an intimate harbor, strong neighborhoods, a surplus of older housing stock, and its proximity to other East Coast cities all have been used to attract visitors, new residents, and businesses. "Whatever you do in a town has to really reflect the character of the town," contends Sandra Hillman. "It is a mistake to try and be something that you are not. Local people will like it if it reflects what they're all about, and people from out of town will like it too."

■ *Long-range planning.* When the Greater Baltimore Committee was formed in 1955, it recognized the need for a comprehensive downtown plan. With privately raised dollars, it hired its own planners and presented the city with a scheme that eventually became Charles Center. The committee and the city later collaborated on the Inner Harbor plan. At the same time, by working incrementally, local officals have allowed for flexibility within their plans. Such adaptability enabled the Rouse Company to propose a change in Harborplace's orientation in the Inner Harbor and meant that the concept of a hotel in the historic power plant could be replaced by that of a family theme park.

■ *Staying power.* Baltimoreans have had to think small and to proceed on a project-by-project basis. But the city has demonstrated an unusual capacity to realize its objectives over decades. Projects have been completed in phases, but the city has returned to older projects to make further improvements as financing, market demand, and public support have increased.

■ *Ability to enlist public support.* Maryland cities must put city bond issues before the public in referendums. Over the past 26 years, 16 bond issues regarding both Charles Center and Inner Harbor have been placed on the ballot, and all have passed. The city's leaders have used the bond issues as a way of educating citizens and enlisting their support.

Baltimore aims to continue finding ways to encourage visitors by increasing its range of evening activities and developing more cultural and entertainment attractions, particularly in the Inner Harbor area. At the same time, city planners will continue to encourage housing around the Inner Harbor and throughout downtown. The recycling of old commercial buildings into new housing stock already is taking place immediately west of Charles Center.

Ethnic festivals increasingly will be held in local neighborhoods as well as in Charles Center and the Inner Harbor. Mayor Schaefer's goal of making downtown Baltimore "everybody's neighborhood" has worked so well that people now feel comfortable going to mingle in their neighbors' streets, and the Inner Harbor no longer needs constant special productions. Twenty-one million people come each year simply because it's a pleasant place to be.

Jay Brodie sums it up:

I think the best thing we have done for the future fiscal health of Baltimore is to position ourselves for continuing progress through two different but related activities. One is the downtown renewal effort which has produced a whole different set of downtown functions than used to exist. Now we have office, hotel, tourism, and service functions . . . all thriving. Secondly, we have helped to bring the neighborhoods alive so that they are attractive places to live with new and rehabilitated housing of every description. And a wide variety of people live here, black and white, with various incomes. Those are the best investments we could have made in the future of the city—and we made them.